The Mobile River

WALTER

THE MOBILE RIVER

With a New Preface

John S. Sledge

Hardcover and ebook editions published 2015
Paperback edition published 2024 by the University of South Carolina Press
Columbia, South Carolina 29208

uscpress.com

Printed in the United States of America

Library of Congress Cataloging-in-Publication Data
can be found at https://lccn.loc.gov/2024020301

ISBN: 978-1-64336-527-5 (paperback)
ISBN: 978-1-61117-486-1 (ebook)

Frontispiece illustration from Peter J. Hamilton,
Artwork of Mobile and Vicinity (Chicago, 1894).

Mobile River and Delta map © Nicholas Holmes III

Published through the generosity of the
A. S. Mitchell Foundation, Mobile, Alabama

For mom,
Jeanne Arceneaux Sledge
Always interested, supportive, and loving

Contents

List of Illustrations

Following page 158

Preface

Not long after this book's original publication in 2015, a friend called. "I read your book," he said. "Boy, you really love that river!" Similarly, but in more formal fashion, Kenna Lang Archer, a Texas historian, wrote in the *Journal of Southern History:* "Sledge clearly feels a particular passion for the Mobile River. He infuses his text with stories, ideas, and people that reflect his longing both to know the history of the Mobile and to make known that history." She applauded the book's strong sense of place and concluded that it made "for very good reading." Of course, such reactions lifted my heart, for I do love the Mobile River, have since childhood, and worked mightily to communicate that, as the following pages will hopefully continue to demonstrate.[1]

Mobile, Alabama, is simultaneously a river city and a seaport. While the region's earliest chroniclers certainly realized this and celebrated it, I felt that some later historians had lost sight of the water's fundamental importance to the city's identity and destiny. *The Mobile River* was born of that belief. Throughout its research and composition, my determination was to focus on certain people and events but to always keep the river itself as close as possible to the narrative center.

After publication it was gratifying to learn just how many people still appreciate the city's maritime significance. Folks came forward to share their own connections, telling stories of forebears who sailed on lumber schooners during the 1920s, worked in the shipyards during World War II, or helped bridge the delta during the late 1970s. Practically everyone claimed a blockade-runner in the family tree.

Ten years beyond *The Mobile River's* publication, much remains the same on the old stream. The bar pilots still guide hulking container ships into port, powerful push boats steer barge strings past the convention center, and Midwestern "loopers" overnight beneath swaying Spanish moss in peaceful delta bayous. Of course there have also been changes, far too many to fully enumerate here. Most significantly in 2019 journalist Ben Raines discovered the wreck of the *Clotilda,* the last slave ship to arrive in America. The discovery made international news and led to the opening of the Africatown Heritage House in July 2023. *USA Today* included the institution in its top ten list of the country's new museums most worth visiting.[2] Whether the wreck itself is fully salvageable remains unknown. Fearing its destruction given such an attempt, some people have advocated an in situ maritime shrine similar to that of the USS *Arizona* at Pearl Harbor. Only time and further careful study will decide. For the present, the wreck is under video surveillance and off limits to commercial traffic.

As for the proposed Interstate 10 Bayway expansion and new Mobile River Bridge, they remain unrealized amid ongoing planning and controversy. Progress is forward but agonizingly slow for frustrated commuters, truckers, and politicians. Meanwhile, the US Army Corps of Engineers pursues a $365 million multiphase project to both widen and deepen the Mobile ship channel. This project will improve the port's access and efficiency in an era of ever larger ships. When completed, perhaps as soon as 2025, the channel will be 55 feet deep and 550 feet wide and include a three-mile-long passing lane in the lower bay, eliminating its exasperating one-way status.[3]

On the environmental front, Alabama Power Company recently bowed to federal pressure and announced a plan to remove and recycle some of the coal ash from its 597-acre retention pond at the Barry Steam Plant. Located riverside at Bucks, not far from the Ellicott Stone, this pond has long worried environmentalists and residents because of potential ground-water contamination or a catastrophic failure that would foul the delta. Removal of a significant portion of the twenty-two million cubic yards of the coal ash will take an estimated 30 years. Nonetheless, the decision represents an important and hopeful advance.[4]

It is unfortunate that the past decade also brought losses. Southern Fish and Oyster closed in 2019 after an eighty-year run, victim of the bridge project. Owner Ralph Atkins Jr. battled condemnation for years but ultimately sold. The venerable tin shed's demolition represented the disappearance of the last bit of genuine old river culture. Similarly, the only World War II–era office building remaining on Blakeley Island fell to the wrecking ball, and in 2020 Hurricane Sally gutted a Confederate earthwork opposite Blakeley State Park.[5]

And then there are the people. I lost my mother, to whom this book is dedicated, in 2022. Shortly after the *Clotilda's* discovery, Joe Meaher—Cap'n Joe in the prologue—died, to the end publicly silent on his ancestor's role in commissioning the voyage. Finally, Nick Holmes III, who drew the delta map on page xiv, and David E. Alsobrook, former director of the History Museum of Mobile who facilitated my research in countless ways, also "crossed the bar."

Despite these changes and losses, I believe *The Mobile River* still does what I intended it to do. Even if you do not have a blockade-runner in your family tree, I hope this paperback edition will encourage you to explore this fascinating river further. If Mobile has a soul, it is there.

John S. Sledge
Fairhope, Alabama
January 28, 2024

Notes

1. The telephone conversation is from memory. For the Archer quotes, see Kenna Lang Archer, *The Mobile River* by John S. Sledge (review), *Journal of Southern History*, 82, no. 3 (August 2016): 660–61.
2. "From history to punk rock: 10 best history museums to visit in US," *USA Today*, January 25, 2024, https://10best.usatoday.com/awards/travel/best-new-museum-2024/.
3. "Port of Mobile harbor construction underway deepening and widening to be completed by 2025," Alabama Port Authority, May 21, 2021, https://www.alports.com/mobile-harbor-construction-begins/.
4. Dennis Pillion, "After push from EPA Alabama Power announces plan to remove, recycle coal ash in Mobile," last modified January 26, 2024, https://www.al.com/news/2024/01/after-push-from-epa-alabama-power-announces-plan-to-remove-recycle-coal-ash-in-mobile.html.
5. Lawrence Specker, "Southern Fish & Oyster, a Mobile landmark is closing," last modified April 29, 2019, https://www.al.com/news/mobile/2019/04/southern-fish-oyster-a-mobile-landmark-is-closing.html. I do not recall news stories about either the old WWII office building demolition or the earthworks damage.

Acknowledgments

By far the greatest pleasure of writing this book has been the many wonderful people who helped me along the way. First and foremost, I must thank Joseph Meaher, who has long had an interest in this project. Joe knows the Mobile River "like any familiar thing" (as was once said of one of his forebears), and he helped me to know it as well through two boat trips and numerous queries answered. Joe encouraged me to seek the assistance of the A. S. Mitchell Foundation in underwriting the book's production costs, and, happily, trustees Augustine Meaher III, David Dukes, Frank Vinson, and Kenneth Vinson agreed. I am indebted to all of them.

Second, I am profoundly grateful to the History Museum of Mobile for its commitment to this project at many levels, from acting as a pass-through for the subvention to scanning photographs and copying documents free of charge. Director David Alsobrook and staffers Scotty Kirkland, Jacqlyn Kirkland, Charles Torrey, Jacob Laurence, Sheila Flanagan, Ellie Skinner, Israel Lewis, and Kathlyn Scott never flagged and, in the process, have become like a second family to me. Quite simply, this book would not have been possible without their involvement.

Many other individuals at numerous local institutions and companies also provided vital and valuable assistance. They include Coll'ette King at Mobile County Probate Court; Jane Daugherty and Amy Beach at the Local History and Genealogy Branch of the Mobile Public Library; Edward ("Ned") Harkins, Zennia Calhoun, Pamela Major, and Jane Pate at Mobile Municipal Archives; Carol Ellis, Chris Burroughs, Nick Beeson, Ben Lang, and Barbara Asmus at the University of South Alabama's Doy Leale McCall Rare Book and Manuscript Library; Greg Waselkov, Bonnie Gums, and Sarah Mattics at the University of South Alabama Department of Anthropology, Sociology and Social Work; Cartledge Blackwell at the Mobile Historic Development Commission; Rhonda Davis, formerly at the Historic Mobile Preservation Society; Judith Adams, Sheri Reid, Jimmy Orum, and James Lyons at the Alabama State Port Authority; Captain Terry D. Gilbreath, harbormaster; Shirley Lampley and Alvin Campbell of the Alabama Department of Transportation; William Harrison III of Harrison Brothers Dry Dock and Shipbuilding; John Hunter of Dockside Services; Patrick J. Wilson and Cap'n Joe Ollinger of the Mobile Bar Pilots; Casi Callaway of Mobile Baykeeper; Jocko Potts, Judy Culbreth, and Lawren Largue at *Mobile Bay* magazine; and Joan Gardner and David Cooper of Cooper/T. Smith Corporation. All of these folks lead busy professional lives but were unfailingly courteous when I came calling.

Other people were helpful on particular aspects of the Mobile's sprawling history. They include Sidney Schell and John Ellis on the Confederate navy, David Smithweck on lighthouses, Sam Hodges and Bill Finch on the delta, Sylviane Diouf on African Town, David Bagwell on water lots, Hudson McDonald on Plateau, Melissa Mutert on the railroad tracks riverside, and Richard Chastang, Noel Andry Sr., Henry Andry, Robert Curtis Andry, and Rudolph Andry on the upriver Creoles.

Others provided help or friendship during the long grind. They include Joey Guess and John Harper at the Promised Land; Anna Guess, who sent fantastic preserves after my river trips; and E. C. LeVert, Tom McGehee, Roy Hoffman, Douglas Kearley, David Newell, Hardy Jackson, Spencer Callahan, Ken Niemeyer, Debby Stearns, Nicholas Holmes Jr., Malcolm Steves, and Ken McElhaney. Special thanks are due Nicholas Holmes III for his fabulous Mobile River Delta map. When I began this project, I knew that I wanted to engage Nick to produce such a map as an accompaniment to the classic Mobile Bay chart his grandfather drew back in 1937, itself never before published in a book. To my great joy, Nick accepted the task, even though I could only pay him for a fraction of his time. Over the course of a long year we compared notes and progress as I composed and he drew, and the collaboration proved one of the most rewarding of my life.

This is now my second book with the University of South Carolina Press, and I appreciate the staff's professionalism and thoroughness more than ever. To Walter Edgar, thanks for introducing them to me, and heartfelt gratitude to Director Jonathan Haupt, Marketing Director Suzanne Axland, Assistant Director for Operations Linda Haines Fogle, and Managing Editor Bill Adams for their marvelous care and skill.

Last, as ever, my family has been my rock. My lovely wife Lynn edited this monster with her usual grace and eagle eye. Our children Matthew and Elena, both out of the nest, used Facebook to express their support and interest from afar. My mother Jeanne Arceneaux Sledge was this book's first reader, and her enthusiastic, early, and continued encouragement has meant a great deal. Though she is my mother, she insists that she knows a good book when she sees it, and so I dedicate this volume to her. Of course, any errors of fact herein are to be laid solely at my door.

Mobile Bay by Nicholas H. Holmes, 1937

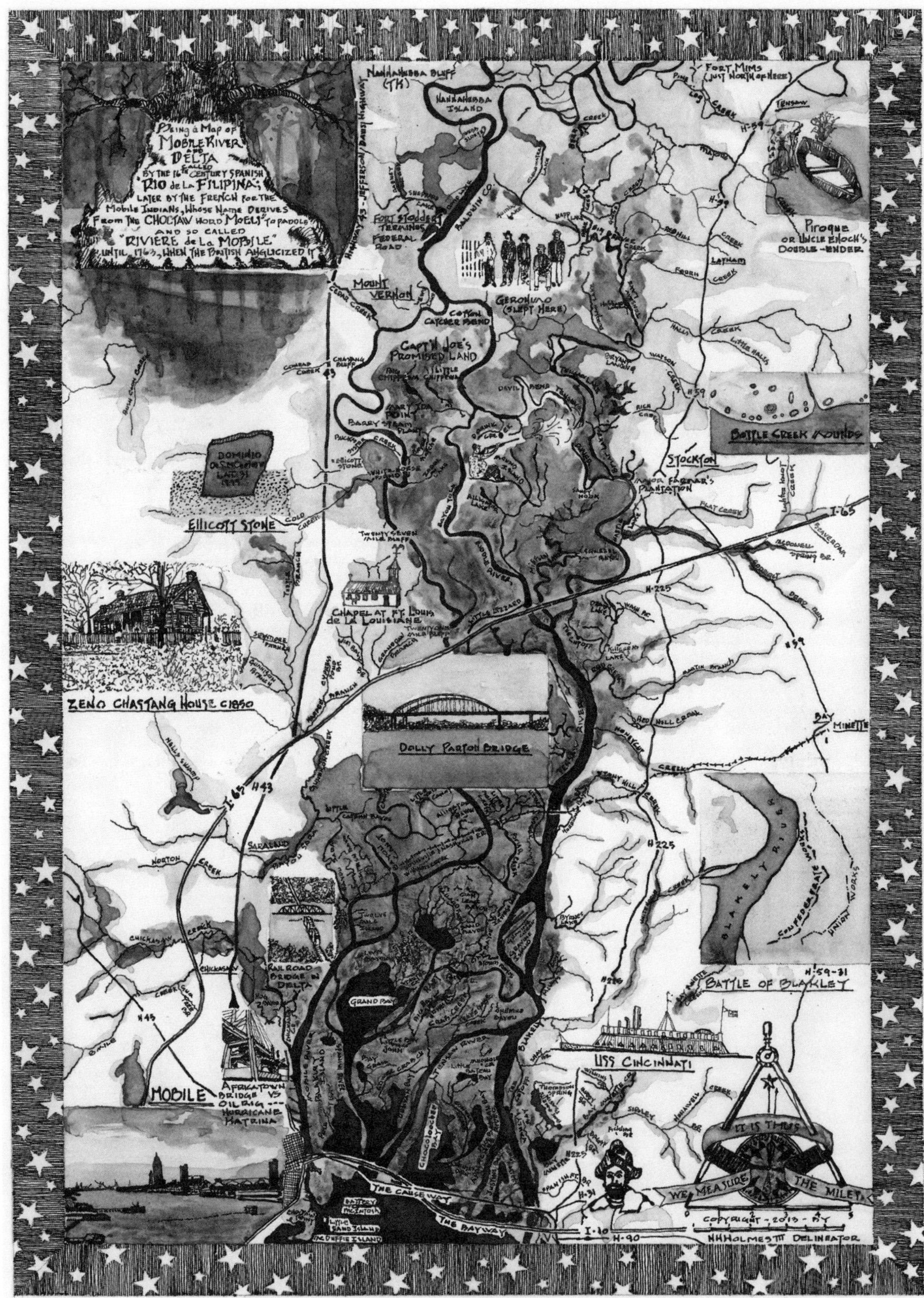

Mobile River and Delta by Nicholas Holmes III, 2013

Prologue

Downriver with Cap'n Joe

Joe Meaher is something of a legend on the Mobile River. His family history has unfolded along its banks, upstream and down, in country, swamp, and city. A descendent of the controversial Timothy Meaher—Mainer, sawmill owner, boat builder, steamboat captain, filibuster financier, slave runner, blockade-runner, and businessman—Joe is a vigorous seventy, deeply versed in river incident and lore and extensively involved in managing his family's timber, farming, and real estate interests. No complete narrative of the underappreciated and fascinating waterway on which he lives is possible without his participation.

Our families go way back. My grandfather and father hunted with his father in the 1930s, 40s, and later when Cap'n Joe was young. In the mid-1970s, his brother Augustine bought my grandmother's Spring Hill Avenue home, Georgia Cottage. The A. S. Mitchell Foundation, with which his family is involved, helped fund all three of my previous Mobile books, the profits of which have gone to the Mobile Historic Development Commission, and over the years Joe or Augustine has consulted me on preservation issues related to historic houses on both sides of the bay as well as at two cemeteries. After my third book, *The Pillared City,* Joe, knowing my enduring love for local history, naturally inquired what was next. "The Mobile River," I replied.

"Have you been on it?" he asked.

The answer was a qualified *yes.* I have always nurtured an interest in the Mobile River and have my own connections to it, though of a markedly different and less intimate character than Joe's. During the 1960s, for example, my grandmother often took me down to the docks to watch the stevedores at work. This was always a favorite outing. While other young boys dreamed of growing up to be firemen, policemen, baseball players, or soldiers, I wanted to be a stevedore and spend my days manhandling exotic cargoes from the holds of salt-streaked freighters.

Ultimately I took a different path but have remained drawn to the waterfront, regularly spending lunch hours at the foot of Government Street to watch the container ships, tugs, and barges ply back and forth. Occasionally there has been the added excitement of touring an accurately reconstructed historic sailing vessel like the *Bounty* or the *Golden Hind* in port, and in the summer of 2002, during the city's tricentennial celebration, I stood with my family on the ninth floor of Government Plaza and thrilled to the tall ships' stately parade.

Ships and harbor craft are not the river's only attractions for me, however. As an inveterate seafood lover, I have long delighted in going to Southern Fish and Oyster at 1 Eslava, a funky riverbank operation that dates back half a century. Standing on the perennially wet concrete floor as rubber-booted and aproned employees drag boxes filled with iced fish and deftly filet the catch or head shrimp, I am taken with the realization that such scenes are immemorial in this town. So I have been beside the river.

As a commuter into downtown from Baldwin County, I cross the Mobile River twice every day through the Bankhead Tunnel, an engineering marvel when it first opened in 1941. Sometimes, if running late, I'll use Interstate 10's George Wallace Tunnel, just south of the Bankhead. It's more recently constructed (1973) and faster but less interesting visually and far more frightening with its hurtling traffic. Whichever tunnel I take though, descending down and down through the well-lit and tiled tubes, the river never even glimpsed either upon entering or exiting, it is nonetheless impossible for me not to contemplate the bulbous prowed ships ghosting just above the Mardi Gras beads swaying from my rearview mirror. So I have been under the Mobile River.

There are also two highway bridges over the river, one on Interstate 65 in northern Mobile County, miles from the city, and the other immediately north of downtown on Highway 90/98, heavily travelled by trucks carrying hazardous loads that are not allowed in the tunnels. On trips upstate or returning, I use the I-65 bridge, officially known as the General W. K. Wilson Jr. Bridge but popularly as the Dolly Parton Bridge for the soaring twin support arches that from certain approach angles look for all the world like, well, what the bridge's nickname implies. Driving across this bridge can feel like flying, with inspiring vistas over the sprawling Mobile River Delta, the second largest in the United States and a natural wonderland of extensive swamps and labyrinthine streams and bayous. Closer to my daily round, when the tunnels are congested by holiday traffic or a wreck, I will sometimes take 90/98's Cochrane/Africatown USA Bridge, sweeping high above the heavily industrialized harbor and then precipitously dropping onto Blakeley Island with its tank farms, retention ponds and forty-foot-high dredge spoil dikes. So I have been over the Mobile River.

But to more directly address Cap'n Joe's query, I had enjoyed a half-dozen waterborne harbor tours up to the time of his telephone call, limited jaunts that departed from the Alabama State Docks, proceeded a few miles to the river's mouth and then returned. The most memorable of these was aboard a small hovercraft that jounced over the chop and, amazingly, onto and around the actual shoreline of Battery McIntosh, or Goat Island, as it's now called, site of a Confederate battery that guarded the city's watery approaches. And, while these are not part of the Mobile's main channel but rather of its delta, I could boast of two visits to the Bottle Creek Indian mounds, an extraordinary prehistoric complex only reachable by water, most directly via the Tensaw River on the bay's eastern side. So, yes, I had been on the Mobile River. On it, beside it downtown, under it, over it, and into the heart of its delta, but of the upper stream, beyond the Cochrane/Africatown USA Bridge where high-rise views show a sinuous, silvery ribbon spooling horizon-ward through marsh and forest, I had no direct meaningful experience.

There matters lay for months, the book project simmering in the back of my mind but a distant prospect given the press of other obligations. Until one summer afternoon Cap'n Joe telephoned out of the blue and invited a colleague and me on a personal guided survey of the entire river, all forty-five incredible miles from Nannahubba Bluff down to Choctaw Point. Hardly believing the opportunity or his amazing generosity, we met him and one of his men on the appointed morning at a Mount Vernon parking lot. "Follow us to the Promised Land," they called from the truck window. There our journey began.

Joe's pride in the Promised Land is evident in virtually everything he says and does. Consisting of acreage on both sides of the river and including farm, swamp, and timberland, this remarkable place is so called because it was customary to name land grants for the closest religious holiday, usually a Saint's day, to the date of the transfer. Joe's family acquired their tract on the Feast of the First Fruits, a celebration of spring harvest and the Children of Israel's crossing the Red Sea into the Promised Land. As we followed the big pickup through a farm gate and down a three-mile-long graveled road, the appellation certainly seemed apt. The land was green, well-tended, and pretty, dotted with grazing sheep and carefully maintained buildings and plantings.[1]

That this cultivated and settled part of the allotment would never flood became evident when we saw the drop-off down to the private landing, a rectangular cut into the riverbank with a small wharf and a few pilings. Here another of Joe's employees met us, and after greetings all around we climbed aboard our conveyance, a twenty-foot aluminum "haul ass boat" with 120 horsepower engines that could easily deliver twenty-five miles per hour. A comfortable and commodious pilothouse promised relief from the fierce sun if such was wanted. Joe's men dexterously stowed several large gas containers, necessary because there are no refueling depots on the river, and some ice chests before casting off and idling out into the main channel. The landing is situated just below the place where the Mobile's main stem divides into two branches, the Mobile snaking southwesterly and the Tensaw trending southeasterly. A large low island between them is part of the Promised Land and the heart of the famed delta. Joe informed us that we would explore the island later on four-wheelers, dwarfed amid giant cypresses and ramrod straight oaks.[2]

As we roared southward, the boat settling gently in the stern and throwing out a large green and white wake, Joe began a running commentary on river history and facts. Like most anyone who has frequented local waterways over a period of decades, he was bitingly critical of the Corps of Engineers in general and the Claiborne Lock and Dam (located in Monroe County on the Alabama River, well above our location) and the Tenn-Tom Waterway (234 miles of locks and dams connecting the Tennessee and Tombigbee Rivers) specifically. These twentieth-century engineering marvels have radically altered the age-old natural patterns of flooding, sedimentation, and salinity throughout the delta. Joe's men nodded in grim confirmation, the pilot explaining that he can now catch flounder off Joe's dock, something unheard of historically, but they taste muddy and are unappetizing. Joe is convinced that this man-made monkeying has allowed a far greater than normal buildup of silt in the swamps, to the tune of several feet in a year in places, and significant incursion of salt-water tides into the lower delta, to the detriment of what used to be good timber.[3]

This was all useful information, but the boat engines were loud, and for long stretches no one spoke, content to take in the scenery and the abundant wildlife. Just south of the landing we saw a mature bald eagle alight, and osprey, egrets, great blue herons, gulls, terns, and brown pelicans were common the entire way. The pilot assured us that, flounder aside, plentiful and edible fish were here for the taking and boasted that he had recently caught a big river cat weighing in at some forty pounds. Other creatures swim these waters too. Scary ones. Only weeks after our trip an eleven-foot-eight-inch alligator weighing a quarter ton was hauled out of the Mobile during a state sanctioned hunt, and grown bull sharks, which can tolerate fresh water, have been tracked upriver as far as Claiborne.[4] Joe was less enthusiastic about eating fish out of the river and vowed that he would certainly no longer swim in the Mobile. This is perhaps a sagacious position, not only because of alligators and bull sharks but because of past pollution issues as well.[5]

We proceeded south, passing the occasional tugboat and barge but few pleasure craft, and the riverbanks displayed an unfolding panorama of spaced wooded bluffs—Chastang's, Seymour's, Twenty-Seven Mile, and Twenty-One Mile—on the western side and luxuriant swamps on the eastern. At times it looked like we were in Louisiana or Florida, the character of the landscape changing from hardwoods and pine to bald cypress, tupelo gum, laurel oak, and palmetto to, just north of the city, open marsh with stunted and scattered trees that stood like mute sentinels, confirmation of Joe's belief that salt-water incursion was killing them. Twelve Mile Island, a nine-hundred-acre onion-shaped mudflat so named for its distance north of the river's mouth, was once heavily timbered but now displayed only a few unhealthy-looking trees amid the bullwhips and palmetto. This is where Big Bayou Canot joins the Mobile, a place notorious for several singularly dark incidents in two different centuries. Rather than take the more commonly used western channel around the island Cap'n Joe chose the eastern one. Our pilot idled back on our speed because, according to Joe, this less-traveled branch has become a graveyard for old barges, some just under the surface and potential navigational hazards. The island yielded little of interest that we could see, but Joe claimed that there was an Indian mound smack in the middle. Walking to it in the heat and through snake- and alligator-inhabited tangles was unthinkable, however.

South of the island, the view broadened, with the Cochrane/Africatown USA Bridge and downtown's skyline set like a miniature tinker toy and play blocks amid a world equal parts land, water, and sky. "The Mobile River has four personalities," Joe said, giving voice to something already dawning on me. "Upland hardwoods, upper swamp, lower swamp, and harbor." That one river could exhibit so many attributes over such a short distance, with concomitant histories to match, struck me as remarkable. It seemed even more remarkable that no one had yet written a book devoted solely to the history of this fascinating stream and its people. The delta and the bay, the Eastern Shore and the area's teeming fish and game are all popular subjects, but the Mobile River gets no respect. It is a workingman's river, broad shouldered, unglamorous, dirty, and rarely considered.[6]

Passing under the bridge, we were now in the harbor, an almost five-mile stretch of industry, commerce, and shipping. Here the river is hemmed by railroad yards, shipyards, concrete wharves, big ships, tugs, cranes, tank farms, silos, warehouses, and loading docks stacked with steel, pipe, wood products, and containers. This is a promised land of a different sort, and Joe's family has interests and holdings here too. Pointing toward a nondescript section on the city side, Joe began dog-cussing a family that had done the Meahers wrong during Reconstruction. Old Mobile is like that. Roots are deep and memories run long. Families have their distinctive quirks, personalities, and relationships that can carry across generations. A bastard who plagued your family in 1870 was as likely to have sired a bastard who sired a bastard and so on down to the bastard who's plaguing you now.

The river widens through the harbor with its turning basins, but we again slowed down, and one of Joe's men took the bow to watch for the big logs that were now more frequent. Having slid downstream for miles, these uprooted, scuffed, and algae-slicked trees bob along and have always posed terrifying risks to navigators on the Mobile. If a boat strikes one at speed the occupants can be thrown overboard or the propellers smashed. Sometimes these trunks are so waterlogged that they partially submerge on end and seesaw up and down with the current. Known as sawyers, deadheads, or sinkers, they are capable of inflicting serious damage.

There is also more traffic in the harbor—push boats behind strings of barges, oceangoing tugs with growling 4,000-horsepower diesel engines, and ships from every corner of the globe. As we glided past the towering hulks of these black and barn-red hulled behemoths with their streams of water, Mobile's importance as an international port and an integral cog in the global economy became evident. Among the vessels we saw that day were the *Torm Camilla,* a 600-foot Danish chemical tanker; the *Tai Honesty,* a Panamanian-flagged 623-foot cargo ship; the *E. R. Boston,* a Liberian-registered ship that is a staggering 958 feet long (that's better than three football fields) and nearly 150 wide; and ungainly-looking in dry dock, the 480-foot pipe-laying ship *Caesar Helix,* brand spanking new with a red hull, white superstructure over the bow, a helo deck atop that, and astern a 300-ton metric crane.[7]

But most impressive was the navy's littoral combat ship *Coronado,* under construction at the Austal shipyard on Blakeley Island, opposite downtown's convention center. The highly polished metallic prow of this 417-foot craft, all angles, peeked menacingly out of its construction bay, looking very much like a modern-day Rebel ironcad (the CSS *Tennessee* was exactly half as long). No doubt Admiral Franklin Buchanan would have preferred this awesome vessel to the underpowered and poorly designed *Tennessee* when he steamed among Farragut's ships. Now completed, the *Coronado* is capable of top speeds around fifty knots, though the official figure is classified, and her capabilities include antisubmarine warfare and mine clearing.[8]

From the bow I caught a good view of Southern Fish and Oyster's tin building, perched precariously at the water, where fishing boats pull right up and offload their bounty. Minutes later we passed the McDuffie Island coal terminal with its conveyors and heaping black mounds and Little Sand Island with its derelict ship used by the Coast Guard for fire-suppression practice. The chop increased, we moved about more carefully, and open water suddenly stretched to all horizons as we entered the bay. Just south a giant cargo ship was approaching, nudged along by tugs, and our pilot deemed it prudent to turn around and head north.

On the return trip we took the channel on the west side of Twelve Mile Island and once again powered up to full speed. By this time the westering sun, the buffeting, and the constant motion had lulled everyone into a trance, and we each kept our own thoughts. For my part I remained in the bow, leaned against the pilothouse, and propped my feet against an ice chest. As the varying scene unrolled in reverse—harbor, bridge, marsh, tree line, bluffs, upper swamp—I fell into a quasi-melancholy reverie haunted by the shades of this river's colorful and rich past: Le Dos Grillé, the Choctaw Indian chief shot through the cheek in ambuscade who calmly plucked the bloody ball out of his mouth, rolled it into the barrel of his own musket, and dispatched his attacker; the iron-handed French explorer Henri de Tonti, vomiting black bile in the last stages of yellow fever at Twenty-Seven Mile Bluff; Aaron Burr held captive at Fort Stoddert, charming the lonely officers' wives while his dreams of empire fled on the icy February wind; young Kazoola, fresh from Africa, naked and terrified as he was hustled off the *Clotilda,* her reeking hulk shielded from prying eyes by Twelve Mile Island's looming mass; Commodore Ebenezer Farrand and his bedraggled Rebel sailors and marines fleeing upriver as spring exploded all along the banks; Albert Stein, the German hydraulic engineer fiercely defending his wrongheaded scouring theory to the bitter end; Madam Rosa Lee and her painted octoroons lounging on plush red divans, ready to relieve sailor boys of their lust and hard-earned gold; General William Sibert coaxed out of Kentucky retirement to oversee the transformation of a swamp into a modern sea port. And so many more, some famous, most not, who made a region and a city and a culture—Indian women and children, coureurs de bois and coopers, redcoats and pirates, flatboat rowdies and steamboat roustabouts, soldiers and generals, jack tars and admirals from too many wars, swampers and cartographers, river rats and railroad lawyers, slaves and teachers, sail makers and oyster shuckers, engineers and riveters, charlatans and healers, politicos and rum runners, bank presidents and society women, architects, musicians and novelists and painters and poets and even a historian or two. All of them actors in a uniquely American pageant of conflict, struggle, and endless opportunity along a river that gave a city its name.

Coasting back into Joe's boat slip at the end of this long and satisfying day, I was grateful to him for such an unusual and stimulating trip and resolved that no matter what other obligations and commitments crowded my horizon this was a story I very much had to tell.

Introduction

"A fine, large river"

The Mobile River proper—that is, the forty-five miles from Nannahubba Bluff to Choctaw Point and the focus of this book—is one of Alabama's shortest rivers. Out of thirty-six, it is an underwhelming twenty-fifth in length, exceeding only such feeble contenders as the Little Warrior (7 miles), Dog (8 miles), Fowl (14 miles), Duck (19 miles), Fish (28 miles), and Styx (41 miles). Comfortably ranking above it on the list are even such little-known streams as the North (77 miles), the Noxubee (140 miles), and the Pea (154 miles), while the Alabama, Chattahoochee, Coosa, Tallapoosa, Tennessee, and Tombigbee—all boasting near or better than two hundred riverine miles within the state's borders—command the top spots.

The Mobile first appears on the map full and wide at Nannahubba, where the Alabama and the Tombigbee meet, but because it empties their waters into Mobile Bay and subsequently the Gulf of Mexico, it usurps them and their multitudinous tributaries. If all of the rivers, creeks, streams, bayous, bogues, branches, swamps, sloughs, rivulets, and trickles that ultimately pour into Mobile Bay are factored into the equation, the Mobile assumes awesome importance and becomes the outlet for the sixth-largest river basin in the United States and the largest emptying into the gulf east of the Mississippi River.

From this broader perspective, the Mobile River Basin encompasses more than forty thousand square miles, including significant portions of Georgia, Alabama, Mississippi, and a little piece of east Tennessee. Its headwaters can be traced into the Appalachian Mountains at Tickanetley Creek, a fine trout stream in Gilmer County, Georgia, roughly eighty miles north of Atlanta and more than seven hundred river miles—that is, measuring by all the twists and turns—from Mobile Bay. If this entire distance is counted as the Mobile's official length—as it often is by geographers, scientists, and the federal government—the river ranks an astonishing twentieth overall among North

Aerial view of the harbor, looking south where the river meets the bay, 1949. History Museum of Mobile Collection. Courtesy of the Doy Leale McCall Rare Book and Manuscript Library, University of South Alabama.

American watercourses, behind the Tennessee and the Colorado but ahead of the Kansas and the Yellowstone systems.[1]

There are many name changes and mergers within this massive watershed, however, not to mention dramatic variations in the character of the landscape itself. From the mountain source, at more than 1,300 feet above sea level, the Tickanetley loses itself in the Cartecay River, which is joined by the Ellijay to form the Coosawattee River. That stream tumbles out of the Appalachian foothills and just north of Resaca meets with the Conasauga, and the Oostanaula River results. At Rome, elevation roughly six hundred feet, the Oostanaula and the Etowah join to make the Coosa, which crosses the Alabama line and continues southwest through forested ridge and valley country. Before all the big dams were built in the early twentieth century, the Coosa was famous for its many falls, rapids, and shoals. At Wetumka, six miles north of Montgomery and less than two hundred feet above sea level, the Tallapoosa flows out of the Georgia Piedmont and presses its muddy waters into those of the Coosa, and the mighty Alabama is formed. Fifty miles west of Montgomery, the Alabama absorbs the Cahaba and then carves its graceful path through a broad coastal plain of limestone, black loam, gravel, and sandy soil all the way to Nannahubba—only six feet above sea level—where it finds the Tombigbee through a series of swamps and tortuous meanderings, one of which is known as the Alabama River Cutoff. The Tombigbee, the dominant stream in the basin's western half, arises in northern Mississippi and flows into Alabama at Pickens County, where it proceeds south, joined by the Black Warrior and Sipsey, as well as numerous other smaller watercourses before it reaches Nannahubba.[2]

A comprehensive historical survey of the Mobile River Basin would certainly have its place, but that is not my intention here. There are already several sweeping overviews of Alabama's rivers, among them *Rivers of Alabama* (1968), by John C. Goodrum et al., and *Alabama: The River State* (1998), edited by Todd Keith, but these give the Mobile limited coverage. More detailed histories of selected rivers within the basin are also available—most notably *Rivers of History: Life on the Coosa, Tallapoosa, Cahaba and Alabama* (1995), by Harvey H. Jackson; *The Tombigbee River Steamboats: Rollodores, Deadheads, and Sidewheelers* (2010), by Rufus Ward; and *Tenn-Tom Country: The Upper Tombigbee Valley* (1987), by James F. Doster and David C. Weaver—but again the Mobile River is only occasionally mentioned. Jackson does not even give it an index entry in his book and glancingly refers to it and the Tensaw as "ill-defined channels."[3]

So the Mobile it is, then, beginning at Nannahubba, and what a strange name that is. It comes, like so many Southern place names, from an Indian tribe—the Naniabas, or "fish eaters," who lived in the Alabama and Tombigbee's fork.[4] This low, swampy land, in reality a large island, was habitable only part of the year, but the thirty-foot-high bluff nearby on the Tombigbee's western bank, where ThyssenKrupp's multibillion dollar plant now busily rolls steel, has never flooded and has long provided a handy northern limit for discussions of the Mobile River. As the nineteenth-century steamboat captains approached Nannahubba (and modern tugboat captains and pleasure boaters too, for that matter), they knew to bear right for the Alabama and Selma and left for the Tombigbee and Demopolis.

The Mobile's northernmost stem—the five miles from Nannahubba down to the Promised Land, known as the Mount Vernon Stretch among watermen—is a truly impressive geographical feature, and if it held these dimensions all the way to the coast it might be a more respected and famous river than it is. Over one thousand feet wide and more than thirty feet deep, it channels a remarkable 39,300 million gallons of water per day as it begins a relatively straight push to the sea.[5] But at the base of the Mount Vernon Stretch, the Mobile assumes a radically different character and splits into two main channels—Mobile west and Tensaw east. From here down to the head of Mobile Bay all of those millions of gallons of water become spread throughout one of the most extraordinary natural landscapes on the Gulf Coast—the Mobile River Delta.

Even experienced outdoorsmen will admit that the delta is damned confusing to navigate. Its 300 square miles include 20,000 acres of open water, 10,000 acres of marsh, 70,000 acres of swamp, and better than 85,000 acres of bottomland forest.

There are more than 250 different waterways that loop and twist and thread through towering stands of cypress and tupelo gum and, closer to Mobile Bay, waving marshy expanses. Promising meanders can quickly become dead ends.[6] Large and small islands, lakes, bays, bayous, and channels bear a bewildering plethora of names—some harkening back to Indian or colonial days, others to the nineteenth century when loggers penetrated the delta's farthest recesses through arrow-straight canals they dug as they went. Feeding into the Mobile's western main channel alone are to be found Alligator Bayou, Bayou Matche, Bear Creek, Black Bayou, Big Bayou Canot, Bayou Sara (originally Saw Mill Creek), Catfish Bayou, Dead Lake, Hog Bayou, Grog Hall Creek, Little Briar Creek, Big and Little Lizard Creeks (a corruption of Lizars, the name of an early French resident of the area); and approaching the city Chickasabogue (in more recent times Chickasaw Creek), Three Mile Creek, Choctaw Pass, and Pinto Pass. Within the vast alluvial plain east of the Mobile lie Alligator Lake, Big and Little Chippewa Lakes, Dominic Creek, Gravine Island, Mound Island, The Basin, Chuckfee Bay, Grand Bay, Lower Crab Creek, Middle River, Raft River, Big Bateau Bay, Chicory Bayou, and so many more.

Visitors have been suitably impressed by the Mobile River Delta since colonial times. The French referred to it as "trembling land," and a nineteenth-century scientist elaborated when he wrote that "much of it is impassable; some of it quakes and sinks beneath the tread, and is covered with tall grass and aquatic plants." In 1797 a geographer noted three broad divisions within its roughly forty-five-mile length—"low rice lands, on or near the banks of the river, . . . level flat cane lands, about 4 or 5 feet higher than the low rice lands . . . and high upland or open country."[7] Immediately after the Civil War, a native Vermonter waxed eloquent on "huge bays and outspread fields of water, so labyrinthean that a stranger, involved in their mazes and impressed by their outré air, would be reminded of the Stygian regions of his classics."[8] But perhaps no one conjured the delta so vividly as the Mobile folklorist and raconteur Julian Lee Rayford. In his 1941 novel *Cottonmouth,* Rayford compared the delta's swamps to the people on their fringes, "some grim, some bitter, some smelly, some sweet and full of sharp fragrance, some inviting, some harmless, some brooding and waiting like the glowering eyes of a wildcat."[9]

Along with its natural divisions, watery magnitude, and pungency, the Mobile River Delta's incredibly diverse flora and fauna have provoked wondering commentary from a wide variety of observers, some well versed in the natural world and others simply awed travelers. In the fall of 1775 the British naturalist William Bartram departed Mobile's rickety wharves in "a trading boat" and was conveyed upstream and across the delta to the vicinity of modern-day Stockton as a guest of Major Robert Farmar, the commandant of what was then British Mobile. Farmar lent Bartram a "light canoe," and for several days the naturalist delightedly explored the environs. In his journal Bartram marveled at the abundant river cane which grew "to a great height and thickness" and fearlessly plunged into "awful shades" where he beheld "stately columns of

Magnolia grandiflora." Deeper in the delta's swamps, the trees were "by far the tallest, straightest, and every way the most enormous" that he had ever encountered.[10]

Of all the trees that grow in the delta—bald cypress, water tupelo, red maple, sweet bay, Carolina ash, magnolia, water oak, and live oak to name but a few—the cypress and magnolia have elicited the most reaction. Shortly after the Civil War, Greville Chester, an English clergyman, collector, and amateur archaeologist visiting Mobile, pronounced the magnolia "almost unrivalled in the vegetable world" for its beauty and was intrigued by the forest floor "gemmed" by its glistening red berries. Almost eighty years later the decline of one of these majestic trees occasioned an article with an accompanying photograph in the *Mobile Register.* Situated at Magazine Point and towering more than one hundred feet high and measuring sixteen feet in circumference, it was known, appropriately enough, as the Great Magnolia Tree. It was thought to be then several hundred years old. The newspaper noted that the tree was a popular surveyor's landmark, used "to determine the boundaries of the 22,000 odd lots in what is known as the St. Louis land tract." While once "a picture of woodland splendor," time and two lightning strikes had not been kind, and, in the words of a nearby resident, it was "slowly dying."[11]

Cypress trees garnered attention because of their height as well as their peculiar knobby knees that poked out of the water. In the eighteenth century the surveyor and naturalist Bernard Romans commented on their "enormous size" and wrote that swamps filled with them were nearly impassable for horses because of the "extremely dangerous" knees, or "spurs," as he called them. In March of 1842 an English visitor to Mobile, James Silk Buckingham, wrote at length about the cypress trees—then displaying their winter brown rather than the rich green of high summer—that seemed to be everywhere around the city. He recorded their height at from eighty to ninety feet and their circumference at from fifteen to twenty feet. "A cypress forest," he wrote, "when viewed from the adjacent hills, with its numberless interlaced arms, covered with this dark brown foliage, has the aspect of a scaffolding of verdure in the air." And like many a newcomer to the Gulf Coast, he was beguiled by their mantles of Spanish moss, "hanging, like a shroud of mourning wreaths, almost to the ground."[12]

Besides its magnificent trees, the delta hosts hundreds of other kinds of plants whose locations are dictated by the subtle and complex choreography of elevation, soil composition, wind, tide, and salinity within the delta. Among these growing things are grasses, shrubs, vines, wildflowers, ferns, mosses, and aquatic and subaquatic vegetation. A short list would have to include giant cane, big cord grass, saw grass, American holly, the nearly ubiquitous palmetto, trumpet creeper, poison ivy, pepper vine, green brier, wild grapes, yellow lotus, swamp hibiscus, ironweed, duckweed, alligator weed, and sea grass. Non-native and invasive species such as Chinese tallow and cogon grass have become major concerns in recent decades, and their impact is easily visible from the causeway across the bay's northern end.

The delta and the bay are continually engaged in an epic ebb and flow that alternately favors salt water and then fresh as well as the respective plants and animals that depend on each. This cyclical flushing has historically followed a seasonal calendar, though upstream dams can radically alter the cycle. During the usually dry late-summer and autumn months, the river levels are low and the Gulf of Mexico advances, swollen by the sun's heat, coaxed by the moon's pull as it approaches Earth's equator, and driven by prevailing southwesterly winds. The bay is brackish to the river mouths, and the lower delta's salinity levels spike and creep upstream. By contrast, during winter and spring the rivers reign, dominating and overspreading the broad delta swamps for months. Salt water retreats, and fan-shaped plumes of fresh water and sediment balloon into the gulf. Historically, this was a most useful series of circumstances for the people who farmed the lower delta. An anonymous cartographer noted on the margin of one eighteenth-century map that "the banks of the river . . . are generally overflowed in the rainy seasons, but it has been observed by persons who have cultivated them, that these inundations preserve the richness of the soil."[13]

The delta's fauna is just as varied and prolific as its flora. There are 300 species of birds, 126 fishes, 46 mammals, 69 reptiles, and 30 amphibians.[14] The birds are a glory, and the delta has long delighted serious watchers. The merest sampling must mention birds of prey such as the bald eagle, red-tailed hawk, screech owl, black vulture, and osprey; shore birds including the laughing gull, American white pelican, brown pelican, kingfisher, white ibis, great blue heron, little blue heron, night heron, snowy egret, and double-breasted cormorant; waterfowl such as the bufflehead duck, canvasback duck, ring-necked duck, harlequin duck, and Canada goose; and nesting songbirds including the brown thrasher, wood thrush, cardinal, bluebird, red-eyed vireo, Carolina wren, towhee, chipping sparrow, and Baltimore oriole. Among the fishes are largemouth bass, bowfin, banded pygmy sunfish, black madtom, bluegill, blacktale shiner, freshwater drum, black crappie, blue catfish, blue sucker, southern flounder, redfish, American eel, Alabama sturgeon, speckled trout, and mullet. The waters also harbor mollusks, marsh clams, oysters, gulf white shrimp, and crabs. The mammal species are not as numerous as the birds or fishes but are nonetheless diverse and intriguing. Among them are white-tail deer, squirrel, red fox, raccoon, opossum, rabbit, wild pig (dating from the Spanish *entradas*), bear, and bobcat. Aquatic mammals including the manatee sometimes visit the delta during the warm months, and when temperatures drop they huddle around the Barry Steam Plant outfall.[15]

Of the reptiles and amphibians, there are more inhabiting the delta than just about any place else in the United States. The bountiful snakes include the deadly cottonmouth and diamondback rattler, as well as the benign banded water snake, hog-nosed snake, and ribbon snake. There are also gopher tortoises, box turtles, and the endangered Alabama red-bellied turtle. But of all the critters that crowd the delta, none has excited as much attention as the alligator. Bartram spied big ones "basking on the shores" and "swimming in the river and lagoons" at the Mobile and Tensaw fork.[16]

That these monsters knew no fear was frighteningly demonstrated for a French marine captain on an upriver trip in 1759. Just above the fork on the Tombigbee, he and his men stopped for the night, pitching their camp on the riverbank. The officer, Jean Bernard Bossu, spread out his bearskin and put a large fish the Indians had given him at his feet for the night. After about an hour's sleep, he awoke with a start as his bedding was dragged toward the water. "I thought the devil was carrying me off," he declared later. But the demon proved to be an enormous alligator—twenty feet by Bossu's estimation. The Frenchman managed to scamper out of his bedding, but his fish was lost. "This story, plain as it is, may pass for a prodigy among those who love the marvelous," he laconically concluded.[17]

Even more astonishing was the experience of a young Connecticut merchant in 1806. William Robertson boarded a small schooner in Spanish Mobile with some trade goods and headed upriver for the American garrison at Fort Stoddert. Near Twenty-One Mile Bluff (roughly where the Dolly Parton Bridge today crosses the delta), the wind died and the vessel lost headway. With her sails hanging limp and the men too tired to pull at the sweeps, the anchor was let go and the schooner lay quietly mid-river. But in what must have been an unnerving sight, Robertson reported that the "water was literally alive with alligators," and many more rested on the shore. Incredibly, the crew took no precautions, leaving the sweeps extended into the water and posting no watch. As a big, bright moon arose and bathed the sails in its ghostly light, the men bedded down on deck. Robertson placed his mattress between the hatch and the mainmast with a mosquito net rigged from the boom. Directly at his head, he recalled, "there was a coop of fowls, and toward morning I was awakened by their extraordinary noise." To his horror he discovered himself sandwiched between "two tremendous alligators," and when he scrambled out from under his mosquito net, he saw "five more on the main deck and one on each sweep." Heart pounding, Robertson shouted, "The vessel is in the possession of the alligators!" In a twinkling the clamor of confused shouts and bare feet thumping the wooden deck yielded to musket shots and enough alligator meat to feed an army. The danger conquered and the chickens saved, the crew made loud fun of Robertson's "two companions on the mattress." Having learned their lesson, however, they pulled the sweeps aboard for what little remained of the night.[18]

Far less spectacular than the alligator but certainly fascinating are the delta's many amphibians—the Southern cricket frog, bird-voiced tree frog, barking tree frog, American bullfrog, Southeastern slimy salamander, Gulf Coast water dog, and the Eastern newt, among others. More visible, and in some cases far more troublesome to even casual observers, are the many insects that make the delta buzz, hum, and whine in summer—gnats and flies; the incredibly riotous cicadas, loudest of all the insects; grasshoppers; primitive dragonflies thrumming the air; beautiful butterflies of many varieties—palamedes swallowtails, sulphers, monarchs; stinging and biting pests such as the fire ant (an unwelcome immigrant through the Port of Mobile, circa 1930), yellow jacket, wasp, and hornet; and, most dreaded of all, the mosquito. In the early sixteenth-century the Spanish castaway Álvar Núñez Cabeza de Vaca said that he encountered "three kinds of them" on the Gulf Coast. "They poison and inflame," he wrote, "and during the greater part of the summer gave us great annoyance." The Indians were just as plagued by them, and Cabeza de Vaca reported that when covered with bites they resembled lepers. The *Aedes aegypti,* or yellow fever mosquito, that later wrought havoc on Mobile's colonial and early American residents, has of course earned its own particularly grim place in history.[19] Then there are the arachnids, some just as irritating and dangerous as the stinging and biting insects, if not more so—chiggers, mites, ticks, scorpions, black widow spiders, wolf spiders, and the gorgeous golden orb spiders, big as a logger's hand.

Contained by red hill escarpments as high as two hundred and fifty feet to the east and west, the Mobile's magnificent delta exists as a dynamic and exotic ecosystem, continually spilling sediment and debris—mud, sand, logs, river cane—into the head of Mobile Bay, growing itself ever southward by degrees—nine hundred feet a century, by one estimation.[20] Thus the big river that begins with such powerful promise at Nannahubba eventually enters its bay in diffuse and complicated fashion through five principal mouths—from east to west the Blakeley, Apalachee, Tensaw, Spanish, and Mobile Rivers. Other than the Tensaw, which at thirty-six miles long nearly rivals the Mobile's main channel, these streams are incredibly short—the Apalachee branches off the Tensaw and is six miles long, while the Blakeley splits off the Apalachee and is only three miles in length. The Spanish River, which splits off the Mobile at the north end of Blakeley Island opposite the city, is a mere eight-mile stem.

The delta will of course figure in this book, as it must, but it will not be the focus any more than the Mobile Basin writ large, for it too has received generous coverage, most recently in "A Wilderness Despite Us: The Magnificent Mobile-Tensaw Delta, How We Have Diminished It, and How We Can Restore It" (December 20, 1998), a *Mobile Register* award-winning special report; Sue Walker and Dennis Holt's *In the Realm of Rivers: Alabama's Mobile-Tensaw Delta* (2005); and Robert Leslie Smith's *Gone to the Swamp: Raw Materials for the Good Life in the Mobile-Tensaw Delta* (2008). While these articles and books treat the westernmost main channel and have much good information, their emphasis is general, environmental, or personal rather than historical and skips among the various waterways. As a result a coherent and full historical narrative, particularly as it unfolded along the banks of the Mobile River and its namesake city's wharves, has remained unwritten until now.

Even with five mouths and countless other smaller outlets dividing its entry into the bay, the Mobile's main channel still manages to be a significant river. The measured discharge at its mouth, just below downtown Mobile, averages a not inconsiderable sixty thousand cubic feet of water per second (compare to four hundred thousand for the mighty Mississippi) and can be even stronger after big rains upstate.[21] But unless a hurricane's storm surge drives bay waters north into downtown—as happened during Hurricane Katrina to a height of twelve feet—the city need not fear flooding from its

Rising tide. When tropical weather strikes, as it did in 1916, downtown flooding usually follows. Erik Overbey Collection. Courtesy of the Doy Leale McCall Rare Book and Manuscript Library, University of South Alabama.

river, and there are no levees as at New Orleans. For, no matter how much rain or flooding occurs above the city, the magisterial delta will absorb it all. The river is tidal all the way up to Nannahubba, though with a tame fluctuation of one to two feet in normal circumstances.

Water temperatures at the Mobile's mouth parallel those of the season—averaging a bathtub-comfortable ninety-five degrees in August, and a refrigerator-cold forty in February. The river nearly froze during the particularly severe winter of 1807, and in less notable cold snaps thin ice sheets hedge its smaller tributaries and the bay's margins.[22] The water's color is endlessly various—brown, black, silver, gun-metal blue, olive green, yellow, coppery orange, molten red, tawny—depending on the season and conditions of light and cloud. If the sun angle is right and there is a chop in the harbor, the river shimmers and explodes with bright white light, dazzling and hurting the eyes. In a short poem penned in 1931, "Green Water Burning," Rayford, who might as well be designated the Bard of the Mobile River, hit it exactly when he wrote: "Flaming little diamonds / dance like demons, / And every wave is crowned with a crest of burning spray."[23] Sometimes, when the weather is muggy and the sky is a dull, headache-inducing porcelain dome, the river can have a viscous quality, its lap heavy and thick. On clear chilly mornings, its surface writhes with mesmerizing wisps and tendrils, and in winter fog it assumes an ethereal, spooky aspect.

The river bottom, where not dredged, is soft and muddy. One diver who explored sunken Rebel wrecks at the Mobile-Spanish river split described it as being "like Cool Whip for several feet."[24] This mud moves with the river, too, and in fact suffuses it, gradually thickening from surface to bottom, billowing into the bay and settling into a bar off Choctaw Point that plagued navigation for centuries. Not surprisingly, underwater visibility is less than two feet in the best conditions. In *Cottonmouth,* Rayford vividly evoked this mud's sinister qualities, writing of murder victims dropped "through a privy into the shallow water and the bottomless-soft mud—mud that was more uncommunicative than a field of snow that's been snowed on and snowed under by fresh snow for three weeks."[25] The Mobile is also a river of mud, then, with many secrets.

Where dredged, the river's bottom is more substantial. As it is described in a boosteristic late-nineteenth-century trade publication, "The canal [that is, ship channel] is dug through a kind of blue, siliceous clay, which is tenacious in character and preserves the shape of the cut."[26] The river current's force continually scours this cut, but without maintenance the ship channel will eventually silt up. During the early 1870s a fierce argument raged about the merits of dredging versus natural scouring at the river's mouth, pitting Yankees and Rebels against each other again, but more of that anon.

Early explorers and travelers on the Mobile were under no illusion that it was in any way a minor stream. In the spring of 1700 Charles Levasseur, a French-Canadian engineer sent to reconnoiter for an advantageous site to establish a fort and town, paddled up the Mobile in a canoe with four men. Just above the mouth he reported a "width of the Seine opposite Invalides" and a depth of "eight armlengths or more."[27] Over half a century later Captain Bossu used nearly the same benchmark, calling the Mobile "more considerable than the Seine before Rouen." He also knew that it originated "in the Apalachian mountains" and was "the rendez-vous of all the Indians who live to the eastward."[28] In 1799 Andrew Ellicott, an American astronomer, mathematician, and surveyor commissioned to determine the boundary between U.S. and Spanish territory, described the Mobile as "a fine large river" and reported "one square-rigged vessel" had easily sailed as far as Fort St. Stephens, more than twenty miles above the fork, and more than sixty-seven north of the City of Mobile.[29]

People were no less impressed in the nineteenth century. Most encountered the Mobile as they were bound downstream for the Port City or upstream after a seaborne arrival there. Prince Bernhard of Saxe-Weimar Eisenach, a Waterloo veteran who afterward traveled widely in the United States, experienced the Mobile as he journeyed south. Near the site of Fort Stoddert he marveled at the river's size, which he estimated as "about half a mile wide."[30] George W. Featherstonaugh, a British geologist and geographer, first observed the Mobile when he traveled in the opposite direction. Featherstonaugh took a steamboat from the city's wharves in 1844, and north of town he compared the Mobile to "the Arkansas in the flatness of surface of the country," most of which was flooded, he guessed, a good ten feet up the tree trunks and river cane for

Busy Mobile River, circa 1910. Among the vessels visible in this extraordinary image are a bay boat (left center), a sternwheeler underway (middle distance), a log raft under tow by a tugboat (middle right), and white hulled fruit steamships berthed at the banana docks. Courtesy Library of Congress.

as far as he could see.[31] Philip Henry Gosse, an English naturalist and schoolteacher, left the city's quays in 1838, and as his steamboat churned upstream he contemplated the pleasing scene. "The river was smooth, and shone like silver, until its surface was broken by the rushing steamer: before us we had a polished surface; behind us we left a rolling sea, enshrouded beneath a long sable cloud of dense smoke."[32]

If it looks like a respectable river north of the city, to the south the Mobile broadens and meets the bay, taking on the more thrilling and, given the right conditions, stomach-churning aspects of the open sea. In 1917 a cub reporter on assignment for the *Mobile Tribune* was conveyed by skiff down to the river's mouth in order to board a schooner. "A stiff wind on Mobile River makes waves as high as a small squall makes in the ocean," he informed his readers. And modern visitors to the harbor are asked "How are your sea legs?" before being ushered aboard a small vessel for their water tour.[33] But it is Julian Lee Rayford who, once again, best understood and related the Mobile's true nature. "A powerful river," he declared, "carrying all the rolling expanse of a commonwealth as it swept on down out to the Gulf of Mexico."[34]

Indeed, the river and the city are nothing without their outlet to the sea. It is Mobile Bay that opens into the wide Gulf of Mexico, tying the region into the immense

Atlantic Basin. Because vessels have been able to sail through the gulf, into the bay, and up the river from anywhere in the world, a long history of colonization, conflict, trade, and prosperity has been made possible. It was into Mobile Bay—"this noble bay," as one nineteenth-century English arrival called it—that the sixteenth-century Spaniards would penetrate, radically altering the lives of the resident natives who had been nourished by the area's abundant resources and caressed by its balmy breezes for thousands of years.[35] The bay, like the delta, figures in this book, too, and it is helpful to have a general understanding of its formation and present geographical configuration before proceeding.

Thirty-one miles north to south, ten miles wide at the head and broadening to twenty-four at its base, Mobile Bay is shaped like a rifle stock, as was aptly noted by one sixteenth-century cartographer, and "a narrow 'Delaware-sort-of-a-bay,'" as an antebellum visitor put it.[36] It is a large brackish sheet of water, only about ten feet deep except for the ship channel running its length, with shallow margins that have long made it ideal for undertow-free swimming, wading, and floundering. An anonymous early nineteenth-century writer provided a fine description of the shore that still obtains: "The beach goes off from the edge of the water with a gradual rise, and forms a foundation to groves of small trees which fringe the environs of the Bay with their undying green. Here and there a noble tree towers over its mates, and shoots into the blue above it—where a diadem of sunlit air settles on its head."[37] The Eastern Shore, with its brown sandy beaches, red clay bluffs, and resorts, has long been the preferred side of the bay for tourists. The western margin by contrast—hard by the ship channel, muddier, its shore cluttered by logs, driftwood, and trash—is the poor man's side.

A long peninsula runs east to west across most of the bay's southern end, terminating at Mobile Point, site of Fort Morgan and much history. Opposite, three miles distant across open water where bay and gulf tumultuously mix, is Dauphin Island, which first provided the French safe harbor. Like all barrier formations, it bears the brunt of powerful gulf storms and, despite man's meddling, is continually resculpted by nature. "Our coast," one eighteenth-century French missionary accurately observed, "changes shape at every moment."[38]

Currents, tides, and waves in the narrow pass between Mobile Point and Dauphin Island can be incredibly powerful, swift, and rough. In the winter of 1854 a British captain sailing out wrote that "the sea (and ground swell on the bar) was tremendous." During the 2010 BP oil spill, fifty-foot poles set in the bay bottom to anchor boom were snapped like toothpicks.[39] Water-borne access to Mobile Bay and the city at its head historically came through this pass via the open gulf, between and over shifting sandbars wherever a deeper channel could be found (at least before regular dredging in the nineteenth century) or from New Orleans and the west through the Mississippi Sound, a relatively safe route protected most of the way by a series of barrier islands. The Gulf Coast Intracoastal Waterway, which greatly facilitates barge and recreational traffic along the littoral, was not completed until well into the twentieth century.

Today's configuration of river, bay, and sea with all its attendant flora and fauna is fairly recent within the Earth's geological time frame. Approximately eighteen thousand years ago, during the last ice age, sea levels were hundreds of feet below those of today. The shoreline stood more than sixty miles south, and Mobile Bay *was* the Mobile River, or at least its valley. The river cut a deep channel on out into what is today open gulf. Dramatic confirmation of this fact was provided after Hurricane Katrina scoured the sandy bottom south of Mobile Bay. Sportsmen began finding significant concentrations of fish in the area, and when a diver investigated, an intriguing underwater "relic forest" of ancient tree stumps was revealed following the meander of the Mobile River's ancient bed, all of it sixty feet deep and ten miles offshore.[40]

With glacial ice so far advanced then—roughly down to the Ohio River—the climate was cooler and drier. Spruce trees grew as far south as Nannahubba Bluff, and various hardwoods dominated the valley. As for the creatures inhabiting this landscape, they included such megafauna as mastadons, camels, ground sloths, and lions. Beginning about ten thousand years ago, the ice retreated, sea levels gradually rose, and the river valley filled in as the waters crept north. The delta began to form where the river and the new bay met, and the Mobile's channel roughly assumed its present course after merging with Big Bayou Canot to its west. Remnants of this evolution are evident in Twelve Mile Island, wrapped between the two ancient streambeds, and the Spanish River, which was originally the lower portion of the Mobile.[41]

When the first human being rested upon the banks of the Mobile River is unknowable, but such an event took place probably sometime between five and ten thousand years ago. The Gulf Coast's dynamic environment, with its changing shorelines, torrential rains, surging floods, howling storms, and shifting streams and land forms, works against the preservation of ancient human remains and has no doubt long obliterated or deeply buried the earliest evidence. But come and settle, people certainly did, as more than enough arrowheads, potsherds, piles of oyster shells, and earthen mounds from their descendants attest—men, women, and children living by the natural rhythms of their distinctive watery world. The Mobile River's human saga had begun.

Part 1

Coming Ahead

1

Indian Stream to *Entrada Española*

Tantalizing archaeological discoveries not far from the delta, such as a beautiful fluted Clovis spear point found along the lower Tombigbee River, indicate that human beings were present in southern Alabama many thousands of years ago. They were nomadic hunters and gatherers, descendants of those hardy Siberians who first crossed the land bridge into North America during the last ice age. It is almost certain that they ranged the gentle river valley that is now Mobile Bay and the coastal woodlands that are now inundated by gulf waters far offshore, but for obvious reasons hard evidence is lacking.[1]

Concrete and much more extensive evidence of human habitation along Mobile River and Bay becomes available for the period beginning about three thousand years ago, when area shorelines had essentially assumed their present configurations. Archaeologists refer to this as the Woodland Period, characterized by more-settled living; a practical mix of hunting deer, small game and birds, gathering nuts and berries, limited agricultural efforts, and exploitation of such estuarine food resources as oysters, clams, and fish; the construction of burial mounds; and the use of sand or fiber tempered pottery to bind the clay and prevent cracking.[2] Woodland peoples were thoroughly at home in their world and adept at utilizing everything in it to enhance survival. Nothing was wasted, and in the benign climate their numbers increased.

Numerous Woodland sites have been identified and dug in the Mobile River delta, providing valuable insight into that distant era. At least three were mapped and briefly investigated during a cultural resources survey of the area during the early 1990s. As simple as these sites are, they provide a useful window into Woodland ways. The first is located on the west bank of Bayou Sara and consists of a small shell midden—or, crudely put, a trash heap. At the time of the dig the midden was roughly nine feet wide by fifteen feet long, just over seven inches high, and steadily eroding into the bayou. Despite these modest dimensions and the instability of the site, a simple shovel test unearthed a fascinating range of artifacts including a deer bone, marsh clam shells, some burned bones, wood fragments, and several sand-tempered potsherds. The site would appear to have been a campsite, occupied for a limited time, where the native people hunted, harvested shellfish, and then cleaned, cooked, and ate their game.[3] From these fragments one can easily imagine what these Indians' life would have been like at this place. Everyone in the group—men, women, and children—participated in hunting and gathering food. Men ventured far afield for large game such as dear and bear for days at a time. Women and children hunted the immediate surrounds for smaller game, perhaps using snares. And everyone harvested the rich waters around them, net-fishing and easily scooping clams out of the brackish shallows and quickly heating them on little wooden grills over small fires. When the men returned from long hunts, there must have been hearty greetings—if they were lucky that is—and people would have turned to butchering and skinning the partially cleaned animals so that some meat could be eaten on the spot, more smoked and hung on strings from house rafters for later, and the hides and bones worked into multifarious utilitarian items such as pouches, moccasins, scrapers, and awls. No doubt much of these people's time was occupied with the getting and preparation of their meals, and when they finished eating they flung the refuse onto the ground to be unearthed by future archaeologists.

The second site is submerged beneath Chuckfee Bay, to the east of Twelve Mile Island and the Mobile's main channel, but originally it would have been above water. The archaeologists reported a badly eroded midden composed mostly of clam shells, with large amounts of pottery scattered around the feature and across the bay bottom. The sherds they recovered were plain or simply decorated and sand tempered, typical of the Woodland Period. They also found part of a turtle shell and fragments of mammal bones. As with the Bayou Sara midden, these items indicate that the Indians enjoyed a variety of readily obtainable foods in their diet, and ceramic vessels were critical to preparing, eating, and storing them. The fact that the site is underwater also provokes intriguing thoughts about how many other early archaeological sites might be flooded and lie yet undiscovered beneath the area's rivers, streams, bayous, and bays.[4]

The third site is on the west bank of Big Briar Creek, east of the Mobile's main channel. It includes a large shell midden eroding into the water, which shovel tests showed to include hundreds of clam shells, as well as turtle, mammal, and bird bones. But the most exciting discovery was a partial human skeleton, including numerous teeth, a right femur, an arm bone, and a shoulder blade. Analysis showed them to belong to an individual well-formed adult male. Though later material was found at the site, because of the type of pottery associated with the skeleton, it is believed to date to the middle Woodland Period. If so, its degree of development further confirms that the Mobile delta's early human inhabitants were well fed and strong.[5]

Woodland customs persisted until about a thousand years ago, when the more sophisticated Mississippian Period began. Lasting roughly until the Spanish *entradas* of the sixteenth century, this period was characterized by large-scale mound building;

elaborate religious ceremony and ritual; better and more decorative pottery; widespread cultivation of beans, maize, pumpkins, and squash; athletic games; extended trade routes; larger towns grouped into chiefdoms; use of the bow and arrow; and more warfare.[6]

One of the gulf rim's most important Mississippian chiefdoms was centered in the Mobile delta on what is called Mound Island, not far from the Tensaw and Middle Rivers. Accessible only by boat via a small stream known as Bottle Creek, the site is an astonishing complex of eighteen earthen mounds, the tallest of which is forty-five-feet high. Since it is heavily grown over now with towering trees and large palmettos that spread their broad fans at eye level, it is difficult to fully appreciate what this place would have been like during its prime Indian occupation seven hundred years ago.

Happily, due to the efforts of many archaeologists and researchers down the decades, a fairly plausible sense of the Bottle Creek site's significance and original appearance can be pieced together. It served as the ceremonial capital of what archaeologists call, somewhat confusedly for the layperson, the Pensacola Chiefdom. They chose this term because of so many associated sites clustered around that city and the general environs, but the Pensacola Chiefdom's influence stretched along the coast in both directions and up the Mobile River system as far as present-day Selma. The people who established this chiefdom had strong ties with the Indians at Moundville to the north and in the Lower Mississippi Valley to the west, and might have even represented a colonization effort of sorts. Given the Pensacola Chiefdom's access to the rich resources of the Mobile Bay Delta, it is easy to see why inland chiefdoms would value its friendship, no doubt making for a wide trade web. In this scenario these Mississippian Indians would have moved into the area, dominating and absorbing the resident Woodland Indians and creating the Pensacola Chiefdom.[7]

Certainly the construction of all those mounds required a high level of social organization and control. They were erected by basketfuls of earth transported from nearby borrow pits and when completed were topped with structures that were occupied by the chiefdom's religious and secular leaders. These structures, now long deteriorated away, had timber posts set into the ground, walls of river cane and mud, and roofs of palmetto fronds. From their lofty platforms the nobles would have looked over a large cleared plaza surrounded by the smaller mounds and earthworks, some of which contained burials. Besides enjoying a better view than their people, the leaders also got better food. In digging the top of the largest mound, archaeologists discovered evidence of superior cuts of meat, plenty of corn, and bigger oysters and clams than those found below. Also, the number of serving vessels recovered indicates that the ruling nobles were well tended by servants or slaves.[8]

Ensconced in the middle of this watery world, the Pensacola Chiefdom depended on good boats to exert its influence, conduct trade, and just manage the day-to-day realities of life in such a place. Like early people elsewhere, these Indians became practiced at fashioning safe and effective dugout canoes. Their construction methods likely did not change much over the centuries, and the observations of Captain Bossu regarding the making of such a canoe in the 1750s by Mobile Indians would obtain for the residents of the Bottle Creek site as well. According to Bossu, the Indians first selected a good tree of the right girth, usually cypress, and then set fire to it. After it fell they laid it on a frame, crudely shaped it, and again used fire along its length after which, he wrote, "they scraped away the live coals with a flint or an arrow." Wet mud might have been used along the sides of the log to control the fire and extensive working with stone and shell tools ultimately produced a sleek and swift river-worthy craft. Some have even been found in Florida with holes drilled into the bow for securing a line. Bossu noted that these canoes were used both for war and for carrying furs, and that the Indians were "very skilled in conducting these little vessels upon their lakes and rivers."[9]

What did these Indians looks like? According to the archaeology as well as later descriptions by the Spanish and the French, they were "well made both men and women," with coppery skin and long black hair. In a strange custom some had flattened foreheads that were the result of being strapped to cradle boards in infancy. This feature was thought to be highly attractive in their culture. Elaborate tattoos were common, sometimes in great whorls, and necklaces and earrings were worn by the more important. Copper and pearl adornments were also popular, but these Indians did not possess any gold, as the Spaniards would soon discover to their keen disappointment. Clothing varied by season and social class. During the warm months men and women went mostly naked, with only loincloths or, in the case of the women, Spanish moss, to cover their sex. In colder weather, deer or other animal skins and feather capes provided effective comfort. Chiefs, such as that of the Coosa encountered by Hernando de Soto in 1540, were sometimes quite impressively attired in beautiful robes or capes, with ornate headdresses.[10]

Warfare was a brisk and brutal business, with the enemy usually dispatched by arrow or club. Scalping was routine. Pitched battles between equal numbers of combatants would have been rare. Ambush or surprise was preferred. Captives were triumphantly paraded back to the home village and either put to work or, if they were important warriors, tortured and killed. Indian torture was a ghastly practice that made many Europeans shudder, but it is not exactly clear how much the Indians were influenced by the Spanish in their techniques, especially the burning or roasting prisoners alive. This was a common punishment during the Inquisition in Europe and no doubt was used on the Indians as well by Soto and possibly others. Sometimes a captive was simply made to kneel and had his brains dashed out by a heavy war club. The more unlucky were stripped, tied to a post, and prodded with sticks, weapons, and burning brands. Indian women, especially those who had lost relatives to warfare, were enthusiastic participants in the proceedings. The prisoner's ears and nose were cut off, his hair scalped, hot coals placed on his head and held down with mud, and his skin gashed. If the victim cried out or was obviously afraid, the punishment was delightedly redoubled. He was expected to bear up, sing a war song, taunt his enemies, and mock

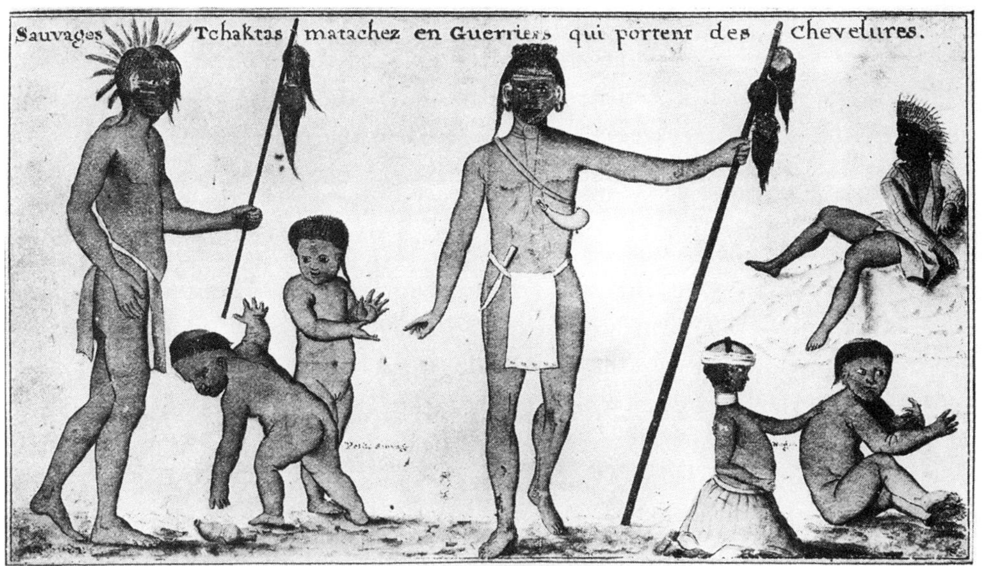

Choctaw Indians. The black child with the strange headgear was probably taken in a raid. Courtesy of the History Museum of Mobile.

the efforts to inflict pain. The end result was always the same, of course, but the warrior's demeanor and pride were everything.[11]

Whether or not anyone was tortured on Bottle Creek's plaza is unknown, though the French encountered the practice among the area's Indians when they arrived much later. There can be little doubt that the plaza hosted games, dances, and ceremonies related to the chiefdom's agricultural calendar. Among the most important of these would have been a green corn ceremony, or busk, to greet the ripening crop in high summer. The Pensacola Chiefdom included numerous small farming villages, and crops were extensively cultivated on the delta's low ground, where regular flooding continually renourished the soil. The success of these crops was crucial to the people's survival, and a good year meant plenty. In celebration there would have been fasting, dancing, and games such as chunkey. This sport was played in an open smooth area, like the plaza, in front of numerous onlookers—some perhaps even betting on the outcome. The action consisted of rolling a disk-shaped stone and having warriors throw spears at it in an attempt to come the closest. Team sports including ball, which was in reality a distant cousin of lacrosse, were also popular and frequently violent. One nineteenth-century account describes a player killed outright on the field, three badly hurt who died later, and more than a dozen who took better than a month to recover. Chiefdoms likely competed against one another, with the losers being deeply shamed. The Indians considered such competition "the little brother of war," and it held great importance within their culture.[12]

In their spiritual life these Indians worshipped the sun, and fire was also important to them. In the early eighteenth century a Frenchman reported that the Natchez Indians kept a perpetual fire burning in their temple. "They say this fire represents the sun," he wrote, "which they worship."[13] It is probable that Bottle Creek harbored such a flame as well, closely attended and maintained atop one of the mounds. The Indians also paid close attention to celestial events, knew how to read the weather—vitally important in hurricane country—and told stories to explain their origins and various aspects of the natural world. They were curious about strangers, if nonthreatening, and that is probably how they initially reacted when oddly dressed white men in an unusual watercraft appeared in the large bay at their doorstep.

Who were they, those first white men? If legend is to be credited, they were a ragtag company of medieval Welshmen led by their prince, Madoc ab Owain Gwynedd, fleeing bloody civil war at home. The old poets mention him and his great voyage but provide no details of his route. Nonetheless, during the sixteenth century the English found the legend useful in reinforcing their New World claims, and during the nineteenth century American intellectuals marveled over unusual ruins in the mid-South and seemingly credible stories of Welsh-speaking Indians. They connected these to the Madoc legend. In a letter dated October 9, 1810, former Tennessee governor John Sevier described an interview he had conducted with an old Cherokee chief almost thirty years earlier. Sevier asked the chief about the origins of some castlelike fortifications and was told they were made by "the White people who had formerly inhabited the country now called Carolina." When asked who these mysterious white people were, the chief told the governor, "they were a people called Welsh, and . . . they had crossed the Great Water and landed first near the mouth of the Alabama River near Mobile and had been driven up to the heads of the waters."[14]

It is indeed romantic to think of a small wooden ship, much battered by the elements, moving up the Mobile River with her salt-stained sail hanging limply while her crew labors at their oars. The men's grunts and the steady bump of their wooden sweeps against rusted iron oarlocks the only sounds in an awesome new green world, as dark eyes wonderingly stare at them from deep in the river cane. Could this possibly have been? Might the Mobile's uncommunicative mud yet yield a jeweled brooch or an iron shield boss dating to the twelfth century? No reputable historian believes so. But there is always the possibility. One of the most distinguished scholars of Gulf Coast history once tackled the subject, and in the end pronounced Madoc "as elusive as a sea-wraith."[15] There we will leave him.

The Mobile Bay area and the Indians who lived there finally enter the realm of written history in the early sixteenth century. In their quest for El Dorado the Spanish had made serious inroads to the Americas. They were settled at Havana, Cuba, and had conquered Mexico and Peru, garnering fabulous wealth in the process. Soon enough they looked to the northern Gulf Coast and the riches it might hold as their next endeavor. Early maps indicate only the most general knowledge of the shoreline, but given the amount of Spanish maritime traffic across the gulf, it was only a matter of time before the lines were to be drawn a little more surely.

The European most generally believed to have been the first into Mobile Bay was Álvarez de Pineda, of whom little is known other than his name and his voyage. He was commissioned by the governor of Jamaica and sent in command of four ships to explore the gulf rim and discover, if it existed, a sea route to the Pacific Ocean. In those days the Spanish referred to the entire northern gulf landmass as Florida and thought it might be a large island. Álvarez de Pineda departed in March 1519 and crossed the gulf, sighting land somewhere along the Florida panhandle and then skirting east and south down to peninsula's end. There he reversed course and followed the coastline all the way to Mexico. During his extraordinary reconnaissance he noted numerous rivers and bays and periodically landed to provision and meet Indians. These Álvarez de Pineda found friendly, and he excitedly commented on gold jewelry "in their nostrils, on their ear lobes, and on other parts of the body." By these adornments he inferred that the northern rivers held "fine gold," and from the natives' mild manner he judged them ripe for "conversion and indoctrination to our Holy Catholic Faith."[16] These assumptions led to much misery for Indian and Spaniard alike in the coming decades.

Álvarez de Pineda's geography was vague of course, and scholars have argued over which river or bay was which on the crude map he produced. At the turn of the last century Mobile historian Peter Joseph Hamilton vigorously championed the Mobile River and Bay as Álvarez de Pineda's Espíritu Santo River, and this has come to be widely accepted and celebrated by modern residents of the city. Hamilton also believed that Álvarez de Pineda's account of ascending a large river and spending forty days careening his ships and trading with the Indians had to refer to the Mobile River, rather than to the Mississippi as some other historians argued at the time. Hamilton was right in his contention that Mobile Bay is more accessible to ships than is the Mississippi's confusing mouth with its multiple channels and mud flats. Despite all of that however, the modern consensus is that the Espíritu Santo was the Mississippi River, which Álvarez de Pineda experienced from its tremendous flow into the gulf—he did not sail up it at all—and the place where he careened his vessels was the Río Pánuco in Mexico. That Álvarez de Pineda claimed he saw Indians adorned with gold, noted many promising-looking anchorages, and did the best he could with his map was more than enough to stimulate further exploration.[17]

Over the next forty years the Spanish launched three major expeditions into Florida. The first of these was led by the dashing figure of Pánfilo de Narváez, whom King Charles V commissioned to explore and exploit the dimly understood new territory. Narváez was well connected and had seen service in Mexico where he had tried to overthrow Hernán Cortés. Physically impressive—tall, robust, and red-haired—he had a nasty reputation for brutality, which among the conquistadors was saying something. The humane priest Father Bartolomé de las Casas, appalled at his needless massacres of friendly Indians, pronounced him "cruel and stupid," and his disastrous Florida expedition more than confirmed the judgment.[18]

Narváez landed in Tampa Bay in April 1528 with five ships, eighty horses, several hundred men, and, surprisingly, ten women—wives who did not want to be apart from their husbands. Also among the company was Cabeza de Vaca, treasurer, high sheriff, and chronicler extraordinaire. From the beginning the *entrada* was a debacle. Narváez treated the Indians in his usual high-handed manner, demanding riches they did not have, mutilating, burning, and setting his savage dogs on them. Constant conflict became the rule. Fruitless forays into the interior chasing mythical gold met with repeated attacks and ambushes. This situation, combined with disease and hunger, took a steady toll on the Spaniards. Alarmed by the course of events, Cabeza de Vaca and one of the women both predicted doom to Narváez's face.[19]

Doom was not long in coming. By autumn their pilot had deserted with the ships, and they were reduced to killing horses for food. In desperation the Spanish constructed five open boats from whatever materials they could scavenge—trees for boards, palmetto and horse hair for rope, clothing for crazy-quilt sails, cypress saplings for oars, and pine sap for pitch—and put to sea. Packed with almost fifty individuals each, the boats struggled westward, landing wherever the Spanish thought food or water could be had. At Pensacola Bay they encountered Indians who promised help but then attacked them in the night. Both Narváez and Cabeza de Vaca were hurt by thrown rocks, and the company miserably rode out a gulf storm offshore in preference to more fighting.[20]

Four days later they straggled into Mobile Bay and pulled some distance up the western shoreline, perhaps as far as the Fowl River. Here they met several Indians in a canoe, who promised to bring them water. One of the company, a Greek named Teodoro, insisted on going with the natives and took a black man with him. The Indians left two of their number with the Spanish as a good-faith gesture and left. At nightfall the Indians came back, but without Teodoro or his companion. The two Indian hostages attempted to jump out of the Spanish boats but were restrained, and their friends fled.[21]

Cabeza de Vaca wrote that the Spanish were "sorrowful and much dejected for our loss." They appear to have sat there in their cramped boats all night, no doubt wondering what on earth to do next. One can imagine the scene—the boats rocking gently on the bay with their huddled occupants conversing in low tones; Narváez himself still dazed from his wound and useless; thirst, coughs; the wind; a night heron's unsettling cry; despair. Landing would have been out of the question.[22]

Morning brought an escalation. According to Cabeza de Vaca, "many natives arrived in canoes who asked us for the two that had remained in the boat." Narváez replied that they would be handed over when the Christian hostages were returned. Among the Indians were several chiefs, "the most comely persons, and of more authority and condition than any we had hitherto seen." The chiefs wore "the hair loose and very long, and were covered with robes of marten such as we had before taken." All in all Cabeza de Vaca thought they made "a brave show." But the danger was real, and as the fruitless negotiations continued, more canoes arrived and attempted to hem in the Spanish boats. The company managed to outmaneuver the Indians and get into the gulf, but the Indians followed, and their demands for their people became more insistent. Finally the stalemate broke when warriors began "to hurl clubs" and "to throw stones with slings." Mercifully the wind came up, and the Spanish made their escape without their erstwhile shipmates, the first Greek and the first black man in local history. Unredeemed, their fates among the Mobile Indians were not to remain a mystery forever.[23] Nor was that of Narvárez's expedition. It went on to further peril and grief, and in the end only Cabeza de Vaca and three others survived the incredible odyssey.

What is most notable about this early contact between Indians and Europeans on Mobile Bay is the distrust and conflict that attended it. At least one historian has theorized that the Indians had advance notice of the company and that the first canoe was a scout meant to ascertain the strangers' wants before they got up toward the delta where the Indian villages were concentrated. There were no women among the larger number of natives who arrived the next morning, indicating that the purpose was to block or kill the newcomers.[24] The Spaniards' reputation doubtless preceded them. Perhaps the Indians had heard of Narváez's tactics already, or endured an unpleasant encounter with some lone wolf pirate or rogue blown off course. In any event, they thwarted Narváez's desperate party, and returned upriver in peace.

Scarcely a dozen years later, Hernando de Soto, a former captain in Pizarro's conquest of Peru, newly minted governor of Cuba, and *adelantado* of Florida, launched his own *entrada*. Though he never saw the Mobile River Delta, he ravaged a large portion of its broader basin, and his destructive trail was to have a far more profound and devastating impact on the region's native populations than Narváez's blundering enterprise. While planning his endeavor in Spain, Soto had actually met Cabeza de Vaca, but rather than being discouraged by the latter's tale of woe, urged him to join the new invasion. The weary treasurer, high sheriff, and scribe declined, having had enough of following bloody conquistadors onto God forsaken shores.[25]

Like Narváez, Soto landed at Tampa Bay with a considerable force—over five hundred men, 237 horses, and hogs for food on the hoof. Over the course of 1540 he carved a ruthless path through the Southeast much as Narváez attempted to do but far more effectively. He entered what is now Alabama somewhere in the northeast quadrant, and knifed down the Coosa River valley, taking august chiefs as hostages, women for his men's pleasure, braves and boys for bearers. Torture, rapine, and murder were trifles to him in the quest for gold and silver. As one chronicler declared, Soto and his men paid "no attention to anything that did not pertain to these metals."[26]

Somewhere along the upper Alabama River, Soto learned the fate of Teodoro and his black companion, when Indians informed him they had been killed at their village and displayed the Greek's dagger to prove it. How long the hapless Christian hostages might have lived among the Indians was not stated, but the fact that they were seized down at Mobile Bay and met their end some two hundred miles north demonstrates the importance of the Mobile River as an effective interior highway.[27]

There has been much scholarly debate over the years as to Soto's exact route and the location of Mobila, the village where the expedition's most desperate pitched battle took place. Some put it toward Montgomery or Selma, others closer to the delta. Most agree, however, that the Spanish were somewhere in the broad fertile swath between the Alabama and Tombigbee Rivers. Mobila was a fortified town, and its defenders were under the leadership of the strong-willed Chief Tascaluza, a giant of a man who upheld the dignity of his position with great fanfare. By the time the Spaniards reached Mobila, Tascaluza was determined to put an end to their depredations and accordingly set a trap.[28]

Lured inside by dancing girls and promises of riches, the Spaniards were attacked by hundreds of Indians who had concealed themselves in huts. The crowded quarters deprived the conquistadors of their greatest advantage, cavalry, and the resulting melee was a vicious affair. The Spanish took losses but managed to fight their way outside, where Soto rallied them for a series of assaults on the town. "We killed them all," one of Soto's men later recalled, "either with fire or the sword." But the cost of victory was high—more than twenty conquistadors killed, almost all the rest wounded, many horses dead, and the baggage consumed in the inferno. Also lost was the only tangible wealth taken during the entire march—some two hundred pounds of river pearls. Nearly broken, Soto's force rested. A fleet was waiting down on the gulf, but rather than flee to safety, Soto wanted to salvage some success from his ill-fated venture. To do anything else meant poverty and shame. Therefore, the *adelantado* turned his veterans north and followed the Tombigbee into what is now Mississippi. Constant fighting marked their progress, and by the following spring, Soto was dead, his body placed in a shroud weighted with river sand and sunken beneath the Father of Waters. The survivors, less than half the original company, made their way down to Mexico, closing one of the most sanguinary chapters in American history.[29]

So much for Soto and company, but what of the Indians? The Spanish accounts put their losses in the thousands. Chief Tascaluza was not accounted for and he may have escaped, but like Soto, his power was crippled. Far worse was to come however, an enemy more fearsome and invulnerable than the most heavily armored and mounted hidalgo—disease. Soto's extended trek through the Southeast introduced a witch's brew of ills that had been theretofore unknown in the Americas—smallpox, measles, and perhaps a variety of pig-borne diseases—to which the Indians had no immunity. Contagion spread like wildfire, far beyond the limits of Soto's track. There is no record of exactly how much of the Indian population succumbed, but one historian has estimated a staggering figure of 90 percent.[30] The effect of this trauma on native world view and spirituality must have been significant, not to mention its impact on the complex and cultivated Mississippian social structure.

Unfortunately for the Indians, Spanish ambitions in the northern gulf country were not yet satiated. But rather than squander efforts in a fruitless hunt for gold, the Crown now decided to launch a bona fide colonization effort, settling Florida and establishing a link with the Atlantic Coast. Accordingly, in early September 1558 Guido de Lavazares, a capable seaman, was dispatched from Mexico on a reconnaissance mission. Proceeding west with sixty men in three vessels—a bark, a lateen-rigged sloop, and a shallop—Lavazares swiftly and expertly probed the coast. Within days he hove into Mobile Bay and was instantly impressed. A notary later took down Lavazares's report, which stated: "This was the largest and most commodious bay he found in that region for the purpose which his Majesty orders." There was more. "The bay is very healthful and has the climate of Spain both in respect to rain and in occurrence to cold." The hopeful testimony continued: "In the bay and its vicinity are many fish and shellfish; there are many pine trees suitable for making masts and yards; there are oaks, live oaks, nut trees, cedars, junipers, laurels, and certain small trees which bear a fruit like chestnuts." On the western shore Lavazares described "yellow and grayish clay for making jars and other things." Indians in "large canoes" darted about checking their fish traps, and corn, beans, pumpkins, and squash were seen surrounding their villages. Lavazares thoroughly explored the bay's margins and at its head found "a copious river," almost certainly the Mobile's main channel, where fresh water was obtained. Álvarez de Pineda, Narváez, Cabeza de Vaca, and Soto had all come within some distance of the Mobile River proper, but it was probably one of Lavazares's nut-brown seamen who was the first European to feel its warm water on his skin. There were no silly references to a gold-laden stream or bejeweled natives. This was a practical enterprise, and the raw materials for survival, if not prosperity, appeared to be in place. Lavazares named his "commodious bay" the Bahía Filipina, for King Philip II of Spain.[31]

The following summer the colonizing fleet arrived, led by Don Tristán de Luna y Arellano. Like Navárez and Soto, Luna was an old conquistador, having served with Francisco Vásquez de Coronado in the quest for the Seven Cities of Cíbola in the American Southwest. But also like them, he found his efforts to be difficult and to end in failure. Luna's expedition was by far the largest to touch the northern Gulf Coast. He had eleven ships; quantities of provisions such as corn, bacon, cheese, vinegar, and wine; tools for clearing land and building; more than five hundred soldiers, a thousand servants, Indians, black individuals, and women; and more than two hundred horses. Luna's immediate superior, the viceroy of Mexico, had his doubts about the inclusion of families, and after it all fell apart wagged a finger: "I told you many times not to take so many married men with wives and children, for experience shows that they are of little effect."[32]

Luna sailed his fleet into Mobile Bay in August, thinking it was actually Pensacola Bay, or Ochuse. Despite Lavazares's enthusiasm for the Bahía Filipina and its resources, Ochuse was known to be a better deep-water anchorage. Once he realized his mistake, Luna disembarked some of the soldiers and horses so they could march east to Ochuse and then sailed the rest of the expedition the less than fifty-mile distance between the two bays. Once safely anchored in Ochuse, Luna sent exploring parties up the Escambia River in hopes of finding it a convenient highway to the interior. But this was one way that Filipina with its extensive river system was far superior, and the soldiers returned with gloomy reports. They found the expedition in dire circumstances, for in their absence a hurricane had struck and sunk or damaged numerous vessels before they could be fully unloaded. Luna's big venture was shaping up to be a disaster before it had even had a chance properly to begin.[33]

Convinced that success meant moving north and getting help from the Indians, Luna divided his force, sending one part overland and the other upstream in small vessels via the Mobile and Alabama Rivers. His goal was the Indian village of Nanipacana (probably in what is now Monroe County, Alabama). But misfortune dogged the Spaniards. Hunger increased, and the Indians, remembering the depredations of Soto a generation before, were understandably skittish. They reacted by melting away with their provender, burning houses and crops, and zinging the occasional arrow into a Spanish breast from cover. Complicating matters, Luna's mental health deteriorated—as his officers put it, "he had lost his reason through illness"—and the command structure broke down amid acrimony and accusation. Soto would have brutally quelled any hint of mutiny, but Luna indulged his disgruntled men in their misery, and the disputes eventually led to a series of lawsuits. The bitterness and disappointment are palpable in the public record that resulted, a boon for historians.[34]

In desperation the Spanish decided to return to the coast, but this time to the more promising Bahía Filipina. "In view of the very bad way in which things were going," a group of officers later testified, "and of the great want from which the people of the camp were suffering . . . the measure considered suitable was that of coming to the [Bahía] Filipina to maintain ourselves upon the shellfish there until the fleet should come." And so the Mobile River hosted its first, but not its last, forlorn little flotilla fleeing defeat and ruin. Crowded aboard makeshift rafts, the Spanish drifted south. It was anything but a routine or easy descent, however. Horses, weapons, clothing, and shoes fell into the river—more potential finds on the Mobile's muddy bottom—and food was scarce to nonexistent. As the officers reported, "many of us had a difficult time; some lost their lives, for the hunger grew so great, and we were so long in getting down the river, that those who escaped from this disaster consider themselves well off to find themselves wherever they may be." Whether the dead were buried beneath the delta muck with a prayer and a hastily crafted cross, or simply eased into the broad silent current to drift astern and sink, the record does not reveal. At last the survivors reached Filipina, then shifted to Ochuse, where a fleet rescued them.[35]

With the departure of Luna's emaciated colonists, the Mobile was once more an Indian stream. It would be more than a century later before a significant number of white men would again float upon its waters or roam its banks, and the natives they encountered were but a remnant of the once proud Mississippian chiefdoms. The Bottle

Creek site was abandoned, though still considered sacred, and its elaborate society forgotten. The Indians in their dugout canoes who ghosted out of small sloughs and bayous onto the delta's larger rivers and lakes to pursue fish and game were still close to the land and understood their environment intimately, but they were also greatly changed.

They called themselves the Mobile, which may have been derived from a Choctaw word, *moeli,* meaning "to paddle," appropriate enough in their riverine surroundings. They were of the Muskhogean family, descendants of Chief Tascaluza's brave people, and they had probably lived at Nanipacana when Luna arrived. By the late seventeenth century they had moved south and were concentrated along both sides of the Mobile's main channel in numerous small villages. Though their numbers were much reduced from Mississippian days—the French estimated that they could field some three hundred warriors—they hunted and farmed as their ancestors had, and their language formed the basis for a trade jargon understood throughout the gulf region. Their immediate neighbors were the Naniabas in the Alabama-Tombigbee fork and the Tahomés along the latter river. Farther north and east were the powerful Alabamas, who frequently made war on the Mobile, often goaded by the English; to the east the Pensacolas (not to be confused with the Pensacola Chiefdom), a small but bellicose tribe; and to the west the Pacagoulas and Biloxis.[36]

It was into this fractured and unsettled world that the French arrived in 1699. As their ships hove to off Dauphin Island, native eyes once again beheld strange vessels with white sails and white men, and no doubt wondered what was to come.

2

Colonial Days and Ways

January 23, 1902, dawned chilly and bright, with a thin mist clinging to the river's placid surface. Quayside, two vessels were bustling with activity, smoke chuffing from their single stacks as they got up steam. The United States revenue cutter *Winona,* a 149-foot iron-hulled twin-screw steamer, and the *James A. Carney,* a 150-foot wooden side-wheeler, were moored at the Mobile & Ohio Railroad Fruit Wharf and the municipal wharf, respectively, only yards apart, loading passengers for what promised to be an auspicious and festive day.[1]

The occasion was the bicentennial celebration of Old Mobile's founding upriver at Twenty-Seven Mile Bluff by the French. A four-foot-high granite marker had already been carefully situated there and covered with a white cloth for the formal unveiling. As the sun rose and burned off the mist, the *Winona* and the *Carney* cast off and began the three-hour cruise to the site.

The temperature steadily climbed into the fifties, and the dark-clothed passengers crowded the rails, marveling at the day's mildness and commenting on the unfolding scenery. Aboard the *Winona* were the Mobile mayor and members of the city council; county officials; representatives of various public boards; the collector of the port; Thomas McAdory Owen, state archivist; Grace King, a New Orleans historian and author; Dr. James Searcy, superintendent of the newly opened Mount Vernon Hospital twelve miles to the north of the site; and members of the Bicentennial Committee. Of the last, none was more invested in the day than the featured speaker, Peter Joseph Hamilton, a forty-three-year-old lawyer and author of the recently published monumental history, *Colonial Mobile.* Aboard the *Carney* were citizens who had paid fifty cents for the "basket excursion," a detachment from Battery A of the Alabama State Artillery with a field piece, and a military band.[2]

At eleven o'clock the vessels reached the bluff. The *Winona* anchored midstream, and her passengers boarded small boats that were pulled to shore without incident. The

Carney angled into the soft bank and dropped a gangplank. Over the next hour people clambered up the twenty or so feet to the site, at that season a brown and sere broom-sedge field, and searched for old bricks as souvenirs or just generally milled about the wooden stage constructed for the ceremony. Hard by the veiled marker towered a moss-hung hickory tree, its branches already budding green in the winter warmth.[3]

The formal activities began with an invocation, and then Hamilton—mustachioed, tall, and reedy, with a scholar's stoop and receding hairline, and clutching a sheaf of papers—took the stage. "We stand on historic ground," he began, as people edged closer. "Here was the first lasting French settlement of the Gulf states, here the cradle of civilization of the Mississippi Valley. In the unbroken forest which two hundred years ago stood in the place of this field, at this same bleak season, after seeing on the river what we see today, armed Frenchmen were cutting down virgin timber, painfully hauling it hither, and building of squared logs a fort overlooking that river."[4]

Hamilton spoke for more than half an hour, broadly sketching the area's colorful history with its "Latin influences," and was frequently interrupted by applause. At last he looked toward the stone and said, "We place thee, lone monument, on a spot still almost as desolate as when Bienville left it for the lasting site at the river mouth; but a spot made sacred by the tears and blood, the life and death of great men."[5] With the conclusion of his speech the veil was solemnly removed from the stone. The small field piece, which had been dragged up the bluff and aimed east, barked sharply, its smoke gently rolling downstream, and the *Winona* answered from anchor with a twenty-one-gun salute. As the reports faded, the band played *Auld Lang Syne, America, Dixie,* and *Yankee Doodle,* with some people singing along. Then, to the crowd's delight, a drummer and a trumpeter stationed just below the bluff struck up a stirring rendition of *La Marseillaise.*[6]

Formalities concluded, the crowd clapped again and broke apart, some heading back toward the vessels and others peering at the stone's inscription. Chiseled on its eastern face, overlooking the delta, it remains clearly legible to this day: "Erected by the people of Mobile, January 23, A.D. 1902, to commemorate the 200th anniversary of the Founding here of Fort Louis de La Mobile by Pierre Le Moyne Sieur d'Iberville and Jean Baptiste Le Moyne Sieur de Bienville."[7] Hamilton no doubt felt good about the day. He had acquitted himself well, and his city had paid appropriate homage to its indomitable founders. He was back in town before dark.

Modern visitors to Twenty-Seven Mile Bluff often wonder, why a fort here? The site is so removed from the coast (almost sixty miles) and from the present-day city of Mobile, as the bluff's name informs, that its choice seems less than obvious. The reasons had everything to do with eighteenth-century power politics, as well as with the Indians who fished and farmed in the vicinity.[8]

As the eighteenth century approached, the French were determined to expand their presence on the North American continent. The Spanish claimed Florida with a fort in St. Augustine and a garrison by 1698 in Pensacola. The English grew and prospered along the eastern seaboard, and their traders and trappers had even begun to penetrate west along the Ohio and Tennessee River valleys. But the vast interior was up for grabs, and the early Mississippi River voyages of French explorers Jacques Marquette and Louis Joliet and by Robert Cavelier, Sieur de La Salle, convinced King Louis XIV to gamble on the effort. Despite the expense and the risks, the potential rewards were significant: a seemingly limitless fur trade, naval stores, extensive mineral resources, new markets in the theretofore inaccessible Spanish colonial ports, and, last but not least, an effective check on future English expansion. The strategy appeared sound. It lacked only the men who could make it happen.[9]

Enter the brothers Le Moyne—Iberville, Bienville, Chateaugué, and Sérigny—a quartet of native Canadians who, by skill, toughness, and force of will, were to plant the fleur-de-lis on the banks of the Mobile River and forge a viable community. Iberville was the eldest, born in 1661, and was appointed leader of the enterprise. A gifted navigator and sailor, he had led the French to victory in a series of battles and sieges on Hudson Bay in 1697. Bienville, born in 1680, was young in years but an experienced, intelligent, and courageous man who had been wounded at Hudson Bay. He had a facility for Indian languages and a strong constitution, always an advantage in the Americas. Once the colony was founded, it was Bienville who would become its most prominent leader. Chateaugué was the youngest of them all, but he also had naval service under his belt. He would act as Bienville's capable facilitator, and he gave his name to Bayou Chateaugué, now known as Three Mile Creek. Sérigny was the second eldest of the four, and, like Chateaugué, would prove crucial in assisting Iberville and Bienville in their more important roles.[10]

Iberville made three voyages to the gulf from 1698 to 1701. During these trips he found the Spanish already in possession of Pensacola Bay, but he successfully established a fort near present-day Biloxi and explored the coastline in both directions looking for the mouth of the Mississippi and a suitable locale for a permanent post. Once found, the Mississippi's mouth (or mouths) was hardly inviting without a good pilot, and the lower Mississippi did not appear promising for settlement because of its low and swampy terrain. Therefore, Iberville concentrated his search to the east. Mobile Bay was too shallow for his oceangoing ships, but its river system was attractive, providing handy access deep into the interior where Indians could be influenced to attack the English colonies.

Happily for such a scheme, the large island at the bay's eastern mouth had a good harbor sheltered by a crescent-shaped spit of land, which the French named Pelican Island. During a later visit Sérigny took a sounding that measured twenty-one feet at low tide, prompting one Frenchman to observe that "vessels of forty and fifty guns would be completely safe here." Iberville and Bienville were rowed to the island but made a horrifying discovery that more superstitious men might have considered a bad omen. As a carpenter named André Pénicaut, who was in the shore party, later wrote, "When we disembarked, we became terrified upon finding such a prodigious number of human skeletons that they formed a mountain, there were so many of them." Bienville promptly called the place Massacre Island, a name that would hold for several years until it was dubbed, less frighteningly, Dauphine, for the French princess (referred to hereafter by its modern spelling "Dauphin"). Some of the Frenchmen on that early shore party speculated that the bones were those of Narvaéz's forlorn sailors, but Pénicaut later learned that they were Mobile Indians who had died in an epidemic and been deposited on the island.[11]

Iberville wanted to know more about the Mobile River and the people who lived there. Experience had shown that it was easier to get into from the gulf than the Mississippi was, and its basin was closer to the English, thus offering obvious logistical advantages for settlement and for building alliances with Indian tribes and sending them forth to create mischief. He ordered a detailed reconnaissance, which was conducted in the early summer of 1700 by Charles Levasseur, a talented engineer and draftsman. Levasseur departed Biloxi in a canoe with four men, entered Mobile Bay, and threaded his way well up the river. He described the Mobile-Tensaw split and learned of numerous small villages and tribes in the region, the latter generally referred to by the French as "petites nations." The bigger tribes were farther north—the Choctaws, the Chickasaws, and the Alabamas. Worrisome, he had heard that "the English were in those nations every day, and that they take pack horses burdened with clothing, guns, gunpowder, shot," which they traded for deer hides. The English trafficked in another commodity as well—slaves. According to Levasseur, they encouraged the bigger tribes to attack the smaller ones, "killing the men, carrying away the women and children whom they sell to the English, each one for a gun, the practice of which has brought great destruction in the neighboring nations, among them the Pensacola and the Mobile."[12]

Levasseur found the Mobile Indians receptive and interested in what the French had to offer in the way of trade and protection from the aggressive Alabamas. He spent a night in one of their riverside villages and wrote of houses with "high walls of earth" that were "roofed with palm leaves, matted with split cane to prevent the wind from carrying away the palm leaves." In another village Levasseur found a large wooden cross that the Indians said the Spanish had left. Clearly, the French were not the only ones coveting the Mobile River and its environs. In his report Levasseur described the Mobilians as "of a strong, merry temperament" and fond of "dance and play almost always." He noted their skill with the bow and arrow, their turkey-feather cloaks, and their cultivation of maize, beans, squash, and watermelon. Their numbers were few, which Levasseur estimated at five hundred, but the Mobilians were comfortably settled on their river and knew how to survive. The French, like the Puritans before them up east, were going to need Indian help if they were to succeed.[13]

Encouraged by Levasseur's report, the Crown ordered Iberville to transfer the main base of operations from Biloxi to the Mobile River. Twenty-Seven Mile Bluff was chosen because it was close to where the Mobilians were concentrated, and the

Indians assured Iberville that the high spot would never flood. Thus it was that on January 4, 1702, Bienville began the move. It started with a small flotilla loaded with supplies sailing from Biloxi to Massacre Island. These vessels included a forty-five-ton ketch, two feluccas, and a freighter.

Watercraft of various kinds were essential to the colonial endeavor. Given the peculiarities of the central Gulf Coast, the French quickly learned which were the most useful and efficient. Like the Indians, they depended heavily upon canoes. These were mostly cypress and longleaf pine dugouts, or pirogues, that ranged from small "two-place" craft that could carry two men and three or four hundred pounds, to fifty-footers that could carry thirty men and several tons. The best of these canoes had seats, steering oars, and sails. Indians and, later, black slaves were frequently used as rowers. Bark canoes are sometimes mentioned in the records, but these were not as easily made on the gulf as in Canada. The French also used canoes made of buffalo skin stretched over willow frames. It is possible that examples of these latter two types were brought along by voyageurs that sometimes trekked into the colony from up north. There are numerous references to *bateaux* and *chaloupes,* connoting a variety of small flat-bottomed or shallow-draft open boats. Larger craft included the felucca, which was basically a sail boat with a lateen rig, sometimes oars or sweeps, and a carrying capacity of a dozen or so men; and the brigantine, a two-masted vessel with only the foremast square-rigged. Brigantines were versatile boats, capable of sailing into shallower bays and inlets as well as navigating across the open gulf. In 1707 a brigantine of better than fifty tons was anchored off Twenty-Seven Mile Bluff and reportedly could navigate even further north. She carried a crew of twelve and made runs to Vera Cruz and Havana for cargoes such as animals and flour. Oceangoing vessels such as frigates and ships-of-the-line, carrying many guns and large crews, were not unknown off Dauphin Island, but these could not cross the bar into the inviting shelter of Mobile Bay.[14]

Iberville discerned that more specialized boats were needed as well and, less than two weeks after ordering Bienville to make the move to the Mobile River, described his instructions for a new barge: "I sent Le Roux, overseer carpenter of the port of Rochefort, and all the ships' carpenters and caulkers to build a pinnace of forty-five tons with a flat bottom, and designed so that it will navigate on the sea as well as in the rivers, and will draw no more than 4 ½ feet when loaded." Such a vessel—essentially an oversized box with a pointed front, oars, a sail, and enough freeboard to manage swells but a minimal draft to ply far upstream over shallow bars—was perfect for Mobile Bay and the labyrinthine delta with its numerous rivers, streams, and bayous.[15]

So began a steady three-way to and fro between Biloxi, Massacre Island, and Twenty-Seven Mile Bluff. Big tents protected the supplies on the island until a permanent warehouse could be erected. Steadily the stuff came in—thirteen barrels of wine (these were Frenchmen, after all!), four casks of flour, a cask of lard, meat, sugar, wheat, wooden shingles, colored beads and red stockings (expected to be popular trade items with the Indians), axes, hammers, saws, pliers, a big clock improbably plopped on the sand, and a hundred other things. Meanwhile upriver, the backbreaking task of clearing the town site began on January 20, nearly two centuries to the day before Hamilton was to deliver his inspirational speech. Working with a will in the cool weather, men felled trees and dressed the trunks for construction and cleared and burned brush, while Levasseur laid out the town. The Mobilians no doubt helped and watched.[16]

The fort took priority and quickly rose on the high bluff. It was small by any standard, only 140-feet square, with pointed bastions fashioned of squared timbers laid on top of one another and fixed at the corners by dovetail notches. According to Pénicaut, who helped build it, "there was a battery of six pieces of cannon which, protruding outside in a half-circle, covered the sector in front and to right and left. Inside, within the curtains, were four fronts of buildings fifteen feet back from the curtains behind them. These buildings were to be used as chapel, as quarters for the commandant [Bienville] and the officers, as warehouses, as guardhouse." Bienville's quarters included a steeply pitched roof and a long balcony running the length of the building with a view of the river. This latter amenity was the first of a very long line to come in Mobile. In the middle of the fort was a *place d'armes* where troops could be inspected and Indians overawed. Plans called for a pointed palisade outside the fort, apparently never erected. On the lip of the bluff a powder magazine was excavated but proved unsatisfactory when it kept holding rainwater.[17]

While the fort was situated well above the river's tawny surface, the rest of the town spread out and downward toward marshy land to the west and a small stream that defined the settlement's northern edge. This was to spell eventual disaster. But for the present the French continued their work. Clearing advanced, with the bigger stumps left in place to rot, while lots were assigned—a large one on the western edge for the priests from Québec Seminary, another for the Jesuits, another for a hospital, and smaller ones for ship carpenters and caulkers, soldiers, coureurs de bois, Levasseur, and Henri de Tonti, a remarkable figure with an iron prosthesis in place of the hand he had lost in a European siege. Tonti was an infantry captain who knew the Americas thoroughly, having traveled with La Salle down the Mississippi, and he would prove invaluable to the new settlement on the Mobile.[18]

By early March, Iberville wanted to inspect the progress on the bluff. He was in Pensacola recovering from a painful injury to his side, but he had begun to feel like traveling again. Though the Spanish were less than thrilled with the French plans, the two countries were at peace, and the Spaniards decided to be helpful for the present. Since both enterprises were tenuous at best, equally threatened by the English and in need of sympathetic assistance from a source closer than Cuba, Mexico, or France, this made great practical sense. Throughout the early colonial period the two small outposts would coexist congenially or uneasily, depending on the official relations between the mother countries—sometimes cooperating by sharing desperately needed supplies, at other times inciting Indian allies against one another or openly warring, as from 1718 to 1721, when Bienville briefly captured the Spanish outpost.[19]

His condition improved, Iberville embarked on his tour in typically blustery late-winter weather. "The water is high," he remarked north of the Mobile River's mouth; "many spots on the mainland on the west side seem flooded, that is, along the banks, far back from the river the land is high. The islands are low, on a level with the water." As he pushed north in a small vessel, he noted the abundance of good timber, "very fine, tall, thick, straight." On his third travel day he arrived at the settlement, where he "found my brother De Bienville there, busy building a fort."[20]

As important as the activities on the bluff were, Iberville did not let them overshadow other considerations. Immediately upon arrival, he had a tall tree cut and made into a mast to be sent down to Sérigny at Massacre Island to replace one lost in a storm. In an effort to cement Indian alliances and reduce the scourge of English slave trading, he had already sent Tonti north, loaded with trade baubles to make peace between the Choctaws and Chickasaws. And the day after he set foot on the riverbank, he ordered Bienville to reconnoiter the large and mysterious delta which the newly risen fort overlooked. Settled into a canoe with several Mobilian guides, Bienville set forth, steering northeast deeper into the flooded swamps. According to Iberville, "he got an Indian to show him the place where their gods are, about which all the neighboring nations make such a fuss and to which the Mobilians used to come and offer sacrifices." Bienville had to give his guide a gun to induce him to take him to the spot, and once they were there the man kept his back turned to the sacred place. This, as it turned out, was the deserted Bottle Creek site. Here, "on a little hill among the canes," Bienville discovered five ceramic (or possibly stone) idols—"a man, a woman, a child, a bear, and an owl." His terrified guide claimed it meant death to touch them, but the unflappable Bienville not only touched them but brought them back to the bluff as well. "The Indians who see them here are amazed at our boldness," Iberville declared, "and amazed that we do not die as a result. I am taking the images to France, though they are not particularly interesting." Intrigued by this passage, several scholars have searched French libraries, museums, and archives for the Mobilian idols, to no avail. Perhaps they yet lie on some dusty basement shelf, waiting for their magic to be rekindled.[21]

By month's end Tonti returned downriver with several pirogues occupied by various Choctaw, Chickasaw, and Mobilian chiefs. With great ceremony the Indians were received in the fort's plaza and invited to inspect gifts that included guns, powder and shot, knives, cooking wares, glass beads, and other attractive knick-knacks. Speaking through Bienville, who was fluent in the Mobilian trade jargon, Iberville instructed the chiefs, "you must not listen to the English anymore, you must drive them away from you." If the Chickasaw did not cooperate, he warned, "we could never be friends with one another and I would carry on no trade with you. I would arm all the Choctaw, Tomeh and Mobilians with guns . . . and you would have the grief of seeing your men slaughtered at the gates of your own village with your women and children." If they were agreeable, however, Iberville promised a brisk trade without the bloodshed or slavery that attended their dealings with the English. With the speechifying concluded, the French officers and the chiefs smoked the calumet of peace and exchanged promises and gifts. Iberville must have been gratified by the speed with which his sovereign's wishes were bearing fruit.[22]

The French had labored hard since their 1699 landfall on the gulf, and in February 1703, they quite possibly celebrated their first Mardi Gras in years. It would have hardly been an elaborate or extended affair—a priest admonishing the flock on the approach of Lent, perhaps a few makeshift masks, raucous song, excessive eating and prodigious drinking—but even the hint of a party has been enough for modern Mobilians to trumpet their city as the "Mother of Mystics."[23] Like Bienville's balcony, that long-ago Mardi Gras represented what was to become another exotic and distinguishing aspect of Alabama's only seaport.

All the while, the town kept abuilding. A few months after the Mardi Gras a Spanish officer visited and was impressed by his French neighbors' dramatic progress. "In one year [they] have made a very elegant fort," he marveled. "They have built more than a hundred very pretty houses in the plaza, and the lands and forests are very good, [so] that if they remain, these will make a great place." The "very pretty houses" were constructed almost entirely of local materials and included two general types—*pieux en terre,* or posts-in-ground structures, and *poteaux sur sole,* or posts-on-sill. Both house types featured upright posts with a clay and Spanish moss wall infill known as *bousillage;* nailed-on exterior siding to protect the *bousillage* from the weather; steeply pitched roofs of palmetto fronds and river cane with, in some cases, ceramic clay tiles running along the ridge line; stick-and-mud chimneys; and packed dirt floors. Masonry hearths and door sills were not uncommon thanks to a nearby brick pit. But there was very little window glass, the roofs frequently leaked in torrential rain, and the interiors were hot in summer and either cold or uncomfortably warm and smoky in winter. There were few if any porches originally, and rickety palisades adjoined most of the houses. These sheltered chickens and livestock or simple gardens. A later eighteenth-century description of Mobile gardens would likely obtain for the Twenty-Seven Mile Bluff settlement as well. According to this account, the fare included carrots, turnips, radishes, leaks, scallions, asparagus, cucumbers, beans, various herbs, and cabbage.[24]

Fort Louis de La Louisiane was named, appropriately enough, for the Sun King. But very soon the French began to refer to their nascent settlement as Fort Louis de La Mobile, or simply Mobile, in honor of their Indian allies. This was off-putting to the French minister of marine, Comte Pontchartrain, who feared the name connoted impermanence, and he wanted it changed. Making light of the request, one of the settlement's officials joked that it could be called Immobile instead, but the original name stuck, and so it remains.[25]

A census taken in early 1704 detailed Mobile's modest beginnings. It listed 180 men "capable of bearing arms," two French families with three girls and seven boys, six Indian slave boys, eighty houses, nine oxen, fourteen cows, four bulls, six calves, one hundred hogs, three kids, and four hundred hens. In addition there were the officers and a few religious. When one considers the immense distances, risks, and effort involved in the colonization effort, the census does not appear too shabby. But the reality behind the figures was troubling. To begin with, the soldiers were hardly worthy of the name. Some were as young as thirteen, others were the sweepings of jails and slums, and all were poorly and infrequently paid. Their daily duties included guarding supplies, transporting the same for long distances, heavy labor in clearing land and building the fort and town, and leaving for extended forays into remote and hostile territory where violent death or torture were real possibilities. Their uniforms quickly wore out, and they were reduced to wearing skins and patched-together garments. They would have been lean and sunburned, with calloused hands and coarse manners. They occupied the lowest social rung in the colony, and Bienville himself called them a "very poor lot and not suitable for war." The Canadian voyageurs and coureurs de bois were freer to come and go and took to living with the Indians where food and female concubines were easily available. Loose morals irritated the priests, but there were no unmarried European women available, and the Canadians would not be denied. The irregular supply ships from France and the poor nature of the surrounding soil meant that the little colony was often pressed by famine, and given the prevalence of disease and the difficulties of the climate, especially the punishing and unrelenting summer heat and humidity, the people often lacked energy for the most basic tasks.[26]

Unfortunately, besides these challenges, the colony was riven by sharp disagreements between two opposing groups: the Bienvillists, who included Bienville, Chateaugué, Sérigny, the Canadians, and the Jesuits, and a faction led by Nicolas de La Salle, a meticulous bean counter whose tracking of the royal warehouse's contents exasperated the Le Moynes. Like many colonial operatives, the brothers engaged in fraud for their own profit whenever the opportunity presented, and accusations would dog them for years. La Salle had the king's ear, or at least those of his own allies in court, and the support of the seminary priests down from Quebec. The resulting charges and acrimony were anything but conducive to Mobile's success. And then came the *Pélican* girls, bringing deadly fever.[27]

Despite the many difficulties in the foreground, Iberville continued to demonstrate his talent for developing and implementing long-term plans. Among the most important tasks was providing Louisiana with marriageable young European women. Iberville was no prude, having fathered an illegitimate child some years before in Canada, but he knew that a settled domestic life depended upon binding unions. Many Canadians had found happiness in willing young native arms, and the church performed a number of early mixed marriages. But soon enough the church decided to discourage such unions, believing that white and Indian issue, known as métis, were less preferable than white children. Iberville hoped that white women of good character would better domesticate the Canadians and provide the colony with new residents far more cheaply than emigration would.[28]

Thus it was that Iberville recommended to Pontchartrain that Louisiana be provided with "a hundred girls." Clergy made the selections, and eventually more than twenty females "reared in virtue and piety . . . who are accustomed [also] to labor and diligence" made the arduous voyage aboard a captured Dutch ship named the *Pélican.* Accompanied by "two gray nuns," they were shockingly young by modern standards—Marie-Catherine Philippe, 16; Marie-Marguerite Dufresne, 14; and Genevieve Burel, 17, to cite but a few—but they were of good families and eager to find husbands and bright prospects in the far-off land.[29]

On July 7, 1704, the *Pélican* sailed into Havana's old harbor for a short layover before the last leg of the voyage. There the girls and crew encountered yellow fever, and by the time the vessel reached Massacre Island near month's end, many aboard were sick and dying. As for those not preoccupied with their physical condition, one can only imagine what they thought of their new surroundings. The old buildings, cobblestone streets, and smiling cool skies of France had been replaced with sand, scrub, water everywhere, endless forests, and swamps, as well as oppressive heat and humidity. On August 1 the smaller vessels ferrying the girls upriver nosed into Twenty-Seven Mile Bluff, to be greeted by an enthusiastic and expectant crowd of men. Bienville, Levasseur, and Tonti were foremost, but all were shocked at the passengers' debilitated condition. Nonetheless, Pénicaut reported that the girls "were quite well behaved, and so they had no trouble in finding husbands." Thirteen marriages were performed in less than three weeks, in fact, and among the betrothed were Levasseur and Tonti, two of the colony's leading prospects.[30]

Unfortunately, even as those from the *Pélican* began to recover, local mosquitoes now carried the virus and had feasted on the residents. As soon as the incubation period ended, the colonists began to take sick. Yellow fever is a ghastly disease, and it would regularly purge Mobile's population until the mosquito vector was discovered in the late nineteenth century. Once a person is bitten by a mosquito carrying the virus, symptoms appear within four days. The onset is characterized by a high fever, flushed face, and chills. Some improvement is not uncommon after the initial sickness, but then more horrible symptoms follow. As a result of jaundice, the skin turns yellow, and severe nausea, muscular pains, and headaches occur. Finally, internal bleeding from the mucous membranes leads to the dreaded black vomit, after which death mercifully ends the suffering. The disease is not always fatal, and those who survive it are immune from further infection.[31]

Levasseur and Tonti were among those stricken. Too sick to be married, they lay in agony. Tonti passed away on September 4, and as Levasseur reached the final stages, that capable officer called for a notary and recorded his dying wishes. These included donations of money to the poor, prayers for his soul, and distributions to his brothers in France and his mother in Quebec. Tonti and Levasseur were among more than forty deaths in the struggling little town, courtesy of the *Pélican.* They were buried in the cemetery, their bodies probably wrapped in winding sheets with no coffins because of the time and trouble involved in making them. No one knows how many Indians perished in the epidemic, but the losses were no doubt staggering. Ten years later a priest would write of his "amazement to see how death has mowed down whole tribes since the arrival of the French in these parts." With November's frost and the end of the plague, Bienville could only glumly calculate the diminished prospects for success in such a terrible place. But only four of the girls had died, and the survivors' marriages soon yielded children and grandchildren, and descendants with family names like Rivard, Saucier, and Alexandre, who would proudly proclaim their heritage hundreds of years later.[32]

Even with a stronger feminine presence, Mobile remained first and foremost a military outpost. The British were a serious threat, and from more than one direction. In 1710 English buccaneers out of Jamaica raided Massacre Island, looting the warehouse, burning a few buildings, killing some cattle, and tormenting the residents before sailing away. Upcountry, Carolina agents attempted to organize large offensives by the Alabamas against Fort Louis. "We are in continual alarms here," one religious lamented. While few of these attacks materialized, one that did was especially traumatic. A force of more than five hundred Alabamas canoed downstream and burned a Mobilian village near the Mobile-Tensaw split. The Mobilian warriors had been well-armed by their French allies and fell back in good order, but the Alabamas made off with a number of women and children. When Bienville learned of the assault, he hurried upstream with his brother Chateaugué, seventy soldiers, some Canadians, and Mobile Indians. They reached the village to find it still smoldering and the enemy gone north. Once the Alabamas caught wind of the pursuit, they knew escape in their heavily laden pirogues was impossible, so they veered into the east bank to continue on foot through the woods. Then occurred one of the most heartrending episodes ever on a river that was to be the scene of far too many in its long history: the Alabamas smashed their pirogues to render them useless and mercilessly, methodically, slaughtered their helpless captives. War clubs and knives rose and fell with practiced efficiency, heads were broken and brains dashed, bodies crumpled, and the Alabamas disappeared into the thickets. When the French and Mobilians reached the bloody spot, they were horrified and anguished. Understandably, the Mobilians wanted immediate revenge, but Bienville was fearful of leaving the fort undefended for too long. He elected to return with part of his force while allowing Chateaugué to continue the chase with the Canadians and Indians. To Bienville's surprise Chateaugué's men caught up with the Alabamas within a few days, killed, and scalped many, and returned to Fort Louis with five prisoners. Rather than host the highly anticipated torture at the fort—Pontchartrain did not sanction French participation in such acts—Bienville let the Mobilians hustle the captives back to their village for death by a slow fire.[33]

Something of the desperation of these forest combats may be appreciated by Pénicaut's story of a Choctaw chief named Le Dos Grillé. The unusual name, roughly translated "grilled back," indicates that he had survived torture or perhaps was an enthusiastic practitioner of it. In 1711 this intimidating warrior and fifteen of his men were on a bear hunt when they were surprised by more than fifty Alabamas. In the initial clash Le Dos Grillé took a nearly spent enemy ball through the cheek. Incredibly, reported Pénicaut, "he drew out the bullet, which had lodged in his mouth, put it in his gun, and with that bullet killed the man that had wounded him." Rallying his men "in a rather high spot," he led a spirited resistance that claimed thirty lives before the enemy retreated. Justifiably proud of his feat, Le Dos Grillé led his braves back to Fort Louis with the scalps to show off to Bienville. "As a reward for their bravery," Pénicaut wrote, "they were presented with gifts of merchandise and were given much powder and lead."[34]

Despite Le Dos Grillé's little victory, the list of problems experienced by the French in the Mobile Bay region in barely a decade of exploration and settlement was long indeed—internal squabbles, profiteering, plague, famine, inadequate manpower, an irregular supply line from France, the inconvenient distance to Massacre Island, desertion, pirate attack, Indian massacres, and constant deterioration of the fort and buildings due to the heat, humidity, and abundant rain. Crises far and near beset the little outpost. In 1706 Iberville died of yellow fever in Havana, and the colony lost its most powerful and able advocate. Two years later a tornado damaged part of the fort, and in what was left there was so much rot that Bienville feared firing the cannon would collapse the bastions, hardly an edifying prospect for a military man. In the spring of 1711 the rains came again, harder and stronger than ever. The creek north of the town flooded "with so much impetuosity," one Frenchman wrote, "that the greater part of the houses . . . have been covered up to the comb of the roof in five or six days." It made no sense to go to the trouble and expense of improving the fort in such a place, and Bienville agreed with those who had long been arguing for a move. In ironic confirmation of Pontchartrain's earlier fear, Mobile proved to be just that.[35]

Despite the negatives, there were positives. The colony was not a failure. The French had established themselves, built alliances with the Indians, and secured the Mississippi Valley into the bargain. The English and the Alabamas remained hostile, but the system of buffer villages was working. Friendly Indians had been resettled in the immediate vicinity—some Chatos down at the river mouth, Apalachees from Spanish Florida on Three Mile Creek, and another small tribe on Bayou Sara. French explorers were ranging farther into the interior, and the trade in deer skins was increasing. There were now French families in the colony and births of white children. The church was established as well, with regular masses, baptisms, death and burial rites, and missions. Pénicaut wrote that the Apalachees, who were Catholic converts, honored the feast day of St. Louis and "dressed very decently: the men wear a kind of cloth overcoat; and the women wear cloaks and skirts of silk cloth in the French style, but haven't the least headdress, going bare-headed." Perhaps most important, the French had learned how to better build, hunt, garden, and survive thanks to their Mobile neighbors. While prospects were not necessarily bright, the endeavor was at least functioning.[36]

The Mobile River's utility as a highway proved itself yet again, this time as the conduit from Twenty-Seven Mile Bluff down to the Oignonets, or onion fields, the new town site at the river's mouth. According to Pénicaut, "all the furniture and merchandise were moved there in boats. Some raft like structures were made, on which the cannon were put and, in general, all supplies and effects that were at the old fort." Heading downstream was a luxury for the boatmen, requiring little effort other than keeping with the current. Their return trips were also easier as their empty craft rode high in the water. Anything of value that could be salvaged from the bluff was loaded and moved, but the deteriorated fort and houses were abandoned and some of the latter burned. The residents were happy about the change of base, and a short time later the arrival of the supply ship *Renommée* seemed a good omen for a better future. "The assistance brought us," mused Bienville, " . . . provides us with courage and gives us hope against the fear we have had of being forced to abandon this colony, which by my care and by my efforts is beginning to take some shape."[37]

The new town site was different from the old one. The river was broader, and the view to the south encompassed Mobile Bay's shimmering waters beneath grand skyscapes of towering thunderheads in the summer and drifting rooster tails in the winter. A low bluff ran along the riverbank, and the land rose gently to the west, reaching elevations of fifteen to twenty feet half a mile away and rising to almost two hundred feet out at what would later be called Spring Hill. The soil was mostly sandy with veins of clay in various places, and swamps bordered the northern and southern ends of the new settlement. Several tributaries fed into the river on the north—Bayou Marmotte (One Mile Creek), Bayou Chateaugué (Three Mile Creek) and Chickasabogue (Chickasaw Creek). Immediately across the river were small islands that would eventually become known as Blakeley, Pinto, and Sand. These were low and marshy, studded with a few pines, and subject to flooding. To the east of these, of course, was the delta, some eight miles wide at this point, with the bluffs of the Eastern Shore on the other side. South of the town several miles was the Rivière aux Chiens, or Dog River, where the French built a warehouse that served as a handy way station between Massacre Island and new Mobile. Below that were Bellfontaine; the Rivière aux Poules, or Fowl River; Mon Louis Island; and then land's end, the Mississippi Sound, and Massacre Island. Small numbers of Frenchmen now lived in all these places, hunting, fishing, subsisting.

The very year of the move, an engineer named Guillaume Philbert Chevillot, who had arrived aboard the *Renommée,* drew a handsome *plan de la ville,* or map of the new town, with extensive marginal notes. The map showed the Rivière de la Mobile along the bottom, with an irregular western shoreline; the bastioned fort with a big flag flying from the southeast corner; twenty neatly delineated squares, each divided into eight ample lots of approximately 80 by 160 feet; and *pinière,* or pine forest, bordering the west. According to the descriptions, the fort was "constructed of cedar stakes 13 ft. high," and inside it were "the governor's house, the magasin where are the king's effects, and a guard house." The officers and soldiers lived outside the fort in barracks or houses. The houses were "constructed of cedar and pine upon a foundation of wooden stakes which project out of the ground one foot and might be called piling, because this soil is inundated . . . in certain localities, in times of rain." Lime for the plaster came "from shell found at the mouth of the river on little islands which bear that name." There was a church, lots for the priests, and the *chirurgien major,* or post surgeon. The map also indicates "a little moat made to carry off water," just south of the fort. One of the new town's most important features was the wharf, or *embarquadère,* off the fort's northeast bastion and angling southeast across the muddy banks and just over the river. This was a crude affair of cedar posts and stretchers topped with wide planks, but it was an all-important lifeline for the little colony. The map shows no street names, but these quickly came—Dauphin, Conti, and St. Louis running east-west a few short blocks from riverbank to woods, and Royal running north-south along the little bluff riverside.[38]

Hopeful as Bienville was, the Crown had determined a new course for the colony. Louis XIV's reign was ending, and the monarch was tired, in debt, and disgruntled with the costly colony. Affairs in Louisiana were turned over to Antoine Crozat, a fabulously wealthy merchant who was granted a fifteen-year charter with a trade monopoly in order to turn things around. Crozat's emphasis was to be on commerce rather than agriculture, and he planned to import more colonists and slaves, develop trade with Spanish Mexico and exploit mining possibilities. He inherited a colony of four hundred white persons, a handful of black individuals, a dizzying array of native peoples, and a governor named Bienville who was only in his early thirties.[39]

Among Crozat's earliest changes was a new governor, who arrived in March of 1713, his vessel booming salutes off Dauphin Island. La Mothe Cadillac, founder of Detroit a few years earlier, was a no-nonsense man of business who brought along a large family. He promptly commandeered Chateaugué's house on Conti Street, despite the latter's protestations. Chateaugué's misfortune aside, Bienville thought one of Cadillac's daughters had "a great deal of merit" and considered marrying her. As it was, he remained a lifelong bachelor. This was just as well, since tensions between him and Cadillac ran high, and the latter was not likely to be a pleasant father-in-law. He was a complainer who had a low opinion of Louisiana's and Mobile's people, and was not shy in saying so. "The inhabitants are no better than the country," he fumed in one letter; "they are the very scum and refuse of Canada, ruffians, who have thus far cheated the gibbet of its due, vagabonds, who are without subordination to the laws . . . graceless profligates, who are so steeped in vice that they prefer Indian females to French women!" The troops were "without discipline," he continued, and overall the colony was "not worth a straw."[40]

It is not surprising that Cadillac's record in pursuing Crozat's new policies was unsuccessful. The Spanish were not interested in trade, mines in the Illinois country yielded nothing of value, and Indian relations suffered. Thanks to the governor's blundering and arrogant manner, a bloody war was provoked with the Natchez Indians on the Mississippi that cost the French valuable lives and required Bienville's personal intervention to resolve. Within a few short years, Cadillac was recalled, Crozat resigned his charter, and the Crown turned to the Scottish rogue and gambler John Law, whose Company of the West was granted a twenty-five-year monopoly on Louisiana trade. Bienville was appointed commandant-general, which, according to Pénicaut, "gave general satisfaction, as no one knew better the wants and resources of the colony."[41]

The succeeding years were eventful and affirmed Mobile's strategic importance. The Alabama Indians had become disgruntled with the English and, while Cadillac was still governor, had asked that the French (less numerous and not so land-hungry as the English) establish an outpost among them. Accordingly, in 1717 Fort Toulouse was erected at the junction of the Coosa and Tallapoosa Rivers, which of course provided a direct riverine supply line all the way to Mobile. According to Pénicaut, several officers and a hundred soldiers were stationed there, "because this is the corridor leading to and from Carolina." Pénicaut certainly understood the geographic importance of Fort Toulouse, but he exaggerated the number of troops—the garrison likely did not exceed forty soldiers at the most. The same year a strong hurricane washed Pelican Island into the theretofore excellent anchorage at Dauphin Island, causing Bienville to hopscotch the capital west, from Mobile to Biloxi to New Orleans—founded in 1718 at an Indian portage on the Mississippi. While the latter city eventually was to emerge as dominant on the gulf, Mobile remained important to the French for its proximity to the Eastern Seaboard and as a trade destination for large numbers of Indians. Tens of thousands of pounds of deer skins passed through the little outpost and accounted for a significant chunk of Louisiana's exports.[42]

The Crozat and Law periods also witnessed the increased importation of black slaves into Louisiana, strengthening what had been an underrepresented race in the colony's diverse human palette. There had likely always been some black individuals in Mobile. In 1707 Bienville owned several black slaves, including two children, Jean Baptiste, age seven, and Joseph, three, and Chateaugué had a black male slave named François Jacemin. The last fathered a child named Anthoine, the first recorded birth of a black child on the Gulf Coast. The mother was a woman named Marie. Labor, of course, was the driving need of the colony, and Indian slaves, who could more easily escape into the woods and blend with other tribes, were not believed to be as satisfactory or hardy as black slaves. Thus it was that ships brought black individuals in ever greater numbers—120 out of Guinea in March of 1721 aboard the *Africaine;* 338 aboard the *Marie;* and 138 on the *Neride.*[43] In 1737 there is strange mention of an "Isle of Vessels . . . near the mouth of the Mobile River," where five slaves were sold by an English ship captain. There are no other references to this island in the records, and it may refer to the mouth of Mobile Bay rather than to that of the river. Whatever the particularities of the incident, black persons had become a common sight on Mobile's rude streets.[44]

They were also ubiquitous on the plantations upriver. At Twenty-One Mile Bluff Plantation, shown on an anonymous map drawn circa 1725, an infantry captain named

Sieur de la Tour Vitrac and his wife, Marie Le Sueur (one of Bienville's cousins), produced naval stores and lived with several orphan children, three servants, and four Indian and more than twenty black slaves. Labor on plantations like that at Twenty-One Mile Bluff would have consisted of clearing and breaking land; cultivating rice, corn, and beans on the flat delta across the river; wood cutting, making tar, raising cattle and hogs, tanning hides, maintaining the buildings, hunting for food, and generally tending to sundry light chores. Some slave men became skilled at trades such as blacksmithing, barrel making, and carpentry. Shirking or misbehavior could have serious consequences, among them beating and branding. Slave women engaged in their share of heavy work, including farming and handling the animals. Midwifery, child rearing, and cooking were also important female roles. The smells emanating from those plantation kitchens must have been mouthwatering, especially those from the distinctive localized dishes that were so ingeniously prepared and served piping hot in pottery, wooden, or pewter bowls—succotash, corn, oysters, venison, squirrel, and gumbo filé seasoned with bay leaves, pepper, onion, and thyme. Slave housing was small, plain, and rough. Most cabins had a chimney and a hearth for cooking, and some had two rooms with a little loft. The dearth of white women remained an issue throughout the history of French Louisiana, and many plantation owners took slave women to their beds, raising large families with them. Some of these women were freed by their masters and were settled with considerable property. This gave rise to Mobile's Creole caste, but that fascinating story must wait yet a bit.[45]

A very good description of a French-era plantation comes from the *American State Papers* in an advertisement for a sale in 1756. The property was located on Seymour Bluff, or the *Grand Ecor des Mobiliens* (Great Bluff of the Mobilians), as it was called until the end of the French period when the natives had relocated. The Indians lived in close proximity to the plantation proper, helping and trading with the French, mixing with the slaves (adding yet another racial variant to the area), and providing a handy early warning system if hostile tribes approached, giving the family time either to hunker down on the place or to fly downstream to Mobile. The advertisement listed the main house as "thirty feet long, on twenty wide posts in the ground, covered with bark, clayed between said posts, with six windows and two doors, with a clayed chimney . . . and a piazza on one side, to the gable end wherof is an appentis [lean-to or shed-roof addition], with a chimney, serving as a kitchen." Other structures included "a fowl house" surrounded by a light paling; "a negro house" sixty feet long by thirteen feet wide set on posts and "bark covered" (this sounds like a barracks meant to sleep many hands); and a big barn, "all which buildings are enclosed with stakes set upright, which form a yard of twenty-five toises square [150 feet]."[46]

Life held plenty of rough edges for the planters, but they certainly enjoyed a greater degree of domestic comfort than their chattel. Something of the quality of daily planter life may be gleaned from the inventory of Joseph Pierre Chastang's worldly goods. Chastang (1736–1815) and his wife lived with their eleven children on St. Louis

Plantation, a 640-acre property with eight cabins near Three Mile Creek. His belongings included furniture, including a bureau, two bedsteads, two cypress tables, seven straw-bottomed chairs, a mahogany table "with falling leaves"; kitchen and dining items such as a gridiron frying pan, a coffee pot, a marble mortar, twelve silver spoons and two ladles; farm tools such as an old plough, four iron wedges, a couple of "old cross cut saws," and miscellaneous tools; three pirogues; a gun; two dozen candle molds; two "worn saddles"; and some "smoothing irons." The inventory makes it clear that these items saw heavy usage. No clothing is listed, but observations made of British Mobile's residents hold true for the French, Spanish and early American periods as well. Climate dictated dress. Men wore "a slight waistcoat of cotton, a pair of trousers of the same and often no coat." In cooler weather they threw on "a kind of surtout, made of a blanket, and a pair of Indian boots." Women also dressed light and were "not very expensive; happy frugality!" Slave clothing was even simpler, sometimes rags, but on the best farms included shoes and, for the women, "a petticoat, and a jacket."[47]

Despite the growing slave economy and New Orleans's founding, Law's efforts were no more fruitful than Crozat's, and in 1720 the roguish gambler was sent packing. The Crown continued to tinker with the colony's organization, and Bienville's fortunes fell, due to his shady dealings, and then rose again when the Crown decided to take over the colony in 1731. Bienville was tapped to be governor once more and served until 1742. Like his brother Iberville before him, he proved a capable strategist when it came to the big picture. In the mid-1730s he built Fort Tombecbe well up the Tombigbee River in order to be closer to the Choctaws and their valuable trade, as well as to better monitor the bellicose Chickasaws. With the construction of this new fort, the French had the Mobile River Basin well-secured—Toulouse on one side, Tombecbe on the other, and at the head of Mobile Bay a busy fort and town.[48]

Even as the French built on the Mississippi and the Tombigbee, they remained committed to improving Mobile. Foremost among its assets was the fort, renamed Condé, now in serious need of renovation. The engineer assigned the task was Valentin Devin, who arrived in 1723. His salary was two thousand *livres* a year. The fort he had to work with was pitiful, "a few small stakes planted side by side," he wrote, the whole business looking more like a "sheepfold" than a military installation. Assigned a workforce of twenty black and five white men, Devin set about shaping the fort into something more appropriate and effective. This involved a great deal of digging and hauling dirt around to sculpt the glacis, the defensive earthworks that would border the permanent brick walls. Unfortunately for Devin all the turned earth attracted the colonists' pigs, which rooted about and frustrated the workmen. Like the thoroughgoing professional that he was, however, Devin pushed forward, and as the months progressed things began to look good. There were corner bastions, sixteen-foot-high brick walls with low parapets, artillery embrasures, and guns positioned on wood platforms. Inside were two long one-story barracks with mansard roofs that could accommodate more than two hundred men, officers' quarters, and a couple of wells, all surrounding an open parade ground. An aqueduct, or *conduit des latrines,* was dug through the glacis so that human waste emptied directly into the river. This is some of the earliest direct evidence for Mobile River pollution, and raw sewage remains an issue to this day, but certainly no one gave it a thought in the eighteenth century. On the riverbank an improved dock was provided, consisting of an excavated slip with a jetty to each side.[49]

The town grew very little throughout the French period and as late as 1760 still only had a population in the low hundreds—soldiers, religious, white families, and black and Indian slaves. The fort, low and brooding, dominated the marshy waterfront, where a few small craft bobbed at anchor or were pulled onto the mud. Frame houses with double-pitched roofs and wraparound galleries sat grandly on some blocks, while plainer homes with little gardens and some poultry and a few pigs inside palings were more common. Weedy, littered empty lots bespoke the slow economy, and there were a few shops; the streets were sandy, muddy, and dusty more or less all at once. A summer visitor stepping onto the little dock at Fort Condé around that time would have inhaled a head-spinning array of scents in the soft air—salt, human and animal waste, wood smoke, pine tar, rotting fish, and perhaps the sulfurous tang of burnt black powder if the arrival had merited an artillery salute.[50]

Hopeful successes aside, Louisiana was hardly a prize as far as the French Crown was concerned. Bienville's best efforts were concluded in 1743 when he asked to retire to the mother country after difficult attempts to pacify the Chickasaws. He had been one of Louisiana's most consistent champions and definitely one of its most complex characters. The passage of this extraordinary figure from the local stage marked the end of an astonishing career that saw cities founded, native peoples subjugated, and the destiny of a region firmly established. Meanwhile, sluggish trade, disease, Indian trouble, and European maneuvering all continued. At the conclusion of the epic struggle between France and England known as the Seven Years' War (there was little fighting on the gulf in what was otherwise an eighteenth-century worldwide conflict), the maps were redrawn. By earlier negotiations and the Treaty of Paris in 1763, France lost the Louisiana territory west of the Mississippi and New Orleans to the Spanish, who had been allied with the British; and the eastern half of Louisiana, including Mobile, to the British. Spain ceded Florida to the British. After more than half a century, the Fleur de Lis was hauled down from the ramparts of Fort Condé, and replaced with the Union Jack.[51]

Mobile was now part of British West Florida, a too-little-known colony in the Americas. The local commandant was Major Robert Farmar, forty-five, a native New Jerseyan schooled in England, and a seasoned veteran. One French official who had corresponded with him appreciated his wit and broad mind, calling him "extraordinary" and a "man of parts," while at the same time recognizing a shrewd and potentially dangerous foe. Farmar arrived beneath Fort Condé's ramparts on October 20 at the head of two infantry regiments—the Thirty-fourth and Twenty-second—and took

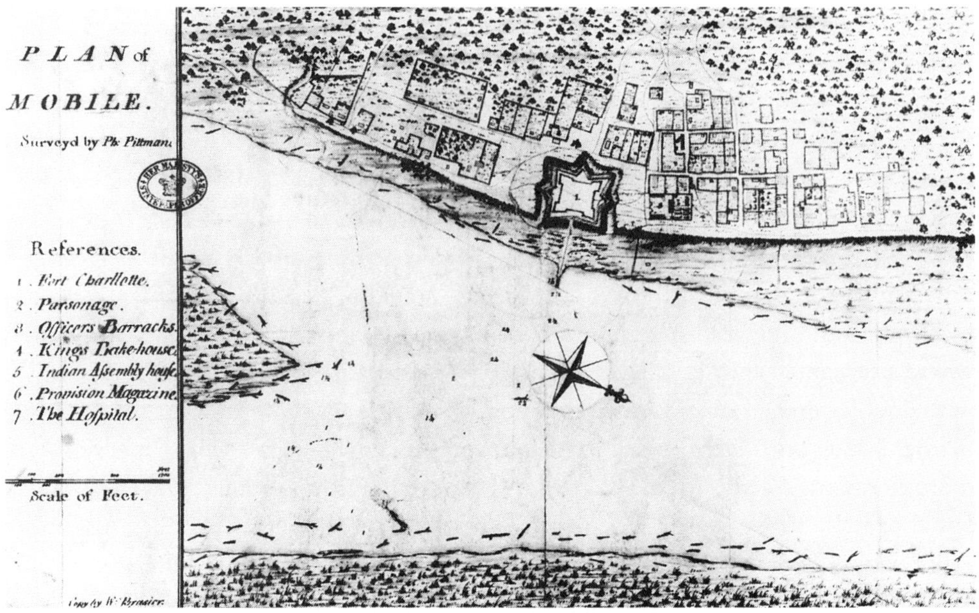

Pittman map, circa 1768. Note the abundant driftwood along the banks. Courtesy of the Doy Leale McCall Rare Book and Manuscript Library, University of South Alabama.

over from the French soldiers, who nonetheless wanted to stay through an important Indian congress coming that November.[52]

Farmar denied them a role in the congress, and over the coming weeks they left the area for good. With his former enemies defanged, Farmar took stock of the fort, renamed Charlotte after the young British queen, and found a great deal wanting. "I am in no small dilemma at present," he wrote to his superiors, and went on to enumerate the bastion's many deficiencies. The list was long. The glacis had been so neglected that it was "all covered with long grass and shrubs that lodged in the rain"; the bricks in the wall and on the parapet were "very much wasted"; the gun platforms "rotten"; some of the cannon dismounted with broken trunnions; the powder magazine needed "repairing and new doors"; the barracks were "in very bad repair" with rotten floors and broken windows; the bake house was "entirely useless"; and to top it all off the very gates "entirely unhinged." Taken in toto, Farmar concluded, the fort was "not tenable against a party with small arms." As for the town proper, it was little better. After surveying it from Charlotte's crumbling walls, he quipped, "this place at present carries the appearance of a little hamlet formed of Negro Hutts, rather than a well peopled town in Canada."[53]

Before he could even mount his own guns or fully unload the supplies ferried ashore by "the very heavy launch" that alone of the British vessels could pass over the shallow bar at Choctaw Point, Farmar was confronted with yet another problem. As shadows lengthened and the nights grew cool with the gentle deepening of fall, Indians representing several tribes began drifting into town for the anticipated congress. Soon there were "near three thousand . . . within two miles of the Fort," Farmar reported, milling about and making a nuisance of themselves. The situation was dicey, and Farmar knew he had to tread carefully. His men were outnumbered and debilitated after months aboard ship in warm climes. The fort was useless for refuge, and help was nowhere near. The Indians, he wrote, were "displeased with the English for taking possession without previously treating with them." They expected presents, food, and liquor, all in great quantities. Farmar quickly assured them that the English "would use them as the French had done" and distributed as many trinkets as could be bought locally—"I am sorry to say it at a very advanced price." Even after the congress, when many of the Indians returned to the forests, others lingered, and Farmar was burdened with "twenty or thirty every day that dine in the house and must have Indian corn to carry to their camp for their children."[54]

The combination of rival tribes and alcohol was always potentially combustible, and on at least one occasion there was a spectacular clash. Happily for Farmar and his weary Lobsterbacks, the trouble was confined to the Indians. It occurred in 1765, as the British were still settling in and important negotiations were ongoing in Mobile to redraw the upcountry boundaries between the various tribes. The scuffle started only blocks from the riverbank, when forty Choctaw warriors led by Chief Red Shoe confronted more than three hundred Creek Indians. (The British referred to the numerous peoples along the Coosa, Tallapoosa and Alabama Rivers by the catch-all title of Creeks; to the French they had been the Alabamas.) Incredibly, Red Shoe and his braves charged their enemy full-tilt and killed many. According to one account, Red Shoe dispatched thirteen by his own hand, even as he was knocked to his knees "and flayed alive for his heroism." Caught off balance, the Creeks plunged into the river and swam across to safety. This saved them, testified one witness, because of the Choctaws' "inability to swim." For neither the first nor the last time, Indian blood mingled with the Mobile's muddy current, and the fracas sparked a war between the tribes that was largely fought to the north. As one venerable Mississippi historian opined much later, this intra-native disagreement was welcomed by the British "as a fortunate diversion."[55]

British hegemony meant different strategic goals from the French, and the changes were quickly manifest. By the Mobile Treaty of 1765, the Choctaws ceded all the coastal lands south of the thirty-first parallel, which included most of the Mobile River. The *petites nations*—the Mobile, the Tahomé, and the Apalachee, among others—that had been so crucial to French success faced the prospect of being absorbed by the Choctaw or moving away. Some stayed; many others relocated west of the Mississippi where, even though the Spanish now governed, most of the residents were French and familiar to them. Ultimately, the indigenous Mobilians, those proud waterborne people who fought Soto to a draw, held the mounds of Bottle Creek sacred, taught the

French how to survive, and gave their name to a river and a bay and a city, faded into obscurity.[56]

Mobile's black residents faced a challenging future as the British West Florida Assembly passed a series of draconian laws. Manumission, something not uncommon among the French, was discouraged. The traditional outlets theretofore enjoyed by slaves—congregating on Sundays, gambling, feasting, and drumming—were all forbidden. Violators were to be "whipt through the streets." Slave drumming in particular was to be a recurring bugaboo among Europeans and, much later, antebellum white Southerners, who feared it as a method of indecipherable communication. Nothing was more agitating to white town folk than the sight of a throng of black persons animated by a drum or more chilling to isolated and outnumbered plantation owners than the haunting, muffled sound of African beats in the humid night air. What if escaped slaves, living as maroons deep in the swamps, were able to call upon their brethren and convince them to rise up and kill their masters? Many slaves did run away into the backcountry, but the Indians rarely accepted them and were treaty-bound to return them. By far the majority of slaves stayed in town and on the farms, performing the colony's heavy work. Not all of them were harshly treated, but many were.[57]

Like the Indians and the black slaves, the resident French population faced changes. Some feared Protestant British religious intolerance and, despite assurances to the contrary, decamped west. Others opted to take the required loyalty oath and stay. Some of them positively prospered. Pierre Rochon, a planter who raised cattle and made tar, got plenty of work as a contractor for the redcoats. He made twenty-two pounds sterling repairing a boat and was hired to do the extensive fort repairs. But the French old-timers like Rochon now found themselves sharing the river and bay with growing numbers of new neighbors. The British governor, George Johnstone, headquartered in Pensacola, had boasted that "West Florida bids fair to be the emporium as well as the most pleasant part of the New World." English settlers followed, some awarded large grants well up the Tombigbee River in what had been wilderness, others finding congenial homes along the Eastern Shore and on the Mobile's western bank. On a survey trip down the Mobile in 1772, the Dutch-born engineer Bernard Romans listed both French and English plantation owners. "At a quarter past nine, a.m.," he wrote of one day's journey, "proceeded past several plantations, as well on the islands as on the main, particularly Campbell's, Stuart's, Andry's, and McGillivray's." Just before lunch Romans landed and bunked with a Frenchman named Simon Favre, who provided "most friendly, genteel and hospitable" treatment. Farmar himself retired to a large farm near modern Stockton where he later hosted Bartram during his travels. By the eve of the American Revolution, there were more than four thousand white residents in West Florida, 325 of these in Mobile. Black residents numbered better than fifteen hundred in the colony, with some five hundred in Mobile, fifty-one of them free. While these were still meager numbers, they represented real growth compared to the stagnation that characterized the French period.[58]

Despite these demographics, however, Mobile carried the reputation of being a dangerous place to live. Dr. John Lorimer, an army surgeon, reported in July 1769 that most of the men were ill. He attributed this to Mobile's semitropical air and heat. Whether inside the fort or confined to quarters, he remarked, the atmosphere was "as close and suffocating as . . . a great oven." The "moisture and damp are very considerable," he continued. These qualities were evident not only against the skin, but also in the area's spectacular sunsets, "nearly the color of claret," and in shoes that became "quite mouldy" if left unworn more than a day. Furthermore, the well water was distasteful and the river full of "innumerable impurities." Fever was common in the summer, and in winter "fluxes, dropsias, and cachexies." Men died in alarming numbers, prompting one official to call Mobile "a black trifle" and "that graveyard for Britons." Less colorfully, a merchant dubbed it "the most disagreeable and unhealthy place in America."[59]

The British found themselves attempting to exploit the same resources as their Gallic predecessors. The deer-skin trade remained vital. Tar and indigo production were important endeavors, as were lumbering, cattle raising, and growing corn, beans, and squash. Johnstone ambitiously brought in vine growers from Madeira to make a stab at wine making and also introduced black Caribbean pearl divers. What the latter thought of Mobile Bay's muddy waters is not recorded. But other than on a local level, only deer skins proved profitable for the government. These skins came in great quantity from the backcountry, where unscrupulous traders supplied the Indians with cheap liquor in exchange. Drunkenness was rampant in the wake of these despicable men, and they delighted in cheating the Indians. In the winter of 1772 a Choctaw chief called Captain Ouma travelled to Mobile and begged for "some regulation" of the rum "that pours in upon our nation Like a great Sea from Mobile and from all the plantations and settlements round about." Ouma cited Favre's plantation as an especial source of the poison. But with almost no British military presence upcountry—Fort Toulouse was never garrisoned and Fort Tombecbe abandoned very early—the Crown had no way of practically policing such matters, even if it had cared to.[60]

Where the British truly excelled was cartography, and several of their maps from this period are extremely accurate and detailed, beautiful productions that are a pleasure to run one's hand across and study. Men such as Romans; Elias Durnford, chief engineer and surveyor general for West Florida; Lieutenant Philip Pittman, a capable assistant engineer; and David Taitt, a proficient mapmaker, fanned out onto area waterways and into the woods, employing the tools of their trade. If one was working on water, these included a spyglass, sextant, compass, and sounding pole or lead line for accurate depth soundings. Typically a lead line consisted of a rope with knots to demarcate each fathom (six feet) of depth and a lead weight with a concave end filled by tallow so the sea floor's makeup could be determined. On land, surveyors utilized compass and chain, wayriser (an early measuring wheel), sketchbook, and pencils. Travel was usually by pirogue with an assistant or two and some native paddlers. While staying at

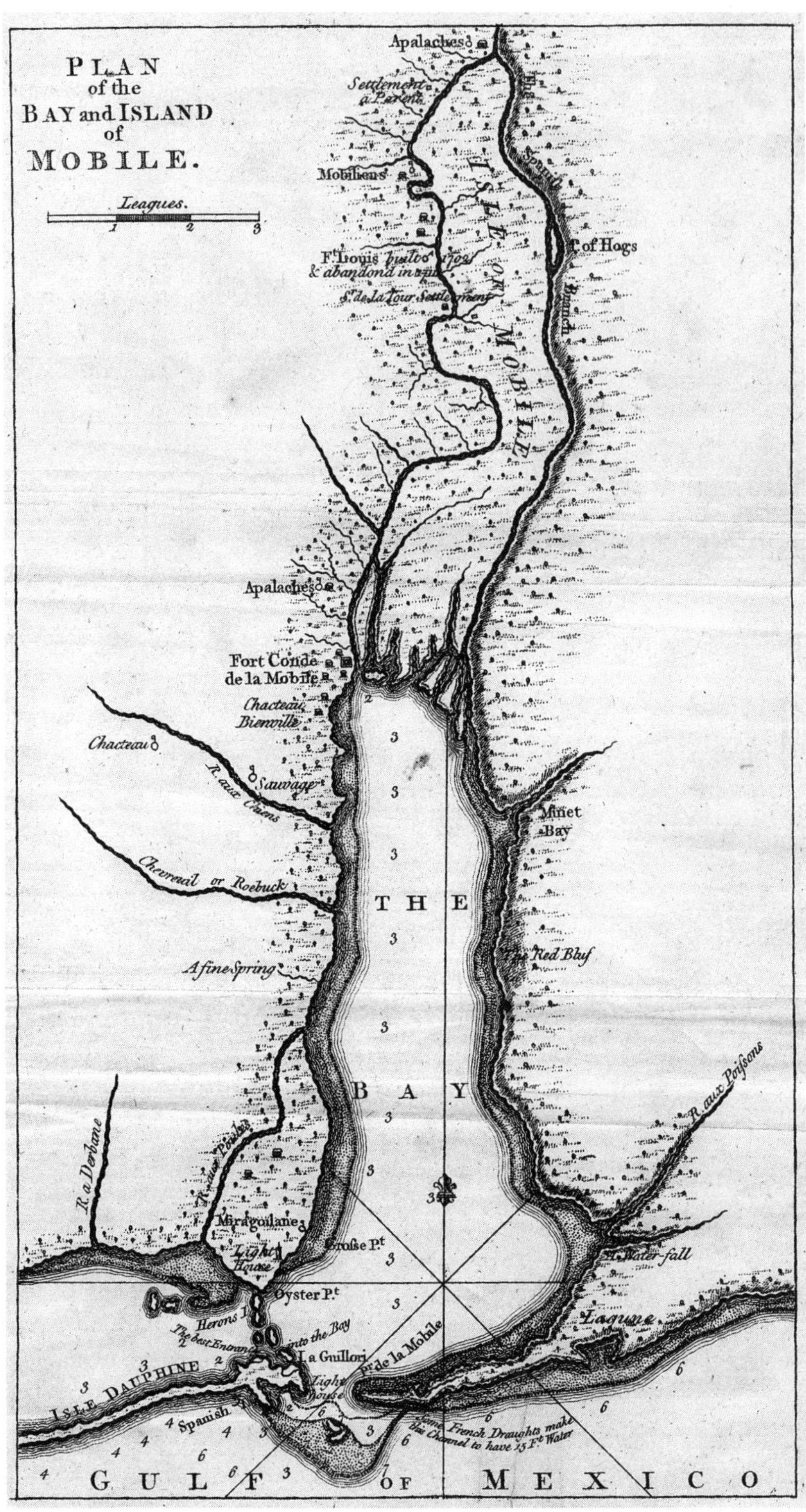

Plan of the Bay and Island of Mobile, 1763. Courtesy of the History Museum of Mobile.

Favre's house during his trip, Romans saw two parties of surveyors headed upstream to "ascertain the boundary between us and the Choctaws."[61]

With firm lines and elegant lettering, these men's maps fluttered off the drafting tables. Among them is an anonymous circa 1766 depiction of the "Bar and Entrance of the Harbour of Mobile," with "Point Mobile" on one side and "Isle Dauphin or Massacre" on the other. Little trees stud the land, and the pass into the bay is finely delineated with shading and dotted lines, notations of "stiff blue clayey ground" in the channel proper and "hard sand" along the margins. Further into the bay a "soft ouzzy" bottom is indicated. About 1770 Durnford produced a "Field Survey of the River Mobile, and part of the River Alabama and Tensa, with the different Settlements, and Lands marked theron." The town of Mobile shows as a tight group of little black squares surrounding the star-shaped fort, and numerous marginal notes identify "marsh land," "low land," and "pine land" up the delta. At roughly the same time, Pittman drew a lovely color "Plan of Mobile," showing the fort in detail and realistically limning the riverbanks and Pinto Island with driftwood. In 1771 Pittman also mapped Mobile Bay, dotting the areas of open water with dozens of tiny numbers indicating the soundings—particularly important the seven feet at bay's mouth, and the ten feet at Choctaw Bar, the latter feature shown as a dotted line looping out in front of the river mouth and town.[62] These two bars had influenced and frustrated mariners since Pineda's coastal voyage more than 250 years before and promised to do so for the foreseeable future. Accurate soundings were absolutely vital to safe navigation, as were good pilots, but more about the pilots in due course.

By far the most spectacular British map is Taitt's 1771 color "plan of part of the rivers Tombecbe, Alabama, Tensa, Perdido, & Scambia in the province of West Florida," illustrating hundreds of square miles of territory. Despite its sweep, the Taitt map is meticulously drawn and presents a fascinating and informative portrait of the Mobile River from "Naniaba Island" to halfway down the bay. The river's upper reaches are chopped by the rectangular-shaped land holdings of the various French and English planters, many of whom are named. The bluffs are shown as little brown-shaded areas, and "Old Mobile" is labeled in the correct spot. Also indicated are "Lizars Saw Mill" on Bayou Sara; delta lands "Overflowed in the Spring"; "Large Canes"; a "Cowpen" on the Tensaw just beyond the split; "Old Indian Fields"; Simon Farve's house hard by Seymour Bluff with Chastang's, Thomas Strothers's and Narbonne's dwellings to the south; the Spanish River; and "Mobille" indicated by a little fort. Blakeley and Pinto Islands are well drawn but had not yet acquired those names and are not identified. Choctaw Point is prominent but not labeled either. What Taitt's map most clearly shows is an area in flux, home to Indians, French, and British making their lives on the ghostly imprints of earlier cultures—"Old Mobile," "Old Indian Fields." Within a decade of Taitt's effort, the map was to be scrambled once more.[63]

By the time of the American Revolution, British Mobile was no more prosperous than French Mobile had been, and it might have been poorer. Visiting the town in

1775, Bartram described it as "chiefly in ruins," with "many houses vacant and mouldering to earth." The inhabitants were a mélange of "French gentlemen, English, Scotch and Irish, and immigrants from the Northern British colonies." The fort was "a large regular fortress." The houses that were occupied were either one-story cypress-frame "filled in with brick, plaistered and white-washed inside and out" or more substantive brick dwellings with big courtyards (yet another favorite Mobile amenity). On the administrative front Farmar had fallen afoul of Governor Johnstone and was locked in a lengthy and expensive court-martial proceeding. The famously argumentative Johnstone had accused the beleaguered commandant of smuggling flour in a coastal flat named the *Little Bob*, one of the earliest in a long line of whimsically christened small craft on area waterways. The issue would take years to resolve, and Durnford was in command of Fort Charlotte when a Spanish fleet appeared on his horizon.[64]

Spain allied itself with the American colonies and France against Great Britain in 1779 and immediately began laying plans to take Mobile and Pensacola. General George Washington needed help on his southern flank, and Spanish attacks in West Florida would divert British attention and resources away from his ragtag army. The task fell to Don Bernardo de Gálvez, governor of Louisiana, a thirty-something warrior who had fought Apaches in Mexico and cleared the lower Mississippi of British troops. Gálvez was proud and aggressive, not one to let bureaucratic obstacles overwhelm him. On January 11, 1780, he departed New Orleans with eleven vessels and a motley but effective fighting force—more than 200 Spanish regulars, 323 white militia, 107 mulatto and black militia, two dozen slaves, and some American auxiliaries. Squally weather delayed them, and several ships ran aground on the bar off Mobile Bay, prompting some officers to call for Gálvez to break off the invasion. Undeterred, the governor refloated the vessels and by February 24 had moved his fleet up to the Dog River. Days later, advance elements reached Choctaw Point with Fort Charlotte in sight. Almost immediately, disgruntled French residents started bringing them intelligence. Delighted, Gálvez crowed, "They love us."[65]

Contemplating matters from Fort Charlotte's decrepit ramparts, Durnford could not have felt good about his chances. The Spanish had begun siege preparations and were manhandling their eighteen-pounder cannons into batteries on the fort's northern and western faces barely a mile away. Mounted on wooden naval carriages, each of these guns featured a nine-foot barrel weighing more than two tons that could throw an eighteen-pound solid shot better than two miles. Their rate of fire was approximately one round every ten minutes, and they were crewed by up to sixteen men. Such fearsome weapons would easily pulverize the fort's brick walls. Once a breach was made, Gálvez's infantry would charge through, forcing Durnford to choose between the senseless sacrifice of his men or capitulation. As if this was not daunting enough, several enemy vessels lay to in the bay some two miles offshore. Among them was the *Valenzuela*, a shallow-draft row galley whose guns, possibly mortars, could pound the fort at leisure. On his side of the ledger sheet Durnford could count the fort's light nine-pounder cannons and a pitifully inadequate force of fewer than three hundred men. They included a contingent of the sixtieth regiment of foot, some Pennsylvania and Maryland loyalists, dozens of black slaves and servants, and fifty-two volunteers from town. Numerous panicked citizens had also crowded into the fort, severely compromising Durnford's combat effectiveness. About all he could do was order the houses standing between him and the enemy to be burned for a clear field of fire.[66]

Eighteenth-century European warfare was a strange business, with the slaughter often bracketed by elaborate courtesies and courtly exchanges between foes. Such a minuet now took place as Gálvez sent an envoy to request Durnford's surrender. "Sir," began the letter carried into Durnford's quarters, "If the number of troops with which I shall invest the fort did not greatly exceed those which you have to defend it, I should not propose to you to surrender; but the great inequality of strength puts us in such a state, that you must either give it up immediately, or you must suffer all the calamities of war." Durnford's reply was polite: "I have the honor to acknowledge the receipt of your Excellency's Summons to surrender immediately the Fort to your Excellency's superior forces." Nonetheless, he insisted, "mine are much beyond your Excellency's conception, and was I to give up this Fort on your demand, I should be regarded as a traitor to my king and country. My love for both and my own honor direct my heart to refuse surrendering this Fort until I am under conviction that resistance is in vain." To conclude the formalities Durnford's and Gálvez's envoys dined together "until near five o'clock, drinking a cheerful glass to the healths of our kings and friends."[67]

Next there occurred one of those Hollywood moments that sometimes actually do happen. Durnford assembled his men on the parade ground and, as he later reported to his superior, "read to them Don Gálvez's summons, and then told them that if any man among them was afraid to stand by me that I should open the gate and he should freely pass." To his gratification, not a man budged. When he shared his reply to Gálvez the troops raised "three cheers and then went to our necessary work like good men." Durnford's determination was almost certainly bolstered when he learned that a British relief force of more than five hundred men was en route from Pensacola. All he had to do was hang on for several days.[68]

For the first but not the last time in its long history, Mobile came under hostile artillery fire. Flame leaped from the eighteen-pounders' muzzles, and great acrid clouds of white smoke rolled across the town as the heavy balls buried themselves in the glacis or ploughed across the top of it and smashed into the walls, scattering dust and broken brick. Durnford's guns thundered in response, while the infantry on both sides sniped and the Spanish sappers pushed their zigzag siege trenches ever closer. For all the smoke and noise, casualties were light. A black slave was wounded early while digging in the trenches, and after more than a week Gálvez's losses amounted to only eight killed and twelve wounded. Durnford lost one killed and had eleven wounded. By the standards of the big battles along the Eastern Seaboard, this was a skirmish. Despite Durnford's efforts, however, the fort's walls were breached by March 12, and the hoped-for relief force had been delayed by abysmal road conditions. Bowing to the inevitable, the noble British officer surrendered his battered fort. Heads held high, the British marched out, with drums beating and flags snapping and stacked arms. "No man in the garrison stained the luster of the British arms," Durnford declared. Gálvez proved a gentlemanly victor, showing concern for Durnford's family and shipping his prisoners to British territory. By the following year Gálvez had overthrown Pensacola and emblazoned his family crest with the phrase "Yo solo" ("I alone"). From the Mississippi to the Apalachicola, West Florida was Spanish.[69]

Once again Mobile's residents were given the choice of taking a loyalty oath or leaving. Happily for the French inhabitants, the Catholic faith was again supreme. For the British the prospect of Spanish government at least promised to be easy. As one planter in the Natchez district stated, "the major attraction of Spanish rule was that there was little or no rule at all for honest citizens." A string of governors presided at Mobile—Grimarest, Favrot, Folch, Lanzos, Perez—but the colonial ways persisted. The Indian trade remained dominant and was increasingly left to the firm of Panton, Leslie & Company. William Panton and John Leslie were a pair of Scottish traders who proved especially adroit at frontier politics. One of their silent partners was the famed métis Alexander McGillivray, whose father was Scottish and whose mother was of a prominent Creek Indian clan. This gave the firm an advantage with the Creek trade along the Coosa and Tallapoosa Rivers, and a Spanish garrison at Fort San Esteban de Tombecbe on the Tombigbee helped with access to the Chickasaws and Choctaws. The company's Mobile office was on Royal Street, and several of their schooners plied area waterways.[70]

The colony grew slowly, and the town of Mobile was somewhat improved. Panton, Leslie & Company and several private landowners were granted waterfront lots on the condition that the parcels would be filled with oyster shells and soil. This leveled off and dried out problem areas, thus reducing the "the putrid exhalations" and pestilence that accompanied them. Royal Street continued to be the thoroughfare closest to the water. The river's marshy western flank began to be covered in places with shells and other fill but was still subject to tidal inundation and littered with driftwood, seaweed, and, on occasion, fish carcasses. In summer it stank to high heaven. The King's Wharf jutted across this waste and into the river just north of what was now called Fuerte Carlota. The siege-damaged fort was repaired and the twelve-foot-wide wharf constructed of heavy two-inch cypress planks. A block north of the King's Wharf stood a significant new enterprise, Montuse's Wharf and Tavern, a lively gathering spot that virtually everyone traveling through town would have visited. Run by Sylvain Montuse, a French cooper turned barkeep, and his wife, Catalina, it offered wine, whiskey, tobacco, oysters, clams, fish, game, and waterfront gossip. South of the fort, Spanish Alley provided amusement to sailors that included gambling, drinking and, no doubt, women of negotiable virtue. For the rest, the town included warehouses and stores along the river; a centrally located hospital; unpretentious houses and a handful of more notable ones dotted about; a simple wooden church on Royal Street; and the cemetery, or Campo Santo, at the western limit. In every direction swamps, marsh, and wilderness stretched for miles.[71]

Just as in French and British times, the population was polyglot. Upriver and even in town there was race mixing aplenty. One cleric grumbled that the Spanish officers "live openly with their mulatto concubines as do many of the people, and they are not ashamed to name the children in the parish registers as their natural children." Free black persons enjoyed greater tolerance and opportunity than ever. They could buy and sell property, sign contracts, and own businesses. There was even an armed black militia with a black sergeant. Otherwise, life in town and on the plantations continued to follow the established rhythms. Hunting, fishing, farming, raising cattle, making tar, wood cutting, mending, sewing, cooking, and childrearing marked the days.[72]

But the wheel was about to turn again. In 1795 Spain signed the Treaty of San Lorenzo with the United States, recognizing the thirty-first parallel and the Mississippi River as the young nation's southern and western boundaries. The treaty also allowed the United States access to New Orleans, thus opening the lower river to more commerce. In Mobile the treaty cut off the vast hinterland, greatly impacting the Indian trade. And from the north came a new breed of settler, the rough-hewn, independent-minded American following the river valleys toward the coast, where trouble with the corrupt and somnolent foreign power controlling the mouth of all those streams was bound to arise.[73]

What the Widow Rochon thought of these developments is not recorded. Just three years before the treaty she petitioned the Spanish government for a little land upriver on which to graze cattle. Her husband, Augustín, Pierre Rochon's brother, had died a dozen years earlier, and like many older single women in the colony, she was handling her affairs as best she could. The mother of nine children, she had led a life that was rich, dramatic and tempered by loss. During the Spanish siege of Mobile, with her husband dead hardly a year, she and her family were holed up at their plantation across the bay when Choctaw Indians raided the place. Several people were killed, the buildings burned, and Rochon and her family captured. The Indians marched them to Pensacola, where they were ransomed by the British and returned to Mobile. Unfortunately for Madame Rochon, her property downtown had fared no better than her plantation. Her house there was among those Durnford "put fire" to, destroying it and all the improvements, including some fruit trees. In the succeeding years she had recovered, however, and was matriarch to a growing clan, actively managing her assets. In her 1792 petition to the Spanish, she declared herself a resident of Mobile. The land she wanted was called "the old fort" and was located about nine leagues distant. The property "has not heretofore been owned or possessed by any person," she asserted, and it would suit her cows nicely. Don Manuel de Lanzos, commander of the Regiment of Louisiana agreed that the land "has been abandoned" and "does not belong to any person." She was granted twelve by twenty arpents, or a little more than four hundred acres. By Christmas her cattle were chewing their cud where Iberville and Bienville had trod and where more than a century later a bookish lawyer would dedicate an engraved stone to keep their memory green.[74]

3

American Dawn

The United States and Spain agreed on the thirty-first parallel as their boundary, but in truth neither nation knew exactly where it lay. It was obviously in the American interest that it should be as close to the coast as possible and in the Spanish that it be farther north. While much of West Florida was as yet lightly peopled—one estimate included forty families along the Mobile and Tensaw Rivers and less than two thousand people in Mobile and Pensacola combined—no one doubted that the Americans were on the way. Opinion was divided among the existing landholders along the rivers, a diverse set if ever there was one, with some hoping to remain under Spanish rule, others chafing for the Stars and Stripes, and some no doubt enjoying the ambiguity and business opportunities presented by fluidity of the situation. Diplomats in Washington and Madrid realized that an accurate survey was absolutely necessary to allay any destabilizing confusion.[1]

To that end a survey party was commissioned with representatives from both nations. The Spanish chose Manuel Gayoso de Lemos, governor of Louisiana, to head their half of the expedition, while President George Washington selected Andrew Ellicott, a Pennsylvania Quaker and clockmaker's son, to lead the Americans. Ellicott was an excellent choice, a talented mathematician and astronomer and no mean surveyor. He had an impressive collection of scientific instruments, perhaps the best in the country, and extensive field experience, having helped lay out the District of Columbia, the city of Erie, Pennsylvania, and several frontier roads. He readily accepted this new challenge and proceeded down the Mississippi to New Orleans to begin the work.[2]

Ellicott quickly realized that getting his heavy and carefully calibrated equipment overland through the swampy wilderness between New Orleans and Mobile presented too many risks and difficulties, so he fitted out a schooner to "follow the coast, and ascend the rivers, to or near the points where the line of demarcation crossed them." His vessel was a fine little shallow-draft forty-ton craft with oak and cedar timbers that he named the *Sally* after his wife. For a crew he picked up a couple of "completely illiterate" British deserters from a privateer, and because he could not find a captain for

Andrew Ellicott. Courtesy of the New York Public Library.

a decent price, determined to do the navigating himself. Also aboard were a cook, a washerwoman named Betsy, and several dozen U. S. soldiers. On March 1, 1799, Ellicott steered the *Sally* out onto Lake Pontchartrain, even as a separate survey party consisting of axmen, chain men, Spanish and American soldiers, and increasing numbers of Indian hangers-on proceeded east from further upriver, blazing the compass line.[3]

March is a stormy and variable month on the Gulf Coast, and the *Sally* beat into contrary winds all the way over to Mobile, where she arrived on March 14. Ellicott thought the little town's situation "handsome" and a few of the houses "tolerably good." He was impressed by the brick fort and thought the local trade "considerable" for so small a place. But real work awaited him upriver, and fighting continued northers and a strong, full current, he inched the *Sally* upstream, taking four days to cover the thirty-three miles to the campsite already established by the land crew.[4]

The place had to have been an agreeable one to the buffeted passengers of the *Sally* as it was located yards from a frontier tavern called Grog Hall. The land party had set up Ellicott's observation tent—worn army issue with an opening cut into the roof—atop Andry Hill, a one-hundred-foot knob named for a French planter who had a nearby plantation at Seymour Bluff on one of the Mobile's tight hairpin bends. (The planter, Simon Andry, like several of his neighbors, kept a black mistress with whom he had many children.) The day after the *Sally* anchored midstream, Ellicott's men had his instruments moved into the observation tent. These included an astronomical clock carefully positioned atop a tree stump and a zenith sector sited on an angle figured off the meridian. The zenith sector was a six-foot-long brass telescope on an alt-azimuth mount with leveling screws and dangling plumb bobs. The telescope was designed to observe objects straight overhead, at or near the zenith, and had a limited range of movement along its two mutually perpendicular axes. Ellicott would have had to lie underneath it on a piece of canvas or sit in a specially designed reclining chair, probably fashioned of canvas and wood so it could be folded. From this extreme angle he was able to observe target stars as they crossed the meridian, time them with his clock, and make the calculations on latitude.[5]

Ellicott pursued his observations into early April, during which the other members of the party lounged in their tents, hunted, fished, bent elbows at the tavern, and misbehaved. In fact, if the testimony of at least two individuals is to be believed, when Ellicott was not wedged under the zenith sector or hunched over his desk calculating angles, he was something of a randy chap himself. A miniature portrait done by a Spanish woman in New Orleans, which Ellicott thought was "an excellent likeness," and a pencil sketch of his profile show him with a pudgy baby face, a small mouth, and heavily lidded eyes. It is not hard to imagine him as a voluptuary. We know by his own correspondence that his private tent had "elegant silk" mosquito curtains and that he ate out of china bowls. Some years later Major Thomas Freeman, one of the surveyors, testified in court that Ellicott had sexual relations with Betsy the washerwoman, whose character "was that of a prostitute, and of the lowest grade." Freeman even claimed that Betsy, Ellicott, and the latter's nineteen-year-old son, a chain man on the party, "slept in the same bed, at the same time." He did not actually see this, he admitted, but he believed it, not in the least because the "old sinner" had once urged him to "take part of his bed with his washerwoman and himself, for the night." Ellicott's opinion of Freeman was equally low. He considered him "one of the greatest rascals and liars in existence" and "expeld him from the camp" before the crew even reached Mobile. But in a letter written in the spring of 1800, John Walker, first clerk of the court at Natchez, who had been along for the entire survey, was also critical of Ellicott and in particular his treatment of Betsy. Walker related that the washerwoman "became deranged" on the last leg of the trip into Savannah and was "chained in a mad-house." He continued: "Mr. Ellicott must feel remorse for forcing her to remain on the line with him during the whole survey against her own wishes and the remonstrance's of his friends." Was Betsy indeed a sex slave who, when not cleaning his linen with her calico sleeves pushed above chapped, reddened forearms, was dragged onto his cot for, as Freeman put it, "beastly, criminal, and disgraceful intercourse"? Or was she a prostitute, paid for favors willingly bestowed? Or neither? Alas, we may never know, Betsy herself having left no record of the matter. But the sorry station and ugly abuse of eighteenth-century servants in general and washerwomen in particular were unfortunate fixtures of the age.[6]

Whatever went on behind Ellicott's silken mosquito curtains during those weeks at Seymour Bluff, the survey project at hand presented certain technical difficulties that demanded attention. Foremost among these was how to shoot the line across the swampy and "almost impenetrable" delta. Fortunately for Ellicott, Andry Hill was elevated above the swamp's dense tree line. "From the top of this hill," he wrote, "we could plainly discover the pine trees on the East side." The solution was to send a party across via small boat through the interconnecting watercourses and have them build a large fire on that high ground opposite. Ellicott had his own signal fire built on Andry Hill, which would allow the two parties to accurately discern their respective locations and measure the angles. But what seemed a good idea presented an unusual difficulty when numerous other woods fires in the vicinity made telling which fire was which uncertain. "It was then agreed," remarked Ellicott, "that the parties should light up, and extinguish their fires a certain number of times; making stated intervals." This worked beautifully, and the next day heavy rain dampened all the fires, and a northwest wind "carried off all the smoke," which allowed for signal flags to be used in daylight.[7]

By April 19 Ellicott had finished his calculations and was bound for Pensacola aboard the *Sally* while the axmen blazed the vista overland from the delta's eastern bluffs. During his time on the Mobile River, he had determined that the actual parallel was almost two miles south of the compass line run from the Mississippi. To mark the exact spot his men erected a brown ferruginous sandstone, nearly three-feet high, on the Mobile's west bank. The stone's north side was engraved "U. S. Lat. 31° 1799" and the south side read "Dominios de S. M. Carlos IV. Lat. 31° 1799." More than two hundred years later, the Ellicott Stone still stands in the woods near the Barry Steam Plant, the oldest above-ground European artifact in Alabama. Despite having been hit by a falling tree in 1917 and blasted with buckshot in the 1970s, it remains in a remarkably good state of preservation. It was to be the only stone marker erected by the survey crew—the line was landmarked elsewhere with simple posts on small mounds—testimony to the significance of the Mobile River for the two nations that commissioned the survey. Ellicott himself opined that the Mobile was "of much more importance to the United States than all the other waters between the Mississippi River and the Atlantic Ocean." All in all, he felt confident in his results, despite their having been obtained "in haste, with a common chain, through thickets, swamps and ponds." His confidence was justified; modern measurements by satellite show Ellicott to have been off by only 799 feet. His achievement was extraordinary.[8]

It also had immediate consequences. Spanish West Florida was now a narrow coastal strip, 450 miles west to east from the Mississippi to the Apalachicola River, and only forty to ninety miles wide. Though Mobile and Pensacola with their harbors and forts remained in Spanish hands, the sprawling backcountry belonged to the United States. Because the outpost at Fuerte San Esteban was well north of Ellicott's line, the

Spanish had to abandon it. The Americans immediately renamed it Fort St. Stephens, and within a few years it would become Alabama's territorial capital. Closer to the actual line of demarcation, now an officially recognized international boundary, the U.S. Congress decided to establish another fort better to protect American settlers, regulate trade through Spanish Mobile, monitor the Indians, and deter rowdies of whatever stripe bent on mischief.[9]

Named Fort Stoddert after Secretary of the Navy Benjamin Stoddert, it was to be a port of entry, seat of an admiralty court of the revenue district of Mobile, and later the terminus for the Federal Road. But first it had to be built. The design, if it can be called such, was for a frontier-style stockade with four bastions. The task fell to Captain Bartholomew Schaumburgh of the Second United States Infantry, a German immigrant and experienced army hand with a strong work ethic and a salty sense of humor. In the summer of 1799 he brought two companies down to Ward's Bluff, situated on the right bank of the Mobile River about four miles below the junction of the Tombigbee and Alabama Rivers. The locale had obvious strategic advantages, perched beside what is today called the Mount Vernon Stretch, a handy choke point between the Mobile-Tensaw split and the delta on one end and the big rivers funneling down from the north. No river traffic, legitimate or otherwise, into or out of Mobile, was going to escape federal oversight.[10]

Schaumburgh reported his progress in a series of dispatches to his superior, Major Thomas Cushing, commanding U. S. troops along the rivers. His first challenge was the climate and its debilitating effect on the men. "I come on but slowly with the Fortifying," he wrote on July 19. "The weather is so extremely hot that I can't work more than eight hours each day." Many of his men were already sick, even though it was not yet peak fever season, and the resources to treat them were woefully inadequate. "Doctor Hogland arrived here without any *thing,*" he complained, "no not even a Chirurgical Instrument—If one of my men should be so unfortunate as to break an arm or leg & should [it] be necessary to amputate the limb, I should have to chop it off with a broad ax." Less drastic remedies included prodigious stocks of brandy, wine, and chocolate "for the use of the hospital." More than a month later, at the end of August, Schaumburgh still claimed that "the sickly state of the men is much against me."[11]

Nonetheless, through the summer and into fall the walls and bastions rose, and guns were mounted. Progress could not come fast enough for Schaumburgh. He intensely felt his exposed position amid numerous potentially hostile forces. "The Savages in this quarter, (meaning the Chactaws)," he explained, "are peaceable, they now & then steal a cow from the inhabitants but they do no other harm." The Creeks, who held sway east of the rivers and on up north, were another matter, "insolent to extreme," and Schaumburgh wished he could "send them to hell." Large numbers of them would wander onto the bluff and ask, "Who gave me permission to come here, cut their trees down & build a Fort." He knew they were being supplied and goaded by the Spanish and the British, and a surprise attack was never out of the question. On November

3 Schaumburgh learned of Creek plans that fortunately failed to materialize, but such rumors served to keep him "upon my guard." According to an informant who had gotten the story "by means of a squaw," a party of three hundred Creeks was to "descend the river" with chickens, under the pretext of going to Mobile. But first they would stop at Fort Stoddert's landing and offer a lower price for the hens. Once Schaumburgh's men were intermixed with the Indians, the latter "would seize and hold them, till they should rob me of every thing they thought proper to take, and in order that I might not suspect their design, they would bring with them their women & children." If there was anything reassuring about this proposed shakedown, it was the appearance that the Indians "had no intention to take hair." Happily for Schaumburgh, his men, and probably the Indians, too, Creek elders nixed the plan "as a bad undertaking." As if this kind of talk was not enough to cause the poor captain sleepless nights, he also heard that "English privateers are cruising between Pensacola, New Orleans & Mobile, and take every vessel they meet with, they have lately taken a vessel richly loaden, belonging to the house of Panton, Leslie & Co."[12]

Further important political developments among the nations active along the gulf rim only served to keep the local situation unsettled. In 1802 Spain returned Louisiana to France, and then Napoleon turned right around the next year and sold it to the United States in the Louisiana Purchase. American negotiators argued that Mobile was part of the deal, but the Spanish denied this and, in an attempt to assert authority, dictated a 12 percent duty on all goods travelling the Mobile River. In February of 1804 Congress responded by passing the Mobile Act, which claimed U. S. ownership of that portion of West Florida between the Mississippi and the Perdido Rivers and designating Fort Stoddert as a customs district. But the Spanish held firm, and American officials and traders grumbled loudly about the inconvenience. In a letter dated March 15, 1804, Governor William C. C. Claiborne of the Territory of Orleans wrote to the secretary of war that the business of the Choctaw trading house in St. Stephens was "subjected to the caprice of a Spanish officer." Claiborne forwarded the complaint of Joseph Chambers, the U. S. factor there, who reported his experience at Mobile. With a cargo of "sixty bales, three hogsheads and one barrel of peltries and furs" bound downstream for the gulf and Philadelphia, Chambers was detained at the Mobile wharves. There, "the officers of His Most Catholic Majesty the King of Spain did . . . demand a duty of twelve per centum upon *their* estimated value of said cargo." Despite being informed that the cargo was "the property of the United States," the Spanish insisted Chambers had to pay $182.68 to be on his way. This he did, but in his report the outraged factor railed that the rivers were the "common highways of nature," and for one government to extract a duty from another "is in violation of a right which ought not to be questioned by nations friendly to each other."[13]

Chambers's words echoed those of President Thomas Jefferson, expressed the previous August in a letter to John C. Breckinridge, a U. S. senator from Kentucky. In his missive Jefferson remarked that the Louisiana Purchase would net the Floridas "all in good time." Rather than provoke an open fight because Spain refused to recognize the Perdido as the eastern boundary of the purchase (the Perdido now marks the border between Florida and Alabama), the Sage of Monticello opted for steady pressure, confident that an influx of grasping settlers and an exhausted Spanish Crown with a depleted treasury would accomplish American desires peacefully. "In the meanwhile," he continued, "without waiting for permission, we shall enter into the exercise of the natural right we have always insisted on with Spain, to wit, that of a nation holding the upper part of streams, having a right of innocent passage thro' them to the ocean. We shall prepare her to see us practice on this, & she will not oppose it by force." But by the following summer, as Chambers's frustrating experience demonstrated, if not exactly opposing it by force, the Spanish definitely were not cooperating. Jefferson wrote to James Madison, secretary of state, on July 5, 1804, and reaffirmed his determination that "we shall enter into the exercise of our right of navigating the Mobile and protect it, and increase our force there *pari passu* with them [Spain]." But despite this official resolve, possession proved nine-tenths of the law. Spain held to Mobile, levied her duties on goods loaded aboard schooners, flatboats, barges, and canoes, and the situation remained in uneasy disequilibrium.[14]

Schaumburgh could have been forgiven for thinking he was holding down the lid on a powder keg. And if bellicose Creek Indians, officious Spaniards, agitated Yankee traders, and roving English privateers were not enough, newly arriving American settlers added their volatile personalities to the mix. The areas north of Mobile became known as the Bigbee District and the Tensaw Settlements, and the Americans were coming in ever greater numbers. They were a rough lot by any measure, accustomed to drinking, fighting, and living with their women without benefit of clergy. A U. S. judge who spent several months at Fort Stoddert in 1804 sent President Jefferson a sobering description. "The present inhabitants," he declared, "are illiterate, wild and savage, of depraved morals, unworthy of public confidence or private esteem; litigious, disunited, and knowing each other, universally distrustful."[15] The only thing missing from this rogues' gallery was an *agent provocateur* to put lit match to the powder, and in the winter of 1807, with icy winds barreling over the region and the Mobile nearly frozen, none other than Aaron Burr appeared on the scene.

Exactly what the former Continental army officer, senator, and vice president of the United States, notorious for killing his rival Alexander Hamilton on the Weehawken cliffs in 1804, was up to in the Southwest has been the subject of much speculation ever since. Burr had engaged in numerous secret meetings with various individuals and corresponded in cipher with the accomplished schemer General James Wilkinson, commanding U. S. forces at New Orleans, about an ambitious plan that was either patriotic or treasonous, depending on one's point of view. The rough elements of the plan involved Burr's descending the Ohio and Mississippi Rivers with a private armed force to link with Wilkinson, detach the western territories from the United States, and invade Mexico. Burr fully expected the American settlers in the territories, disgusted with

Spanish misrule, to join his cause. If the darkest interpretations of Burr's intentions are true, he intended to set himself up as king in the conquered territory with his daughter, Theodosia, at his side. That he thought of his adventure in lofty terms is confirmed by a letter to Wilkinson in 1806, wherein he declared, "The Gods invite us to glory and fortune; it remains to be seen whether we deserve the boon."[16]

Unfortunately for Burr, Wilkinson decided that they did not, and it would be better to expose the plot than to aid it. He alerted Thomas Jefferson and the Spanish, who had been paying him to spy for decades. With Burr now wanted and rumored to be somewhere on the Mississippi, the backcountry was abuzz. On January 7, 1807, Silas Dinsmoor, the Choctaw agent at the foot of the Natchez Trace, wrote to a friend: "We are all in a flurry here hourly expecting Colonel Burr & all Kentucky & half of Tennessee at his back to punish General Wilkinson, set the negroes free, Rob the banks & take Mexico. Come & help me to laugh at the fun." Three days later Burr was apprehended with several boats and about sixty men. Arraigned in Washington, Mississippi Territory, he jumped bail and disappeared into the wilderness.[17]

Shivering at his desk in the hamlet of Wakefield, situated on a bend of the Tombigbee River near what is now McIntosh Bluff, Harry Toulmin mulled the situation. Appointed judge for the Mississippi Territory by Jefferson a few years earlier, Toulmin was an impressive figure who would prove more than equal to the unusual challenges attending his position. Born in England in 1766, he had become a Unitarian minister before immigrating to Virginia in 1793 and embarking on a distinguished legal and political career. Settled at his frontier post, he took as his main objective keeping the peace along the line of demarcation where diverse residents rubbed elbows amid growing tensions. A charismatic leader like Burr who could rally the settlers or incite the Spanish was the last thing the scholarly judge needed. In a letter to an American army officer at Fort Stoddert, Toulmin was matter-of-fact and calm. "Burr is still in concealment," he wrote, "but I fully expect he will make his appearance in a day or two."[18]

As Toulmin guessed, Burr not only made his appearance, but he did so in the very hamlet where the judge had penned his letter. It happened on the blustery night of February 18, 1807, when the fugitive was recognized by a young federal land registrar named Nicholas Perkins. Burr had stopped to ask directions at a little tavern, and by the firelight Perkins was immediately struck by the stranger's "extraordinary" appearance. The young man later recalled that "he had on a white hat with a brim rather broad than otherwise, a long beard, a checked Hankerchief around his neck, a great coat belted around him to which was hanging a tin cup on one side and a butchers knife on the other." Most striking were the stranger's glittering dark eyes. Refusing to stay at the tavern, the stranger and a companion rode on, while Perkins hastened south to Fort Stoddert where he tipped off Schaumburgh's successor, twenty-nine-year-old Lieutenant Edmund Pendleton Gaines. The young officer favored Andrew Jackson—tall, lean, and rugged with a high forehead crowned by a thick comb of upswept hair. Like Jackson, Gaines recognized the importance of decisive action, and he immediately took to horse with Perkins and several soldiers. They soon confronted Burr and his companion on the Pensacola road. The exchange was brief. "I presume sir," said Gaines, "I have the honor of addressing Colonel Burr." Ever evasive, Burr replied, "I am a traveler in the country, and do not recognize your right to ask such a question." Unfazed, Gaines came to the point: "I arrest you at the instance of the Federal Government." Burr then tried to intimidate the officer: "You are a young man, and may not be aware of the responsibilities which result from arresting travelers." Unmoved, Gaines quipped, "I am aware of the responsibilities, but I know my duty."[19]

Taken back to the fort, Burr was treated with great courtesy and in short order won over everyone around him. Gaines's wife, Frances, who happened to be one of Judge Toulmin's daughters, and the few other wives at the lonely outpost were completely charmed by this dashing, improbable personality in their midst, and the men respected his daring historic accomplishments. During the two weeks he was held at the fort, Burr enlivened Gaines's dinner table, played chess with his wife late into the night, and comforted his ailing brother in an adjacent room. But Gaines realized there was always the potential for trouble with a man like Burr, a fact further impressed upon him when a Spanish officer from downstream called and asked to see the famous prisoner. Gaines refused to allow it, and after the officer left he confided to Perkins that he was "suspicious the Spanish would endeavor to rescue Colonel Burr." This was a frightening prospect for the earnest American officer. Fort Stoddert was isolated and undermanned, and what soldiers were there were mostly ill and poorly equipped. There was also the very real possibility that Burr might become a focus for the restless settlers seeking to at last wrest Mobile from Spanish hands. Desperate to be done with the whole business, Gaines asked Perkins to escort the prisoner all the way to Washington, D. C., for trial.[20]

On the morning of March 5 Burr was marched out of the fort and down to the landing by Perkins and a file of dragoons. In the words of one of his nineteenth-century biographers, "as the boat, with its crew of soldiers glided past the few houses on the river's bank, all the ladies, it is said, waved their handkerchiefs, except those who were obliged to put those weapons to tenderer use." One of these women is supposed to have even named a son for the intriguing colonel. After an arduous journey back east with his guards, Burr was tried and acquitted. He moved to Europe shortly thereafter. Contemplating it all later from his writing desk, in a letter to Madison, Judge Toulmin shared his own theory as to what Burr intended when he jumped bail. Because the colonel had friends and contacts in the region, Toulmin believed that his destination of choice was the Tombigbee, "calculating that the people of this country would eagerly flock to his standard, that they could then immediately take possession of Mobile." Pensacola and New Orleans were no doubt next, with Mexico the greatest prize of all. Burr himself never said, of course, but during the Texas Revolution of 1836 he exclaimed to a friend: "There! You see? I was right. What was treason in me thirty years ago is patriotism today!"[21]

Toulmin and Gaines no doubt breathed sighs of relief once Burr exited their territory, but none of the fundamentals had changed, and where the great conspirator failed, the notorious Kemper brothers meant to succeed. Nathan, Reuben, and Samuel Kemper were a trio of frontier rowdies with a burning hatred for the Spanish. In the summer of 1810 they took Baton Rouge and booted out the Spaniards, declaring an independent Republic of West Florida. Exploiting the moment, Madison, now president of the United States, quickly annexed what were called the Florida Parishes (those areas of Louisiana north and northwest of New Orleans), and the Kemper brothers set their sights further east. Reuben became the main instigator in the Bigbee District, and together with several other residents he formed the Mobile Society. In a letter written on July 19 to Cayateno Perez, the Spanish commandant at Mobile, a man named Joseph P. Kennedy declared that "this Society has its origin in the oppression which we have suffered from the Spanish Government in detaining a country which the Supreme law of the State has declared to be ours." Kemper, Kennedy, and the brothers John and James Caller agitated in the area for weeks, whipping up resentment and refining their plans. Surveying the situation with a gimlet eye, Toulmin knew trouble was imminent, but he was determined to keep the peace and enforce the laws. In a letter to James Innerarity, an agent for Panton, Leslie & Company in Mobile, he grumbled about Kemper in particular, who he said talked in a "high style." The judge continued: "He even indirectly has the assurance to threaten me with his future vengeance—should he *eventually* be injured by the warnings which I have in several letters given to the people of this country to be aware of being seduced from the allegiance to the laws of the union." An officer at Fort Stoddert offered an equally jaundiced opinion of Kennedy, whom he labeled "without *real* talents, yet in a seditious intrigue, or for the low arts that secure popularity, he must be acknowledged eminent." Kemper responded in typical fashion when he called Toulmin "a base Devil filled with deceptive and Bloody Rascality."[22]

By November the bullying and name calling were done, and the Mobile Society made its move. Mortified, Juan Vicente Folch, the Spanish governor at Mobile, offered to drop the 12 percent duty if Toulmin could induce Kemper and his confederates to abandon their enterprise. But it was too late. Their blood up, Kemper and more than one hundred followers crossed Nannahubba Island and worked their way down the delta's eastern side. Scouring the surrounding farms and plantations for arms and provisions, they were mostly frustrated. The French, Creole, and British residents were not affected so much by the tariff, and they were less than enthusiastic about losing precious larder to a band of wild-eyed American revolutionaries. The filibusters took what they could plunder and were greatly cheered when a keelboat arrived from their Baton Rouge allies loaded with whiskey, corn, flour, and bacon. Then things began to unravel. In a fatal error Kemper divided his force, sending a portion of it under the command of Major William Hargrave, an old Revolutionary War veteran, across the delta in the keelboat. Kemper opted to march the rest of the men and the horses back around across

Nannahubba and down the west side where he would rejoin forces and strike Mobile from the north.[23]

The keelboat reached the Mobile River without incident and hove into Sawmill Creek (now called Bayou Sara) opposite Twelve Mile Island, where Hargrave settled down to await Kemper. In the meantime the weather had deteriorated, turning cold and wet. In an effort to cut the chill, the filibusters stoked several large fires, guzzled the whiskey, and broke out a few fiddles. Unbeknownst to them, "an evil old man in the neighborhood" slipped downstream and told the Spanish that the filibusters were drunk and off their guard. Acting quickly, Folch dispatched two hundred regulars and citizen volunteers by boat, who arrived at Sawmill Creek shortly before midnight.[24]

Marching nervous armed men across swampy unfamiliar ground in the dark toward a foe, even an unprepared one, in hopes of springing a surprise attack is never a sure thing. One of the Spanish soldiers fired too soon, and Hargrave was able to mount a ragged defense. There were shouts, flintlocks flashed brilliant yellow and orange in the misty air, acrid smoke drifted over the camp fires, and men fell. This was shooting at shadows and silhouettes, but when the brief clash was over, four filibusters were dead and several wounded. Ten were captured, hauled down to Mobile and clapped in irons. They were subsequently sent to Havana where they languished for five years behind the stone walls of Moro Castle. Kemper, Kennedy, and all their fiery rhetoric about how they would overthrow "ancient Mobile" were defeated. To make sure they got the message, General Wilkinson ordered U. S. troops to help the Spanish protect the port town from further such incidents.[25]

It was an ironic turn of events to say the least: the American government too timid to seize vital territory it believed it rightfully owned, its citizens infuriated by an unjust tariff imposed by a foreign power, and its armed forces actually helping that foreign power maintain a hold on the disputed real estate against its own people. The settlers' frustration was soon backed by the editorial imprimatur of the region's first newspaper, the *Mobile Centinel.* An ungainly printing press had been floated downstream in early 1811 by a pair of entrepreneurs—John B. Hood of South Carolina and Samuel Miller of Tennessee. In their first number, printed on May 30 at Fort Stoddert, they wrote that "the original intention of the Editors was to have issued their paper from the town of Mobile; but they cannot yet congratulate their fellow citizens on the possession of that spot, to this country so important—other persons can, perhaps, give better reasons why we have it not in possession."[26]

Time was on the Americans' side, however. Governor Folch, Captain Perez, and the threadbare troops at Fuerte Carlota could only wait and watch as developments to the north continued to build toward what most considered an inevitable outcome. By 1811 the Federal Road was completed down to the juncture of the Alabama and Tombigbee Rivers, where travelers could either float down to Fort Stoddert's landing or utilize ferries to cross Nannahubba Island and gain the Mobile's west bank. The road had been authorized by the U.S. Congress several years before to get mail from Georgia to the newly acquired city of New Orleans, and after the Creek Indians agreed to let it traverse their lands, gangs of workmen had cut it through the forests of what is today southern Alabama. The original goal had been to move the mail in three days from Coweta, Georgia, to Fort Stoddert, but in practice seven days was the norm. Travel on the Federal Road was rough and dangerous, but it quickly became a thoroughfare into the Gulf South from the more populous Eastern Seaboard. Settlers came in ever growing numbers, and tensions mounted with the Creeks.[27]

As the terminus for the road, Fort Stoddert was now more important than ever, and its garrison increased to several hundred men. But as Edmund Gaines's brother, George—the very one nursed by Burr—later recalled, "The place proved unhealthy & the troops in 1805 and '6 were sent to St. Stephens to spend the sickly months, leaving a small garrison to take care of the fort. . . . After this the summer encampment was established on a hill called Mount Vernon 3 miles west of Fort Stoddert." Situated back from the river swamps on higher ground, Mount Vernon cantonment became a bustling military post. The soldiers' days were defined by ever-present discipline, constant drilling, and patrolling. No one doubted that serious fighting could erupt at any time, what with the rapidly shifting fortunes and intentions of so many nations and players in the region. But for the present the political irresolution continued while the young officers at Mount Vernon studied their manuals of war and their men practiced with the musket and bayonet.[28]

South of the line of demarcation, a number of Americans had sworn allegiance to the Spanish king and were comfortably ensconced. Among them was a Connecticut Yankee named Josiah Blakeley, who, on February 28, 1812, wrote a lengthy letter to a niece back home describing the surrounding country, his circumstances, and hopes for the future. "Mobile, the great object of contention at this moment between the United States and the Spaniards," he explained, "contains about 90 houses, all of wood and but one story high." He reported a brisk coastwise traffic: "Packet boats and other vessels are constantly running between this and New Orleans; passage about three days." There were only about twenty white families in Mobile, "those French, Spanish, Americans, and English." But he went on to state that he was "acquainted on both sides of the river, for a hundred miles up, with all the best people." Other than a Catholic church in Mobile, "for 500 miles north, I do not believe there is a church or clergyman." As for the incoming settlers, Blakeley thought them "almost savage." After describing how the Mobile River "disembogues its waters into the bay by several mouths," Blakeley revealed that he owned several islands in the lower delta—the one opposite the city shaped like an elongated lobster claw was later named for him—but that until the "unfortunate dispute" between the United States and Spain was resolved, "it is impossible for me to either sell or cultivate these lands." Even so, he did not doubt their value and was confident that with American rule he would prosper. "Cattle and hogs do well upon them," he wrote, "and no expense. Upon them I have about 30 head of cattle and hundreds of hogs, the hogs wild. I shoot or catch them with a dog. On one of these islands I have a small house and plantation, called Festino." This was on Polecat Bay, near Coffee Bayou, and the paradise Blakeley made it sound like—"the orange, fig, quince, and peach; all do well"—is difficult to imagine today with roaring interstate traffic, shibuilding, and scummy tailings ponds nearby.[29]

Not long after Blakeley's letter went north, events accelerated. In April, Congress formally annexed Mobile into the Mississippi Territory, and in August the territorial governor ordered the creation of Mobile County with a sheriff, militia districts, and even a local government for the town. But by far the most important development was Congress's declaration of war against Great Britain. Because Britain and Spain were allies, Mobile and Pensacola suddenly represented dire threats to the nation's underbelly. If the Royal Navy was given access to these ports, what had been an irritating situation could suddenly become potentially fatal to the body politic. It was time to act, and in February 1813 the secretary of war ordered General Wilkinson to take Mobile and Pensacola. Given the order's travel time from Washington and the requisite preparations, Wilkinson did not embark until that April, when he sailed from New Orleans with five gunboats, scaling ladders, and eight hundred men. Open war on the Mobile River looked to have arrived at last.[30]

The approach by Wilkinson's force presented anything but an intimidating picture, however. His vessels ran aground; he almost met, as he put it, "the unprofessional end of death by drowning instead of shooting"; boats collided, fired on one another, and generally blundered into Mobile Bay. By April 13 things were more under control with the gunboats anchored off the town, and the infantry and artillery, reinforced by four hundred men down from Fort Stoddert under the command of Colonel John Bowyer, dug in around it. Inside Fuerte Carlota, Captain Perez hunkered with about 130 underfed scarecrows. He was cut off and doomed. Under a flag of truce, one of Wilkinson's officers delivered a note to the trapped Spaniard. "Sir," it began. "The troops of the United States under my command do not approach as the enemies of Spain, but by order of the President they come to relieve the garrison which you command, from the occupancy of a post within the legitimate limits of those states." No doubt grateful that he was confronted with a surrender demand rather than burnt powder and cannon balls, Perez quickly assented. Terms and conditions were hammered out over the next two days, and on the fifteenth the Spaniards marched out and boarded American transports for the short voyage to Pensacola. When the last *soldado* exited the gates and passed the glacis, one American artillery company and two infantry companies entered the fort. An artillery salute was fired by the land batteries, and the vessels in the bay responded in kind. The Stars and Stripes was hoisted up the flagpole, and Wilkinson commanded that "the call of *all is well* is to be repeated by the sentinels every hour, beginning at the guard-house and passing to the right." A pass was required to go into town, and the men had to wear their uniforms when they did so.[31]

As one of the surrender conditions, a Spanish officer presented Wilkinson with a complete inventory of the fort's armaments and munitions, all to be paid for by the

U. S. government. Despite the lack of foodstuffs that had plagued the garrison, the inventory shows it to have been well supplied with the implements and accessories of war. On the list were two eighteen-pounder French cannon, six twelve-pounders, two eight-pounders, three brass four-pound swivel guns, thousands of cannon balls of various sizes, canister, grapeshot, forty barrels of charcoal, eighty-three fireballs, seven steel spikes, 139 pounds of buckshot, forty powder horns, forty bayonets, a blacksmith's anvil, two tin powder funnels, nine crowbars, two melting ladles, seven whip saws, two fascine hatchets, twelve cedar buckets, a lightning rod, and a large launch "without oars or sails." All of these, as well as the brick fort that held them and the town and lands beyond, had fallen to the Americans without, as Wilkinson proudly put it, "the effusion of a drop of blood." Wilkinson then moved on Pensacola, but it was decided to postpone that action, and he threw up a small fort on the Perdido River instead. Down at the mouth of Mobile Bay, he had a semicircular sand and timber redoubt erected that was named after Colonel Bowyer. At long last, from Nannahubba to the Gulf of Mexico, the Mobile River's waters caressed only American soil.[32]

The backcountry was a different story. Dissatisfied with an assimilation plan that had attracted some of their tribesmen and alarmed by the Federal Road's growing traffic, more traditionally minded Creeks argued for a return to the old ways. Encouraged by British agents and the powerful eloquence of the Shawnee Prophet Tecumseh, these Redsticks, so named for their painted war clubs, became embroiled in a civil war with a faction that was friendlier to the white population. The picture was complicated by the large number of métis who had relations on both sides of the conflict. Many white residents expected the spat to explode into a war with the United States. Surveying the situation from Tennessee in the summer of 1812, General Andrew Jackson, whom the Creeks would soon call Sharp Knife, welcomed the opportunity. "Our settlements on the bay and river of Mobile will require to be strengthened," he wrote in the Nashville *Clarion,* "and to strengthen them a part of the country inhabited by the Creeks will be indispensable to us. Fortunately, the crimes of this nation have supplied us with a pretext for the dismemberment of their country."[33]

Mobile and the métis inhabitants along the rivers all the way up toward the cutoff were attractive targets for the Redsticks. Some of the métis were wealthy and owned plantations, cattle, slaves, taverns, and ferries. The Redsticks resented their assimilation and success, and some nursed even more personal grievances and slights based on earlier encounters and confrontations. Isolated raids and pillaging had already set people on edge, and when a force of Redsticks journeyed to Pensacola for gunpowder, bullets, flour, and corn, the residents of the Tensaw decided to intervene. On July 27 a force of métis and white militia led by Colonel James Caller ambushed the Redsticks at Burnt Corn Creek. James was one of the Caller brothers who had been involved in the ill-starred Kemper Rebellion, and his foray into Indian fighting did not go much better. Dandied up in "a calico hunting shirt, a high bell-crowned hat, and top boots, and riding a fine bay horse," he managed to surprise the Indians at their breakfast.

After routing them, Caller's men began plundering the pack train, but in their distraction and disorganization they were counterattacked. They panicked, and Caller lost his horse, boots, pants, and finally himself, wandering in the woods for days after the clash clad only in the hunting shirt and his drawers. Casualties were low on both sides, but the Redsticks were emboldened, believing their foes to be weak and unworthy. Sensing victory, they plotted their next move.[34]

It came at midday on August 30, the drum beating the call to dinner, when more than seven hundred Redsticks under the leadership of William Weatherford, a métis himself, and the Prophet Paddy Walsh rushed the carelessly left-open gates of Fort Mims. Located about forty miles north of Mobile, not far from the Alabama River above its juncture with the Tombigbee, this was a rude stockade surrounding the frame home of Samuel Mims, a métis who had made money in the deer-skin trade. There were several other buildings in the one-acre compound, including a kitchen, smokehouse, spinning house, and blacksmith shop. The palisade had firing ports cut into it all around, but there was no elevated fire step, meaning the enemy could use these openings to fire into the fort if they gained the walls. During the recent troubles, several hundred people—militia, white and black individuals, métis, friendly Indians, and many children of all colors—had sought the refuge of the place. It was overcrowded, noisy, dusty, and sweltering in high summer's heat and humidity. Due to poor preparation, gross incompetence, and drunkenness on the part of Major Daniel Beasley, the fort's commander, the Indians achieved complete surprise. Whooping, "painted red or black and stripped to the buff," and brandishing their fearsome weapons, they poured into the compound.[35]

Ten miles downstream, Judge Toulmin was worried. Major Beasley had sent him a note "but this morning," Toulmin fretted, indicating that rumors of an Indian attack were unfounded. That there had been one was obvious, however. "What the result is we do not know," Toulmin wrote, "but the smoke of burning houses in that quarter are now seen on the riverbank at Fort Stoddert." In the ghastly backwash that accompanies all human violence, terrified refugees soon engulfed Fort Stoddert and continued on to Mobile. "Some pushed off by water, others fled by land in the darkness of the night," Toulmin later wrote, "and the whole face of the country exhibited a scene of consternation and distress." The judge thought it wise to remove his family further from the scenes of destruction, and they joined the flight south. "The river was strewed with boats from fort Stoddert to Mobile," he recalled, "and here many have no shelter and no means of support." During the following days more smoke rose from scattered locales as the Redsticks continued raiding and burning plantations and farms all over the Tensaw and up between the forks of the Alabama and Tombigbee Rivers.[36]

A handful of people had, incredibly, escaped the carnage at Fort Mims—some militia, sixteen settlers including a few women, and an African girl—and, as their first-hand accounts became known, the entire country was seized with rage. Beasely had been among the first to die, they reported, struggling to shut the gate. For more than an hour it was more battle than massacre as the defenders gave a good account of themselves and killed many Redsticks. But then the buildings were set afire, and the force of numbers told. The end was horrific as warriors scalped and killed the white people and hated métis. Women were disemboweled and babies dashed to death. Many settlers were captured and hustled north. The final casualty figures have since been the subject of much debate. Weeks after the massacre a reinforced burial detail counted 247 settlers, "men, women, and children," as well as more than one hundred Indians "covered with rails, brush &c." The precise numbers will never be known, but the event was of catastrophic proportions. Property losses were also great. After the war Tensaw settlers filed claims for more than 5,400 cattle, 2,500 hogs, hundreds of horses, thousands of bushels of corn, and dozens of slaves lost or stolen.[37]

Down from the north Andrew Jackson came like an avenging angel leading his Tennessee Volunteers and their Choctaw and Cherokee allies. Into the fall of 1813 Jackson's force campaigned through the upper reaches of Creek Indian country, laying waste to villages with fire and sword. Farther south, the settlers took heart in the heroic encounter known ever after as the Canoe Fight. While it did not occur on the Mobile proper but rather on the Alabama River, the Canoe Fight easily ranks as the most famous water-borne episode (not counting the Battle of Mobile Bay) in the history of the entire basin. It was a brief and bloody affair involving nine Indian braves, "all painted and naked except their flaps," in a long canoe and Sam Dale, Jeremiah Austill, James Smith, and a free black man named Caesar in a rude square-bottomed dugout. Dale was an imposing figure, more than six feet tall, 190 pounds, and widely known on the frontier. When the Indians saw his canoe approach, the chief cried, "Now for it, Big Sam." The white men tried a volley, but only one weapon discharged, and then the boats bumped together. While Caesar held the canoes with an iron grip, the occupants swung their rifles at one another over his unprotected head. Dale split the chief's skull open, and the Indian fell to the bottom of the canoe dead. Another he bayoneted. Within minutes all the Indians were killed and thrown into the river. From the western bank the militia cheered "loud and long." As for the Indian witnesses on the opposite bank, it was no doubt a sobering sight and a grim lesson that their American foes were anything but cowardly or inept.[38]

By the following March of 1814, Jackson dealt the Creeks their death blow in a tight curve of the Tallapoosa River known as Horseshoe Bend. More than five hundred warriors were killed on the field, some 250 more were shot or drowned as they tried to swim the Tallapoosa, and hundreds of women and children were captured. Only weeks later William Weatherford presented himself to his foe at Fort Jackson, built at the juncture of the Tallapoosa and Coosa Rivers on the remains of Fort Toulouse. Weatherford begged for an end to the fighting and protection and provisions for the starving Creek women and children. Jackson was impressed by Weatherford's bearing and bravery and spared his life. In the Treaty of Fort Jackson that followed, the Creeks ceded all of their lands west of the Coosa River, twenty million acres and more, encompassing much of present day Alabama. The Mobile River Basin was now well and truly an American possession. Down on the coast however, things were still unsettled. The Spanish held Pensacola, a British fleet was somewhere over the horizon, and marauding Redstick diehards were still active. His work not yet done, Jackson and five hundred troops climbed aboard boats on August 11 and headed downstream for Mobile.[39]

On the twentieth they reached Fort Stoddert, where Jackson found the thirty-ninth regiment under Major Uriah Blue in good order. Determined to press on to Mobile, he departed the following day, but a rainstorm forced him to the western bank. This was at Seymour Bluff, where Simon Andry's widow, Jane, offered him a warm bed under a good roof. But Jackson was no Ellicott in love with his creature comforts. He demurred, supposedly telling the kindly widow, "Madame, I am a soldier still." After sleeping either aboard a boat or in a soggy tent on the bluff, the general embarked the next day and by some unfortunate mishap lost his sword in the river—another artifact awaiting discovery.[40]

Jackson's soldiers and volunteers no doubt appreciated his sharing their lot. Like their commander, these men were battle-hardened and mentally tough, travelling light and fast. The typical private wore shoes, pants, leggings, a shirt, waistcoat, jacket, knapsack, and hat. Weapons included a tomahawk and knife stuck in a belt and a .69 calibre Springfield musket, five feet long and weighing ten pounds. This was a smoothbore and not especially accurate, but with a fifteen-inch bayonet attached and leveled at close quarters it was intimidating and lethal enough. If wounded, soldiers' prospects were usually poor. Amputation, gangrene, and horrible suffering were the most likely results. After the initial British attack on Fort Bowyer, the American officer defending wrote that the "surgeon reports one man lost: owing to the want of Surgical Instruments as he was compelled to amputate his arm with a razor. The Man shortly after expired." The men ate meat, corn, bread, and whatever else they could forage on the way. Six soldiers constituted a mess, their cooking done in an iron skillet and served on tin plates, the eating accomplished with knives and forks or grubby fingers. They slept in canvas tents, usually on the ground. Discipline was strict, especially under Jackson, and when they were free on the town, drinking and whoring, ever the enlisted man's entertainments, constituted the most popular pastimes. Cowardice, unwonted cruelty, and panic were not unknown in a fight, and grumbling about army life was ubiquitous in camp and on the march. Most men would have preferred to be home, but they met their responsibilities admirably and so helped make a nation.[41]

On August 22 the flotilla finally reached "Mobile Town," where Jackson found the garrison healthy and well provisioned. Almost immediately he sent out patrols to help protect settlers and plantations "exposed to marauding parties," and a small contingent was dispatched down to Fort Bowyer to resupply and strengthen it for a possible British assault. If such came, Jackson knew that his best chances of protecting Mobile rested there. If the British got up to the town, it would go badly for the Americans. As had so often been the case at critical junctures in the past, Fort Charlotte was in deplorable condition and not likely to withstand a siege by the finest military force in the world. The brick walls were weak and the barracks too deteriorated to shelter men, so they quartered in town while officers pitched their tents in the middle of the fort's plaza.[42]

Jackson established his headquarters in a rough dwelling near the river. His days were hectic and full as he began inspections of the surrounding area and engaged in a flurry of correspondence. The overall military picture looked bleak. The British were pursuing attacks in the north and planning more on the Gulf Coast. The Americans had been humiliated and routed on the Chesapeake and Washington burned. The government remained intact but without a permanent address. As to the enemy's southern strategy, Vice Admiral Sir Alexander Inglis Cochrane had written London that the "three thousand British Troops landed at Mobile" would be joined "by all the Indians with the disaffected French and Spaniards." This combined force would then drive "the Americans entirely out of Louisiana and the Floridas." On the twenty-seventh Jackson got valuable hard evidence of this plan when James Innerarity appeared at his door and requested a private interview. The local agent for John Forbes & Company, the successor to Panton, Leslie & Company, was a conscientious Scotsman who might have been presumed to remain loyal to the interests of his homeland. Jackson perhaps was suspicious initially, but not after Innerarity, tears streaming down his face, handed him two letters. They had been sent by the agent's brother, John, in Pensacola and contained frightening news. "Great events are in Embrio and will soon develop themselves," one of them read. "Your situation is critical. The grand Fleet consisting of 14 Saile of the line and a grate number of transports arrived at Bermuda from B. bringing 25,000 of Lord Wellingtons army." Among these troops were supposedly two black regiments. New Orleans and control of the Mississippi Valley was the ultimate aim, but John Innerarity feared Pensacola would be thrown open to this force by the Spanish, whence Mobile would be an easy target. Jackson's blood must have been boiling by this point. At Pensacola the British could arm and supply hostile Indians to wreak more havoc in the backcountry, incite American slaves to rise up against their outnumbered masters, and make Mobile Bay a lake for the Royal Navy. From there, New Orleans would be a pushover. Clearly now, everything hinged on Fort Bowyer and the pitifully small force behind its ramparts.[43]

On September 12 Major William Lawrence squinted anxiously out as four British warships, two sloops and two brigs, approached from the sparkling gulf. The vessels worked their way toward the mouth of the bay, taking soundings to find the channel. The *Hermes,* a twenty-gun sixth rater that drew a little more than eight feet, stood into the bay and dropped anchor. This was a lightweight vessel by the standards of eighteenth-century naval warfare, unfit for joining a line of battle against much bigger ships of the line. But to the Americans about to face her wrath, she was doubtless a discouraging sight. Most of her guns were thirty-two-pounder carronades, affectionately dubbed "smashers" by British seamen. In combination with her three sisters, she represented overwhelming odds. Bowyer had eleven guns, some of them antiquated, and 158 men. Its garrison confronted a total of seventy-eight guns and six hundred men on the sea side and on the land side sixty royal marines and 180 Indians who were preparing to assault the vulnerable fort's rear. Once Bowyer fell, the British would move up the bay, where those fearsome carronades would pulverize Fort Charlotte's brick walls and sweep away the gently moldering houses of the straggling little town.[44]

On the afternoon of the fourteenth the marines and Indians were within eight hundred yards of the fort and opened fire with two small guns. The Americans responded immediately, and Lawrence was able to report the enemy "silenced by a few shot." The land force thereupon decided to pull back and let the navy do the dirty work. The following afternoon, the duel began. Lawrence's men stood to their guns, and soon the British ships were "enveloped in a blaze of fire and smoke." A lucky shot cut the *Hermes*'s cable, and she drifted onto a shoal, where the Americans raked her, causing great loss of life aboard. Disabled, she was set afire and abandoned by her crew. She burned into the night, the orange flames luridly flickering and dancing on the bay waters, and at 10:00 p.m. Lawrence exulted, "we had the pleasure of witnessing the explosion of her Magazine." The report was audible all the way up at Mobile, where the agonized Jackson thought it was the fort. After he discovered otherwise, the delighted general intoned that "the gallant Lawrence, with his little spartan band, has given them a lecture that will last for ages."[45]

Unexpectedly bloodied by this stout defense, the British drew off and were forced to change their plans. Denied Mobile as a base of operations, they had to find another way to take New Orleans. In the meantime Jackson was done tolerating the Spanish thorn at Pensacola. He marched north and thence across Nannahubba Island to attack it from the land. It fell on November 7, and the British no longer had an anchorage on the gulf. They ultimately attacked New Orleans in January 1815, where Jackson and his multicultural force par excellence—pirates, Creoles, black men, Indians, Mississippians, Tennesseans—mowed them down in droves. Hoping yet to salvage something from their wrecked southern strategy, the British attacked Fort Bowyer once again in early February, this time with more than two dozen ships and several thousand men. It fell, but before they could mount an invasion north, word arrived that a peace treaty had been signed at Ghent the previous Christmas Eve. The war was over. Admiral Cochrane dashed off a note of congratulations to General Jackson, and his fleet hove away. The Mississippi Valley, the Mobile River Basin, and the Gulf Coast were secure at last.[46]

After its long colonial century Mobile was now to be organized and governed on democratic Yankee principles. Elections were held in 1814, and commissioners were chosen, among them James Innerarity (president), Miguel Eslava (treasurer), Benjamin Dubroca, and Peter Hobart. They were sworn in by Blakeley and represented a cosmopolitan range of backgrounds and abilities. Innerarity, who was Scottish, was perhaps the most influential businessman in town; Eslava was Spanish and had served as Mobile's *ministro de la Real Hacienda,* or treasurer, during the 1790s; Dubroca was of French extraction and held a large land grant that fronted on Bayou Chateaugué; and Hobart was a Vermont carpenter who was soon to design and build the first courthouse and jail. These officials were empowered to, among sundry other things, "lay a tax on stores, retailers of spirituous liquors, wheel carriages, and billiard-tables." Town limits were agreed upon, running from Choctaw Point west "in a straight direction to the western bank of the Bayou Chotage [Chateaugué], at a point lying two hundred yards above the place on said Bayou Chotage, called the Portage; thence down the western bank of said Bayou to its mouth; thence down the river and bay of Mobile to the place of beginning." A harbormaster was appointed, and three wards were established, to be patrolled by two policemen.[47]

The town fathers were interested in advancing Mobile's commercial interests above all other things, but they faced several disadvantages. To begin with, crumbling Fort Charlotte and its weedy earthen glacis sprawled across valuable acreage and hogged riverfront property. Second, the Choctaw Bar allowed only vessels drawing eight feet of water to access the town by the river's main mouth. Many ships had to jog eastward into the mouth of the Spanish River, which had a little more depth, and sail up and around Blakeley Island, dropping down to the city from the north. If winds and tides were not just right, frustrating delays resulted. And last, because of this navigational challenge, a new town founded by none other than Josiah Blakeley across the bay on the Tensaw River, just where it bifurcated into the Apalachee and Blakeley Rivers, was blossoming. Soon there were brick quays on the Tensaw, better than one hundred houses, and numerous stores. In 1820 a British merchant wrote that Mobile and its upstart rival were "contending violently for the privilege of becoming that great emporium which must shortly spring up in the vicinity of this outlet for the produce of the young fertile state of Alabama."[48]

Ultimately, Mobile prevailed, its competitor undone by rampant land speculation and several vicious yellow-fever epidemics. Perhaps just as important, Mobile, for all its troubles, had gotten an earlier start and was more established. As for the other shortcomings, Choctaw Bar would have to wait, but Fort Charlotte could be torn down. The army wanted to keep it for a while, but Congress authorized its sale in 1818, and two years later it was bought by the Mobile Lot Company. The glacis was leveled, the brick walls blasted by barrels of black powder, and bit by bit the venerable old pile succumbed. No one batted an eye at the demise of Mobile's most prominent and storied landmark, battle-scarred and rich in associations from Bienville, Cadillac, and Farmar to Gálvez, Perez, and Jackson. It impeded progress, and its demolition provided the practical Americans tons of useful fill for the marshy river margins. If trade was to flourish in Mobile, those had to be improved quickly.[49]

Everyone agreed that the riverfront needed work. Its utility was greatly impaired by the swampy strip between Royal Street and the water. Tides regularly ebbed and flowed across this zone, making it unfit for development. In addition, driftwood, oyster shells, seaweed, wrecks, rubbish, and refuse were scattered in profusion along its length. Only two large wharves crossed the muck and fingered over the water, decrepit holdovers from Spanish times. But when the state of Alabama passed legislation that extended ownership to private citizens who improved theretofore useless submerged lands, numerous individuals carted in fill and erected little sheds and rickety wharves. Impatient with this disorganized clutter and convinced that it was "dangerous to the health of the city," town fathers claimed the right to remove the offending intrusions and build their own wharves. To back their contention, they pointed to an act of Congress passed on May 26, 1824, that granted the city everything between the high-water mark and the river channel. Armed with this seemingly ironclad authority, the city set to work. A blizzard of lawsuits resulted as multiple owners, some citing Spanish grants, others state law, and the city the congressional act, confronted one another. One of these cases, *Pollard v. Hagan,* in which Pollard claimed he had been sold the land by the federal government and Hagan that the Spanish had originally granted it to him, ultimately made it all the way to the U.S. Supreme Court in 1844. Hagan was represented by a brilliant Alabama lawyer named John Archibald Campbell, who later became a Supreme Court justice himself. In the resulting decision, which became famous, the court agreed with Hagan, ruling that by earlier precedent Congress had no right to confirm and grant land after Alabama became a state. This became the Equal Footing Doctrine, which held that when a state was admitted to the Union, it was on an equal footing with the original thirteen. Congress was therefore required to respect Alabama's right to award or sell these submerged lands to whatever entity it chose. Thus the water lots, as they came to be called, could only be granted by the state and not the federal government. The city's claim was invalid.[50]

Throughout the teens and twenties, the marshland was filled with every manner of item, from clean sand, brickbats, cobbles, cotton bales, and broken barrels to timbers, ballast, and partially sunken hulks. Dry land was built up and a new street run north and south. Named, appropriately enough, Water Street, this development enhanced the riverfront, and more wharves began to be built, some erected by the city and many more by private landowners. In June of 1815 James Wilson contracted for a twenty-foot-wide wharf "to commence at high water mark at the east end of Dauphin Street, and to extend in a direct line toward the channel of the Mobile River to where the water has a depth of nine feet." Out at the end the wharf was to "have wings next the stream," and there were also to be "jutters for weigh offices near the low water mark." It was to be built with the same materials and methods as almost all of nineteenth-century Mobile's wharves. This meant cypress posts driven by a heavy drop hammer floated for the over-water work, and strings, caps, braces, and yellow-pine planks affixed with large square nails. Savvy carpenters knew to nail the planks grain-downward, so if they cupped, it would be in concave fashion, shedding water and making for longer deck life. Given the harsh Gulf Coast climate, decking usually needed replacing about every fifteen years, whereas the pilings were good for decades. Early Mobile's wharves were tough, utilitarian structures, but even so they eventually weathered, bent, warped, twisted, or came apart under constant forces. Some were repaired and maintained, some were not. In a strong hurricane everything but the pilings would be smashed and carried away. Most of the early wharves were of the standard table design, but the best were solidly constructed and expensive. In 1823 a newspaper advertisement solicited "some person to fill up the street above the water mark and Water Street eastwardly 200 feet and to lay a barrier in front of same of good solid logs at least one foot square of pine or cypress, also to run out a table wharf from the center of the Street 40 feet wide by 250 feet long." The pilings were to be "ten inches square" and the "planks 3 inches thick." This kind of improvement usually represented an investment of between five and ten thousand dollars, as much as a good brick store. Some of the wharves had buildings on them, warehouses, counting houses, shelters, boathouses, worksheds, and the like. Because the waterfront was now so busy and animated, the city approved "public Commodes" on the wharves as a "great convenience to all the citizens living near the water." The concept of human excrement plopping into the water apparently did not deter people from drinking river water in the winter when it was thought "wholesome," nor did the presence of live fish thrashing in traps hung off the Government Street wharf. There, in the autumn of 1824, William Robertson had petitioned for the right to "erect a Fish Market House on the borders of the channel... for the preservation of live fish." The market also included wooden stalls that Robertson provided to "any fisherman" desirous of "carrying fish to their customers after the regular market hours to any part of the city."[51]

American Mobile's beginnings were modest, but they were promising. On February 7, 1822, the *Mobile Commercial Register* took stock of the town and reported almost three thousand residents "of all colors," 240 frame houses, a bank, a post office and custom house, two churches (one Catholic, one Protestant), 110 stores and warehouses, a courthouse and jail, boardinghouses, three bakeries, and "six well constructed wharves already built, and two or three more about to be commenced." A devastating fire in 1827 retarded progress somewhat (more about that in chapter 10), but the very next year what most impressed a visitor was that warehouses on Commerce Street—recently laid east of Water Street, one hundred feet wide and running three blocks from Government Street to St. Francis Street—would soon "present an entire brick front form one end to the other, with the exception of one or two lots." Early travelers marveled at Mobilians' ingenuity in extending their usable waterfront over what had been boggy land. "One entire street, I am told, has been built on the river," one of them wrote of Commerce Street, "and the enterprising citizens are fast founding another." This was to be Front Street, and upon its completion the riverfront was to be well built-up with stores, sail lofts, warehouses, offices, cotton presses, coffee saloons, barrooms, oyster houses, livery stables, and hardware stores.[52]

River traffic was initially dominated by shallow-draft lighters, schooners, and brigs coming in from the bay and gulf and flatboats, barges, keelboats, and pirogues floating down from the hinterland with cotton, corn, and naval stores. Flatboats and keelboats were exhausting and difficult to power upstream, so crews usually broke them up and sold the wood after arrival in Mobile. The city bought the gunwales and recycled them for street curbs. But three important developments radically enhanced the river's importance and utility in both directions for merchants and residents. The first was the arrival of the steamboat, the second was the federal government's commitment to improving the harbor, and the overarching third was the explosion of cotton growing in the fertile Alabama Black Belt and Mississippi prairie. The first two made efficient commerce possible, and the third provided a staple that the world could not resist. With the intersection of these developments, Mobile's golden age began.[53]

The earliest steamboats were primitive contraptions with low-pressure boilers that could only achieve a few knots, barely enough to breast the Mobile's current. But hopeful entrepreneurs formed steamboat companies, and the first successful trip up the Tombigbee to Demopolis took place in 1819, to be followed in 1821 by a ten-day run to Montgomery by the *Harriet.* Just as exciting was a congressional appropriation of twenty-five thousand dollars in 1826 to deepen the river's channel. The Dog River Bar and the Choctaw Point Bar were at last to be dredged to a greater depth, opening the city's wharves to bigger ships. These improvements were to take years, and indeed they proceed apace, but no longer would civic leaders and businessmen have to worry about their city's poor accessibility not receiving the federal government's serious consideration. Mobile's future looked bright—billowing sails, whistling calliopes, and King Cotton sovereign over all.[54]

4

Calliope Song

The United States Mail steamer *Southern* gently glided between two of Mobile's wooden wharves in the mild May air. She was no ocean racer but rather a low-pressure packet making her regular run through the Mississippi Sound to New Orleans and back. It was 1842, and the passengers shouldering their baggage and preparing to step onto the wharf that day represented an interesting range of antebellum types. They included W. Addle, a twenty-two-year-old soldier; a "land proprietor" named Toulmin who may have been a son or grandson of the deceased judge; two merchants; a "Yanke"; a "pedlar"; a laborer; a "loafer"; and Miss E. Norton, a twenty-year-old "Lady of Pleasure." Mobile was undeniably an American town now, but it was also a seaport with a long and colorful colonial history, and travelers still found its people exotic. Two years later a visitor wrote, "You can see as great varieties of character in the streets of Mobile as any city of its size in the union.... Here goes a staid, demure faced priest & behind him is a dashy gambler. Here goes a quiet Quaker merchant and there is your Mississippi 'buster,' 'half horse & half alligator with a touch of snapping turtle & a cross of lightning.'" There were also sailors "ready for devilment of any kind," beggars, "Pretty Creoles," pale "sewing girls," "painted vice," and "wretched" Choctaw holdovers forlornly hawking "light wood."[1]

But before Addle, Toulmin, Miss Norton, and the others aboard the *Southern* could get into town and join this throng, they first had to navigate the wharf and the immediate waterfront. Nineteenth-century sensibilities were certainly inured to the unsettling sights and pungent smells that defined the era, but even by those standards Mobile's waterfront was daunting. A clergyman who landed in 1840 described the area "about the wharves" as "very filthy and stinking." Four years later a German paleontologist who passed through agreed, writing: "I was astonished by the filthiness of the city of Mobile. When we left the steamboat an atmosphere of horrible odors met us, permeating all the dirty streets which were bordered on both sides with green gutters." Municipal authorities acknowledged the problem and had struggled with it for years. It arose anew every spring as warming temperatures exacerbated matters. In April 1840 a

Grand Mobile, circa 1835. An evocative sketch by John Pierce Wachsmith.
Courtesy of the History Museum of Mobile.

grand jury urged town fathers to do something, as they found "the Wharf all along the river is now in a state and condition that threatens the worst consequences, not only to the convenience of the Community but to the health of the people." There were more than thirty table wharves jutting into the river between One Mile Creek and Government Street, and while some were in active use, others were neglected. The slips between these wharves had become repositories for every conceivable type of driftwood, junk, and wreckage, all of which continually accumulated muck, sand, slime, dead fish and crabs, and more mess. As if this were not bad enough, wooden sewer pipes emptied their foul, iridescent effluvium directly into the river, where it greasily eddied and swirled amid the pilings, lapped back onto the shore, and was ultimately swept out into the bay. After heavy rainstorms the "green gutters" and streets that terminated at the water discharged torrents of horse manure, tobacco spit, urine, vomit, whiskey, blood, dirt, fruit rinds, and dead dogs, cats, and rats into the evil mix. No one would have looked askance if Miss Norton chose to place a scented handkerchief to her face as she gingerly crossed this disgusting sector.[2]

Disagreeable sights and smells were not the only hurdles to getting into town. A northerner described the area immediately back of the wharves as an animated working waterfront of patient mules, stamping horses, rattling wagons and drays, "lazy, laughing singing negroes," roustabouts, clerks, and hurrying travelers. Another visitor recalled "hackney carriages ... and a host of porters" loudly soliciting "passengers and luggage at every arrival." In addition to the animals, conveyances, and people, there was a veritable obstacle course of barrels, crates, boxes, burlap bags of coffee and flour, stacks of lumber, heaps of firewood, mounds of cordage, piles of coal, and big four-hundred-pound cotton bales seemingly everywhere—on the boats, the wharves, and even stacked along the sidewalks near the river. Everyone noticed them, and most commented upon them. In 1860 the *Mobile Daily Advertiser* decried teetering tiers of cotton bales, the paths between them so narrow that "lady passengers . . . found some difficulty in getting their hoops through." The same clergyman who complained about the reeking wharves correctly observed: "Mobile is a city of cotton. It is to be found in the quay warehouses, sidewalks, everywhere." By 1840 hundreds of thousands of bales of the white stuff were moving through town. Cotton trade dominated the first half of the nineteenth century, and it remained important into the 1930s. A British traveler who declared that the staple "has made Mobile and all its citizens" did not exaggerate. Nineteenth-century Mobile meant cotton. "Look which way you will see it," one Yankee arrival remarked, "and see it moving; keel boats, steam boats, ships, brigs, schooners, wharves, stores and press houses." And then there were the people associated with the business—merchants, factors, lawyers, bankers, insurance agents, weighers, stevedores, screwmen, sailors, planters, and slaves. They were ubiquitous, and had only one topic of conversation. After a three-day sojourn, the Yankee quoted above sighed, "I must have heard the word cotton pronounced more than 3000 times."[3]

With foreign threats eliminated, the Indians mostly removed by the mid-1830s, and a vast swath of excellent agricultural land selling for as low as $1.25 an acre, what had been a steady stream of settlers into Alabama and Mississippi became a flood. The federal government sold more than a million acres in the latter state in 1833, and the white population doubled by 1836. Many of these settlers brought along coffles of slaves, and soon there were more black than white residents in the most fertile upcountry counties. Large farms were established along the Tombigbee and Alabama Rivers, and an absolute mania for growing cotton prevailed. As one Natchez lawyer noted, it was as if "a new El Dorado had been discovered; fortunes were made in a day . . . where yesterday the wilderness darkened over the land with her wild forests, to-day the cotton plantation whitened the earth."[4]

It is not surprising, given the quality of the land and the proliferation of chattel slavery, that cotton production reached staggering levels during the antebellum years. The United States supplied roughly half of the world's supply, and 80 percent of that was grown in Georgia, Alabama, Mississippi, and Louisiana. Cotton exports exploded in quantity and value, from 350 million pounds worth $25 million in 1831 to 500 million pounds worth $65 million just four years later, and the gulf ports of New Orleans and Mobile benefitted the most. New Orleans passed New York City as the busiest American export town in 1834, and Mobile was not far behind. The number of bales shipped out of Alabama's seaport tells the tale—103,065 in 1830; 238,014 in 1835; 319,876 in 1840; and nearly half a million or better all through the 1840s and 1850s up to the Civil War.[5]

The world's nineteenth-century cotton trade followed a triangular route, dictated and dominated by New York merchants. All those thousands of bales were shipped from Mobile and her sister Southern ports like New Orleans, Charleston, and Savannah to a European city, usually Liverpool, England, or Le Havre, France, where they were quickly distributed. The ships then sailed back across the Atlantic to New York, loaded with emigrants and general cargo. From New York the vessels completed the triangle by sailing for Mobile and the other cities with ballast plus a thousand necessaries that included coffee, oats, whiskey, bells, bobbins, ribbons, hats, shotguns, hoes, knives, and scythes, as well as the finer appointments that people on the plantation or in the town house required—china, crystal, and silverware for the dining rooms; and pianofortes, marble mantels, and the latest editions of *Godey's Lady's Book* for the parlors. There was an old saying in the antebellum South that when a man died the only thing the region provided was the corpse and the pine box. Everything else—his suit, his shoes, his watch and chain, his ring—had been manufactured somewhere else. Mobile was the third busiest port in the nation by 1860, but the trade imbalance suggested by that old saw was buttressed by real numbers that revealed a drastic gap—$38 million dollars of exports and a mere $1 million in imports. Cotton accounted for 99 percent of the former, with cedar logs, staves, turpentine, rosin, pitch, brick, leather, and lime making up the difference, while all those everyday goods and fancier goodies constituted the imports. Only the most nervous economic prognosticators were troubled by the matter, however. Fortunes were being made, and progress and prosperity were the watchwords.[6]

The Mobile River represented a vital segment of cotton's route out to the spinning mills of New England and Europe, and commercial life in the seaport at its mouth was almost completely dominated by the many nuances of the trade, from unloading the bales at the wharves to brokering lucrative deals with faraway buyers and insuring the freight. Most of the actual cotton plantations were further upstream, well above Nannahubba Bluff, and every one of them had its own landing. But there were a few landings along the Mobile, too—at Three Mile Creek, Twenty-One Mile Bluff, Seymour and Chastang Bluffs, Cedar Creek, the Arsenal at Mount Vernon (formerly Fort Stoddert), and some others. These served the boats for replenishing firewood, and the scattered Creole and white farmers as connections to the outside world. The occasional bale of cotton or barrel of turpentine could be trundled out for delivery, and hardware, cloth, or dry goods picked up and hauled back to plain cabins. The majority of cotton, however, was loaded in market towns such as Montgomery, Selma, and Claiborne along the Alabama River, Demopolis on the Tombigbee, and at the hundreds of individual landings in between. European travelers were astonished at the dearth of towns along the rivers and marveled at how cotton bales were slid down long plank chutes where there were high bluffs, as at Claiborne. "There was something truly western in the direct, reckless way in which the boat was loaded," Frederick Law Olmstead observed in the 1850s. Each bale flew down at a "fearful velocity," he wrote, and bounded onto the deck where it was arrested by "a barricade of bales previously arranged to receive it." Vessels often began their voyage at Montgomery with only a few hundred bales aboard, and passengers like Olmstead had plenty of room to roam, but by the time they reached Mobile there could easily be several thousand bales stacked everywhere conceivable, crowding the passengers and leaving the boat's lower deck awash.[7]

Once arrived at Mobile, the cotton was muscled ashore and loaded into quayside brick warehouses. Almost every bale was under the direct management of one or another of the many cotton factors or commission merchants in town, the majority of whom kept offices along Commerce and Front Streets. In many cases upcountry planters had already made arrangements with their favorite factors and merchants, usually friends of long association, and sometimes these businessmen had even advanced the planters money ahead of the sale. One such factor, Duke Goodman, moved to town from Charleston in 1831 and advertised his services in the *Mobile Commercial Register.* "From his long experience, personal attention, and promptness," Goodman's third-person ad read, "he hopes to obtain a liberal support from his friends." Goodman's usual fee was 2.5 percent of the cotton's sale price, for which he handled all the details of shipping and insurance. Cash advances were made at 8 to 12 percent interest, and for modest fees Goodman would order whatever the planter or his family needed from abroad. This latter service was usually provided by commission merchants, but

Wrestling cotton into a warehouse. This image dates after the Civil War, but the task remained the same as it did before that conflict. From *Mobile in Photo-Gravure* (Mobile, 1892).

Goodman, like other businessmen, could be either factor or commission merchant as need dictated. He had the contacts with agents and merchants locally, in New York, and abroad and could effectively broker cotton deals or order household items with minimal fuss. Included in his extensive and carefully cultivated network were planters, lawyers, bankers, insurance men, merchants, municipal and county elected officials, foreign buyers, steamboat and sea captains, stevedores, work-gang foremen, draymen, and counting-house clerks. He was extraordinarily successful, eventually coming to own several wharves, numerous buildings in town, and more than a hundred slaves, most of whom labored on the wharves and in the cotton warehouses.[8]

Happily for Goodman and the planters who depended on his business acumen, foreign cotton sales did not depend on time-consuming overseas correspondence, but rather were readily secured from representatives of British and French companies with local offices. In fact, there were so many British cotton merchants working in Mobile that a short street perpendicular to the river was called the English Channel. Despite the easy familiarity that prevailed among those used to the trade, however, these were not deals made on a handshake and a promise. Nothing was left to chance, and every aspect of the transaction was governed by contracts that delineated each party's expectations and responsibilities. Among the most important of these documents was that between the factor and his agent. The latter individual provided the means of getting the cotton thousands of miles across perilous seas. According to one example from

1850, the agent provided a brig that he pledged "shall be kept tight, stanch, well fitted, tackled, and provided with every requisite, and with men and provisions for such a voyage." The factor, for his part, agreed to provide "a sufficient cargo of freight for ballast from one port to another on her voyage." He was allowed up to twenty "lay days" in Mobile for getting the cotton ready for the trip, and he promised that it would be "delivered alongside of the vessel, within reach of her tackles." Upon the brig's safe arrival at Liverpool, the factor was obligated to pay four thousand dollars "lawful money of the United States." On top of that he was responsible for "all foreign port-charges, pilotage, and dues incurred by the vessel on her voyage." Failure on either party's part to abide by the contract was subject to "*the penal sum of eight thousand dollars.*" In order to protect themselves from potential disaster, each party would have purchased insurance available from either a local or an out-of-town company, several of which maintained downtown offices. In Mobile, factors routinely bought policies from the Hartford Insurance Company, Aetna, Southern Insurance Company, the City Insurance Company, and the Marine Dock and Mutual Insurance Company. In 1852 a newspaper article held that anyone who suffered uncovered losses had only himself to blame, "for every faculty is now at hand for insurance."[9]

The cotton sold and the contracts signed, the fluffy bales had to be made ready for the long sea passage and loaded aboard ship. Mobile's facilities for storing, pressing, and loading cotton were some of the best in the South. An 1851 issue of *Hunt's Merchants' Magazine* described them in admiring detail. They included forty-eight wharves, "some of them noble ones," that could accommodate forty-two thousand bales at once and forty-two fireproof brick warehouses that had an overall capacity of 310,000 bales, most of them concentrated on the north end of the working harbor. The magazine noted that the warehouses covered "40 acres of ground—quite a little farm, if it all lay together." In addition, there were twelve cotton presses, capable of reducing seven thousand bales a day.[10]

Adequate wharves and warehouses were critical, but presses were absolutely vital to the success of the cotton trade. When the bales arrived from upcountry they were enormous and bulky, bound in burlap and rope. While steamboats and flats could easily accommodate these ungainly bundles, more efficiently sized bales were wanted for seagoing ships, where space was sold at a premium. Accordingly, as quickly as practicable once it landed on the wharves, cotton was moved into warehouses and pressed. The cotton press was essentially a big open-ended wooden box, with cast iron plates, or followers as they were called, above and below that could be simultaneously scrunched against the bale by large screws or a system of levers. These were operated either by hand, mules, or, come midcentury, steam. A good press could quickly reduce a bale to a third of its original size, after which it was retied, weighed, classed, and sent quayside, where knowledgeable eyes saw and approved. As reported in *Hunt's Merchants' Magazine,* "The compressing is as well done in Mobile—ship's captains say better—than at any other seaport." After delivery alongside a vessel, the reduced bales were hoisted aboard by longshoremen and then stowed by the screwmen, specialized workers who used powerful jackscrews to pack the bales tightly into the ship's hold.[11]

Even by the hard measure of other nineteenth-century waterfront tasks, screwing cotton was difficult work. Charles Erskine, a sailor who knew the gulf ports well, recalled an occasion when he had to help pack a vessel in New Orleans. It was, he declared, "the most exhausting labor I had ever performed." The southern heat and humidity only made it all the more trying. "We wore nothing but trousers," he wrote many years later, "with a bandana handkerchief tied over our heads. The hold was a damp, dark place. The thermometer stood at nearly one hundred, not a breath of air stirred, and our bodies were reeking with perspiration." To keep themselves in rhythm and good spirits, the men sang a sea shanty that included the verse "Were you ever in Mobile Bay, / Bonnie laddie, Highland laddie? / Yes, I've been in Mobile Bay, / Screwing cotton by the day, / My bonnie Highland laddie, ho!" By the evening of the fourth day Erskine and his mates had earned "eight silver Spanish dollars" for their trouble and could take pride in a job well done—"it would have been impossible to find space enough left over to hold a copy of *The Boston Herald*."[12]

To the surprise of most travelers, the majority of antebellum Mobile's waterfront labor was performed by white workers, frequently German and Irish immigrants. Erskine was a white Bostonian, and a Maine pastor and author who visited remarked that "free labor seems to have driven slave labor from the wharves and from the streets." There were still plenty of black workers to be seen, however, especially on the steamboats and in the locally owned warehouses where slaves like Goodman's labored. These men worked incredibly hard and developed their own songs to go with their tasks. The best known of these locally inspired ditties was "Roll the Cotton Down," which went, in part, "Oh, roll the cotton down, my boys, / Oh, roll the cotton down! // . . . A pleasant place is Mobile Bay, / a rollin' cotton all the day." The city's waterfront was surely a lively and noisy place when all that cotton was coming and going. At other times it could seem eerily deserted, especially during midsummer when the cotton plants were green and growing upcountry, the rivers low, and a blanket of haze spread over the entire region.[13]

Cotton meant money for Mobile and its enterprising citizens, or some of them, and one of the manifestations of this newfound wealth was good architecture. Away from the wharves, antebellum Mobile was distinguished by beautifully designed and proportioned public buildings and townhouses. First-class architects such as the brothers James and Charles Dakin, James Gallier out of New York, and local craftsmen including Cary Butt and Thomas James worked from the latest pattern books and exploited the region's abundant timber and clay for lumber and bricks to erect these wonders. During the 1830s such columned Greek Revival masterpieces as Government Street Presbyterian Church, Barton Academy, the Marine Hospital, and Oakleigh mansion graced city streets, and by the 1850s local cotton merchants were building brick Italianate townhouses with big eave brackets, florid cast-iron fences and balconies, and side-hall entrances flanked by double parlors with pocket doors. Along the principal thoroughfares such as Government Street and Springhill Avenue, wealthy families cultivated flowers and fruit trees on their spacious lots. Once visitors left the unpleasant wharves behind, they were usually impressed by Mobile's physical presence. In the 1830s the English parliamentarian and world traveler J. S. Buckingham gave a lecture at the newly erected Presbyterian church, a building he felt was "unsurpassed . . . in chasteness of style and elegance of decoration in the United States." With its monumental Ionic columns, stunning coffered ceiling, and "luxurious, sofa-like pews," all expertly designed and executed, the church set a very high standard. Government Street also interested Buckingham, "lined with rows of trees on either hand, protected by an excellent flag-pavement at the sides, and already ornamented with some exceedingly handsome public structures, and private mansions and dwellings." Nearly twenty years later, an English traveler named John W. Oldmixon also admired "wide, sandy Government Street" and especially how wagons and carriages whispered along it at speeds of up to an exhilerating fifteen miles an hour. Oldmixon possessed a keen eye for architecture and liked what he saw in Mobile. "Columns, porticos, rich cornices, handsome verandahs meet the eye everywhere," he wrote. "It is a city of villas, the upper part standing in their own small gardens." About the same time the Swedish novelist Fredrika Bremer visited and was carried away by it all, gushing, "I like Mobile, and the people of Mobile, and the weather of Mobile, and everything in Mobile; I flourish in Mobile."[14]

Concurrent with fine buildings and fragrant flowers was a glamorous social scene. Winter was the season. There was minimal danger from fevers or epidemics then, the cotton trade was robust, planters and their culture-starved wives were in town, and the parties and balls related to Mardi Gras were in full swing. Mardi Gras was greatly changed from the earliest French celebration at Twenty-Seven Mile Bluff. Most historians agree that American observances of the holiday in Mobile owe their origins to Michael Kraft, a native Pennsylvanian who worked as a cotton broker. During some impromptu 1831 New Year's Day revelry, Kraft and a few friends broke into a Dauphin Street hardware store and lifted hoes, rakes, gongs, and cowbells. The motley assembly forthwith made a little racket outside, called on some female acquaintances, and drank to one another's health. They had such a good time they formed themselves into the Cowbellion de Rakin Society and in subsequent years elaborately expanded their routine to include masks and a ball. A decade after Kraft's first parade, cotton-trade apprentices formed the Strikers Independent Society (the name refers to how these men marked the bales, striking them, for loading aboard ship). Other mystic societies followed, and Mardi Gras proper, the day before Ash Wednesday each year, became the focus and culmination of the social season. Hard-headed businessmen were not blind to the advantages of a strong social atmosphere in a busy commercial environment. The editor of the *Mobile Daily Advertiser* wrote that young men's "association together for the purpose of affording amusement, and oftentimes instruction for themselves and their friends, tends, greatly to destroy that acerbity of feeling which the clashing interests of business are always calculated to engender." Social and commercial ties were close and firm thanks to Mardi Gras, and to this day professional, family, and personal relationships between the Black Belt and Alabama's port city continue to be nourished by the custom.[15]

Quieter and even more select pleasures included a number of salons presided over by wives of the elite. The most famous of these was that of Madame Octavia LeVert, consort of Dr. Henry LeVert, a physician. Madame LeVert had traveled extensively in Europe, seen French salons firsthand, met Queen Victoria, and published an account of her adventures in 1858. Guests in her Government Street rooms included elected officials, prominent businessmen and planters, belles, actors, painters, musicians, and occasional celebrities including Miss Bremer, Henry Clay, and Washington Irving, who declared, "She is such a woman as occurs but once in the course of an empire."[16]

More publically accessible was the theater, which Mobilians and visitors to the city embraced with gusto. Once again, practical observers recognized the importance of quality diversion to a productive business climate. In 1849, the *Alabama Tribune* noted that the theater appealed to the many who had come to town "principally on a double errand—business and pleasure." A planter could thus spend his day down on Commerce Street chewing the fat and smoking Cuban cigars with his factor, a British sea captain could handle a little business with his consul in a Royal Street coffee saloon, and a local iron founder could secure a deal for a fresh supply of Scottish pig iron from an agent touring his furnaces, and all could then reunite with their wives at an elegant hotel like the Mansion House, Hotel Waverly, or Battle House for turtle soup, oysters, and Madeira wine before going out to an evening performance. Noah Miller Ludlow had one theater or another in town—they frequently burned down—throughout the antebellum period. One of these seated 700 and featured a pit and two boxes. Blacks were relegated to the upper tier of seats, but this area had to be subdivided again because light-skinned Creoles (sometimes called quadroons or octoroons based on the amount of black blood they were thought to have) refused to sit among darker-skinned individuals. The Royal Street Theater was even bigger, with a seating capacity of over 1,500. A steady stream of actors and actresses that included Tyrone Power, Jim Crow Rice, Miss Phillips of Drury Lane, Mlle. Celeste, Junius Brutus Booth, Ole Bull, and Charlotte Cushman all trod the local boards during the antebellum era. So did Joe Jefferson, who died of yellow fever while in town, and his widow and young son were comforted and fed by the compassionate Madame LeVert.[17]

There were ruder amusements in town, of course, never more memorably described than by John O'Connor, a native Ohioan who visited during the 1840s. "With the exception of New Orleans and Havana," he wrote much later, "there was no commercial mart on the Gulf of Mexico as thriving as Mobile, when I first visited the place, and I doubt if there could have been one found on the face of the globe . . . where crime, debauchery, and lawlessness of every description reigned rampant to such a fearful extent." The worst area was a downtown block known as Shakespeare's Row. This consisted of three-story brick buildings surrounding a big interior courtyard that was entered by arched gateways from opposite sides. Open balconies wrapped the second and third stories, and numerous small staircases led up to the various rooms. "Every one of these rooms was occupied for gambling purposes," O'Connor reported. "While those portions of the Shakespearian row which faced on either street were occupied by mercantile offices, banks, jewelry stores, tailoring establishments, money brokers, coffee-houses, billiard saloons, and restaurants, its courtyard was one vast gambling hell." The wagering went on all night, he declared, and "the rattling of faro-checks and the spinning of roulette wheels could be heard without cessation." In addition to gambling dens, O'Connor observed "dance houses of the lowest order" where little was left to the imagination. "Lewd women with their more degraded associates drove decency to cover with their abandoned talk and gestures," he lamented. "Boatmen, longshoremen, and sailors spent among these abandoned harlots their hard earnings, and drank the poisonous fluids which maddened their brains, and made them, but too often, commit deeds of blood and violence." That O'Connor's vivid descriptions were not exaggerated is demonstrated by a petition dated September 2, 1847, and signed by several leading citizens, protesting against one barkeep's custom "of giving 'whore balls' in the most public and popular streets in this city." The petition stated that these balls "continue very late, often the crowds do not disperse until daylight, they frequently end in broils and affrays which are pregnant with evil, and are injurious to the citizens of the city." Genteel revulsion or no, vice continued to flourish along the waterfront and proved as difficult to clean up as the dirty wharves.[18]

Despite the commercial success that brought all of these things, good and bad, no one involved with traffic into or out of the city was completely happy with the port. The river was to blame. The Mobile's current is powerful and helps maintain impressive depths throughout the stream's length. Even off the ends of the downtown wharves, brigs and schooners could safely anchor in nine to twenty-two feet of water. But at the river mouth the water fans into the bay, losing considerable force. This allows tons of mud, silt, and sand to cease tumbling and scouring along the bottom and gently settle into a thick ridge known as the Choctaw Bar. If nature was left to her own devices, as she was throughout the colonial era, the average depth over the bar at high tide stood at about seven feet, not enough for oceangoing vessels, even during those years.[19]

After Congress appropriated funds to improve Mobile's maritime access in 1826, a ponderous "dredging machine" began work off Choctaw Point. The record does not indicate the design, but in all likelihood it was either a bucket-ladder dredge or a grapple dredge, both of which were steam-powered. The former consisted of a series of scoops positioned along a swinging conveyor mounted on one side or through the center of the vessel. Once over the desired location, the crew swung the ladder down and started it so that the scoops bit into the bottom and brought the spoil topside where it was dumped onto flats and later emptied out in the bay. The grapple dredge consisted of wooden barge surmounted by a dipper that took large bites out of the river bottom

Mobile Harbor, 1851. Note the steamer to the left, moored in a slip. Courtesy of the History Museum of Mobile.

and lifted them into the sunlight. Both kinds of machines were cranky and subject to frequent breakdowns, but by 1831 a ten-foot-deep channel had been cut through the formidable ridge that constituted the bar.[20]

This helped navigation somewhat, but the bar and the swampy terrain below the city opposite it remained the source of much agitation and comment. In 1846 a visitor remarked on the "prodigious quantity of drift timber, of all sizes, and in every stage of decomposition" that "lay stranded far and wide along the shore." Thirteen years later in an article in *DeBow's Review* on the climate and fevers of the Southwest, the area was described as "a cypress swamp, with its margin resting on an immense deposit of *silt* and drift-wood, and which presents a foul and suspicious appearance." But at least one person who braved the driftwood and muck was intrigued. In the winter of 1835 the Irish actor Tyrone Power rode down to Choctaw Point and was pleased by "an extensive view of the Bay of Mobile" and "many little rivulets . . . the sides of which were decked by a hundred different shrubs and plants." Power's most vivid memory of this excursion was not the view or the flora, however, but a naked Indian that he and his guide encountered in the act of "laving . . . his coal-black shining hair" with water poured from a gourd. Small numbers of Choctaw Indians were common in Mobile throughout the early nineteenth century, and Power's encounter with one of the tribe was similar to others noted by antebellum travelers. Close to the city as it was, Choctaw Point was semideserted and wild.[21]

The initial cut across Choctaw Bar was only about two hundred feet wide, and officials recognized that vessels needed help steering into and out of the river mouth. In an effort to improve navigation, a forty-three-foot conical brick lighthouse was erected in 1831 amid the clutter on the point. The lighthouse featured eleven lamps and a fourth order lens more than two feet high, all calculated to be visible up to fourteen miles away. A keeper was hired and lived in a little frame one-and-a-half-story house close to the tower. There are three contemporary illustrations of the Choctaw Point Lighthouse, one a very early photograph and the other two romantic color renderings, but each depicts the swampy surroundings and driftwood jumble that characterized the site. Unfortunately, the handsome new lighthouse was almost useless either by night or by day, when it was a readily identifiable landmark. Oldmixon's experience was not atypical. He bought passage out of town aboard "a beautiful schooner" commanded by a "gay, good-looking, fast young fellow" who wore "a most fanciful velvet cap." They departed on a calm day, the water's surface brushed by cats-paws, and slowly moved south. "The glassy surface of the bay was like a mirror," Oldmixon later wrote, "as we crept along among the innumerable drift logs by the lighthouse, and—got aground! for it was low water, and we drew eight feet, an unheard of depth for any vessel under 300 tons; but she had been built for a revenue cruiser." Eager to be on his way, Oldmixon instead was stranded on the Choctaw Bar. "It was very tedious in the bay on the mud," he groused. The dashing captain managed to distract his passenger with some unappetizing "beefsteaks and dough-boys." At last a "breeze and a thunder-gust brought us down the bay, and we anchored in a fog among the town of cotton ships."[22]

This was the Lower Fleet. While the Dog River and Choctaw Point Bars restricted deep draft access into town, the lower reaches of the bay, just inside the sheltering land spit tipped by Mobile Point, presented no such difficulties. Here larger ships rode at anchor, attended by dozens of smaller vessels, or lighters as they were generally called, offloading cargo and running it up to town or bringing down cotton from the wharves to be screwed into the big ships' holds. Brigs and schooners were easily loaded in town and could and did make coastal and transatlantic voyages, but without the Lower Fleet, Mobile's viability as a cotton port would have been severely compromised. Where the river failed, the bay provided a solution, though businessmen still chafed at the inconvenience and delay that resulted.[23]

Oldmixon was quite taken with the spectacle. "This is a curious sight," he wrote; "it is quite a town of ships; a little floating community; thirty miles from Mobile, and four or five miles from the nearest shores and pine forests." Sometimes these ships remained anchored for weeks, until they could acquire a full cargo. During this time the captains and sailors could attend religious services at a nearby floating bethel and frequently took steamers into town for rest and recreation. On the eve of the Civil War an Episcopal priest and novelist from up East named Joseph Holt Ingraham journeyed to Mobile and hove into the bay "just at sunrise." There, spread out before him, was the Lower Fleet with its forest of masts tipped by the rosy dawn light. "This fleet consisted of nearly a hundred ships and barks," he wrote, "and had a fine appearance, extending for a mile or two in length. To and from its anchorage plied the smoking Bay steamers, and among them sailed a graceful cutter, the vigilant watcher of the coast." The stretch of bay up to Mobile, Ingraham marveled, was "lively with vessels of all kinds, moving on every possible course." At Choctaw Point, town came into view and "did not strike me as interesting. Its approach is disfigured by marsh land, covered with old logs, and the forests crowd close upon the city." Once into the harbor, however, "there was a good display of shipping at the wharves, vessels of light draughts, and a fine view of steamers, taking in and discharging cotton, the great staple."[24]

More than four-story-brick cotton warehouses, columned public buildings, polite salons, elaborate hotels, spacious theaters, the ineffectual Choctaw Point Lighthouse, or the big ships of the Lower Fleet, steamboats were the defining objects of antebellum Mobile. According to one contemporary list, there were fifty of them working the local waterways. They ranged in size from twenty-six tons to more than 440 and bore colorful names such as the *Cuba, Wild Duck, Eliza Battle, Illinois Belle, Forest Monarch, Heroine, Lucy Bell, Magyar, and Emperor.* Even so, compared to the overall steamboat tonnage at New Orleans—80,993 in 1842—Mobile was a distant second with just shy of 7,000 tons, but that was enough to make for constant river and bay traffic, as Ingraham noted, and put her well ahead of both Charleston and Savannah.[25]

They were ingeniously designed contraptions, smaller than the behemoths that plied the mighty Mississippi but beautifully adapted to the peculiarities of local river travel where shallow water and tight bends were frequent realities. The typical mid-nineteenth-century steamboat was essentially a big raft with paddle wheels and a superstructure. Captains liked to boast that they could "run on dew," and this was not far from the truth. Drafts from two to four feet were the norm, even when the boats were loaded, which allowed them to penetrate far beyond where light schooners could go. The best boats had three decks with a square pilothouse perched atop. The main deck was mostly open to allow for easy loading and unloading of cotton bales and other cargo. If the boat was a side-wheeler, as most antebellum vessels on the Mobile were, the kitchen, boilers, engine, and paddle wheels were boxed and situated in the center. Above the main deck was the boiler deck, a misnomer, since it consisted of a long saloon flanked by small passenger cabins. Each of these had two doors, one into the saloon and the other onto an outside gallery that ran all the way around the vessel. Next was the hurricane deck, which featured a smaller structure that housed the officers' cabins. This was known as the Texas, so called for being separate from the boat's passenger population as the Republic of Texas was separate from the United States. The pilothouse was centered over the Texas, and the most elaborate ones looked like big cupcakes decorated by fancy jigsaw carpentry. From this high vantage the pilot steered the vessel by use of a large polished wheel that employed ropes to move the rudder. The steamboat's most distinguishing feature, of course, was the pair of tall black smokestacks forward the pilothouse—the height increased draft and engine efficiency. These vented the wood fires that stoked the boilers and belched thick smoke and fiery embers when there was a real head of steam. Steam whistles were used for signaling and releasing pent-up boiler pressure, and by the 1850s the finer vessels carried impressive calliopes with keyboards, which played cheery tunes to amuse or distract those on board or ashore.[26]

Buckingham rode one of these vessels down from Montgomery and found the trip anything but relaxing. "The engine was a high pressure one," he recalled, "and gave out a burst of steam from a tall chimney, at every revolution of the wheels, the sound being like the hard breathing of some huge mastodon laboring under the asthma." The beds and meals were perfectly satisfactory to the well-traveled Englishman, "but the tremulous motion communicated by the high-pressure engine, through all this range of cabins, occupying as they did the space which covered the engine itself, was so great as to render it almost impossible to write, and very difficult even to hold a book steady enough to read." The Scottish geologist Sir Charles Lyell found himself on the Mobile in 1846 and was especially disconcerted when the crew blew out the boilers with blasts of steam. This was an absolutely necessary and frequent procedure in the Mobile's muddy waters, lest the works end up, in popular river parlance, "crusted, rusted, busted." Lyell wrote that "when they clear the boilers of the sediment collected from the river-water, it is done by a loud and protracted discharge of steam, which reminded us of the frightful noise made by the steam gun exhibited at the Adelaide Gallery in London."[27]

Despite these sometimes alarming sounds, the better Mobile River boats provided no little degree of comfort, as Buckingham admitted. The steamer *James Battle,* launched in 1860, represented the epitome. It featured an opulent saloon with big chandeliers, tables with "different colored cloths, embedded in various designs around the edges, and fringed with gold lace and gold tassels," and in the ladies cabin a "magnificent $1,000 piano" was situated in front of a large gilded mirror. A wood-burning stove provided heat in the winter. Steamboat food ran the gamut, but again the best was very good indeed, with boiled oysters, fruit, and game on the bill of fare. If the weather was decent and one had a good cabin, a steamboat ride could be a pleasant thing. The English naturalist Philip Henry Gosse wrote of his "unabated delight" during a moonlit cruise upriver.[28]

As for the roustabouts, stevedores, rollodores, and firemen aboard the vessel—usually slaves, sometimes Irishmen—steamboat travel meant back-breaking toil. The men lived and worked on the main deck, wrestling cargo into place or unloading supplies. They scrambled ashore at landings to cut and load firewood and maneuvered the big cotton bales with heavy iron hooks, while overseers kept an eagle eye and applied the whip to anyone caught shirking. Accidents were common, and a fall overboard midriver meant almost certain death. In between stops the men played dice, and at the end of the day they were known to break out a fiddle and a banjo. Bed was a rough bit of burlap right on the deck or propped against a cotton bale. The stewards enjoyed an easier lot in general, and on the quality boats were well fed and given good clothes in order to be presentable to the passengers. Even so, their welfare depended on careful attention to detail and enduring insults or rudeness in silence.[29]

Because Mobile was simultaneously a seaport and a river town, there were numerous support services for both oceangoing and riverine maritime interests. In addition to all the offices and warehouses connected to the cotton trade previously noted, these included steamboat-agent offices that sold passenger tickets; ship chandlery firms that provided rigging, tar, hemp, belaying pins, leather goods, hatchets, and brooms; sail-making lofts where both men and women sat at tables or clambered over and around immense cotton duck folds suspended from the ceilings, all the while pushing heavy needles and thread through the cloth; sawmills that could fashion any shape or size of beam needed; foundries where steam boilers were made and repaired; and, last but not least, shipbuilding outfits where carpenters, caulkers, and mechanics were capable of turning out anything from barges, yawls, tugboats, and schooners to three-decked steamboats with every appointment like the *James Battle.* In the spring of 1856 the *Mobile Daily Advertiser* extolled several local firms and their admirable abilities. Foremost among these was "Messrs. J. M. & T. Meaher," whose bustling shipyard on Chickasabogue Creek had already launched the *Wm. Jones, Jr.,* the *Czar,* and the *Southerner.*[30]

Timothy Meaher. From Marie Bankhead Owen, *The Story of Alabama* (New York: Lewis Historical Publishing Company, 1949).

In the long and sometimes dark history of the Mobile River, no other family was to be more closely associated with its triumphs and its tragedies than the Meahers, and no member of that determined group was more capable and strong willed than Timothy Meaher. An Englishman who met him early in the Civil War wrote that he was "a character—perhaps a good one. One with a grey eye full of cunning and of some humor, strongly marked features, and a very Celtic mouth of the Kerry type." A photograph of him as a young man shows a full face framed by dark mutton chops, slightly downturned mouth, and an even gaze. Born in 1812, he was a native Mainer, the son of an Irish immigrant. At age twenty-three he moved to Mobile, no doubt attracted by stories of the fabulous riches to be made in the cotton boom there. Eventually five brothers and a sister would join him, but within twenty years only his brothers James and Byrnes and sister Abby had survived the rigors of climate and river life along with him.[31]

Timothy Meaher's river career began modestly when he signed as a deckhand aboard the *Wanderer.* "She was a peculiar river boat," he told a newspaper reporter late in life, "having five boilers—one flue and four cylinder boilers. She had only one engine, a very large one. . . . She was nine feet deep in the hold, and her model was similar to that of a sea-going vessel, with a bowsprit forward and her draft was five feet light. . . .

Little running was done at night." He worked hard aboard the *Wanderer* and various other vessels, learning the numerous twists and turns of local waterways, the subtleties of riverboat nomenclature, and how to handle rough men. His diligence paid off. He soon became a mate and by the early 1840s was a captain in his own right. The *William Bradstreet* was his first steamboat. Others followed, including the *Orline St. John* (named after a former girlfriend), the *Czar,* the *Roger B. Taney,* and the *Southern Republic,* "all built at Mobile, owned and commanded by myself." Meaher's strong sectional sympathy for his newfound home is clearly revealed in the names of the last two vessels. Taney was chief justice of the United States Supreme Court during the Dred Scott case in 1857. And, as secession loomed, Meaher ardently advocated Southern independence.[32]

In addition to success afloat, Timothy Meaher began acquiring property along the river north of downtown and lived at the mouth of Three Mile Creek. By 1847 he owned a large tract between that stream and Chickasabogue, which became known as Meaher's Hummock, and in partnership with his brother James (local wags referred to them as the firm of Jim and Tim) operated a plantation, shingle yard, blacksmith shop, and a shipyard where they built steamboats, schooners, at least one ship, and "numerous barges and scows." According to his obituary in 1885, James Meaher "was a quiet, modest and unobtrusive man of sterling integrity and stainless honor. He was one of those men whose word was as good as his bond. He never took a drink of liquor during his entire life." The brothers made a good team: "Captain James looked more specially after the financial part, and Captain Tim attended to the running of the boats, and knew the rivers like any familiar thing." Byrnes was not listed as a partner with his brothers, but his professional dealings were intimately bound up with them nonetheless. He got his start as a mate under Timothy and before long was captain of the *Czar.* He owned a plantation in Grove Hill, not far upcountry. The only girl of the brood, Abby Meaher lived with Timothy until 1853 when she married a wealthy San Francisco banker. A family genealogy published in 1890 described her as "a lady of culture, a good linguist and a practiced Catholic . . . , rigidly plain in dress and benevolent in the extreme." Besides their business enterprises, steamboats, and land, the Meahers also owned slaves who sweated in the shipyard and manhandled the timber and cotton. Byrnes Meaher had nineteen slaves in 1860, James twenty-two, and the J. M. and T. Meaher partnership held three. Ironically, given his subsequent history, the extent of Timothy Meaher's slave ownership has proven harder to pin down. He does not appear in the 1850 or 1860 Slave Schedules of the United States Census. He almost certainly did own human beings, however, and in a common practice would have paid other owners to hire out their slaves' labor to him. On the domestic front James and Timothy married sisters, also native Mainers, in Tim's case the governor's niece, and they all lived and prospered by the muddy river at their threshold.[33]

Mark Twain made the Mississippi River pilots famous, but on the Mobile the captains got all the glory. They were the lords of the river and frequently had larger-than-life personalities that long outlived them in memory and lore. Timothy Meaher was typical of their combination of raw-boned ability, coarse humor, shrewd business acumen, and thoroughgoing river sense. Sometimes, like Timothy, captains owned shares of the boats and companies they worked for, and sometimes they simply shopped their services. Many of them worked at one time or another for Cox, Brainard & Company, the largest shipping outfit in town with more than twenty vessels. This firm ran regular packets up the Tombigbee and Alabama Rivers and over to New Orleans, even employing a German musician called Professor Funk to play the calliope aboard one of its boats. It also dominated the lightering business between the city and the Lower Fleet. One of the owners and captains was Owen Finnegan, a native Irishman who plied the rivers for more than fifty years. In typical fashion he had worked his way up from the bottom. "I landed in Mobile in the year 1847," he later recalled, "on the steamboat *General Taylor,* in the capacity of a watchman of the boat." By 1852 he was involved with Cox, Brainard & Company. and reaped the profits from "a large and profitable trade." Finnegan owned and captained many boats during his long career, the best known being the *Maggie F. Burke,* named for a granddaughter and fated to suffer a collision on the Mobile in 1884. His reputation both on the water and in the company office was sterling. Waterfront habitués joked that he was the only captain "who could kick up dust in the middle of the river." In 1904 an article in a Black Belt newspaper admiringly held that "his name is not only known favorably in Mobile, but in every hamlet, hill and dale from the Coosa's rapids to the gulf, and to the farthest branches of the Little Bigbee is his name a household word."[34]

The most belligerent captain on record was Robert Otis, "the combative, who ruled the deck of the invincible *Cuba.*" One contemporary recalled that Otis was "small, compact, distressingly quiet, and made few friends." He was quick with his fists, on one occasion bloodying a rival captain on the Dauphin Street wharf over some perceived slight and on another beating his own pilot so badly the man needed a surgeon's ministrations. Most memorably, when another boat crowded his vessel, threatening damage to the wheelhouse, boiler deck, and guards, he "rushed to his room and soon after emerging leveled a shot and fired at the pilot." The man was badly wounded near the eye, and Otis was tried, convicted, and heavily fined for the act, but he escaped jail time. More physically intimidating but nowhere near as difficult as Otis was Captain George W. Cloudis, "a steamboat man from foretop to fetlock." Cutting a trim two-hundred-pound athletic figure, Cloudis abjured liquor but was "an inveterate coffee drinker." Jesse Cox, one of the firm's principals, was the gentlest and most kindly regarded captain on the river. He lived near Montgomery on a bluff overlooking the Alabama, with a "charming wife" and "interesting children." River folk loved to tell the story of how Captain Cox once comforted a bereaved young mother. She had boarded his boat with the small white casket of her dead child, and when she was informed that it was customary for caskets to be stowed in the servants' quarters on the main deck, she objected and dissolved into tears. Cox hastened down, and when he ascertained the problem, told the cabin boy to "order the chambermaid to prepare a stateroom in the ladies' cabin for this little one. Under these circumstances we have no rules." Of such variety were the men who commanded those fantastic boats.[35]

Ordinary people loved to watch the steamboats come and go, and some departures were attended by enthusiastic impromptu displays. In the fall of 1914 the *Mobile Register* published an interview with an elderly resident about his memories of antebellum steamboat travel. He had been a boy then, but his recollections were yet vivid. They included the story of dozens of black roustabouts gathering at the bow of a steamer to serenade their sweethearts and wives come to bid them farewell. Even as the boat disappeared upstream, the old Mobilian said, "the roustabouts could be heard in the distance with their many voices singing that old popular tune, 'Good-bye, mah Honey, I'm Gone.'" More thrilling for loosely supervised local urchins, such as the interviewee had once been, was when boats cleared the wharves and their powerful side wheels began churning up the water and generating a wake. Such an occasion offered too much temptation to be resisted, and in a sight "never to be forgotten," up to one hundred boys plunged into the river, "taking as we used to call it, 'the waves.'" It was an insurance agent's nightmare, impossible to imagine now.[36]

While adults were not inclined to jump into the river and swim after the steamboats, they did love to watch them race. Sometimes the competition was spontaneous and of short duration, say from the wharves down to the river mouth, but at others it was long planned and attended by spirited discussion and high-stakes betting. One of the latter kind occurred sometime in 1854, when the brand new *William Jones, Jr.*, commanded by Byrnes Meaher took on the *Cuba* and the fearsome Captain Otis. The affair was witnessed by a "mere lad" named James Fleetwood Foster, who shortly after the turn of the century wrote down his steamboat reminiscences for the *Wilcox Banner*, a Black Belt newspaper. "Well do we remember the great crowds that thronged the entire river front," Foster wrote. People jammed the wharves, leaned out of second- and third-story office windows and pushed onto balconies. Women were just as excited as the men, "to the extent of requiring the arms of the sterner sex to prevent their dropping from their stands and falling into the river beneath." Foster was pulling for the *Cuba* with her jaunty raked smokestacks and snapping banners, while much of the crowd liked the *William Jones, Jr.* "With hearts beating like kettle drums we heard the gang planks fall with heavy splash upon their hardened decks," Foster's tale continued. "The black smoke poured from the tall chimneys so thick that it seemed to seek its exit by force." Once situated in the stream, the *Cuba* shot away, chased by the *Jones.* "The happy blacks in shirts of red and blue were crowded upon the forecastle freight pile, and with caps in hand kept time to the songs of defiance as they yelled the superiority of their favorites." Unfortunately for the many spectators ashore, "the river soon became clouded by the thick smoke from the many smaller crafts and nothing could be seen until the gradual turn of the broad sweep that leads to Spanish River and many were the conjectures as to the loss and gain of each." Even after the racers disappeared, the crowd lingered, anxiously awaiting some news from a "down boat." Soon enough

Mobilians got the word that the *Cuba* made Nannahubba seven minutes ahead and ultimately beat the *Jones* to Montgomery by three hours. "Of course the usual excuses for a beaten craft came in," Foster commented; "some pipe out of order, wheel picked up a log, or not in exact time."[37]

Despite the popularity of these river races, the local press worried about the potential for disaster among so many spectators. "We must protest again, in the name of public safety," an editorial in the *Mobile Register* chided on August 11, 1859, "against the usual morning race between the *Junior* and the *Crescent*, when they meet at the mouth of the river, and thence up to town. If it is not discontinued, there will be a burst up, and some dozens of our best citizens will be blown into the air and water. We give the warning. If the hosts do not heed it, the passenger's [*sic*] better do it."[38] This was not the fulmination of some fussy green eyeshade. Steamboats faced many natural and man-made perils on the river. These included sawyers that could hole a boat, sinking her or forcing her listing to the bank; shifting sandbars that could ground a vessel and cost valuable time; collisions with pilings, wharves, or other boats; fire from a live ember landing among the cotton bales; and, most frighteningly, as the editorial noted, a burst boiler. Steamboat boilers were subjected to terrific pressures, especially during races, and given the developing technology of the era, they were frequently known to fail, with horrific results. It had happened in Mobile before, just off the Dauphin Street wharf, and this was no doubt foremost in the newspaper editor's mind when he penned his warning.

Authorities were well aware that steamboating was attended by many dangers and as early as 1826 enforced state inspection laws. One of these stated that boats running between Mobile and Blakeley "or places on either of the rivers Mobile, Alabama, Tombeckbee, or their tributaries" were subject to "thorough survey and examination by the board of harbor master and wardens of the port of Mobile." Craft had to be "staunch, well-provided and *river-worthy* for the space of at least one year thereafter" in order to receive a certificate. If a vessel failed to be certified and suffered a calamity that resulted in a lawsuit, "the burthen or proof, shall rest upon the carrier." But even a conscientious captain, a professional crew, and a fresh certificate hanging in the pilothouse were no guarantee of safety, as the experience of the *Ben Franklin* was to prove.[39]

March 13, 1836, was, the local press mourned, "a day of disaster and gloom." The *Ben Franklin*, a sturdy side-wheeler under the command of Captain H. A. Slade, was scheduled to leave the Dauphin Street wharf at 10:00 a.m. She was jammed with passengers, and a crowd of people, including many women and children, had gathered on the wharf to wave goodbye. With everyone aboard, the captain cast off but ran afoul of a neighboring vessel's anchor line. The crew successfully freed the boat, and the *Ben Franklin* backed into the channel, where her engine fully engaged. "The paddle had scarcely made three revolutions," a newspaper reporter wrote, "before a terrible explosion took place. Those on shore, and there were hundreds . . . , heard a deep report, like the dull sound of a heavy piece of artillery, followed instantaneously by a sharper report, and still another in quick succession." For some reason the boilers had exploded, and "the forward part of the boat, including the boilers, the boiler deck, pilot-house and chimneys, were seen blown out, as if from the mouth of a vast mortar, and among the flying fragments human bodies were wheeling thru the air, to an immense height." The boilers themselves were catapulted into the river, where they sank hissing amid "volumes of vapor." In what was probably an understatement the reporter wrote that those ashore were "filled with distress and alarm," exacerbated no doubt when a mangled body blown two hundred feet high and one hundred yards from the boat landed on the Dauphin Street wharf "a bloody and disfigured mass." Dozens of people were in the water, and the scene aboard the stricken vessel was a "ghastly horror."[40]

Providentially for the passengers and crew of the *Ben Franklin,* the mishap occurred in broad daylight in the middle of the harbor, where rescue and relief were immediately at hand. In another bit of good luck, because the force of the blast had been forward the loss of life turned out to be relatively light compared to those in other such incidents around the country. Among the fifteen or so killed outright, most were crewmen—the pilot, three firemen, two deckhands, the cabin boy, and a carpenter, plus a few passengers. A dozen more were badly hurt and five only slightly so. Two days later the captain wrote to the newspaper and declared that "there was no local cause for an explosion." He stated that he had personally checked the boilers and not seen any reason to "believe that they were unsafe or defective in any respect." Several engineers who studied the matter pinned the cause on human error, "some imprudent person having placed some obstacle in the way to prevent the safety valve from being raised to its usual height, to give full vent for blowing off steam."[41]

Eleven years later the passengers and crew of the steamboat *Tuscaloosa* were not so fortunate in the particulars of their boiler explosion. Like the *Ben Franklin,* the *Tuscaloosa* was scheduled to leave from the Dauphin Street wharf, but the departure was set for 8:00 p.m., and a violent January storm was lashing the river. Rain came down in sheets, serried rollers funneled into the river mouth from the bay and marched upstream, conspiring with a strong southeast wind to pin the vessel against the wharves. More steam was the answer, and, her side wheels chopping the water fiercely, the *Tuscaloosa* at last got into the channel and turned north. The strain on the engines must have been too great, for just a few miles north of town, right at the southern end of Twelve Mile Island, two of the boilers exploded. Almost immediately the boat caught fire, and then barrels of gunpowder stored on deck caused a secondary blast. Crippled, the boat veered into the bank and her stern swung out into the current. Whether or not she hit the river's west bank or the west side of Twelve Mile Island is not specified in any of the accounts, but it hardly mattered. This is the lower delta, and the marshy land on all sides was flooded by high water. In an article the following morning the *Alabama Planter* reported, "The ladies were then lowered from the upper cabin and sent ashore in the yawl. Some escaped by swimming and on temporary rafts. On getting to shore, it was almost impossible to get a dry footing, the tide being so high as to cover it almost entirely." The river was in a perfect froth. Battling the waves, some of the men "climbed trees, and some of the ladies stood almost to their necks in water." The explosion and fire were visible from town, but relief did not arrive for three hours, when the *James Hewett* finally pulled alongside.[42]

All of the survivors were rescued and brought back to town, but many bodies could not be recovered until the following day when the weather abated. Another steamboat then brought down ten victims. These unfortunates, "shockingly mangled," were laid out on the wharf, and an inquest was held over them by the coroner. Identification proved difficult, and the scene was not for the squeamish. One body "had its head blown clearly off," and others were "burned almost to a cinder." The *Alabama Planter* assured its readers that it presented a sight "too terrible and dreadful to witness without the most painful emotion." Some were identified by personal belongings, in the case of second clerk Blue Pasteur, a "shirt button with his initials on it," or a distinctive tattoo, such as the image of an anchor on the forearm of deckhand W. Turner, who was found floating in the river with a boat hook fastened in his clothes. Throughout history human tragedy has brought out both the best and the worst in people, and the destruction of the *Tuscaloosa* was no different. Immediately after the explosion, it was proudly reported, the ladies, miserably shivering in the water as they were, refused to board the rescue boat until the wounded had been loaded. But in the following days the public and officials were outraged when scavengers were discovered at the wreck "stealing everything of value they could lay their hands on—breaking open trunks, rifling bodies, and in short gorging themselves, like wild beasts, on the desolation produced by this awful calamity." Incredibly, several of these "scoundrels" even made it known that they would deliver the bodies "if paid for at the rate of ten dollars each." The newspaper thought they deserved lynching, "superior in its promptitude and severity to the law." The ultimate death toll was never exactly determined, as the number of passengers was uncertain, but most estimates run from fifteen to thirty lost. As for the survivors, they gathered at the Waverly House and praised the captain for his efforts. In a unanimous decision they voted to present him with a "service of silver plate . . . to consist of a massive waiter and two tumblers, with an inscription expressive of the reason of the presentation."[43]

The loss of the *Ben Franklin* and the *Tuscaloosa* were by far the most dramatic steamboat disasters during the antebellum era on the Mobile River. It is somewhat curious, however, that neither of these episodes remained lodged in popular memory to the degree of the burning of the *Orline St. John,* commanded by Timothy Meaher, on the Alabama in 1850 or the *Eliza Battle,* a Cox, Brainard "floating palace" captained by S. Graham Stone, on the Tombigbee in 1858. Casualties were only slightly higher in each of those incidents, but both vessels caught fire with full loads of cotton and drifted downstream like blazing torches as horrified passengers leapt into freezing waters, some women with their dresses in flames. The *Eliza Battle* became known as "the phantom steamboat of the Tombigbee," and her story was featured in Selma folklorist

Kathryn Tucker Windham's phenomenally popular 1969 book, *13 Alabama Ghosts and Jeffrey*. As for the *Orline St. John,* she was rumored to be carrying a large sum of gold, and the wreck site attracted treasure hunters for decades. These stories have been oft told and published and need no repetition here. Suffice it to say that both events were closely connected to Mobile and its people, and both occasioned much comment and discussion throughout the Mobile basin and indeed the South.[44]

Even as steamboats dominated transportation, their demise was being laid down in the form of gleaming iron rails on chert rock roadbeds. Railroads were originally conceived to enhance river traffic by linking different streams. But soon enough the speed and efficiency of trains told, and steamboats dwindled in importance and numbers. Progressive Mobilians recognized the importance of good rail connections and believed that if they could link the Port City with the Ohio River valley, they could siphon off some of New Orleans's business. A committee was formed to tackle the project (Duke Goodman was an early member), and a feasible route was surveyed all the way to Cairo, Illinois. Investors signed on, politicians and boosters promoted the idea in other states along the proposed route, and by the spring of 1861 the line was completed to Columbus, Kentucky. The Civil War prevented its completion to Cairo, however, and thoroughly wrecked what had been done. But the early numbers had been promising, and frustrated businessmen could only dream of how many bales of cotton might have been diverted from the Crescent City. After the war railroads would become ascendant, significantly impacting both the physical appearance of Mobile's waterfront and its place as a successful seaport, but for the present the promise was more tantalizing than tangible.[45]

Sectional tensions mounted through the 1850s, and thoughtful merchants worried about what a war and a blockade would do to their city's economy. Many Mobilians hailed from the North, especially New England, or had close business ties with New York and Boston, and they knew the results were likely to be disastrous. Whether or not Timothy Meaher expressed any such concerns is not known, but his subsequent actions certainly would not seem to suggest it. Meaher's enthusiasm for his adopted homeland and its peculiar institution was already evident in his family's slave ownership and his choice of boat names. He upped the ante considerably when he decided to give material support to William Walker's rash attempt to establish a new slave society in Nicaragua and doubled down a few years later when he financed, planned, and executed a daring scheme to import slaves illegally from Africa directly into Mobile. The latter incident constitutes a major element of the Mobile River's history, but it is a story for a later chapter. Meaher's support of the filibusters was not so successful and merits briefer notice.

William Walker, the so called grey-eyed man of destiny, was a Nashville-born doctor and lawyer who became an active filibuster. He invaded Baja, California, in 1854, and Nicaragua the following year. The United States recognized his regime in the latter country in 1856, but it quickly fell apart, and he was returned to the states. Undaunted, he launched a second Central American expedition, a portion of which departed from Mobile in December of 1858. Walker had promised to establish slavery in Nicaragua in order to attract Southern investors, and it definitely worked in Timothy Meaher's case. In fact, the irascible river man went so far as to provide a schooner in which he had an ownership interest, the *Susan,* captained by Harry Maury, to transport 120 of the filibusters. Many of these were Mobile men, tough customers with "revolvers and bowie knives." One observer remarked that they were made up "mostly of the class found about the wharves . . . with here and there a Northern bank cashier who had suddenly changed his vocation." This motley assembly boarded the *Susan* and was towed down to the Dog River Bar, whence the schooner sailed on her own to the lower bay. Suddenly becalmed there, she was overhauled by a United States revenue cutter and boarded. Tense and delicate negotiations ensued, with the federals demanding surrender and the filibusters refusing. When Captain Maury told the federal officer he would hold him as hostage, the man was unperturbed and shouted to his crew to ignore that fact and open fire on the *Susan* anyway. A standoff developed instead, with neither side having enough fire power to overthrow the other. The vessels anchored close until a heavy fog descended and Maury was able to slip away.[46]

Cheered by their narrow escape, the filibusters nonetheless failed in their overall mission. The *Susan* ran aground off Honduras, and her people had to be rescued by the British sloop-of-war *Basilisk.* Luckily for the frustrated filibusters, the British were sympathetic and ferried them back to Mobile, arriving on New Year's Day. Locals could not have been more delighted. "On the first day of the new year," the *Mobile Register* reported, "in the midst of the festivities and congratulations of our citizens, they were surprised by the unexpected appearance of Capt. Maury in one of our most popular thoroughfares, with his banner flying over him and a train of a large number of the adventurers." New Year's became the equivalent of a Mardi Gras parade, and "the welcome was indeed generous and cordial." The British officers were given a banquet and "the freedom of the city in recognition of their kind treatment of Walker's disappointed and unfortunate followers."[47]

Northern men detected the chill in the air, and those unwilling to cast their lot with an increasingly bellicose South packed their portmanteaus and headed home. After the election of Abraham Lincoln in November 1860, there was no longer any doubt on the secession question. Stephen A. Douglas was in town for the returns and depressed by what was to come and retired early to his hotel room. Meanwhile, down on Commerce Street a cotton factor conceded to a client that the market was "unsettled by the election news," but he naively predicted that "in a few days . . . confidence will be restored and things will move on as before." He was wrong. War was coming to the Mobile River once more, and the opening act was about to be played at the Mount Vernon Arsenal, where worried federal troops keenly felt their isolation and vulnerability.[48]

5

Rebel River

South Carolina seceded from the Union on December 20, 1860. Reaction across the region was immediate and electric. From Norfolk to New Orleans crowds gathered around liberty poles, cheered, and formed units of "minute men." In Mobile a one-hundred-gun salute thundered downtown, and there was a military review and fireworks. "The bells are ringing merrily," stated one dispatch, "and the people are out in the streets by hundreds, testifying their joy at the triumph of secession." Caught up in the excitement was a young woman named Kate Cumming, soon to become a nurse and famous diarist. "The city was one blaze of light from the illuminations," she recalled; "scarcely a window in the whole city was not lit. The noise from the fireworks and firearms was deafening. Speeches were made, processions paraded the streets with banners flying and drums beating, and in fact everything was done to prove that Mobile at least approved of what South Carolina had done." Mobilians thoroughly enjoyed the moment or, if they did not, kept their counsel, and anticipated a similar move by Alabama. Governor Andrew B. Moore had called a state convention in Montgomery for January 7 to consider the momentous issue.[1]

Into this agitated environment came the USS *Crusader*, a 545-ton screw steamer fitted out as a gunboat. She was by any measure a mean-looking craft—sleek black hull with a white band punctuated by gun ports, a sharp prow, and slightly raked masts with a smokestack just aft the mainmast. In spite of what alarmed Mobilians might have thought when her wolfish profile appeared on their horizon, her mission was completely routine. For the past several months she had been chasing down slave ships in the Caribbean and doing it quite well. On January 2 the secretary of the navy ordered her commander, Lieutenant John N. Maffitt, to take the vessel into Mobile to cash a prize-money check with the collector of the port. Maffitt was no callow shavetail but rather an experienced forty-one-year-old naval officer. He had been born at sea in 1819—his widow said he considered himself "a son of old Neptune"—and joined the navy as a midshipman at age thirteen. His prior service included a stint on the fabled *Constitution* and decades with the U.S. Coast Survey. He knew the South well, having been mostly raised in North Carolina, but was a conscientious officer and not likely to brook any nonsense from inflamed rowdies looking for trouble.[2]

The *Crusader* drew twelve feet, and so she anchored just off the Dog River Bar while Maffitt was rowed ashore and proceeded on up to the city to conduct his business. Alabama was still in the Union, but the sight of a warship flying the Stars and Stripes in Mobile Bay was too much for the local fire-eaters and hotheads who had been carousing since word of South Carolina's secession. A harebrained plot was hatched to seize the *Crusader*, and Maffitt soon heard of it. Not one to be caught off guard, he cleared his vessel for action, got up steam, and promptly called on the editor of the *Mobile Register* and another leading citizen. Maffitt was direct, stating "that if steamers approached me with hostile intent I would open my broadsides and sink them in fifteen minutes with every desperado on board of them." This had the desired result, and the scheme was "reluctantly abandoned." Maffitt cashed his check and took the *Crusader* back into the gulf. He would return to Mobile soon enough but in a very different guise from that of a loyal United States officer.[3]

In Montgomery, Governor Moore decided to act. Georgia governor Joseph E. Brown had already seized that state's federal forts and arsenals, and on January 2 he had urged the Alabama governor to do the same. If Moore was waffling, the *Crusader* incident convinced him that action was absolutely necessary before the federals had a chance to reinforce their Alabama garrisons. These included Forts Morgan and Gaines at the mouth of Mobile Bay and the Mount Vernon arsenal near the site of old Fort Stoddert. By 1861 this last facility was much improved. Authorized by Congress in 1828, it had been constructed where the earlier cantonment had stood, on the higher ground three miles back from the river. It included a thirty-five-acre main post with numerous two- and three-story brick buildings and a horseshoe-shaped ten-foot-high brick wall. There was ordnance machinery in place, a blacksmith shop, and significant stores of powder, ammunition, and weapons. Moore knew that its seizure would instantly choke off arms to other federal forts in Florida and Mississippi, not to mention that it would provide his own state forces with an impressive capacity to wage serious war. Thus it was that on January 3 he ordered state militia to take it and the bay forts.[4]

When the order clacked into the Mobile telegraph office, it was instantly attended to by the state militia colonel stationed there. By 11:00 p.m., four companies had mustered down at the city wharf. Even though this was a daring and potentially deadly undertaking, they were attired in full parade regalia that would have made the grizzled butternut veterans at war's end hoot in derision. The units included the Mobile Rifles, clad in dark green coats and shakoes with white plumes; the Washington Light Infantry in scarlet; and the German Fusiliers and Gardes Lafayette, the last under the command of Captain Belloc, duded up in European frippery. In high spirits, these troops loaded their scaling ladders aboard the waiting steamer and eagerly filed onto the deck. The vessel pulled into the river channel and pushed upstream, reaching Mount Vernon just before dawn.[5]

Inside the arsenal seventeen federal troops commanded by Captain Jesse L. Reno were fast asleep. Why they did not take precautions—including posting a sentry—is unknown, since secession fever was widespread, and in fact President James Buchanan had declared that very day to be set aside for "Humiliation, Fasting, and Prayer" nationwide in response to the crisis. But asleep they were when the Mobile militiamen scaled their walls and dropped into the compound, then opened the main gate and surrounded the armory. Completely surprised, Reno and his astonished soldiers offered no resistance, and within minutes the state of Alabama was in possession of a fine brick military facility, 20,000 stand of arms, 150,000 pounds of gunpowder, 300,000 cartridges, and much else besides. Eager to save face, Reno wrote to his superior that afternoon: "I did not make, nor could I have made, any resistance, as they had scaled the walls and taken possession before I knew anything about the movement." He went on incredibly to argue that, because it was "impossible for me to hold this place with my seventeen men, I trust that the Department will not hold me responsible for this unexpected catastrophe." Only a fool would have believed such a move by the Southerners "unexpected," and as for Reno and company's supposed inability to defend the arsenal, the *New Orleans Bee* was less certain of their helplessness. "Had they not been taken by surprise," it opined, "and they had been so disposed, they might have given some trouble and shed some blood, as the arsenal is defensible against musketry and their number was more than a third of their assailants." Nonetheless, the pattern was repeated at Forts Morgan and Gaines, which fell with equal ease the same day to other units dispatched from Mobile. Surveying these seizures in Georgia, Alabama, and elsewhere two weeks later, a writer for the *New York Times* expressed frustration and fury, ranting that the U.S. government's military officers "either through cowardice or in sympathy with treason, have offered no resistance to the capture of Federal property; at the first summons of an incompetent and undisciplined rabble in uniform, they have hauled down the flag every American soldier is bound in honor to save from dishonor with his life; and have surrendered their trust to treason."[6]

In a letter to Buchanan the afternoon of the capture, Moore explained his actions to the lame-duck executive. "I received such information as left but little, if any, room to doubt," he wrote, "that the Government of the United States, anticipating the secession of Alabama, and preparing to maintain its authority within this State by force, even to the shedding of blood and the sacrifice of the lives of the people, was about to re-enforce those forts and put a guard over the arsenal." His move was, therefore, "but an act of self-defense, and the plainest dictate of prudence." A soldier who participated in the arsenal seizure thought it all a cakewalk. "The defenses around Mount Vernon seemed totally underprepared," he said. "If it is like this everywhere, Buchanan may as well raise the white flag now."[7]

At last, after these audacious acts by the governor and militias, the state convention met and on January 11 voted Alabama out of the Union. Once again Mobilians spilled into the streets and wildly celebrated. According to one witness, a "secession pole" was erected at the foot of Government Street and a "Southern flag ... was run up amid the shouts of the multitude and thunders of cannon." The crowd then moved over to the Custom House where speakers extolled the glories of independence while ladies cheered from the Battle House balcony across the street. Militia and cadets marched to and fro downtown, jamming the square and blasting "salvos of artillery." At night Government Street was transformed into an "avenue of light" by burning tar barrels, and everywhere downtown "rockets blazed, crackers popped, and the people hurrahed and shouted as they never did before." In common cause, municipal authorities voted to change the names of Maine, Massachusetts, New Hampshire, and New York Streets to Palmetto, Charleston, Augusta, and Elmira respectively.[8]

After the bombardment of Fort Sumter in early April, the shooting war was on, and Mobile's sons flocked to the colors. One of the first big departures took place on April 14 when the Mobile Cadets and Washington Light Infantry boarded the steamboat *St. Nicholas* for the voyage to Montgomery and then by rail to Virginia. Gone were the garish green and scarlet coats these troops had worn on their arsenal adventure. Now they tramped along in "stout, serviceable gray, specially selected for a rough campaign." According to the *Mobile Daily Advertiser*'s man downtown, "the wharves, the balconies on Front Street, the boat which was to carry the soldiers away, and those lying adjacent were densely crowded, and after the last *adieu* had been waved, Dauphin and St. Francis Streets were thronged to their fullest capacity with the returning multitudes." As the *St. Nicholas* got under way, the Alabama State Artillery fired off a salute from the wharf, and all the boats rang their bells in support. The reporter was wise enough to guess that the "gay smiles and waving 'kerchiefs" that had seen fathers, sons, husbands, and brothers off were likely to be replaced by "tears from bright eyes" when night fell. For many if not most of the brave soldiers aboard the *St. Nicholas,* the coming years were to be filled with unspeakable suffering, struggle, and, too often, death.[9]

As the weeks advanced, Mobile was steadily transformed into a wartime town, and commercial activity along the wharves and down the bay slackened. Northern ships in the Lower Fleet up anchored and departed, while foreign vessels lingered, hoping for a last load of cotton before the anticipated blockade. In early May the *London Times* reporter Russell visited and provided some interesting descriptions of Mobile and its transition, as well as fascinating insight into Timothy Meaher's character. He was on a Southern tour and departed Selma for the Port City aboard Meaher's *Southern Republic,* a magnificent three-decker. The river was high, and the vessel made good time, her calliope playing the "wild strains of 'Dixie'" at every landing. Captain Meaher was clearly invigorated by recent events and held court in the saloon, telling rowdy stories and showing off his tattooed and scarred "South Caroliny niggers," urging them to rub their bellies and dance to show "how happy they were." Russell was not taken in for a minute, nor were the grinning planters and merchants gathered around. They knew these exotic scarified specimens with their filed teeth were really among those Meaher had arrogantly and illegally imported directly from Africa under the authorities' very noses only months earlier. As for the slaves being happy, Russell quipped that when cutting wood ashore or stoking the boilers, "they don't seem to be in the possession of the same exquisite felicity." Russell related Meaher's exchanges with these river slaves matter-of-factly, but even so they are highly distasteful, not to say offensive, to modern sensibilities, and starkly illustrate the distance between 1861 and today.[10]

Whether or not he was relieved finally to step onto the quays at Mobile, Russell did not say, but after the riverboat scenes, his readers certainly are. The hurly-burly of the cotton trade was largely dormant, but the waterfront looked just as it had to antebellum travelers—"a fringe of tall warehouses, and shops along-side, over which were names indicating Scotch, Irish, English, many Spanish, German, Italian, and French owners." Meaher hurried on up to Three Mile Creek, while Russell took a "large, well-lighted" room at the Battle House, "a fine building of the American stamp." After registering with a "Vigilance Committee" on the lookout for abolitionists, the indefatigable reporter sallied into town, which he thought bore a "'kinder-sorter' resemblance" to Malaga, Spain. Everywhere were "oyster saloons, drinking-houses, lager-bier and wine shops, and gambling and dancing places." He was charmed by the public market, "crowded with negroes, mulattoes, quadroons, and mestizos of all sorts, Spanish, Italian, and French, speaking their own tongues, or a quaint *lingua-franca,* and dressed in very striking and pretty costumes." Still, there could be no escaping the fact that things were not routine: "The citizens were busy in drilling, marching, and drum-beating, and the Confederate flag flew from every spire and steeple." Overall, Russell was impressed and thought these Southerners he had met "never will, never can be conquered."[11] Despite the correspondent's confidence, however, civil and military authorities were worried. Their city had fully cast its lot with the nascent Southern republic and would be vital to The Cause, but much work needed doing. Despite the capture of Morgan, Gaines, and the arsenal, Mobile was woefully vulnerable by sea, river, and land and almost wholly unprepared for the attack or siege that was sure to come.

Mobile's strategic importance was obvious to even the most casual observers. With a population of almost thirty thousand, it was the fourth largest city in the Confederacy, and as a seaport it ranked second only to New Orleans. Its river system, ever an asset, provided a superior interior supply route, and its rail connections, but imperfectly realized before the war, suddenly took on enormous significance. Besides the Mobile & Ohio which reached all the way to Columbus, Kentucky, there was the Mobile & Great Northern Railroad by the fall of 1861, which ran from Tensaw Landing in Baldwin County to Pollard, Alabama, where it then linked with lines to Montgomery and Pensacola. With the completion of the Mobile & Great Northern, troops, matériel, and supplies could be securely shuttled between the eastern and western theaters. After Corinth, Mississippi, fell in early 1862, this looping route became the only east–west rail link available to the Rebels. Its military utility was demonstrated on several occasions during the war. The best known of these occurred in the summer of 1862, when twenty-five thousand soldiers were shifted from Tupelo to Chattanooga through the Port City. For days rail cars brimming with troops trundled into Mobile, where the men then crowded the wharves for steamboat transport across the bay and their next ride on the Mobile & Great Northern. As long as Mobile and these railroads remained unmolested, the Confederacy would enjoy an internal cohesion that could keep the war going far longer than otherwise.[12]

Alabama's port city had other advantages besides its water and rail connections. These included five hospitals; flour mills and grist mills; a distillery; saw and planing mills; a textile mill; disciplined fire and militia companies; a large black labor force; plentiful, well-watered high ground west of downtown, where military encampments were soon established; and, perhaps most important, the maritime outfits and industrial concerns along the waterfront. These included at least one dry dock south of Government Street, numerous warehouses, shipyards, machine shops, and foundries. Among the last was the Phoenix Foundry on Water Street, which advertised "Ship and Steam Engine work, Sawmill, Machine and Brass Foundry work of all kinds, cast, turned and finished as well as jobbing and smith's work in all its branches." In 1861 the Phoenix employed twenty-eight men, including an architect, two finishers, ten machinists, three blacksmiths, five pattern makers, two foremen, two boilermakers, two molders, and a carpenter. Not far away stood the Mobile Foundry, which had eighteen employees, ten of them machinists. Of the machine shops, some little more than holes in the wall with a chain fall, a grinder, and tools scattered about, others more sophisticated, the most important was the Park and Lyons Machine Shop at the corner of State and Water, north of Government. This firm's energetic owners, Thomas W. Park and Thomas B. Lyons, were enthusiastic Confederate supporters and wasted no time in scoring a government contract to bore out rifle barrels to better fit with the ammunition at hand.[13]

Authorities had no intention of leaving this plum on the gulf to its own devices. Governor Moore declared that "Mobile must be defended at whatever cost," and to that end he authorized a ten-thousand-dollar expenditure on Forts Morgan and Gaines. Every penny was needed and more. These forts were built of brick and were more than adequate to defend against old-style vessels such as the *Hermes* with smooth-bore guns. But against the rifled cannons now carried by the Union ships, they were completely at risk and likely to be reduced to rubble in a sustained bombardment. Russell visited them and found Gaines "merely a shell of masonry," but he thought Morgan presented "a formidable sea face." Both were filled with men hard at work making improvements. Beyond these forts, Mobile was undefended. The Mississippi Sound, dredged in 1831 through the efforts of John Grant, was wide open to the west, and if the federals ran the forts and got into the bay, nothing was to prevent their light-draft gunboats from steaming directly up to the city, which they could assault either directly via the Mobile or Spanish Rivers or through a roundabout backdoor route up the Tensaw, Blakeley, or Apalachee and across the lower delta and so anchor opposite the city's waterfront that way. Civilians felt the exposure and danger. Kate Cumming wrote of that first summer, "The city was in a most defenseless state, and could have easily been captured, and no doubt would have been had the fact been known to the enemy." She was worried and "did not know how soon the war ships would pass Fort Morgan and throw shells into our midst." She reported that some people buried their family treasures, while others kept them packed in trunks ready to evacuate at a moment's notice. In the event of an attack the town bell would ring and all women and children were immediately to leave. Along with the anxiety came privation. Life's little luxuries were the first things to be missed, foremost New England ice, which no longer came into port. "We were fast awakening to the distressing fact of our great dependence on the North for almost everything," Cumming moaned.[14]

The state legislature hardly calmed any nerves when it resolved late in 1862 that Mobile "must never be desecrated by the polluting tread of the abolitionist foe . . . ; [the] port must never surrender, but must be defended from street to street, from house to house, and at last burned to the ground rather than surrender." Despite impressive official resolve, however, the earliest defensive efforts were comical, if not pitiful. The city's first naval squadron consisted of sailboats and large rowboats each with a small cannon mounted in the prow. One observer dubbed the little fleet "a most absurd and childish farce," and General Jones Withers, fresh out of office as Mobile's mayor, grumbled that "the idea of our caricature gunboats being a protection to the coast trade is to me simply ridiculous." One intriguing letter written on January 5, 1862, to Major Danville Leadbetter, an army engineer tasked with building the city's defenses, indicates that local innovators were at least experimenting with some unusual ideas, but they lacked the foresight to take even simple wartime precautions. "It may be proper to state that the submarine apparatus in the river was boarded and sunk by some reprobate during a night of last week," the correspondent reported. There are no other known references to this vessel or to who had built it. Does it still lie deeply buried under Mobile River mud, awaiting discovery, or has it long been obliterated by subsequent riverfront projects? In any case more serious efforts by land and sea, including below the waves, were in the offing, and Mobile's defenses would go from laughingstock to formidable.[15]

The Confederate high command continuously reorganized and shifted the boundaries of its departments during the war, and Mobile was variously part of Department No. 1, which included south Alabama; the Department of Alabama and West Florida; and the District of the Gulf. An array of Confederate army and naval officers came and went in the top spots. The army officers included Major General David E. Twiggs, who preferred his headquarters at New Orleans; Major General Braxton Bragg, famously argumentative but a good organizer; Brigadier General Samuel Jones, a capable artillerist; Brigadier John H. Forney, wounded and in need of a calm post; Major General Simon Bolivar Butler, popular and productive; and finally, from May 19, 1863, to war's end, Major General Dabney H. Maury, a native Virginian, West Point graduate, and Mexican War veteran. Maury tackled his new responsibilities with gusto and made his headquarters in the Port City, which he later remembered as "altogether an interesting and agreeable command." Maury had a trim Vandyke and the weathered, hard face so typical of nineteenth-century Americans used to lives in the elements, but he was short and people made fun of him for this. One of his men described him "as 'every inch a soldier,' but then there were not many inches of him." The troops called him "puss in boots" because of his proclivity to wear thigh-high leather cavalry boots that nearly consumed him. Despite the frequent command changes, however, the overall defensive strategy pursued by all of these officers remained more or less constant, and each of them pushed it to the degree that their own competency, limited resources, and circumstances allowed. The elements of this strategy included the ongoing strengthening of Forts Morgan and Gaines; the construction of Fort Powell on a shell island flanking Grant's Pass; the erection of land and floating batteries, as well as the placement of channel obstructions and underwater torpedoes to protect the riverine approaches to the city; extensive lines of earthworks surrounding the city on all its landward approaches; and the development of an effective naval force, which, if not able to lift the blockade, would at least hold the bay. After the fall of New Orleans in April of 1862, many locals expected Mobile to be next, and state officials ordered the construction of shore batteries at Choctaw Bluff on the Alabama River and Oven Bluff on the Tombigbee. These would at least protect the state's rivers if the coast was lost. As a precaution the ordnance machinery and tools at Mount Vernon arsenal were shipped to Selma, and the battery that had been thrown up there earlier abandoned. As far as any offensive action was concerned, the closest efforts to it were private attempts to develop a submarine boat that could operate outside the bay and, of course, blockade-running, which constituted a lifeline as well as an important morale booster.[16]

The numerous channel obstructions and flanking batteries directly protected the Mobile River proper and its closest approaches. The likelihood of these doing much more than slowing down a determined assault was doubtful if Union forces once got into the bay, but Mobilians and the men charged with their protection were not willing to leave the matter to fate. They would do all that the available money, labor, and technology allowed. Leadbetter had begun work on these defenses, and after he was promoted in October 1863 the effort was taken up by Lieutenant Colonel Viktor von Scheliha, a former Prussian army officer and a talented, if somewhat fussy, engineer. After the war von Scheliha wrote a treatise on coastal defense in which he provided detailed explanations on exactly how the defensive works were built. Channel obstructions composed of pilings and rubble were an important defensive strategy at Mobile, and, barring inclement weather or military activity, there were probably very few days throughout the war when steamboats, flats, and laborers could not be seen somewhere around the bay or in the rivers setting piles and dumping brickbats. According to von Scheliha, pilings were viable at depths of up to twenty-five feet, a requirement perfectly met by the Mobile's many mouths. Most pilings were of yellow pine, twelve to fifteen inches in diameter, with "their bark on." Because the bay and river bottoms were composed of mud and sand, the easiest method of setting these posts was with a high-pressure steam nozzle. One end of a long hose was attached to a valve on a steamer, and the other, with the nozzle, was loosely roped to the piling. Four men were needed—an engineer and three laborers to guide the hose and pile. Once they were in position, the engineer opened the valve, and the men pointed the pile and gently lowered it as the steam jet forced aside the water and blew open a depression on the bottom. "The steam was allowed to play until the funnel had reached a depth of four and even five feet," von Scheliha wrote, "when the noose was detached from the pile and the valve shut. So soon as the pressure of steam ceased, the mud closed the funnel-shaped hole in the bottom around the pile, which stood now as firmly as if driven by a good steam pile-driver." Given the ease of this procedure, it is hardly a surprise that thousands of pilings were placed during the war, and, where they do not interfere with navigation, they are still present. Some of the pilings were tipped with sharp iron caps or chained together to strengthen them even further.[17]

Von Scheliha believed that in order to be of the most utility, pilings had to be set in serried paired rows across a channel—perhaps as many as nine doubled rows deep—with each doubled row separated a certain number of feet and the intervening space filled with rubble. Old bricks and construction rubbish were thrown directly among the pilings, and in the narrow stretch of open water between the paired rows, scows, flats, barges, and decrepit steamboats were loaded with debris and sunk. The effectiveness of this method may be appreciated by the remark of a Union engineer tasked with clearing the rubble immediately after the war. He wrote that all the debris had "gradually settled into a species of concrete very difficult to remove." Where a narrow passage needed to be preserved for their own navigation, the Confederates used chains and booms as simple gates. In the event of emergency loaded flats or old hulks were kept anchored alongside so that they could be quickly towed into the opening and sunk to block passage. After much labor the obstructions off Choctaw Point formed a large trapezoid with the narrow end pointed south. The mouths of both the Mobile and Spanish Rivers were effectively covered by this arrangement, and gaps were left in four places to allow for friendly vessels. Unobtrusive stakes or lone pilings acted as steering markers for captains and pilots, but navigating the upper bay and rivers could still be dicey for Southern shipping, especially in fog or dirty weather. This was graphically demonstrated on a murky February night in 1863 when the Rebel gunboat *Selma* steamed down the bay to launch a surprise attack on the federal blockaders and ran directly into an obstruction at the Dog River Bar instead. She began to sink, but her crew managed to work the pumps and get her aground in shallower water. Carpenters from Mobile got her patched and she was able to steam back into the harbor where she went straight into dry dock. Needless to say, the attack was aborted, and the Confederacy was temporarily denied the services of a much needed warship.[18]

Besides the pilings and obstructions, beginning in 1863 the Rebels began using torpedoes, or mines, as they would be called today. Maury accurately described them as "beer casks charged with gunpowder." They were usually coated inside and out with pitch and activated by a primer. They could either be anchored to small cribs on the river and channel bottoms or simply weighted and allowed to float. Cheap and easy to produce, hundreds of these devices were sown in local waterways and between Forts Morgan and Gaines. Because of the harsh and corrosive conditions to which they were subjected, they sometimes misfired, but overall they did deadly service and were truly feared. During the Mobile campaign, nine federal warships and a launch were blasted by torpedoes, most famously the *Tecumseh* during the Battle of Mobile Bay, with total casualties more than two hundred killed and wounded. Admiral Henry K. Thatcher, who eventually brought the city under the direct threat of his vessel's guns, declared that the torpedoes "are the only enemy we regard."[19]

Pilings, sunken wrecks and torpedoes were not sufficient for Confederate authorities, however, and along with these defenses they ordered earthworks, fortifications, and floating batteries to be built at Choctaw Point, the southern end of the Pinto Island spit, in the water east of the Spanish River channel, and across the bay at Spanish Fort, Blakeley, and on the lobster-claw-shaped islands coursed by the Tensaw, Blakeley, and Apalachee Rivers. Army engineer Leadbetter began this work and by the time he was transferred had more or less completed the installations. The Choctaw Point battery, four guns hard by the lighthouse, was part of a more extensive line of earthworks and forts that circled the entire city—there were eventually three such lines—but because better coverage of the river mouth was desired, another battery was constructed out from the point on a sand spit. In addition, Pinto Battery was erected in four feet of water, three-quarters of a mile south of that island. This placed the installation less than 150 feet from Choctaw Pass, the main channel into Mobile harbor and close to the Spanish River mouth as well. Spanish River Battery was situated 3,500 feet to the east, in shallow water alongside that stream. All of these batteries presented significant construction challenges. Workers began by sinking hundreds of piles within the projected outline of each battery. Huge clusters of pilings were concentrated where the guns were to be positioned in order to support their tremendous weight. Once all of the pilings were set, a terreplein was formed by a large frame filled with rubbish and dirt. In the autumn of 1862 a deserter described the rest of the Pinto Battery's construction to the federals: "Upon this [terreplein] is a heavy timber foundation and wall of large timbers with casemates for guns; the whole is strongly cased by railroad iron." Pinto Battery initially mounted four guns. Spanish River Battery was similarly built, though with eight guns at first, and in the winter of 1863 another deserter described it as a timber and sand installation "protected by a double thickness of railroad iron." A couple of small floating batteries, boxy casemated rafts mounting one or a few guns that could be towed to wherever needed, supplemented these works. Across the bay elaborate earthworks and fortifications protected the city from a land assault from Pensacola or up the Eastern Shore, and the batteries on the Apalachee and Blakeley Rivers guarded Mobile's watery back door.[20]

In May 1863 the upper-bay batteries were all renamed to honor the mounting sacrifice by Southern soldiers. Choctaw Point Battery became Missouri Battery for that state's losses; Pinto Battery was named Battery Gladden in memory of Brigadier General Adley H. Gladden, killed at Shiloh; Spanish River Battery was rechristened Battery McIntosh for Commander Charles F. McIntosh, killed near New Orleans; Apalachee Battery became Battery Tracy for Brigadier General Edward D. Tracy, an Alabamian killed at Port Gibson, Mississippi; and the installation in the Blakeley River was named Battery Huger for Lieutenant Commander Thomas B. Huger, also killed in fighting near New Orleans. The following month von Scheliha took over Mobile's defenses and surveyed all these works with a knowing eye. They looked good but not good enough for what he feared was coming. Furthermore, the constant action of wind, wave, and frequent rain continually degraded them. Determined to improve on what he had found, von Scheliha informed Alabama governor T. H. Watts that McIntosh and Gladden "are being reconstructed entirely." He left no doubt as to the magnitude of the task, telling the governor, "Your Excellency may form an idea of the difficulties in our way from the fact that over 120,000 cubic yards of earth are required for the construction of the parapets, bomb-proof traverses, etc.; that the earth has to be brought from a point over 10 mi. distant and that the eng. Dept. has only 4 small flats and one steamboat at its disposal to do all this work." Despite these challenges, he declared that "excellent progress is being made by pushing on the work day and night."[21]

So who, other than the very busy carpenters, engineers, and soldiers—too few—was doing all this backbreaking work? Officials had tried to entice white citizens to help early in the war, promising $2.50 a day and rations, but there were few takers. Slaves, however, had no choice, and they were put to work in gangs guarded by white overseers. Mobile had a large black population, but authorities also imported plantation slaves. In the fall of 1862, for example, the governor asked upstate planters for six hundred black workers. "The owners will be allowed a dollar a day for each slave," he promised, "to commence from his embarkation on river or railroad; transportation, subsistence and medical attendance will be furnished." Planters were requested to provide tools, clothing, and bedding. When not enough planters participated, officials sent impressment officers out to force compliance, but this action was extremely unpopular and politically risky. Once in town, the slaves were housed in cotton warehouses and presses along the river. These utilitarian structures had been planked and furnished with chimneys but still constituted primitive quarters. They were woefully overcrowded, and because they were close to the swamps at Choctaw Point, many of the people were consistently sick with fevers and pneumonia. Beginning at 7:00 a.m., the slaves were marched out to the earthworks, where they ditched and trenched almost without respite. One observer remarked: "It would be a novel sight to one unaccustomed to the presence of the sable race, to witness the crowds of darkies employed in building the fortifications. They are in such numbers that they look like ants on the side of an ant hill." The bemused detachment of this observer was about the closest to compassion that the unfortunate slave laborers could expect. Although conscientious officers such as von Scheliha wanted them healthy and well fed for efficiency's sake, harsh treatment was all too common. Von Scheliha admitted that "abuses have existed, and, unfortunately are existing yet." Perhaps even worse off than the slaves were the captured black Union soldiers. These poor men, frequently still clad in their filthy and tattered blue coats with the buttons cut off, were objects of special contempt and wrath. According to the testimony of Private Joseph Howard of Co. F, One Hundred and Tenth Regiment of U. S. Colored Infantry, he was taken prisoner in north Alabama in the fall of 1864 and sent to Mobile to "work on the fortifications." Howard was one of almost one thousand "Forrest Negroes," so-called because they had been captured by the legendary Confederate cavalry general Nathan Bedford Forrest. Once in the Port City, Howard and his compatriots were "kept at hard labor and inhumanly treated," he reported. "If we lagged or faltered or misunderstood an order we were whipped and abused, some of our own men being detailed to whip the others." Rations consisted of "corn-meal and mule meat." Fortunately for Howard, he was able to steal a skiff and slip down the river and into the bay, where he was rescued by a Union gunboat.[22]

The last piece of Mobile's defensive strategy was its naval squadron. Like the army, the navy changed commanders several times, but by September 1862 it had settled on Admiral Franklin Buchanan, an experienced hand who had served in the Mexican War, superintended the U.S. Naval Academy, and commanded the *Virginia* at Hampton Roads, besting two federal ships. (A wound forced him to miss the renowned fight with the *Monitor.*) Perhaps most important, Buchanan got along well with the army and was widely liked and respected. Surely no one envied him his task, however. The federals held undisputed sway over the gulf, had a large base on Ship Island off the Mississippi coast, and occupied Pensacola, with its navy yard and deep harbor, and New Orleans, with its vast maritime resources and shipyards. To top it all off, the Union navy enjoyed the services of Admiral David G. Farragut, one of the most accomplished seamen of the age. Simply defending Mobile Bay promised to be an enormous task, but Buchanan was nothing if not aggressive, and he nurtured the hope of eventually taking his vessels into the gulf and slugging it out with his enemy. Certainly Farragut expected nothing less—he and Buchanan had been messmates in the old navy—and he admonished his captains that if his former comrade sailed out, to "bag him and do not let him get back into the bay."[23]

Mobile River served as the epicenter of Confederate naval efforts. A naval yard was established near Hitchcock's Press at the foot of Charleston Street with a dry dock and marine railway, and other wharves were utilized at Dauphin and St. Anthony. The mostly undeveloped riverbank along Blakeley Island proved handy for some of the work, too. The government also arranged deals with independent civilian contractors to build new vessels or fit out partially constructed ones at private yards, and a few patriotic citizens pursued their own maritime schemes in machine shops. During the war two vessels were converted into warships at Mobile, two others built outright, four

Admiral Franklin Buchanan. From J. Thomas Scharf, *History of the Confederate States Navy from Its Organization to the Surrender of Its Last Vessel.* Albany, N.Y.: Joseph McDonough, 1894.

armor-plated and fitted out, and three armed. In addition, several smaller boats were constructed, and private interests launched a few torpedo boats (called Davids because their small size and deadly ability was likened to that of the Old Testament hero) and bona fide submarines. Farther upstream, a naval yard was established at Oven Bluff on the Tombigbee, and several ironclads known as Bigbee Boats were begun there but were never finished because of material shortages. On the Alabama, far from the coast, the Selma Ordnance and Naval Foundry constructed vessels, most famously the *Tennessee,* that were floated down to Mobile and finished and turned out cannon such as the 6.4-inch Brooke, an 11-foot-long instrument of death that weighed more than 10,000 pounds. The guns had to be shipped separately and mounted in Mobile lest their awesome weight ground the vessels en route. Last, the biggest ship of them all, the *Nashville,* a 270-foot side-wheeler that one of her officers called a "tremendous monster," was begun in Montgomery and then sent downstream. Had time and resources allowed, the Confederates could have counted on a sturdy little fleet of at least eight ironclads and three gunboats, enough in fondest Rebel dreams or darkest Yankee nightmares to break the blockade, retake Pensacola and New Orleans, and steam into New York harbor with defiant banners waving.[24]

In the beginning there were no ironclads, however. Other than the armed launches, hardly worth consideration, Mobile's first decent Confederate vessels were a pair of wooden side-wheel steamers christened the *Morgan* and the *Gaines.* These ships were privately built by Otis's shipyard, the *Morgan* completed between Charleston and Texas Streets and the *Gaines* between Canal and Madison Streets. Each was about two hundred feet long with a thirty-eight-foot beam, north of eight hundred tons with a draft of roughly seven feet, steam-powered and capable of about ten knots, armed with ten guns, and crewed by a little more than one hundred officers and men. As they lay alongside the river being fitted out, these ships were the object of much public interest. On February 14, 1862, the *Mobile Register* reported on the launch of the *Gaines.* "Every available space in the neighborhood was filled up to the very ways," the article began, "and though the deck was crowded there were nearly as many persons under the boat's bottom as on board." Carpenters cut away the supports, but the vessel "hung for some time" until other vessels and jack screws could coax some movement, "but when she started she went, the smoke rising from the ways as if in answer to the signal gun that announced her in motion." Amid cheering, the *Gaines* settled into the river close by her sister the *Morgan,* and the paper noted that the ships were "near enough alike to pass for twins to an unskilled eye." A few weeks later, after test runs in the rivers and bay, the newspaper followed up and announced that "the *Gaines* is the best sea boat, but the *Morgan* can run where nothing else can." The Rebel brass decided to celebrate its growing flotilla with a procession. This took place on March 9. "The *Morgan* led off from the wharf," according to the paper, "in front of the Independent Press, and was followed by the *Gaines,* which lay a little above." Their crews lined the rails and colorful flags flapped from their diminutive masts, while small boats crowded the river and crowds exulted.[25]

Eager to participate directly and to help, the public materially contributed to Mobile's ship-building efforts. A Women's Gunboat Fund was established, and the press approvingly listed contributions from all over the state. One lady sent a gold chain in memory of her father; the women of Bridgeville forwarded "jewelry, produce, etc."; and local belles "gave their jewelry and table plate, their pin cushions and fancy articles to the 'women's gunboat.'" Glad to encourage the public, officials invited the newspaper's editor to tour the *Morgan* and the *Gaines* and take a little cruise on the latter. "The new boats are a splendid success," he crowed, "a triumph of the ship building capabilities of this city and the South." Avid to exploit the new boats, the high command ordered the *Morgan* and the *Gaines* to break the blockade at once. They steamed out on April 3 and met two federal vessels just beyond the bar. Shots were exchanged with no damage or casualties on either side until the Rebel vessels sought the protection of Fort Morgan's guns. If what one of her officers said about the *Morgan* was true, discretion was definitely the better part of valor. "Her steam pipes are entirely above the water line," he remarked, "and her boilers and magazines partly above it, so we have the comfortable appearance of being blown up or scalded by any chance shot that may not take off our heads." Mobilians were disappointed, and some were critical, but until they had ironclads in their fleet there was little chance of achieving anything decisive.[26]

For more than a year, from May 1862 until early 1864, there was only one ironclad available to defend Mobile Bay, and it was hardly state-of-the-art. The *Baltic* was a side-wheel river tug purchased by the state of Alabama and hastily converted. One hundred eighty-six feet long, thirty-eight feet in the beam, and drawing a little more than six feet, she was protected by armor plating and cotton bales and mounted six guns. Her profile was typical of Civil War river ironclads, low, angled, and brooding with a tall smokestack forward and the side-wheels arching high aft, and no doubt when seen through a spyglass at several thousand yards the vessel looked dangerous enough. But the *Baltic* was woefully underpowered and at best could achieve only about five knots. It took her almost twenty-four hours to steam from town to Fort Morgan. Furthermore, she was anything but sound. One of her officers described her as "rotten as punk, and . . . as fit to go into action as a mud scow." Fortunately, the Yankees did not know any of this, and her dark outline in the bay was enough to make them nervous about launching an attack without overwhelming force. Buchanan was determined to augment his sorry flagship and engaged in a flurry of activity and correspondence to insure that when Farragut did finally steam into the bay, he would face a fleet of iron rather than wooden gunboats and a converted river tug.[27]

In order to achieve his goal, Buchanan had to create his department and administration almost from scratch. When he arrived in the Port City, he surveyed his command and its resources and remarked: "I have neither flag-captain nor flag-lieutenant, nor midshipman for aides; consequently, I have all the various duties to attend to from the grade of midshipman up. My office duties increase daily, which keeps me in the office until 3 o'clock, and then in the afternoon I visit the navy yard, navy store, ordnance, etc." On the positive side he was mostly satisfied with his sailors' early performance during their drills. "Their exercises at general quarters I have seldom seen equaled," he noted admiringly. "Our little squadron will do its duty." Soon enough, however, these common Rebel webfeet gave him headaches. As an officer aboard the *Morgan* groused, "To call the *Morgan*'s crew sailors would be disgracing the name. Out of a hundred and fifty not one is even *American*, much less a Southerner." Unsettling as that seemed, they were a rough lot to boot, more pirates than jack tars, "a desperate set of cutthroats." Buchanan concurred, stating: "There are on board some of these Steamers some of the greatest vagabonds you ever heard of. One or two hung during these times would have a wonderful effect." Buchanan did not hang them, but he quickly imposed strict naval discipline and routinely clapped malefactors in irons. He also harangued his officers, familiarizing them with regulations and ordering them to wear gray uniforms. The latter command was necessitated when a lieutenant reported to the admiral for duty wearing, Buchanan gasped, "*a black coat.*" It did not take long for Buchanan's growing contingent to realize that they were expected to be a professional military organization. There were fits and starts and ongoing bad behavior aplenty, especially drunken episodes and whoring, ever the sailor's solace, but these men were brave. As one of their officers admitted, they "never were backward in a fight."[28]

Daily life aboard Buchanan's ships and in the various batteries guarding the rivers was generally spartan, but when not patrolling down the bay, the vessels anchored in the river with the pleasures of town close by. For those in the batteries, there was constant fortification work and foul weather to be endured, but leave was regular, as were visits by civilians and military brass aboard small boats and yawls. Nathan Bedford Forrest and Raphael Semmes both toured Battery Gladden, as did soldiers' wives, girlfriends, sweethearts, and friends. On New Year's Eve 1864, a Confederate lieutenant stationed in Battery Gladden wrote of drinking the old year out with his comrades and concluded that "it was a merry crowd before morning." One Rebel webfoot aboard ship described a not altogether unpleasant routine to his wife. "We are in four watches," he wrote, "which gives me two days on duty and two days off. On my liberty days I go on to shore at half past nine and find some friends and acquaintances with whom I consume the time until 2:00 p.m. I then return to dinner (and by the way we live very well) and remain until after quarters at 4 and then go ashore until tea time. It seems precisely like living a very short distance from the city." Even Buchanan was able to unwind occasionally and have a little fun. During a river tour and ball aboard a larger steamboat attended by the Alabama governor, a military band played, "and dancing was soon got up in the splendid saloon." According to a journalist along for the ride, Buchanan, "who was looking on, joined in this, and naturally by doing so created a great deal of confusion and merriment, at which he was in high glee." Church services in town were routinely attended by religiously inclined officers and sailors. More comfortable sleeping arrangements were another advantage of their time on the Mobile River as opposed to down the bay. Some men were quartered in waterfront warehouses, and others slept in tents on open flats lashed alongside such vessels as the *Baltic,* whose casemated interior was insufferably hot during the warm months.[29]

Steadily Buchanan's squadron increased. The *Huntsville* and *Tuscaloosa* were built at Selma and floated downstream to Mobile where they were armored and fitted out. Iron plate, of which there was never enough, came from the Shelby Ironworks in central Alabama and in some instances from enterprising private citizens. On August 10, 1863, the *Mobile Evening News* described several men at "one of the upper wharves" diving "in about thirteen feet of water and groping in the mud to find some gunboat iron." According to the paper, the iron had been sitting on a flatboat when swells from a passing steamboat tipped it into the stream. The men used a block and tackle to raise the pieces, for which they got seven dollars each. But for the most part decent iron plate was as rare as hen's teeth, and authorities were continually juggling their sources and cannibalizing other projects to meet their quotas. Good engines were equally precious, and those put into the *Huntsville* and *Tuscaloosa* came from the Columbus Naval Iron Works in Georgia. Even though these vessels were small ironclads with only four guns each, the new engines proved incapable of delivering even as much headway as the sluggish *Baltic.* Buchanan was sorely disappointed when they struggled to breast the Mobile's current, and he decided to use them as floating batteries instead, supplementing the river batteries and Eastern Shore defenses. Unfortunately, like all vessels of the type, they proved terribly disagreeable for men to live on.[30]

Far more effective and impressive was the *Tennessee,* also built and launched at Selma. From the beginning there were high expectations for this vessel, and her launch was occasioned by pageantry and celebration. None other than Captain Timothy Meaher was present aboard the *Southern Republic,* which was to escort the new boat downriver. "About midday there was heard the sound of a gun," one Confederate officer recalled, "and immediately afterwards the *Tennessee* was shot into the swift current like an arrow, and the water had risen to such a height that she struck in her course the corner of a brick warehouse, situated on an adjoining bluff and demolished it. This was her first and only experience as a ram." Despite this inauspicious start, Captain Meaher towed the *Tennessee* on down the river, the *Southern Republic*'s calliope shrieking "Dixie" as they went. People lined the banks and cheered, and in Mobile big crowds joined Buchanan and other top brass turned out to see their best hope arrive.[31]

The *Tennessee* was the Confederacy's strongest vessel, and she looked just as mean as she was. Built of heavy pine and oak timbers more than two feet thick and plated with five inches of iron bolted to the wood, she was more than two hundred feet long and almost fifty feet in the beam, displaced more than one thousand tons, drew thirteen feet (a serious problem in the rivers and bay), and carried four boilers, two engines, and six guns. For weeks she lay in the river, as carpenters, mechanics, and engineers got her finished. Supplies, especially good iron, were sometimes problematical, and Buchanan had to beg, borrow, buy, and confiscate whatever was needed. There were frustrating delays, occasioned by snafus such as predrilled holes in the armor plate that did not properly align with the bolts in the timber and misplaced parts. Buchanan chafed at the inefficiency of the civilian contractors, in particular, and called one of them "an old woman" because of his inept blundering. Getting iron plates affixed to those areas of the craft just below the waterline required workers to run long timbers through the gun ports and heave the *Tennessee* over on her side against the muddy bank. Then the men could wade into waist-deep water to bolt the required plates in their proper place. Compared to the *Baltic, Huntsville,* and *Tuscaloosa,* the *Tennessee* was a behemoth, with a gun deck, berth deck, and orlop deck all connected by ladders and small square hatches. There were officers' quarters, crew's quarters, magazine, storage, and an engine room. Even though she only carried six guns, they were rifled, and the fore and aft guns were pivot, which meant they could swivel to fire in three different directions. Kate Cumming went on a tour of this fearsome warship while it lay in the river. "It is a ram, and has many a dark-looking corner where the men are to be stowed away in case of a battle," she wrote, a little unnerved. "All looked very mysterious. I certainly felt I should not like to be one of the crew." As for the crew, they were the usual foreigners, boys, and unskilled coal shovelers, all "hard characters" in Buchanan's estimation.[32]

With the completion of the *Tennessee,* Mobile was now one of the most heavily fortified and best protected cities in the Confederacy. All the strategizing and planning by top officials such as General Maury and Admiral Buchanan and engineers including Leadbetter and von Scheliha, and the prodigious grimy labor and effort of countless soldiers, sailors, carpenters, shipwrights, mechanics, slaves, prisoners, and civilians had made the city well-nigh impregnable. Or at least that was the general belief. Late in the war a *New York Times* article detailed Mobile's defenses as they had been described by deserters. It listed the three lines of earthworks circling town and noted that the middle line contained "forty-two redoubts which mount 125 guns of various calibre." The average redoubt held four guns, and the "gunners are well protected by traverses, and in many cases, by bomb-proof." The paper told of seven shore batteries on the west side of the bay down to the Dog River and enumerated "Battery Gladden, mounting eight guns," "Battery McIntosh, mounting eight guns in front and two in rear, and anchored," and a one-gun floating battery nearby, all of which thoroughly covered the mouths of the Mobile and Spanish Rivers. Then there were the pilings and the torpedoes, "which the rebels have literally sowed . . . for many months past." The lethality of these infernal devices was made manifest when two deserters from the *Tuscaloosa* struck one in their yawl "and were blown to atoms by it." The *Times*'s information was by and large accurate. Late in 1862 an English merchant named W. C. Corsan traveled through Mobile and articulated its defensive strengths: "the forts at the entrance of the bay; shore batteries all the way up; then lines of obstructions sunk, one within the other, across the channel below the city, these commanded in turn by water-batteries and iron-clad rams waiting inside to pounce upon any assailant" and, of course, the protective earthworks around the city, and, "to crown all, the power of concentrating an army of 100,000 men at Mobile, by railroad, in a very few days."[33]

The grim reality for the South, of course, was that the kind of manpower Corsan referenced was impossible to gather without leaving other theaters deserted. Reinforcements could be hurried by rail into the Port City, but even in the best of circumstances their numbers were bound to be inadequate. Throughout the war Mobile never had many more than ten thousand soldiers and sailors to man its ramparts and warships. As well constructed as the earthworks and forts were, they could not hold out for long if the defenders were thinly spaced. Ironically, one willing source of local manpower was viewed with extreme mistrust and suspicion by the high command. This was Mobile's free Creole population, who still lived in the houses and farmed land deeded to their eighteenth-century forbears and even owned slaves. On November 20, 1862, the Alabama State Legislature passed an act "for the enrollment of the 'Creole Guards' of Mobile." The act empowered Mobile's mayor, at his discretion, to "enroll such male Creoles between the ages of eighteen and fifty years who wish to be enrolled." They were to be formed into companies but "confined exclusively to the defense of the city and county of Mobile." While local officials and state solons may have been comfortable with this unusual move, Richmond was decidedly cold about formally accepting them into the army. Almost exactly a year after the act was passed, General Maury wrote to his superior in the Rebel capital and suggested that the war department "is not exactly informed about the people I have reference to." He endeavored to give them a little history lesson. "When Spain ceded this territory to the United States in 1803," he explained, "the creoles were guaranteed all the immunities and privileges of the citizens of the United States, and have continued to enjoy them up to this time." He admitted that many of them had "negro blood in the degree which disqualifies other persons of negro race from the rights of citizens, but they do not stand here on the footing of negroes." They were, he continued, "very anxious to enter the Confederate service, and I propose to make heavy artillerists of them, for which they will be admirably qualified." In conclusion, the harried Mobile general begged, "please let me hear at your earliest convenience if I may have them enrolled in a company, or in companies if I can find enough of them to make more than one company." James Seddon, secretary of war, answered in the negative. "Our position with the North and before the world will not allow the employment as armed soldiers of negroes," he wrote. Only a month later von Scheliha proposed to Alabama senator Clement C. Clay that he be allowed to develop and train a corps of black engineers. He believed such a group would be more motivated and efficient than slave labor and ultimately cost the government less. He too was rebuffed, and the Creoles remained a small local home guard.[34]

Meanwhile out in the gulf, the blockade was tightening, and more Union ships were prowling off the mouth of Mobile Bay, including more than a dozen wooden ships and four turreted monitors. Farragut was planning a run past the forts combined with an infantry assault on both the forts. If all went well, Morgan, Gaines, and Powell would be reduced and captured and lower Mobile Bay would become a lake for the Union navy. The brazen exploits of the dashing blockade-runners would be put to a stop and Mobile's strategic significance crippled. The city might hang on behind its forts and obstructions for a bit, but the Rebel river that defined it, sustained it, and linked it to the world would be corked to the south and threatened from the north by blue-clad cavalry driving for Selma. "The prospects of the Confederacy look gloomy," an officer in Battery Gladden confessed late in 1864. "Our armies are steadily diminishing. Where can we recruit?"[35]

6

Rebel Defeat

While Confederate authorities concerned themselves with strengthening Mobile's defenses and the troops at Forts Morgan and Gaines warily eyed Union warships in the gulf, several private citizens were busy developing semisubmersible and submersible vessels they hoped would break the blockade. The most notable of these were the *American Diver* and the *Hunley*. A little later the CSS *Saint Patrick* was built by a private contractor with government oversight. While postbellum Lost Cause legend portrayed such efforts as desperate and crude amid the wartime hurly-burly—the *Hunley* was said to have been converted from an old boiler—the reality was that these craft were carefully conceived, designed, and constructed. The *Hunley*'s subsequent sinking of the USS *Housatonic* off Charleston, South Carolina, was one of the American Civil War's most dramatic firsts, and it wrought a revolution in naval warfare.

The idea of using submarines to even the Confederacy's naval imbalance dated almost to the war's beginning. Only two months after Fort Sumter, a Tennessee preacher, chemist, and inventor named Franklin G. Smith wrote a letter to the *Columbia (Tenn.) Herald* that was reprinted in numerous Southern newspapers, including the *Mobile Register*. "Excepting our privateers the Confederate States have not a single ship at sea," Reverend Smith lamented. But he had a solution. "Throughout our Southern seaports, men of a mechanical turn and the right spirit must go to work, maturing the best plans for the destruction or capture of every blockading ship. From the Chesapeake to the mouth of the Rio Grande, our coast is better fitted for submarine warfare than any other in the world. I would have every hostile keel chased from our coast by submarine propellers." Smith declared that a successful submarine must be "cigar shaped for speed—made of plate iron, joined without external rivet heads, about 30 feet long, with a central section about 4 x 3 feet, driven by a spiral propeller, a fishtail sculler, or, (far better) by a steam engine occupying the after part of the boat." There is evidence that several such vessels were subsequently built by Smith, including one sunk at Memphis, and perhaps the "submarine apparatus" referred to in the January 5, 1862, letter to Major Leadbetter as having been sabotaged in Mobile River.[1]

Such early attempts are shadowy and difficult to document because they did not involve the government, frequently took place in secret, and left no paper trail. But in the spring of 1862 a trio of determined inventors fled New Orleans and arrived in Alabama's Port City, bringing Mobile's submarine history more fully into the light. They were Horace Hunley, a thirty-eight-year-old lawyer and sugar broker; James McClintock, a thirty-two-year-old engineer, machine-shop owner, and former riverboat pilot; and his partner Baxter Watson, about whom little is known. Hunley was the front man and represented the hope of the enterprise. Because of his wealth, business network, and social polish, he proved to be an effective salesman and fund-raiser. McClintock was the operation's mechanical brains, having puzzled the engineering challenges and drawn the plans, and Watson assisted. While still in the Crescent City the three had built a submarine known as the *Pioneer* and actually received a letter of marque from the Confederate government to operate her as a privateer. But when Farragut took the city they scuttled the boat in Lake Ponchatrain and brought their scheme to Mobile.[2]

Desirous of official support if they could get it, the men called on General Maury and explained their plans. Maury was only a little older than Hunley, but he was also a blooded veteran whom they might well have expected to be cynical of newfangled ideas. Nonetheless, he proved to be open-minded and intrigued by their presentation. He did not give them any money, but he did endorse the project, and, more concretely, made the resources of the Park and Lyons Machine Shop available to them. The partners surely viewed this as a godsend. While the shop was not as large as some they had known in New Orleans, it was more than adequate, with a foundry, several open-sided worksheds, and assembly yards. It had all the requisite tools and equipment that would be needed, including chain falls, hoists, pulleys, forges, weights, tongs, and hammers, not to mention a competent labor force. In addition to this excellent facility, the New Orleans men gained important new partners and allies. They were the shop's owners, Park and Lyons, as well as a British-born mechanical engineer named William A. Alexander. The latter had enlisted in the Twenty-first Alabama Infantry but because of his mechanical skill had been assigned to the machine shop to supervise the rifle-barrel boring work. Maury specifically ordered Alexander to quit that job and devote his full energies to helping Hunley's team. Also taking a great interest in the project was one of Alexander's comrades, twenty-two-year-old First Lieutenant George E. Dixon, who would later captain the *Hunley* on its final and decisive voyage.[3]

The men went to work, and by year's end they had a submarine boat almost ready. This was the *American Diver,* or *Pioneer II* as it was sometimes called, and though precise drawings and descriptions are lacking, its general appearance and design were not dissimilar to those recommended by Reverend Smith in his early letter. Essentially it looked like a big cigar, or, as McClintock put it, "twelve feet of each end was built tapering or molded, to make her easy to pass through the water." Bow planes allowed the boat to dive, and it was steered by a single rudder. Propulsion was McClintock's biggest engineering challenge, and he invested considerable energy attempting to develop and install an electric motor, and when this failed, a steam engine, which proved impractical. "There was much time and money lost," the frustrated engineer later said, and he was forced to rely instead on human muscle power turning a long propeller shaft to move the boat. The *American Diver*'s crew consisted of five men, four seated on a bench to turn the shaft and a fifth who stood erect in the bow, his head poking up into a short conning tower with glass ports. Early tests, whether in the river or bay is not clear, though most references indicate the bay, revealed an unanticipated and unusual problem. When the vessel was submerged, the captain had difficulty knowing whether the craft was under way, "as there are no passing objects by which to recognize the fact of motion." After the war McClintock admitted to British navy officials that more than once the men "continued working the crank while all the time the boat was hard and fast in the mud." Even when moving, the *American Diver* managed only a pitiful two knots. Her sole weapon consisted of a torpedo in tow. The method of attack was to dive beneath an enemy and the pull the torpedo into the ship's side, after which the submarine would retreat.[4]

Despite the imperfections and difficulties, by February 1863 it was decided to send the *American Diver* on the offensive. This meant getting Admiral Buchanan's approval. He had authority over what happened in area waters, and he was a far tougher sell than Maury. Nonetheless, in the end he was willing to try anything, and the *American Diver* was towed down the bay with the intent of attacking the blockading fleet. The result was a disaster. Just off Mobile Point the currents were fierce and there was a heavy chop. The little vessel foundered when seawater poured into her open hatches. Fortunately the crew scrambled out, but the boat was lost and Buchanan remained unconvinced. "I never entertained but one opinion as to the result of this Boat," he growled, "that it would prove a failure." Buchanan's skepticism stemmed not only from the engineering challenges, as yet not satisfactorily overcome, but also from the shallowness of Alabama's coastal waters. Even if the boat had worked, he observed, it could not be effective "against the enemy off the harbor as the blockading vessels are anchored in water too shoal to permit the boat to pass under them." Disappointed, but undeterred, Hunley and company redoubled their efforts back at the machine shop.[5]

Unfortunately for Hunley's personal finances, he had spent most of his available funds on the *American Diver*, and he was thus forced to find investors and expand the partnership. Luckily investors proved easy to recruit, not only for the novelty of the enterprise but also because the Confederate government promised citizens 50 percent of the value of any enemy ships sunk. Patriotism and profit made a compelling combination. Hunley's new team became known as the Singer Submarine Corps, named for Edgar Collins Singer, a Texas gunsmith and mechanical engineer who had invented the Singer Torpedo. Singer was in town on a navy contract to seed the rivers and bay with his new device, which operated by a simple plunger. His opinions on the best way to deliver a torpedo by submarine were earnestly sought by Hunley. Other partners included A. A. "Gus" Whitney, J. D. Breaman, R. W. Dunn, and James Jones. The budget for the new submarine was a hefty fifteen thousand dollars, of which Whitney bought a one-fifth share. Probably for this reason the craft was sometimes called Whitney's Submarine Boat. Hunley himself was reduced to purchasing a meager four-hundred-dollar share.[6]

Once again the workmen at Park and Lyons bent to their task, and parts for the new vessel began to accumulate under the sheds. Conscious of prying eyes, the Submarine Corps decided to move the construction phase into the Seamen's Bethel located eight blocks south on Church Street and only three blocks from the river. Built in 1860, this was an elegant brick church with Gothic windows and doors, bracketed eaves, and a modest steeple. It had been provided to improve spiritual services to seamen in port, but with the departure of the Lower Fleet and the blockade, it was empty and available. Banging and rasping away with hammers and saws, carpenters removed the pews and floors to allow the submarine's keel to be laid more efficiently. Even in the bethel though, security was somewhat lax. Much later an old Mobilian recalled his childhood during the war years. "I was a small boy at the time," he remembered, "and would go every evening with the boys in the neighborhood to witness this part of the construction and to play about the boat." A Rebel deserter told Union officials that he had seen the boat "in all stages of construction at Mobile." If anything then, the new venture was an open secret, and anxious parties on both sides awaited more news.[7]

Shortly after the turn of the century, Alexander wrote a detailed description of the submarine's construction. His memories have been a standard reference for years, but after the *Hunley* was raised from the ocean floor in 2000 and carefully examined, certain inaccuracies in his account became evident, understandable given the fact that he was remembering events forty years in the past. According to Alexander, a cylindrical boiler was cut in two and then expanded with the addition of two twelve-inch-wide longitudinal strips. The bow and stern were fitted with cast cones, which made the vessel "30 feet long, 4 feet wide, and 5 feet deep." Alexander even produced a drawing, which showed a long straight-sided tube with abruptly pointed ends, crewed by nine men. In reality, as quickly became evident after the *Hunley* was raised, the submarine was anything but a slap-dash contraption. Several people commented on the fact that when viewed bow on or from above the vessel looked like a porpoise, with gently tapering ends. Indeed, during the boat's construction the partners began calling it the *Fish Boat* (only after its transfer to Charleston was it known as the *Hunley*). This was clearly more than an obligatory moniker for a vessel intended to maneuver beneath the waves. The boat actually looked like an exotic sea creature. Not surprisingly, this elegant appearance was not the result of a repurposed old boiler. Modern analysis shows the *Fish Boat* to have been beautifully designed and fabricated. It was fashioned of forty-two wrought-iron plates meeting together with no overlap and affixed to interior butt straps. The outside rivet heads were hammered flush, to reduce drag, and the bow and

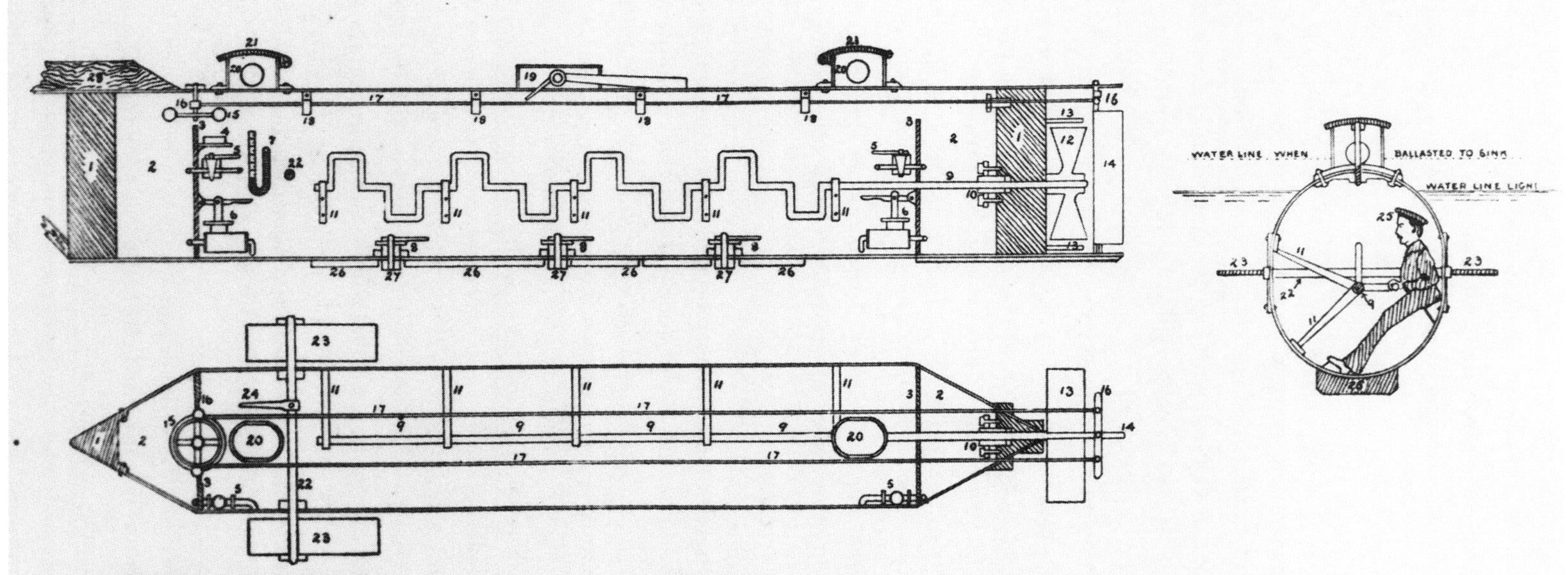

From sketches by W. A. Alexander.

CONFEDERATE STATES SUBMARINE TORPEDO BOAT H. L. HUNLEY. LONGITUDINAL ELEVATION, PLAN, AND TRANSVERSE SECTIONAL VIEWS.

1. The bow and stern castings; 2, water-ballast tanks; 3, tank bulkheads; 4, compass; 5, sea cocks; 6, pumps; 7, mercury gauge; 8, keel-ballast stuffing boxes; 9, propeller shaft and cranks; 10, stern bearing and gland; 11, shaft braces; 12, propeller; 13, wrought ring around propeller; 14, rudder; 15, steering wheel; 16, steering lever; 17, steering rods; 18, rod braces; 19, air box; 20, hatchways; 21, hatch covers; 22, shaft of side fins; 23, side fins; 24, shaft lever; 25, one of the crew turning propeller shaft; 26, cast-iron keel ballast; 27, bolts; 28, butt end of torpedo boom.

Hunley sketch by Alexander. From *Official Records of the Union and Confederate Navies in the War of the Rebellion,* series 1, volume 15 (Washington, D.C., 1906).

stern were made of specially cast iron pieces. The length was forty feet, not thirty, the boat was four feet high, and crewed by eight men rather than nine.[8]

Other details Alexander got right, such as the rudder, bow and stern ballast tanks, sea-cocks that could be opened to flood the tanks, iron castings fitted to the keel that could be released to lighten the boat in an emergency, the dive planes operated by a lever, the mercury depth gauge, a compass, the paired conning towers with hatchways sealed by rubber gaskets (though he misremembered the exact dimensions—they are twenty inches wide and Alexander stated sixteen), and the "wrought iron ring or band" surrounding the propeller "to guard against a line being thrown in to foul it." But once modern researchers had cleaned out the *Hunley* and studied it further, they were even more impressed by the vessel's engineering. To begin with, the crank shaft did not run down the center of the boat, as Alexander had indicated in his drawing, but rather off-center. Had the shaft run down the center, the men could have sat erect along their wooden bench as they turned it, but this would have unbalanced the craft, necessitating the use of heavy counterweights on the opposite side. Instead, with the shaft off-center, the men were required to hunch over it as they turned it. This balanced the vessel's center of gravity and eliminated the need for bulky counterweights. And while the men's position was anything but comfortable—one recent writer called the boat's interior "an ergonomic nightmare"—their labors were nicely assisted by a set of differential gears that turned the propeller, multiplying and smoothing their force. In contrast to the *American Diver,* the *Fish Boat* could manage four knots, still slow but workable. A series of small glass deadlights ran along the top of the vessel to help illuminate the interior, and the conning tower had larger glass portholes that allowed the pilot to steer visually when conditions allowed. Once the vessel was submerged, a candle provided minimal light, and its flame also served to alert the crew when the oxygen level was falling. Last, to enhance the effectiveness of the deadlights and the meager candle the interior was painted white. In sum, McClintock had done his homework, and the *Fish Boat* represented a state-of-the-art submarine for its day. Given the right conditions and a properly trained and drilled crew, there was every reason to expect this vessel to make history.[9]

Come July 1863 it was finally time to launch the submarine and put it through its paces. Unlike the *American Diver,* which appears to have been mostly tested in the bay, the *Fish Boat* was first operated in the Mobile River downtown. This was a sagacious choice for several reasons—the river was deeper than the bay, confined and more protected, and less prone to heavy chop, which had done in the earlier sub. Getting the vessel out of the bethel presented a minor difficulty when workmen had to cut away some of the interior columns to make room. But once they did, what had been an open secret became public knowledge. The trim *Fish Boat* emerged through the bethel doors and, as one man later described the event, "was placed upon a wagon and taken to the slip at the foot of Theatre street where she was launched into the Mobile River." People crowded the banks that July as the *Fish Boat* cavorted about the river, diving, surfacing and proceeding from point to point. At last, on July 31 the vessel's full range of capabilities was demonstrated for a gaggle of Rebel brass that included Admiral Buchanan, General Maury, Capt. J. D. Johnston (soon to have command of the *Tennessee*), and General James E. Slaughter, one of General Bragg's confidants and a capable artillerist. Hunley himself was not present that day, having left shortly before on a journey through the South—whether on some sort of secret mission or to try and shore up his declining business fortunes is not certain. Nonetheless, the other partners and mechanics were on hand to see the results of their handiwork. The demonstration took place, just as the initial launch had, off the Theatre Street wharf. The crew clambered into the vessel through the narrow hatchways one at a time, holding their arms over their heads to squeeze through. Once inside they took their places along the bench as the pilot stood in the bow and checked his compass. With the officers and a large public watching from the banks, the *Fish Boat* cast off and, towing a live Singer Torpedo at the end of a two-hundred-foot tether, steered toward a coal flat anchored mid-river. Summers are insufferable along the Gulf Coast, and the vessel's interior must have been infernally hot, the men laboring in shirtsleeves. Just offshore the pilot depressed the diving planes, and the vessel disappeared. He then lit a candle as the men turned their crank and the *Fish Boat* glided down into Mobile River murkiness. At twenty feet the boat leveled and passed under the flatboat. The men kept driving the vessel forward until the torpedo hit the coal flat and a terrific explosion confirmed their success. No doubt there were lusty cheers onshore, but aboard the cramped vessel with its sweating iron walls and close atmosphere the men were rocked by the concussion and thrown off their rhythm. They quickly restarted their cranking, however, and soon the *Fish Boat* broke the surface well beyond the smoking remains of the flat. Exhausted, overheated, and panting for breath, the crew threw open the hatches to raucous celebration from the dazzled witnesses, Buchanan not least among them. Convinced now that the submarine indeed had military utility, but equally certain that Mobile Bay was not the place for it, he wrote to the commander of naval forces at Charleston and offered him the boat. "To judge from the experiment of yesterday," the admiral declared, "I am fully satisfied it can be used successfully in blowing up one or more of the enemy's Iron Clads in your harbor." Thus, during the second week of August, the *Fish Boat* was hoisted out of the river, placed aboard two railroad flatcars, and covered with a heavy tarp. The army lieutenant in charge of getting the submarine loaded predicted a brilliant future: "It will become in a very short time one of the great celebrities in the art of defense and attack on floating objects." And so it did, though not without first killing several brave crews that included Hunley and Thomas Park among them. But all of that was in another theater, and the tale has been thoroughly and often told.[10]

The *American Diver* and the *Fish Boat* were not the only submarines to course Mobile waters during the war. Late in 1864 another such innovative vessel was completed at the naval yard in Selma and sent to the Port City. On June 16 of that year the chief of the ordnance works there, Catesby ap Roger Jones, wrote to General Maury about the submarine: "It is to be propelled by steam (the engine is very compact), though under water by hand. There are also arrangements for raising and descending at will, for attaching the torpedo to the bottom of vessels, etc. Its first field of operation will be off Mobile Bay, and I hope you may soon have evidence of its success." The Union learned about the vessel as well when a spy named Edward La Croix described it as a "torpedo boat, length, about 30 feet; has water-tight compartments; . . . is propelled by a very small engine, and will just stow in 5 men." La Croix further reported that this boat was "a good sailer on the river and has gone to Mobile to make last preparations for trying its efficacy on the Federal vessels."[11]

The new vessel was the *St. Patrick,* designed and built by a man named John P. Halligan, a private contractor, though he soon scored a naval lieutenant's commission and was placed in command of the boat. La Croix had gotten some of his facts wrong, but overall he was not far off. The *St. Patrick* was in reality a little bigger than the *Fish Boat,* being almost fifty feet long, six feet wide and ten feet deep. By all accounts its steam engine was good and moved the boat efficiently on the surface. As Jones noted, once submerged, the crew, of whom there were seven counting Halligan, manually cranked the propeller. The method of attack was a twelve-foot boom attached to the bow with a torpedo on the end (a mode perfected by the *Hunley* as superior to towing, especially in rough water where the torpedo could be dangerously tossed around). Once in Mobile, Maury was most anxious that Halligan immediately take his craft on the offensive. This was after the Battle of Mobile Bay, and the Union navy had the run of the lower bay and was even probing the upper defenses. But Halligan proved timid, and he dithered. Exasperated, the desperate general wrote to the high command that he had told Halligan that if he did not "attack at once I would place an officer in charge of her who would." In response the officious contractor lieutenant "placed his affairs in the hands of a lawyer and procured from Richmond a transfer of his boat to the naval commander of this station." Since the Battle of Mobile Bay and Buchanan's wounding and capture, Mobile's naval command had now devolved on Ebenezer Farrand, who was not as interested in cooperating with the army as his predecessor had been. Maury appealed to President Jefferson Davis to break the deadlock, and the executive ordered Farrand to give the vessel to the army. Maury then assigned command of the *St. Patrick* to an eager young naval officer named Lieutenant John T. Walker. But when Walker boarded the vessel, he found that Halligan had absconded with several vital parts and was ensconced in the Battle House Hotel. Using what Maury termed "energetic and good management"—one can imagine the confrontation!—Walker "recovered . . . the necessary machinery and thinks he can operate tomorrow night." On the night of January 27, 1865, Walker finally got under way, and attacked the Union gunboat *Octorara,* lying off the Eastern Shore near the mouths of the Blakeley and Apalachee Rivers. It was a harum-scarum affair, with the *St. Patrick* approaching on the surface and scraping against the *Octorara*'s side, the torpedo misfiring, and a Yankee tar grabbing the smokestack while his mates poured musket fire down onto the submarine.

The *St. Patrick* broke off the attack and returned to Mobile, playing no further significant role in the war. Maury was satisfied by Walker's attempt, but the overall army commander for the region was disgusted by all the shenanigans leading up to it. "The navy at Mobile is a farce," he groused. "Its vessels are continually tied up at the wharf; never in cooperation with the army."[12]

Confederate authorities and ordinary citizens had high hopes for these endeavors, but despite the *Fish Boat*'s spectacular destruction of the coal flat and the *St. Patrick*'s daring nocturnal assault on the USS *Octorara,* none of them loosened the blockade a jot. As the war progressed, the material shortages suffered by Mobilians expanded beyond the New England ice noted by Cumming to include virtually everything under the sun, from ribbons and buttons to coffee, sugar, and paper. The situation was so bad that in the autumn of 1863 hundreds of poor women marched down Dauphin Street carrying signs that read "Bread and Peace" and "Bread or Blood." Armed with hatchets and household items such as brooms they broke into stores and looted food and clothing. Maury called out troops to quell the disturbance, but the sympathetic soldiers refused to act. Finally the mayor appeared and promised relief to the rioters. Their energy expended and some immediate need satisfied by this rampage, they were mollified by his speech and dispersed. In the aftermath the mayor was as good as his word, forming relief committees that helped somewhat, and though there was ongoing want, there were no further crises like the Bread Riot.[13]

If the blockade could not be broken by submarines, torpedo boats, or wooden gunboats like the *Gaines, Morgan,* or *Selma,* it could be penetrated by daring captains aboard fast vessels. Tempted by handsome profits to be made running cotton down to Cuba and returning with military and civilian supplies, ship owners and their captains frequently made the attempt. On August 8, 1862, the *Mobile Register* reported that "a fine schooner was to be seen just about sunset yesterday evening, lying off Matthew's Press, concerning which all we are able to state is that she ran in yesterday morning in the face of the blockade, and that her cargo consists chiefly of powder, lead, caps, salt, coffee, cavalry sabers and soap." Such arrivals at the city's doorstep by light-draft runners were always an occasion of great excitement among locals, and those with waterfront contacts took to giving the captains their personal shopping lists. Confederate authorities were interested only in military cargo, but many a Mobile wife delighted in a small package handed her by an old salt that included needles and thread, calico, paper, ink, and perhaps Cuban cigars for the man in her life (if he was still at home) and hard candy for the children. The writer Augusta Jane Evans was happy when one captain promised to bring her "the finest gold pen in Cuba" on his next voyage, freeing her from the inelegant steel nibs she had been using. Mobile being Mobile, liquor was among the most popular imports, and one vessel's haul during a single voyage included a keg of bourbon whiskey, a keg of brandy, twelve boxes of sauterne wine, eleven boxes of champagne, twelve large cases of gin, and twelve bottles of Jamaica rum.[14]

Blockade-running was dangerous to be sure with the Union navy continually on the prowl, but the odds favored it dramatically. During the war there were more than two hundred attempts at Mobile, and better than 80 percent of these were successful. While any and all kinds of vessels were used, the slower ones were soon captured, and the captains and owners, some of them foreign, grew to depend on a newer style of fast steamer that rode low in the water and could outrun the swiftest Yankee warship. One of these was the British vessel *Denbigh,* jokingly called "the mail-packet" by Union sailors for her regular runs into and out of Mobile Bay. The *Denbigh* was an iron-hulled side-paddle steamer launched in 1860. She was 182 feet long, 22 feet in the beam, and registered at just north of 162 tons. She drew about seven feet and so could run directly up to the city over the Dog River and Choctaw Bars, carried twenty-one officers and men, and was a greyhound on the gulf, boasting a top speed of almost fourteen knots. This remarkable dash was the result of feathering side wheels that could whirl at thirty-nine revolutions per minute. The *Heroine* was another successful blockade-runner; an iron-hulled side-wheeler like the *Denbigh,* she was 179 feet long, 19 feet in the beam, 214 tons, and ultra fast. Not surprisingly, given the attractive profit margins—as much as 500 percent—as well as the added joy of tweaking the hated Yankee, Captain Timothy Meaher turned his hand to blockade-running and built the *Grey Jacket* at his shipyard. This vessel was a marvel of expert nautical design and workmanship. A Union captain later opined that she was "one of the most perfect sea boats he ever saw"—and Meaher himself strode her deck during her runs.[15]

Getting into Mobile Bay required thorough knowledge of local waters, and savvy captains such as Meaher knew they had three choices. The least attractive was the Pelican Channel, a shallow approach that crossed the old anchorage at Dauphin Island first used by the colonial French more than a century and a half earlier. The main channel ran north–south just off Mobile Point and crossed a bar with twenty-one feet of water. Finally, to the east was the Swash Channel, a twelve-foot-deep course that hugged the Fort Morgan peninsula. The main channel could be difficult to navigate, especially at night, and was closely guarded, so blockade-runners generally favored the Swash Channel where Confederate batteries at the fort and field pieces to the east could keep the Union ships at a safe distance. Given that most captains preferred to race in or out in the dirtiest weather imaginable in order to better screen their vessels, the risks of running aground were significant. Nonetheless, these intrepid gamblers succeeded again and again, to the frustration of their Union adversaries. Farragut called the *Denbigh*'s captain a "bold rascal" and vowed "if I get him he will see the rest of his days of the war [in prison]."[16]

No other aspect of the Civil War at sea contains as many wild scenes of derring-do as blockade-running, and Mobilians thrilled to the triumphs and deeply regretted the failures of these captains. Two local incidents stand out for their excitement and consequences—the successful entry and exit of the CSS *Florida* in late 1862 and early 1863 and the capture of Meaher's *Grey Jacket* on New Year's Eve 1863. The *Florida* was a sleek Rebel warship with three raked masts and double smokestacks. She steamed out of Havana on September 1, 1862, to make the run into Mobile. Her captain's aim was to recruit a full crew there and acquire accessories needed to fire his guns. Circumstances were less than ideal for this voyage. Not only was the *Florida* unable to fight if cornered, but her small crew was wracked by yellow fever. Undeterred, the vessel's captain set his course and trusted to the fates. He was John Newland Maffitt, the very same who had sailed into Mobile Bay as a loyal United States naval officer just before the war and threatened ruin to secessionist hotheads. Now a Rebel sea captain in gray, Maffitt steered his fast new ship north. On the afternoon of the September 4, his lookout sighted Fort Morgan, and Maffitt reveled in the gorgeous scenery. "There was not a cloud in the sky," he later wrote, "or a zephyr breath on the sea, to disturb the serenity of the surroundings." While it was a pretty day to be out on the water, it was folly to run the blockade in such weather, and Union ships steaming his way soon took Maffitt's mind off the view. In an effort to bluff his way in, he ordered the British flag raised and put on a full head of steam. The ten-gun warship USS *Oneida* attempted to cut him off, but when Maffitt sheered his vessel directly toward the blockader, the Union captain hesitated. It was now "dash ahead, trusting to fortune and a clean pair of heels," Maffitt wrote, and at a distance of only eighty yards the *Oneida* opened fire and was soon joined by two other pursuers. Amid a hail of "rapid and precise" gunfire, Maffitt lashed himself to the rail while shrapnel and splinters flew about him and men were wounded aboard. Aloft in the rigging where sailors were setting the top gallants to increase speed, one man lost the bottom of his foot; on deck another a finger; and below decks a third his head when a round shot crashed through the side. On the *Florida* plowed, Maffitt grimly holding her side. "The loud explosions, roar of shot and shell, crashing spars and rigging, mingled with the moans of our sick and wounded, instead of intimidating, only increased our determination to enter the destined harbor." Finally the *Florida* reached the range of Fort Morgan's guns and the Union warships fell away. She anchored inside Mobile Bay at last, where the *Morgan* and *Gaines* steamed toward her, "their crews cheering as they approached."[17]

Because of the yellow fever, the *Florida* was quarantined immediately, but during the following days visitors thronged the battered ship's sides in small boats, shouting up congratulations. From the city a proud Buchanan wrote to Maffitt, "You will please inform the officers and crew that as Admiral commanding this station I fully appreciate their gallantry." For his part Maffitt was relieved to have discharged his duties so well. Too ill to as yet visit the city, he became a celebrity nonetheless—"The papers are full of it"—and he wrote that his cabin "is like a flower garden." His female admirers also sent "jellies, cakes and delicacies." Maffitt and his skeleton crew soon healed well enough to leave their shell-shot vessel and recover more fully in town. The *Florida* was anchored off the Dog River Bar, and workmen traveled down to begin repairs. As for his Union pursuers, there was no adulation. The captain of the *Oneida* signed his incident report to Farragut "with great mortification" and was relieved of command as soon

CSS *Florida*. From J. Thomas Scharf, *History of the Confederate States Navy from Its Organization to the Surrender of Its Last Vessel*. Albany, N.Y.: Joseph McDonough, 1894.

as the news reached Lincoln's desk. Secretary of the Navy Gideon Welles was furious and became an international laughing stock. A flurry of official correspondence ensued aimed at insuring such a breach never happened again.[18]

By January 1863 the *Florida* was at last ready to make the run out, and Buchanan suggested that Maffitt paint the vessel "lead color" to reduce her visibility. On the stormy evening of January 16—"the pilot said it was too dark to see Light-House Island"—Maffitt made his move with "all the steam and canvas that could be applied . . . over rugged seas." He was chased, but he had the advantage and the *Florida* escaped. Her subsequent career as a commerce raider was devastating to the Union merchant fleet, driving up shipping rates and forcing American vessels to seek foreign registration. Years later, Admiral David D. Porter called the navy's failure to capture the *Florida* on her runs into and out of Mobile Bay "the greatest example of blundering committed throughout the war." But the former commander of the CSS *Alabama*, Admiral Raphael Semmes, who knew whereof he spoke, declared the episode "the most daring and gallant" in a war that had been full of them.[19]

Timothy Meaher—rich, influential, determined—was not as fortunate as Maffitt when it came to the blockade. In late December 1863 he loaded his *Grey Jacket* with 513 brand-spanking-new bales of cotton, 25 barrels of rosin, some turpentine and tobacco, and with 22 passengers and crew sailed past the Choctaw Point Light, down the bay, and out into the gulf. It was the proverbial dark and stormy night—"a gale and very heavy cross sea"—ideal conditions for such an attempt. Just off the Mobile Bar *Grey Jacket*'s ghostly stack of sails was spotted by the USS *Kennebec*, which immediately gave chase. Meaher's vessel was fast, and she quickly outpaced her pursuer in the darkness. Piling on canvas in a full gale could have negative consequences, however, and as *Grey Jacket* smashed across the swells in howling wind and driving rain her masts and spars were damaged and her engine broke down as well, effectively crippling her. On the morning of December 31, *Kennebec* caught up. "I fired a gun across her bow," the Union captain reported, "when she hauled down her colors and hove to." Whether or not Meaher, a native Mainer, appreciated the irony of being apprehended by a ship named for that state's most important river is unknown, but his blockade-running career was finished. His passengers and crew were transferred to the USS *Colorado,* while he, the chief mate, and the lead engineer were sent into New Orleans aboard the captured vessel.[20]

In the Crescent City the trio was separately interviewed. Meaher stated that he was born in Maine but had lived in Mobile for thirty years. "I am a citizen," he continued, "of the *State of Alabama, to which I owe allegiance*" (italics original). He then claimed that he had sailed out of Mobile Bay under the American flag, that he was the sole owner of the cargo, and that he was Havana bound. The mate contradicted Meaher in his interview, stating that the *Grey Jacket* sailed "under English colors and had no other." He also reported that the vessel was owned by Timothy and James Meaher together and that they only owned half the cargo. *"The balance was for Confederate government account."* This was damning and confirmed by a document found on board and entered as evidence. It was titled *"Memo. of agreements made between Messrs. Meaher & Bro., owners of the st'r Gray Jacket, and Henry Meyers, major and ch'f ord. officer, acting for the gover't of the C. S."* According to the memo, the Confederate government had supplied the "whole cargo of cotton, and will make over to the owners of the vessel one-half of the cotton, in consideration of which the owners do agree to deliver the other half, belonging to the government, at Havana, free of further charge, except the one-half of the expenses of compressing and storing incurred at Mobile." The government was also to be given "at least one-half of the carrying capacity of the steamer in the return voyage." This, in a nutshell, was how blockade-running worked, and Meaher had been caught red handed.[21]

Nothing in Meaher's life to this point would suggest that he lacked audacity, and several months after the interview he filed what he termed "a claim, and *answer* to the libel." One can only imagine the incredulous smiles that must have greeted Meaher's subsequent shaggy-dog story. He had been living at Mobile when the war began, he admitted, but afterward "gave no aid" to the Rebels. His sole interest was to protect his considerable assets. The only way to do this, he believed, was to get them out of the country. "And he now avers," the official account of his claim read, "the truth to be that his right of property in the said steamer and in her cargo, which was *full and complete while the same were in the port of Mobile,* continued to be full and complete after he had gotten upon the high seas with the intent of escaping from the power and control of the States in rebellion." Perhaps suspecting that this ridiculous argument might not do the trick, Meaher further stated that in any case he was covered by a presidential pardon dated "8th December, A. D. 1863." This pardon "declared to all persons who had participated in the existing rebellion ... that a full pardon is granted to them and each of them, with restoration of all rights of property except as to slaves and in *property cases where rights of third parties shall have intervened,* upon the condition that every such person shall take and subscribe an oath ... that he is not embraced by the exceptions made by the same oath." He had taken this loyalty oath, Meaher said, on March 18, 1864. He met the conditions and was due a full pardon and "a bar to any future proceedings." That the man who had illegally imported slaves and supported filibusters before the war, enthusiastically endorsed secession, escorted the formidable ram *Tennessee* down the Alabama River with his steamboat's calliope shrieking "Dixie" the entire way, and brazenly run the blockade in collusion with the Confederate authorities could say any of this with a straight face is ample evidence of just how audacious Timothy Meaher could be. He had gotten far by such techniques, but his bold claims were summarily dismissed. The *Grey Jacket* was converted into a Yankee gunboat and its cargo seized by the United States government.[22]

While Meaher wangled with the federal authorities in New Orleans, Admiral Buchanan decided that the *Tennessee* was at last ready for action and ordered her down the bay. The massive ironclad was commissioned on February 16, 1864, "the colors hoisted," and James D. Johnston appointed captain. Johnston's subsequent entries in the vessel's log vividly illustrate how involved and challenging just getting the *Tennessee* to its appointed station proved to be. The main problem of course was that the ironclad drew thirteen feet, and both the Choctaw and Dog River Bars were several feet shallower than that. Anticipating the problem, Buchanan had ordered several camels built. These "were huge boxes curved to fit the sides of the helpless *Tennessee,*" remembered William Rix, a Vermonter who had been trapped in the Port City by the hostilities. "They were so constructed that after having been put in place and water let in by an aperture in the bottom, they would sink to the required depth. Then, after slinging the ship to them by chains passed under the bottom, and pumping out the water, the buoyancy would be sufficient to float the whole over the bar, 'like wanton boys swimming on bladders.'"[23]

But the *Tennessee* was so ponderous and heavy that even getting her to the river mouth began to look like a Herculean task. On February 20 Johnston wrote in the log that Buchanan came on board at eleven that morning, and the vessel was taken in tow by the *Baltic,* which then proceeded upriver with her charge. The intent was to round Blakeley Island and steam down the Spanish River, a common route that avoided Choctaw Bar. Just north of town, however, the *Tennessee* grounded. She was successfully refloated but again grounded several hours later. The CSS *Selma* then "passed a hawser to the bows of the *Baltic* to assist in towing," but still the big ironclad would not budge. There she sat for an inglorious week until two other steamers were lashed alongside of her and at last pushed her forward. The following day just after lunch, Johnston recorded that the *Tennessee* had finally anchored in "5 fathoms water and veered to 15 fathoms chain. Spanish River Battery bearing due south, distance 1 mile." And there she sat for a month, waiting for the camels to be finished by the frenzied carpenters in the naval yard when disaster struck. As Rix described the incident, "the camels were at last completed and the calkers at work during the last night filling the seams with oakum when an awkward foot upset a can of turpentine, which by some means became ignited, and both fabrics were utterly destroyed." Exasperated, Buchanan ordered them rebuilt, and the *Tennessee* returned to the naval yard.[24]

By mid-May everything was again ready to make the attempt, and the *Tennessee* was taken in tow by the *Morgan* with a seven-inch hawser, and the steamer *Magnolia.* "At 1:45 p.m.," Johnston recorded, "the *Morgan* parted her hawser, and the wind catching the *Magnolia,* drove her on the banks, where she became jammed by the ship. Got out kedge from starboard at 2:30 and commenced kedging and backing the ship around." The kedge was an anchor that was thrown out some distance from a ship and used to pull, or warp, the vessel afloat again. Between the kedge and the other vessels, the ironclad floated free and by suppertime came "to anchor near the obstructions in 2 fathoms." Choctaw Bar thus bypassed, the vessel was ordered on south—but the camels could not provide enough buoyancy to ride over the nine-foot depth at the Dog River Bar. Buchanan was beside himself. "What folly to build vessels up our rivers which cannot cross the bars at the mouths," he fussed.[25]

Fortunately, Buchanan had anticipated the problem, and extra camels were standing by. With three of the big boxes now flanking each side of the *Tennessee,* they were pumped dry and the warship steadily elevated to a seven-foot draft, "like a giant on stilts," as Johnston put it. On May 18 she got over the bar, and Buchanan wrote to a friend, "I wish you could see the *Tennessee,* she is a man-of-war." Finally arrived at Fort Morgan, the excited admiral wanted to sally forth immediately and smash his erstwhile shipmate. Maddeningly, the *Tennessee* grounded again, and when she was refloated the weather and sea conditions were unfavorable for an attack. Furthermore, the element of surprise had been lost. Farragut, brass spyglass pressed to his eye, was studying this fearsome new vessel, and, though sobered, he was confident. "Let him come," he remarked of his old comrade. "I have a fine squadron to meet him, all ready and willing." Much as he would have wished to, however, Buchanan was fated to be a defender rather than an aggressor. Farragut had all the ships, ironclads, and troops he needed, and as his fleet gathered off the Mobile Bar, the Confederates knew the great contest was nigh.[26]

On the evening of July 27 the *Denbigh* ran safely out of Mobile Bay, the last blockade-runner to do so. Several others, including the *Heroine,* were trapped as the Union noose closed. Early on the morning of August 5 Farragut headed in, his powerful warships in a line, with weaker vessels lashed to their port sides where they were protected from the fort's big guns and their engines could help power the warships. The USS *Brooklyn* led the van, with Farragut's flagship *Hartford* second and the turreted ironclads *Tecumseh, Manhattan, Winnebago,* and *Chickasaw* just ahead and to starboard, closer to the fort. Opposing this awesome fleet were Fort Morgan (Gaines was too far away to play a role), the torpedoes and obstructions, and the *Tennessee, Gaines, Selma* and *Morgan,* drawn up across the approach, just inside the bay. Aboard the *Tennessee,* a Rebel lieutenant described the scene: "It was a grand sight to see when [the vessels] were all in line, the monitors leading slightly and the wooden vessels lashed together, two and two." The Confederate sailors were mesmerized: "we had ample time to witness the pageant, for such it was for half an hour, before it became a bloody, fiery reality of war. The water was smooth as a millpond, and the tide was flood, which fact argued a determination on the part of the enemy to come in anyway, for in case of being disabled their vessels would float in." That was vintage Farragut.[27]

Watching the drama unfold from the Union side, an assistant surgeon aboard the *Lackawanna* witnessed the first shot from Fort Morgan, "looking exactly as if some gigantic hand had thrown in play a ball toward you." Then all hell broke loose as tongues of flame and great billows of smoke enveloped fort and fleet. In order better to see the action and direct events, Farragut climbed into the rigging where he was famously secured by a small rope tied by the signal-quartermaster. Farragut later called the Battle of Mobile Bay the "most desperate I ever fought," but his grit and seamanship left little doubt as to the outcome. When the *Tennessee* made its move, the *Tecumseh* veered to engage and promptly hit a torpedo that lifted her stern high into the air and sank her in moments, with ninety-four aboard. Horrified, the captain of the *Brooklyn* started backing his ship's screws, and the Union fleet bunched up in front of Morgan's batteries. As Rebel shot wrought fearful havoc and carnage on the Union decks, Farragut rebuked the *Brooklyn*'s commander and issued his immortal command, "Damn the torpedoes, full speed ahead!" Fortunately for the federals, no other torpedoes worked that day, though they could hear them bumping and thudding against their hulls as they steamed into the bay. Wet powder and barnacles, oysters and teredo worms clustered on the striker mechanisms were to blame.[28]

Meanwhile in the city, citizens could just discern the distant rumble of cannon fire. Breakfasting in their Government Street house, two young women, Frances Mosby and Lou Mendenhall, heard frantic ringing of bells that became a "pandemonium of sound." The women sprang from the table, hastily donned bonnets, and headed for the riverfront. All along the route were excited residents, and "we girls locked arms and joined the crowd on the sidewalk. The confusion was indescribable, but we soon learned the cause. At sunrise that morning Admiral Farragut had formed his line of battle to attack the Forts." Some panicked and began immediate plans to evacuate, but cooler heads felt confident that even if the forts and Buchanan's little squadron failed, the upper bay batteries and obstructions would protect them. By such little self-reassurances did Mobilians such as Mosby and Mendenhall cope.[29]

In a little more than two hours after getting under way, Farragut's fleet had successfully run past the forts and anchored well inside the bay. But Buchanan left his foes little time to lick their wounds, and shortly after nine o'clock steamed straight for them. The Union vessels hastily up-anchored and the battle joined. The *Tennessee* may have appeared invulnerable, but she had two significant design flaws—exposed steering chains and a tall smokestack. Both were almost instantly shot away, depriving the vessel of control and engine draft. Sitting amid the towering warships and the lower profile monitors, the *Tennessee* belched destruction in every direction, her sailors sweating and coughing inside her casemate at their smoky guns. The Union ships fired at the behemoth again and again, with no more apparent effect, wrote one contemporary, than "a musket wad or popgun pellet might be expected to produce on a buffalo's skull." While the wooden warships ineffectually rammed the *Tennessee,* watched their shot ricochet off her iron sides, and collided with each other, the *Chickasaw* clung to her quarter and hammered away with eleven-inch shot. The nearby *Manhattan* got in fewer shots, but they too were fearful. The same young Confederate lieutenant who had admired the peaceful nautical ballet that preceded the battle described one of the thundering reports from the *Manhattan.* It produced a "blast of dense, sulphurous smoke" that enveloped the *Tennessee*'s portholes as "440 pounds of iron, impelled by 60 pounds of powder admitted daylight through our side where, before it struck us, there had been two feet of solid wood, covered with five inches of solid iron." Incredibly, there were no casualties from this shot, but under the constant pounding the *Tennessee*'s casemates weakened, splinters flew across her decks, and Buchanan was badly wounded. At 10:00 a.m. Johnston decided that no more could be done, and "with almost a bursting heart," ordered the *Tennessee* surrendered. As for the rest of Buchanan's little flotilla, the *Selma* had been captured, and the *Morgan* and *Gaines* fled close to Fort Morgan, the latter vessel badly damaged and sinking. The Battle of Mobile Bay was over. Twelve Rebel sailors were killed, twenty wounded, and 280 captured. Farragut counted more than three hundred casualties, nearly one-third of those aboard the *Tecumseh* and most of the rest aboard the *Hartford* and *Brooklyn.* It was then, and still remains, by far the fiercest and most sanguinary combat ever waged on Mobile waters. It also marked a turning point in naval warfare. The future clearly belonged to iron and steam. Wood and sail were done.[30]

There yet remained one little drama to play out, however, and that concerned the fate of the gunboat *Morgan.* The vessel's captain "felt exceedingly anxious to save her to the Confederacy," but he worried that running up to Mobile seemed "impossible in a noisy, high-pressure steamer, making black smoke, to pass the enemy's fleet unobserved or to elude the vigilance of his gunboats." He went ashore to inform Fort Morgan's commander that he intended to scuttle the vessel and try to flee in small boats. But he had not reckoned with his executive officer, Lieutenant Thomas Locke Harrison, who swore that "the *Morgan* was the only vessel now left to the navy in those parts and she was more needed now than ever before, and that she was too valuable to give up." In another Hollywood moment akin to that inside the ramparts of Fort Charlotte eighty-four years before, Harrison lined up the men on deck and informed them of his decision. Those who wanted to join him in the attempt should cross to the starboard side; those who wanted to be put ashore should go to the port side. Harrison proudly nodded his approval when, "all hands went to the starboard." As for the *Morgan*'s captain, "a timid man," Harrison briskly told him "the *Morgan* was going to town," and the chagrined skipper stayed locked in his cabin during the entire affair.[31]

It was, a soldier at Fort Gaines later recalled, "a regular conflagration of gunpowder all the way up the channel." In the wee hours of the morning after the battle, a Union lookout spotted the *Morgan* headed north behind a trail of black smoke. Within minutes one vessel after another gave chase. Among them was the *Kennebec,* which banged away with her eleven-inch gun and smaller pieces. But in the darkness and smoke the Union sailors lost sight of their quarry, and by sunrise the *Morgan* was steaming hard for the obstructions off Choctaw Bar. Thinking her a Yankee gunboat, the skittish defenders sank a rock-filled boat in the gap, and *Morgan* was brought up short. She had been hit only once during her flight, but her pursuers broke off the chase, not wanting to hazard Batteries Gladden and McIntosh. A small steamboat hurriedly came down from the city, and, working in concert with the *Morgan,* managed to push aside the obstructing hulk enough so the gunboat could pass. Safely though the defenses, she then "stood up to the city with colors flying." It was a small triumph to be sure, but it was something.[32]

Within days of the fleet action in the lower bay, Forts Gaines and Powell were captured and Fort Morgan besieged by sea and land. The wounded Buchanan was taken to Pensacola to recover, and Farragut began to contemplate his next move. Fully expecting an attack on the city itself, Maury ordered all of his officers to send their families away. People living near the city's outer defenses were instructed to abandon their homes, and hundreds of trees were cut down to provide clear fields of fire. Farrand replaced Buchanan, and though the wounded admiral had once called him "respected," others felt differently. "The present incumbent is not much thought of," wrote one man. Buchanan's successor might have been an argumentative mediocrity, but he did not have much of a naval squadron to work with in any case. It consisted of the *Morgan,* the floating batteries *Huntsville* and *Tuscaloosa,* the gigantic but not yet fully armored *Nashville,* and the weak and underpowered *Baltic,* whose plate had been cannibalized for the *Nashville.* There were also civilian vessels that the government would soon impress—the trapped blockade-runners *Heroine, Mary,* and *Red Gauntlet* and the steamboats *Black Diamond* and *Southern Republic* which could do service transporting troops and supplies. Timothy Meaher owned two of these vessels—the *Red Gauntlet* and the *Southern Republic*—and though he had been no slouch when it came to supporting the cause, having them summarily seized probably did not set well with him. The Bigbee Boats were still under construction upriver and would not be ready anytime soon. Offensive action with such an assemblage was out of the question. Farrand's role would be to support Maury and land operations across the bay.[33]

Even though Fort Morgan still held out, Farragut was pleased with his position. On August 12 he wrote to his wife: "I have quite a colony here now—two forts, a big fleet, and a bay to run about in." Curious to see just how well fortified the city was, he made a reconnaissance north three days later. The water was too shallow here for his big ships, but the monitors and gunboats could maneuver well enough. By mid-morning Farragut was within three miles of the defenses with a few ironclads and four lighter craft. Hunkered down in Battery Gladden, Lieutenant William Mumford recorded a "clear and quite warm" day. "Seven of the enemy's gunboats came within sight of the city during the morning," his diary continued, "and at 10 minutes to 2 o'clock, p.m. opened fire upon the bay batteries. About thirty shots were fired." The *Chickasaw*, which had so punished the *Tennessee* earlier, opened fire with her forward turret on the *Morgan*, anchored behind the obstructions. According to another witness, "the little *Morgan*, safe behind the water entrenchments, at last began to bark, like a little dog." All of the shots by both sides fell short or were way off target. Amid all the booming, Farragut studied the defenses carefully, and, as he later wrote to Welles, "until these obstructions can be removed, there will be no possibility of our reaching Mobile with any of our light-draught vessels." Watching from shore, Rix bluntly remarked that "so effective was this water line . . . that Farragut's fleet might as well have attempted to sail through the Green Mountain Range." The federals retired, leaving residents of the city cut off from the sea and wondering when the inevitable attack would come.[34]

On August 23 Fort Morgan surrendered at last, and Farragut wrote to Welles: "I am now a little embarrassed by my position. We have taken the forts at the entrance of Mobile Bay, which is all I ever contemplated doing for more reasons than one. I consider an army of twenty or thirty thousand men necessary to take the city of Mobile and almost as many to hold it." The admiral was tired and ailing. "I have now been down in this Gulf . . . nearly five years of six," he informed the secretary, "and the last six months have been a severe drag upon me, and I want rest, if it is to be had." His higher-ups dithered over the request for weeks, but by late November Farragut was sailing for New York aboard the *Hartford*. For the time being Mobile was to be let alone, but eventually Union might would come around to forcing its defiant citizens to pledge their allegiance to the Stars and Stripes once more.[35]

The endgame was played in the spring of 1865 in a combined army–navy operation. The army commander was forty-seven-year-old Major General Edward Richard Sprigg Canby, known as Sprigg, a native Kentuckian with a shaved visage—rare for Civil War generals—and a limited record that included graduating next to last in his West Point class, Indian fighting, and holding the New Mexico Territory for the Union. The navy was under the direction of Rear Admiral Henry K. Thatcher, a forty-nine-year-old Mainer who had resigned from West Point to join the old navy. Canby thought it best to attack Mobile from the east, taking the fortifications at Spanish Fort and Blakeley and then hitting the city itself through the watery rear approaches. This strategy would avoid the city's formidable triple defense line and cut off it from resupply or reinforcement from outside. In order to execute his plan Canby moved two columns toward the head of the bay. The strongest consisted of thirty-two thousand men from the 13th and the 16th corps. This force advanced from Forts Morgan and Gaines up the Eastern Shore of Mobile Bay. The second column was much smaller, thirteen thousand men who marched west from Pensacola. Supporting the operation were fifteen vessels under Thatcher. These included monitors such as the *Chickasaw,* and side-wheel double-ender steamboats including the *Octorara* and *Metacomet.* The latter vessels, with a rudder on each end and reversible paddle wheels, were especially designed for service on narrow waterways.[36]

By any measure the odds against the Confederates were long. Maury had only nine thousand soldiers to command and a remnant navy whose new commander had an aversion to "strenuous" service. Once the federal intent became clear, Maury sent all the men he could spare across the bay. The general in charge of Spanish Fort's defenses was Randall Lee Gibson, a Louisianan and planter aristocrat who had seen heavy action at Shiloh, Chickamauga, and Atlanta. Maury was only able to give him 1,800 men to defend earthen fortifications that stretched more than a mile and a half across broken country. As the Union forces concentrated in their front and began probing and firing on the defenses, Gibson admonished his men, "You must dig, dig, dig. Nothing can save us here but the spade." Just to the north, at Blakeley, Brigadier General St. John R. Liddell, a Mississippi planter's son, had just shy of three thousand soldiers thinly spaced behind his crescent-shaped earthworks. The old town of Blakeley, "a pretty village . . . surrounded by pine woods," was mostly deserted and a far cry from the robust town that once rivaled Mobile.[37]

Sitting in Battery Gladden on the rainy morning of March 27, Mumford and his comrades could hear firing "in the vicinity of Spanish Fort." It was too hazy to see anything, but Mumford reported that "the cannonading was quite heavy and continued all day." The *Heroine* steamed for Mobile with General Maury and some casualties that evening but ran against the obstructions surrounding the battery. The damage was not severe, but Maury took a small boat into town and a larger steamer had to come and help extricate the *Heroine.* The following day brought continued heavy firing, and Mumford reported that the *Nashville* "was struck several times." The heaviest attack thus far on Spanish Fort came late April 4 when seventy-five Union cannon engaged in a sequenced barrage. One Confederate described the Union line as "one blaze of artillery." The thundering was easily audible in Mobile, where one resident marveled that "the windows of our houses . . . rattled as if the old buildings were in an ague, and people were lulled to sleep by the music of death."[38]

A wounded Rebel soldier evacuated with other casualties aboard the *Heroine* on the night of April 5 later provided a colorful and lively description of getting from the Eastern Shore to Mobile during the awesome federal bombardments. George S. Waterman lay on the deck, using his penknife to find a "soft plank," as the vessel steamed upriver for Blakeley and then Mobile. Hoping that they would not be spotted, the captain had ordered no lights or unnecessary noise. But as Waterman recalled, mixing in the present tense to give his account immediacy, "the very engine strokes and beat of the paddles seemed distressingly loud in the calm of the night. All hands on deck crouch behind the railings." The pilot and captain conferred in whispers, the pilot asked for a sounding, and the leadsman reported "two fathoms, sandy bottom with black specks." As the vessel eased north of Blakeley the captain ordered full steam and a river run for town. "Pointing her sharp nose into the teeth of the wind," Waterman wrote, "the *Heroine* passes the batteries with a rush, her wheels beating a devil's tattoo as they plow up the green water." Alerted to her at last, the Union guns opened fire. "Clippity clip!" Waterman wrote. "That shot grazes a stay and makes it sing.... The sky is scored and blistered with the shells and balls, the heavens shine like the ceiling of a circus tent blazing." Undaunted, the captain and pilot stood to their stations while the shot whistled through the rigging and plunged hissing into the river. Incredibly, the vessel avoided any direct hits, and Waterman's pounding heart began to calm when he heard the mate tell the captain, "we ain't in any more danger now from sparks ... than a maiden of two and forty summers." Relieved, Waterman declared that "luck did favor us." Arrived at the city, he and his comrades were transferred to various private homes to recover.[39]

Anxiety ran high in the city what with the steady sound of gunfire and the incoming streams of the wounded and the exhausted. B. B. Cox, who had been about nine years old during the siege, recalled much later how he had joined the crowds along the waterfront "to see and hear the bursting of the shells, the booming of the cannon and the rattle of musketry." On the night of April 8, when the Union batteries unleashed their full force, William Rix hurried down to Front Street and sat on a balcony "watching the sublime pyrotechnics and listening to the awful roar of the battle." Steadily the steamers came and went, taking over supplies and removing the wounded. Folding under the Union pressure, Gibson abandoned Spanish Fort on the night of the eighth, some of his men straggling north up to Blakeley, others by steamer and small boat over to the city. One soldier remembered the pell-mell scramble to get out. "Looking out on the water," he wrote, "we saw a yawl pulled cautiously to shore. In we plunged, rushing up to our necks in water, and throwing our guns in first, pitched into the boat, head over heels, laughing, sputtering, struggling." Cox encountered these Johnny Rebs when they disembarked at the town wharves, "shoeless, hatless, coatless and hungry."[40]

April 9 brought the final assault against Blakeley. Safely removed from the heat of battle at Battery Gladden, Mumford grimly recorded the day's events. "At 6 o'clk, p.m. the enemy advanced on our lines in two strong columns and carried the entire works. ... Our entire forces were captured with the exception of a few who swam to Batteries Huger and Tracy. Our lines were very weak, the men being about two yards apart. Batteries Huger and Tracy are the only barriers left to prevent the enemy from reaching the city." Out in the bay to his front the young lieutenant counted fifty-nine "vessels of all classes." The Battle of Blakeley (or Blakely, as it was often spelled by military authorities at the time) was the last significant land clash of the American Civil War, fought on the very day Robert E. Lee surrendered at Appomattox. Casualties were light compared to some of the war's earlier battles—116 killed, 655 wounded, and 4 missing for the federals, and about 100 Confederates killed and nearly 3,000 captured, including several generals. Black troops played an important role in the decisive Union attack, and in the confused aftermath of the fighting there were claims that these soldiers shot down unarmed Confederates. The 51st U.S.C.T.'s white officer gave these accounts credence when he said that "the niggers did not take a prisoner, they killed all they took to a man." Other officers stepped in and defused the situation. Not all the black troops felt moved to exact revenge, however. One met his old master and shared a canteen. Batteries Huger and Tracy fell over the next two days and Mobile lay completely open to capture. Writing in his postwar memoirs Ulysses S. Grant was none too happy about the cost of these late battles. "I had tried for more than two years to have an expedition sent against Mobile when its possession by us would have been of great advantage," he grumbled. "It finally cost us lives to take it when its possession was of no importance, and when, if left alone, it would within a few days have fallen into our hands without any bloodshed whatsoever."[41]

After Blakeley, Mumford reported "great excitement in the city," as a general and none-too-organized evacuation got under way. But the men at Battery Gladden were to serve as a rear guard to keep the Union vessels from getting up the Spanish River. Throughout the day of April 10 Mumford observed frenetic activity along the city's waterfront where vessels were being loaded with supplies. Just before lunch a federal gunboat approached and Gladden opened fire, holding it at bay. The next day Mumford and his men were ordered to get out themselves. "Rolled all the shot and shell into the bay," the lieutenant wrote. "All of the implements were broken up. None of the guns were spiked; the truck wheels and elevating screws were thrown overboard." At midnight the men were taken off their exposed position by the *Heroine* and deposited on the wharves amid the confusion. "The men, though low spirited, behaved well." With alarm bells and cries of consternation for accompaniment, Maury marched what remained of the army out of town, while Commodore Farrand prepared a makeshift flotilla on the riverfront. Sailors, pilots, and coal heavers were deserting left and right, vanishing into the throngs, but eventually a diverse little fleet consisting of the *Nashville, Morgan, Baltic, Black Diamond, Southern Republic, Red Gauntlet, Virgin, Mary,* and *Heroine* steamed north for Selma. When it was learned that the city had already fallen, Farrand took the Tombigbee River for Demopolis instead. The unwieldy *Huntsville* and *Tuscaloosa* were scuttled at the head of the Spanish River, where they yet lie deep under water and mud.[42]

April 12 was Mobile's fateful day. At sunrise the last Confederate cavalry rode out of town, firing thousands of cotton bales as they went. Citizens rushed in behind them and put out the blaze, however, saving most of the valuable commodity. For the moment there was a power vacuum, and, as in conquered cities throughout history, a mad rush of looters descended on anything left unguarded. "The streets were filled that morning as in the season of Mardigras," wrote Rix, "and the tide in the different thoroughfares set in one direction, converging toward the government warehouses on Water street." Citizens battered down the heavy wooden doors and helped themselves to the hoarded contents. "All day long," Rix continued, "like a colony of ants, men, women and children were rushing through the streets in jealous fear of not getting their share." He particularly noticed a woman, "once of the better sort," who was trundling home a barrel of flour while nearby "a brawny Irish woman" struggled by "with a side of bacon balanced on her head and as many hams as her arms can clasp." Fascinated, Rix watched as fat melting in the April sun dribbled onto her "panting bosom." Coffee, sugar, and rice were popular with the crowds, as were weapons and military accoutrements. Rix was astounded to see women and children carting off "loads of sabers, and bayonets and Springfield rifles, which were found in the original cases." Last, the gleeful rabble reached the boxes of rockets and signal torches and ignited them in a manic fury. Rix could only shake his head at the spectacle. "The wonder was that the mob was not self-quelled by being blown to atoms." But the most bizarre sight came later when "two huge pyramids of cotton, with a steamboat presumably under them," floated downriver. Perched atop the snowy mounds was a bald-headed septuagenarian "white with lint" and proudly holding aloft Old Glory. He was an old merchant and a loyal Union man who had managed to secrete his cotton well up Eight Mile Creek, a tributary of Chickasaw Creek, until the Rebel fleet had passed. He then headed to town triumphant, and, according to Rix, eventually collected more than $150,000 from the federal government for his cargo.[43]

The federals did not need long to reassert order. Thatcher ferried eight thousand bluecoats across the bay and landed them immediately below town, occupied Batteries Gladden and McIntosh, and moved a gunboat and several river monitors "directly in front of the city." "Sir," he and General Gordon Granger, the 13th Corps commander, wrote to Mayor Robert H. Slough, "your city is menaced by a large land and naval force. We demand its immediate and unconditional surrender." Years later Cox clearly recalled seeing the mayor hurrying out the Shell Road to meet the federal infantry, barreling along in his carriage pulled by two white horses and flying "a very large white flag on a long pole, which could be seen at a long distance." "The city has been evacuated by the military authorities," the mayor informed the Union officers who met him. "Your demand has been granted, and I trust, gentlemen, for the sake of humanity, all the safeguards which we can throw around our people will be secured to them."[44]

Flags snapping, drums beating, fifes shrilling, long muskets shining in the sunlight, and brass buttons flashing on blue coats, the Union troops marched into town as people either sullenly stood by or unleashed their long-repressed feelings toward the Union. One ardent Southerner could hardly contain his spite in a letter to his sister. "I have a sad tale to tell you," he began. "At about 4 o'clock the advance of the Yankee army reached the city at the same time one of their boats . . . arrived at the foot of Govt St. As soon as the negroes and puerile white people saw the boat at the wharf they rushed down the street shouting and hurrahing." Mingling with the troops aboard the vessel, they clapped and cheered "the detestable Yankees." "Soon the deck was crowded with the colored 'gemmin of Africa 'scent," he disgustedly continued, "and their white livered brethren." Cox, being a youngster, was intrigued by the marching soldiers. "The city was resonant with every patriotic refrain," he wrote, "from the Star Spangled Banner to John Brown's Soul is Marching On. Every one realized for the first time, as he listened to the 'tramp, tramp' of orderly files, that 'the boys' had come." Rix headed for the Custom House, where he just missed a speech by General Granger. A man in the crowd condensed the general's remarks for him: "O, it is all rose-color. Granger says it is a free country—do as we damn please—only we must not show our noses on the street after dark." The troops stacked arms and went into bivouac, white tents blossoming all over town. The black troops were quartered down at Choctaw Point, the least desirable place, but these men were well used to such petty indignities from their own commanders.[45]

With Mobile under military occupation and civic order fully restored, Union authorities assessed their spoils of war. The army counted four hundred heavy guns mounted within the earthworks and a large supply of ammunition and military stores. Down on the river Thatcher found twenty thousand bales of cotton. The navy yard was intact, "but most of its contents had been destroyed, except some lumber and a quantity of soft coal." There were a few steamers, barges, and small boats, which the navy confiscated. The dry dock was still serviceable, and all of the foundries, machine shops, warehouses, presses, and offices along Front and Commerce Streets were in good condition. Despite the general lack of destruction, a correspondent for the *Cincinnati Daily Commercial* newspaper found the city "a sad picture to contemplate." The people looked "distressed," he wrote, and the stores were "occupied only with the flies and the dust." There was no money "save the scrip of the Confederacy," now worthless. Kate Cumming, just returned home after her exhausting and depressing hospital work, wrote that if "the plague had entered the city it could not have had a gloomier appearance." She was also upset by the new social order. "We came across a number of negro children," she fumed, "and I politely asked them to let us pass, but they very rudely said, 'The middle of the road is for you and the sidewalk for us.'"[46]

While soldiers and civilians got used to one another in town, Thatcher put his sailors immediately to work sweeping the waterways of torpedoes and "blowing up and removing the obstructions in the main ship channel." This was dangerous and costly work, and in the days after the surrender two tugs, a launch, and a gunboat were sunk by torpedoes. On April 13 the armed tug USS *Ida* hit a torpedo near the Choctaw Point obstructions. One of the shaken sailors later said that "her smoke stack must have gone fifty feet into the air." In his report to Thatcher the captain wrote that her timbers were crushed, her boilers burst, and she sank in ten feet of water, "directly in mid-channel." One man was reported missing, another had his leg broken in two places, and the cook was "scalded on the left arm." The following day the gunboat USS *Sciota* struck a torpedo in twelve feet of water while running across the bay. "The explosion was terrible," her captain declared, "breaking the beams of the spar deck, tearing open the waterways, ripping off starboard forechannels, and breaking fore-topmast." Four men were killed and six wounded.[47]

A far greater national calamity occurred on the evening of April 14, Good Friday. Rix was the first Mobilian to learn of it shortly thereafter while "strolling alone, in the cool of the evening, about the docks and the deserted wholesale marts that face the water." While standing on Front Street, "I saw on the distant water a boat approaching, and knew by the regular lift of the oars, as they flashed in the setting sun, that it was a man-of-war's yawl. An officer was seated in the stern, holding in one hand the tiller, and in the other a roll of papers." The boat glided up to the wharf, and the officer "leaped ashore" with a brief salutation to Rix. "After he had gone, the sailors, with some circumlocution, informed me of the assassination of President Lincoln." Worried about possible unrest or official retribution, Rix hustled home. To his surprise, however, when the news became generally known, Mobile's citizens "appeared to be more painfully affected than the army." As for the rank and file, Rix remarked that it fell on them "like the cold pattering of a rain." The officers were stony faced, "wrapped in official reserve."[48]

The city's war was over, but the last of Maury's forces and Farrand's naval squadron were still afield and afloat desperately hoping yet to fight another day, or at least to avoid capture. The army evacuated Mobile along the Mobile & Ohio railroad tracks. There were roughly 4,500 men in the depleted ranks, protected by a rear guard of Louisiana cavalry. A federal brigade pursued, and there was a brief skirmish at Whistler, where the Rebels attempted to burn a bridge. The federals drove them off with light losses, and the chase continued upcountry. To the east strong Union columns marched north from Blakeley and Pensacola, bound for Montgomery where they planned to link with General James H. Wilson's rampaging cavalry. There was no resistance on these latter routes. "Country very lonely indeed," one Yankee wrote. "Trees green, woods full of beautiful flowers." The few houses they encountered were "miserable huts," each of them "inhabited by from 10 to 12 white-headed children." The troops got news of Lee's surrender on the twenty-second, when they entered the little hamlet of Greenville. The men cheered and fired their weapons into the air. "For the first time," a private wrote, "the roar of guns of the 16th corps proclaimed the glad tidings of peace—upon that afternoon—amid the pines of Alabama."[49]

Meanwhile, Farrand's ragtag flotilla labored upriver unmolested. George Waterman had left the mansion where he was recovering from his wound and was aboard one of the vessels. He later recalled that "the waters of the Mobile glistened at prow or stern as each craft hastened to its proper position. The river was quite full, and rising, its current swift and strong." They soon passed Fort Stoddert, "made famous in the days of Aaron Burr." Waterman somewhat proudly and not inaccurately described the old hero as an "early secessionist." William Lochiel Cameron was also with the fleet. "I was a very small, young, and not especially significant officer attached to the *Nashville,*" he wrote in an article for *Confederate Veteran* magazine published half a century afterward. "Although the river was deep, it was narrow and crooked," he recalled of the Tombigbee portion of the journey. "Our vessels were long and wide and every once in a while we were onto the bank, first on one side and then on the other." But rations were plentiful—"salt horse, salt pork, molasses, hard-tack, navy beans, rice, coffee, sugar"—discipline lax, and "the weather was charming. The trees along the banks of the river were just covering their limbs with a lovely green, and the birds were singing merrily as they flew from bough to bough." At night they tied up to old stumps and were lulled to sleep by mocking birds. "The swash of the water as it rapidly flowed against the sides of the vessel also tended to sooth the troubled mind." The ship's steward bargained with area planters for "fresh meat, vegetables, milk, chickens, eggs, etc." In exchange the planters asked for the salted meat the sailors had on board, rather than worthless Confederate money. Surely many children witnessed this ungainly river fleet, and though no such written accounts were found during research for this book, they would have carried the memory into old age, regaling wide-eyed grandchildren about their Civil War, when the giant ironclads, tall-masted blockade-runners, and big steamboats appeared in their river.[50]

As the fleet pushed upriver, Cameron and his comrades soon encountered exslaves floating downstream, bound for Mobile and the pleasures of unbounded freedom. The first of these meetings took place late one afternoon while the *Nashville* was tied to the bank. The junior officers were enjoying a smoke under an awning when one of the men spied "an object just appearing in sight up the river." As it got closer, it "proved to be a canoe, or dugout, in which were a negro man seated in the stern and a negro woman in the bow, in the center there was what appeared to be a large-sized trunk. This outfit made quite a picture framed against the bank of the river just across, upon which was the reflection from the setting sun." When the canoe got closer, the man shouted up, "Ain't you-all's Yankee man's boat?" This assumption was undoubtedly due in part to the fact that the officers were all wearing blue, which experience had shown to be better for the sea service because Confederate gray was badly stained by salt water. "You are all right: come on board," was the reply. "The arrival of these negroes suggested some fun," Cameron wrote, and the resultant episode makes painful reading for modern sensibilities. The man "was middle-aged, as black as a crow, and looked like a 'green one.'" He wore a "cutdown plug hat, the top resewed on with white cotton yarn." The war over, he had "see-seeded" from his master and "brought the old woman along." The officers suspected the trunk contained looted goods, and put the man through an elaborate, highly ritualized interrogation. At one point an old skull was presented to him, and he was ordered to place one hand upon it and recite, "Alas, poor Yorick! I knew him well." "The expression on the faces of both darkies was irresistible, and the crowd had difficulty in repressing their laughter," Cameron chuckled. In due course, after the man had been made to straddle a barrel, the trunk was searched and found to contain silver and jewelry. Then the fun turned to viciousness. "You darned thieving nigger," snarled a midshipman, "get off to your boat with your woman. I will see that the property you intended to steal is returned and will also inform the owner that we 'put you through' and gave you the last we had in the shop." The quartermaster was then ordered to "put these niggers into their boat and shove her off." Cameron assured his readers that the trunk, which still bore the owner's name and address, was soon returned. He further went on to state that he and his comrades were all "gentlemen and would not have imposed any needless cruelty upon a man on account of his color." Yet only a few paragraphs further on, he revealed that the other vessels had been visited by "large parties of negroes" who likewise thought they had fallen in with the federals. They were taken on board and passed from bow to stern with "a gentle application of the 'cat'" for their error.[51]

After several days on the river the flotilla at last reached Demopolis where the vessels and the men became a sensation. The local Confederate commander reported to General Taylor that "there are eighteen boats here." They included, besides those already named, a crazy aggregation of steamboats, tugs, barges, and pleasure boats picked up en route. As a precaution a battery was thrown up downriver, and Farrand posted a picket boat. But most of the men either sampled the joys of civilian attention in a new town or deserted and set off downstream for Mobile again. Cameron and one of his comrades found solace in the parlor of a Mrs. McDonald and her "two handsome daughters." These ladies treated their dashing guests to "strawberries and cream out of real china plates with silver spoons" with "lemonade from cut glass tumblers" to drink. This idyll came to an inevitable end in early May when the fleet unmoored from its gentle refuge and headed back downstream to be formally surrendered at Nannahubba Bluff.[52]

The Confederate army and navy in southern Alabama were surrendered and disbanded on May 4 and May 8 respectively. Taylor and Canby had held a preliminary meeting on April 29 at Magee's Farm, twelve miles northwest of Mobile, and agreed on the particulars in advance. Taylor and an aide arrived at that meeting in their threadbare uniforms on a railroad handcar pumped by two black men to face Canby, a brigade, and a regimental brass band. It was a cordial affair, with everyone relieved the fighting was finished. The band struck up "Hail, Columbia"; Canby ordered "Dixie," and Taylor said "Hail, Columbia" was more appropriate. Bottles of champagne were popped, and Taylor joked that these were "the first agreeable explosive sounds I had heard for years." The formal surrenders took place in Citronelle, in northern Mobile County where Taylor and Farrand each signed the papers. Canby was a gentleman throughout and insured generous terms, allowing the ex-Confederate soldiers and sailors to keep their side arms and promising them transportation to their homes. The relief of tension throughout the area was immediate and welcome. "Oh, what a glorious

My interest in Mobile's waterfront dates to childhood, when my grandmother first took me down to the Alabama State Docks to watch the stevedores. I got a subscription to *Port of Mobile* magazine shortly thereafter and thrilled to the exotic covers by artist Jim Gray. Courtesy of the Alabama State Port Authority.

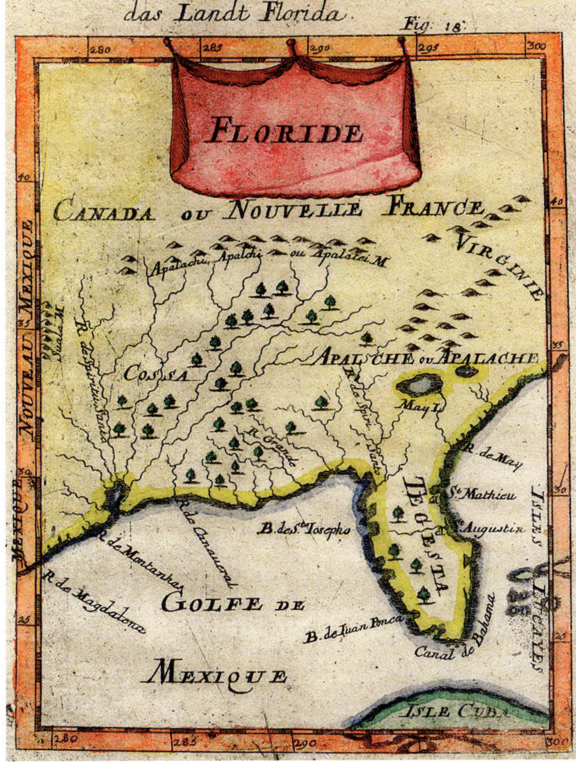

European knowledge of the Gulf Coast developed slowly, as this 1690 map demonstrates. The Rio de Spiritu Santo to the left is almost certainly the Mississippi River. The Mobile is one of the unnamed streams toward the center. Courtesy of the History Museum of Mobile.

Henri de Tonti was a capable frontier diplomat and one of French Mobile's early leaders. He died of yellow fever in 1704. Courtesy of the History Museum of Mobile.

Old Mobile town plan, 1702, probably drawn by Charles Levasseur, a talented engineer and cartographer. Courtesy of the Archives Nationales.

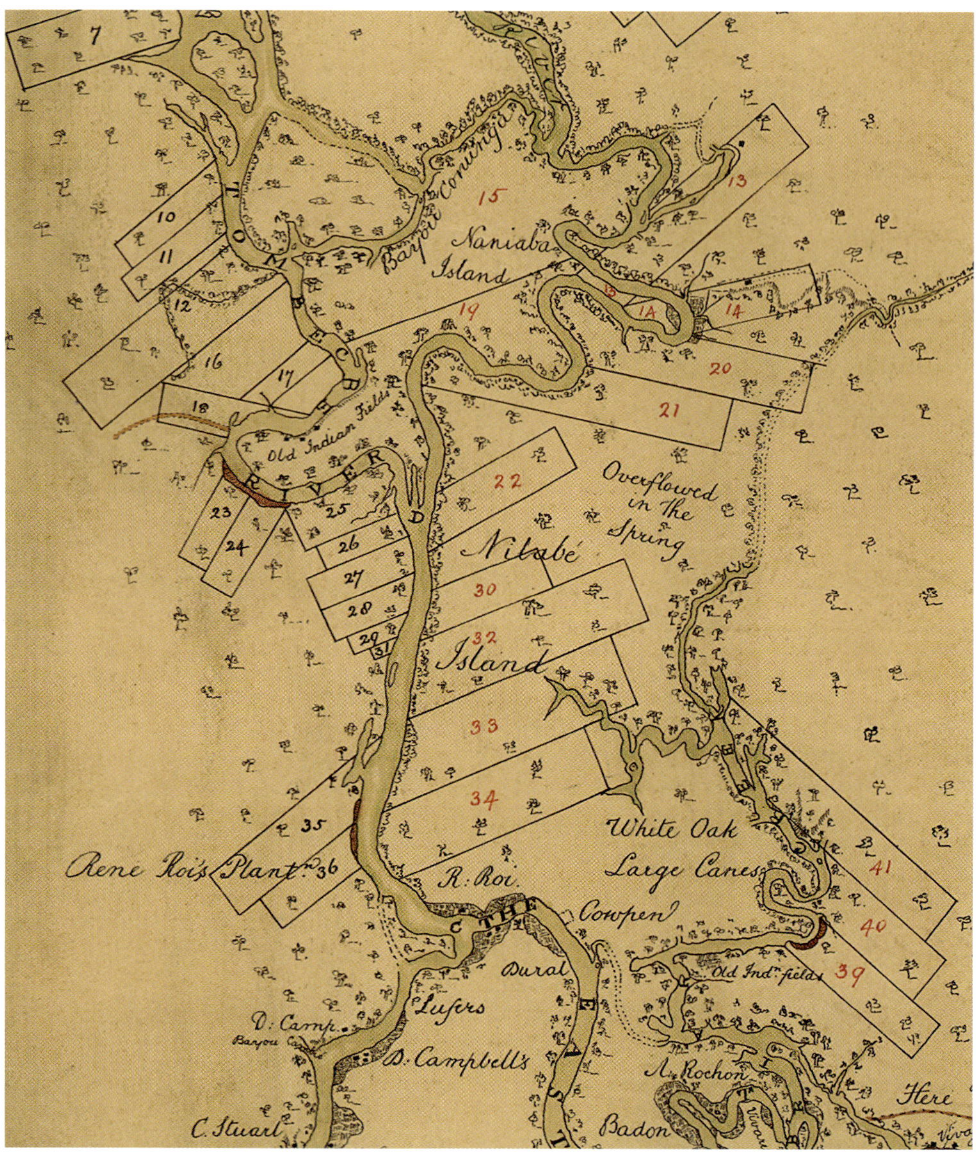

Detail, David Taitt's 1771 West Florida map, showing the upper Mobile from Nannahubba to the Tensaw split. The long narrow lots were typical of the colonial era, when every plantation needed river access. Courtesy of the Library of Congress.

FACING: *Mobile, 1842,* by William Bennett. The city's bustling antebellum harbor and waterfront are depicted from the river's east bank, most likely Pinto Island. The sailors in the foreground are sealing their boat's hull with tar. Courtesy of the History Museum of Mobile.

Choctaw Point Lighthouse and the tender's cottage. Despite this picture's bucolic tone, the site was a pestilential swamp covered by logs and junk, and the lighthouse was virtually useless to mariners. *Harper's Weekly,* May 31, 1862. Courtesy of the Mobile Municipal Archives.

The Confederate ram *Baltic,* dismissed by one of her officers as "rotten as punk" and little better than a "mud scow." Nonetheless this hulking ironclad prowled the bay and harbor to the war's very end. Courtesy of the Mobile Municipal Archives.

Hunley: The Beginning, by Paul Bender. This 2000 painting accurately depicts the submarine's earliest successful tests with a towed torpedo. Unfortunately for the boat's pilot, the Mobile's waters were never this clear, and he would have depended more on guesswork than visuals. Courtesy of Paul Bender.

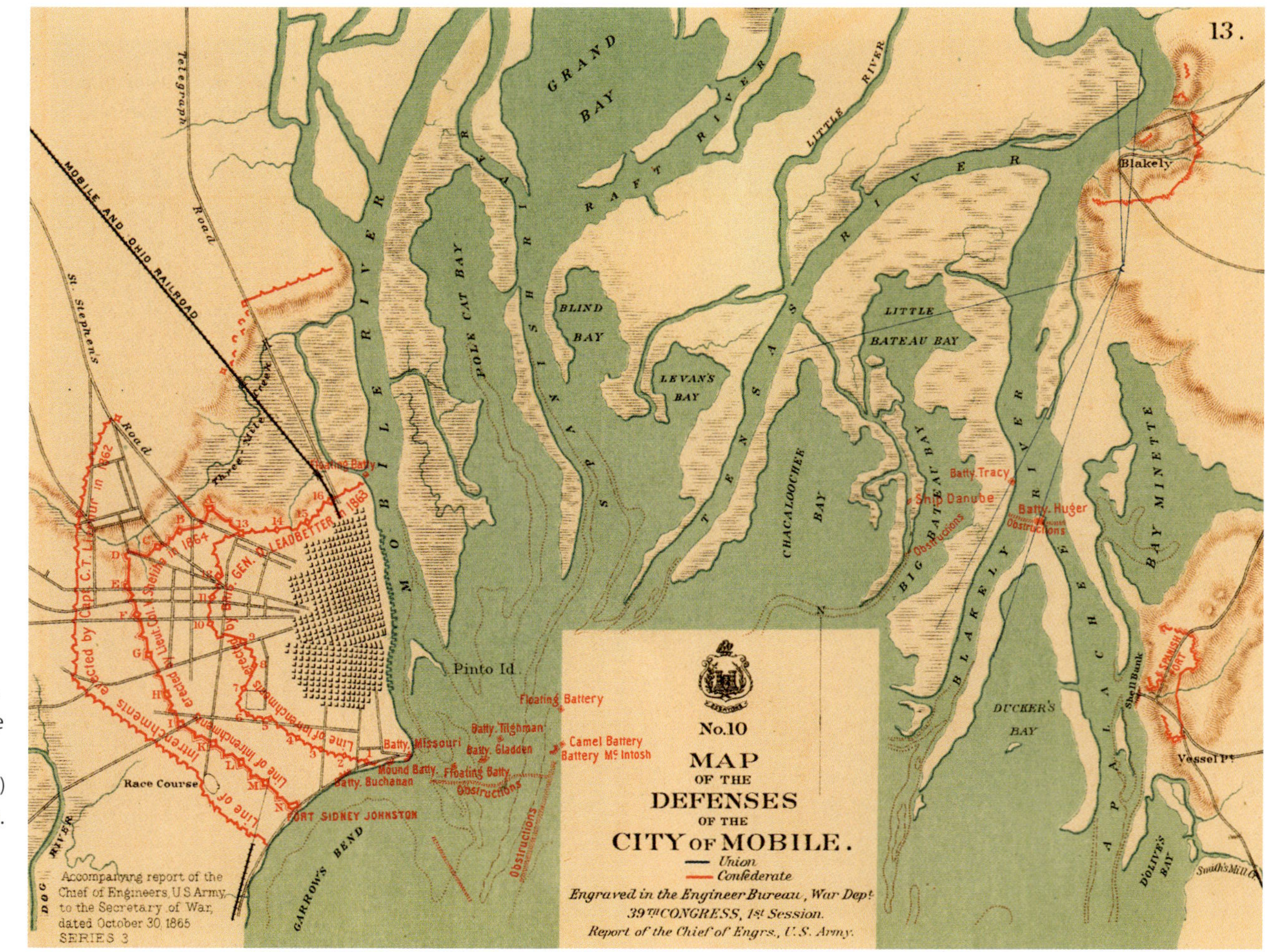

Federal engineers drew this map of upper Mobile Bay's defenses after the fall of Forts Morgan and Gaines. Their cartographic skills were superb, but they switched the Blakely (as they spelled it) and Apalachee Rivers' names. From *The Official Military Atlas of the Civil War.* Courtesy of the Mobile Municipal Archives.

Detail, the magazine explosion's aftermath. Hundreds of people and animals were killed, and burning vessels drifted downstream. From *Harper's Weekly,* June 24, 1865. Courtesy of the Mobile Municipal Archives.

Albert Stein, a talented hydraulic engineer who let his preference for scouring over dredging become an obsession that retarded port development. Courtesy of the History Museum of Mobile.

FACING: Mobile's harbor and waterfront painted in 1895 by the sea captain William Challoner. The romantic couple in the painting is not as incongruous as one might think. Well-bred nineteenth-century Mobilians frequently took to the harbor for pleasure. Courtesy of the Historic Mobile Preservation Society.

City of Mobile, painted in 1899 by R. D. Wilcox. Steamboats loaded with cotton bales were a common sight on the Mobile River until the 1930s. Courtesy of the History Museum of Mobile.

An early postcard view of the Alabama State Docks. Mobilians were proud of their new port facilities. What better way to set them off than by florid azalea displays? Courtesy of John Hunter, Dockside Services.

Bankhead Tunnel under construction, as depicted by Roderick D. MacKenzie. The tubes were assembled at ADDSCO and subsequently floated out into the river and sunk. As this pastel indicates, the welding went on day and night. Courtesy of the History Museum of Mobile.

Cudjo Lewis in old age, painted by Emma Langdon Roche. Lewis lived until 1935, last of the *Clotilda*'s smuggled slaves. He never ceased longing for Africa, but he was never bitter. Courtesy of the History Museum of Mobile.

Mobile waterfront painted in 1984 by Lee Hoffman. The air of desertion and quiet amid so much evidence of heavy commerce is not uncommon at certain times dockside. Courtesy of Kaye Hoffman.

termination of things," exulted one Union officer camped near Montgomery. When the news reached a work party digging earthworks on the Tombigbee, one of the men shouted "the war is over, throw down your spades and let the Fort go to Hell. We don't want it." Just north of the Mount Vernon Stretch, the *Octorara* began firing celebratory salutes, and a company of Iowans at Mount Vernon whooped it up, fished, and sallied onto the river in small sailboats. Rebel soldiers were already passing through the area in numbers, and many showed themselves willing to chat with their erstwhile foes and share a pipe or plug of tobacco.[53]

The vessels in Farrand's river fleet were to be turned over at Nannahubba. As the boats steamed downriver, the men relaxed and let their thoughts wander. Waterman was aboard the *Southern Republic* and wrote that "my attention was drawn to the fragrance of magnolias, honeysuckles, and jasmines amid the pines of old Fort Stoddert." On May 10 the flotilla anchored in the broad watery expanse just below Nannahubba Island, where the Mobile River is at its widest. They were met by the Union ironclads *Cincinnati* and *Chickasaw* and the tinclad *Nyanza*. The Union officer in charge of the proceedings, Fleet Captain E. Simpson, paroled 112 officers, 285 sailors, and 24 marines. "We, the undersigned," read the document, "prisoners of war belonging to the Confederate naval forces serving under the command of Commodore Ebenezer Farrand, in the waters of the State of Alabama, this day surrendered by Commodore Ebenezer Farrand to Acting Rear Admiral Henry K. Thatcher, United States navy." They agreed that "we will not hereafter serve in the navy of the Confederate States, or in any military capacity whatever, against the United States of America." The formalities done, the men mixed together, and Cameron wrote, "I found myself in the quarters of the young officers on board the *Cincinnati* drinking iced wine and smoking Havana cigars, having eaten a 'square' meal with them as an honored guest." The ex-Confederates were loaded on board the *Southern Republic* and taken to Mobile, the calliope tooting "O Ain't I Glad to Get Out of the Wilderness!" When Cameron and his comrades reached the city's wharves, a large crowd of black people stood watching. Among them the young parolee spotted none other than "the same darky" with the plug hat sewn with white yarn that he and his fellows had tormented upriver. "I did not," he sheepishly admitted, "renew the acquaintance with Sam on that occasion."[54]

In the days following, various Union officers inspected the Rebel vessels and reported on their condition and recommended whether or not they could be reused or sold for scrap. The gigantic *Nashville* grounded at Nannahubba as the river fell, and she could not be moved until it rose again. She was found to be but lightly armored, weak-hulled, and not coppered, making her unfit for salt-water service. Thatcher ordered her armor salvaged and sent to Pensacola, and the hull sold. The *Baltic,* surprisingly, was found to have a good hull but rotting decks and upper works. It was recommended that she be used as "a steamer for towing purposes." The *Morgan* was judged a good "Western river boat" with yellow pine construction, a pair of twenty-six-foot-wide side wheels, and "four cylindrical double-flue boilers." She was battle-scarred—"three shot holes on the starboard side close to the water's edge, patched with copper and canvas"—and her hull needed caulking. It was recommended that she be auctioned "for the benefit of the government." The steamer *Black Diamond* was found to be "well constructed," with two-and-one-half-inch hull planks, three bulkheads, and four rows of stanchions supporting the main deck. She was also recommended to be sold. The civilian vessels that had been impressed by the Confederates or joined the fleet in flight were left to their various fates. The *Southern Republic* would continue to ply area waters, but Timothy Meaher renamed her *Republic,* and he soon abandoned the stream that had made his fortune. "I quit the river," he told a newspaper reporter in 1870, "when the colored citizens demanded cabin passage." He continued residing at his Three Mile Creek abode, however, managing his business interests and property, watching the tides, and wangling with the African men and women he had smuggled before the war. The *Heroine* was converted into a bay boat, ending her days running happy couples and excursionists, some of them black, over to the Eastern Shore and back.[55]

The city of Mobile had escaped the hostilities intact. But it was a heavily fortified and armed garrison town and the focus of significant military campaigns on sea and land, and immense quantities of ammunition and ordnance had accumulated in its environs. With the fighting ended, Union authorities began collecting all of this deadly stuff and storing it in Pomeroy and Marshall's Warehouse at Commerce and Lipscomb Streets, some ten blocks north of Government Street. On Wednesday, May 25, the army hired a large number of freed blacks to help unload a newly arrived train loaded with artillery shells. Witnesses were alarmed by the "happy-go-lucky" attitude manifested by these workers as they laughed, tossed the ammunition back and forth, and even smoked pipes around loose gunpowder. Perhaps lulled by the postwar mood, the supervising officers were not paying close attention. No one knows exactly how it happened—a dropped percussion shell, a carelessly tossed match—but at exactly 2:15 p.m. the Pomeroy and Marshall's Warehouse was ripped by a titanic explosion.[56]

Six-year-old Peter Joseph Hamilton, the very same who would movingly evoke Mobile's founders forty-seven years later at Twenty-Seven Mile Bluff, was with his mammy, playing in his front yard more than a mile away. "I was on top of the fence," he later wrote, "when we felt what I should from my tropical experience now call an earthquake, indeed two or more in succession and, as we looked fearfully toward the city, over it swept a black cloud, dividing in two in the wind, as I have since seen in Vesuvius." Down by the river a returning Confederate veteran was stunned. "In an instant the air was filled with brick and debris of every kind," he remembered, "flying in every direction." Another witness provided a lurid description of "bursting shells, flying timbers, bales of cotton, balls of rosin, bars and sheets of iron, bricks, stones, wagons, horses, men and women, and children co-mingled and mangled into one immense mass." The explosion was felt as far as one hundred miles away. The warehouse was obliterated and a ten-foot crater left in its place. Eight surrounding blocks were instantly leveled, and windows shattered all over town. At the Battle House Hotel a large party of ladies and gentlemen at table were showered with falling plaster, lath, and debris; at the foot of Church Street, three-quarters of a mile away, a man was blown into the river; horses and mules were killed outright by the concussion; and all around the vanished warehouse fires raged and ammunition continued to explode. On the nearby river all was chaos. The captain of the tugboat USS *Cowslip* described what he found when his vessel steamed to give aid. "The schooner *Orville,* loaded with hay, was lying very near some burning barges and in imminent danger. I took her in tow and brought her to a place of safety on the opposite side of the river. I then steamed up the river to where the *Kate Dale* was burning, to see if there were any persons on board in need of assistance." Two men were missing from that boat and a Rebel parolee on board had been struck dead by the concussion, but had not a mark upon him. The *Cowslip* took two other vessels in tow in a desperate bid to get them away from the fires. They included a bark "then at anchor opposite the burning pile and against which the hulk of a burning steamer was drifting," and a steamboat with her upper works wrecked.[57]

Sailors, soldiers, and civilians rushed to the scene. "Not a warehouse in that portion of the city was left standing," wrote a reporter, "and thousands of men worked hour after hour among the debris, bringing forth one after another of the writhing and dead victims." As in the steamboat disasters of antebellum days, bodies were laid out on the wharves. Many were too burned or mutilated for identification. After the initial shock General Granger organized a more effective response, and the civilian authorities cooperated closely. The total number of dead was never accurately determined. The accident had occurred at the height of a week day, and hundreds of people were in the area working or just lounging. Many were transient ex-slaves. "Most of them have no marks or papers by which they can be identified," declared a local physician, "and I am unable to learn their names." The final death toll was placed at between two and three hundred and more than two hundred injured were taken in by the city's hospitals.[58]

Mobile's physical, financial, and emotional scars would take decades to heal. Because of the magazine explosion, Water Street was a "continued wreck" from St. Michael Street to the site of the blast, and many corner buildings in that quadrant of town were "razed within a few feet of the ground." Ten thousand bales of cotton were consumed in the fires, many of which were privately owned and had represented the hope of some economic recovery for destitute merchants and planters. Property losses were near one million dollars, but insurance settlements were out of the question in the postwar South.[59] And then there were the accumulated losses of the war itself—the dead and wounded most of all, impoverished families, severed business relationships with the north, lost or confiscated assets from houses to ordinary tools to steamboats. Miles of now useless earthworks impeded travel and irritated locals with blowing dust and clinging mud. Water-filled trenches became breeding grounds for mosquitoes, and thousands of ugly stumps dotted the landscape. As for the river that had given the city its existence and its name, it still flowed south and out into its grand bay. But four years of warfare and commercial neglect had left the harbor virtually unusable. Silted slips, sunken and half-sunken vessels, iron-tipped pilings, and hidden torpedoes all needed attention if the city was to regain its former influence and glory. Everyone agreed that everything depended upon the river, and yet even there old enemies were about to clash again.

7

"Mobile Harbor: What shall we do with it?"

USS *Hartford's* sharp prow knifed through the warm, deep-blue gulf waters as she steamed eastward to Mobile Bay. South of Sand Island Lighthouse, she took on a pilot and was guided into the main ship channel, whence she bore north directly for Alabama's Port City. It was yet early morning, June 4, 1902, and in contrast to the scenes of blood and thunder she had endured almost forty years earlier, the *Hartford* was now embarked on a peaceful celebratory visit. Old-timers would have certainly recognized her noble profile, but she was a different, improved vessel. For one thing she had been reconfigured as a barquentine with a fore-and-aft-rigged mizzenmast rather than a ship, as during the Civil War. This made her more maneuverable in tight spots and represented a change that Farragut, a blue-water man forced to fight mostly brown-water battles, definitely would have welcomed. Her poop deck had been removed and the hulking black pivot guns or yore replaced by efficient and deadly five-inch breech-loaders and a quartet of Maxim machine guns. Additionally, her hull had been reinforced, and she was fitted with powerful modern engines and steering apparatus. In recognition of her distinguished past, her old wooden wheel was preserved amidships and employed when she was under sail power alone. Near the wheel stood a large oak panel deeply engraved with Farragut's immortal words, "Damn the Torpedoes! Go ahead!" Her complement included 21 officers and 478 landsmen training to be sailors, more than 100 more hands than she carried on that fateful August day in 1864.[1]

Opposite the "frowning ramparts" of Fort Morgan, *Hartford* paid homage to the *Tecumseh* and its unlucky crew, entombed beneath thirty feet of water and a layer of mud. In a traditional ceremony still observed by U.S. naval vessels visiting the Port of Mobile, a salute was fired and a wreath reverently tossed upon the waves, after which the ship proceeded on up the channel. By late morning *Hartford* passed Choctaw Point, her men standing on the yards in their dress whites and jaunty caps, while Captain W. H. Reeder surveyed the waterfront. It was both similar to and different from the

USS *Hartford,* circa 1900. Courtesy of the History Museum of Mobile.

Front Street, circa 1895. Courtesy of the History Museum of Mobile.

riverside of the antebellum and Civil War years. Choctaw Point was swampy and cluttered with driftwood, as ever, but its ineffective lighthouse was history, and the Republic Creosoting Company was in operation not far inland, augury of a new industrial era for that troublesome bit of real estate. Steamboats, mostly stern-wheelers now, were still a common sight, as were brick cotton warehouses and the three- and four-story commercial and office structures with balconies lining Front and Commerce Streets. Trains were obviously the preferred and dominant mode of transport ashore, and multiple railroad tracks ran down the middle of both Front and Commerce, which were jammed with boxcars and flatcars.

One other dramatic change from earlier days was the near elimination of finger wharves crowding the shore. Much of the river's west bank was now controlled by larger corporate entities and the city, which used a combination of long marginal wharf berths with big open sheds and metal-clad warehouses punctuated by occasional piers and slips, better accessible by the oceangoing vessels that routinely called at the port. The L & N Railroad owned 2,200 feet up to Government Street that included a freight depot, passenger depot, and banana houses; the Mobile & Ohio Railroad had the section between Government and Dauphin, where the United Fruit Company had erected a long warehouse alongside the tracks. Abutting this property and extending northward 1,550 feet, a busy municipal wharf where the river boats called and the bay boats were berthed was maintained by the City of Mobile. Between Adams Street and One Mile Creek, the Mobile & Ohio Railroad had a grain elevator, an overhead conveyor, a coal chute, multiple cotton and hemp sheds, and eight angled piers divided by slips. At the harbor's northern-most reaches, near Three Mile and Chickasaw Creeks, was a concentration of sawmills, planing mills, and wood yards with log booms in the water to capture the thousands of cut trees sent downstream by delta swampers. No doubt Captain Reeder's experienced marine eye also saw and appreciated the plentiful and sophisticated ship-building and repair facilities, with dry docks, ways, foundries, machine shops, pattern shops, and salvage yards on both sides of the river. He would have found the harbor to be alive with vessels of every size and description, from the aforementioned stern-wheelers to barks, four- and five-masted schooners, oceangoing steamers, white-hulled "fruiters," stubby-nosed harbor tugs, dredges, coal barges, fishing yawls, oyster boats, skiffs, and perhaps even a pirogue or canoe here or there, representing the oldest and surest means of Mobile River conveyance.[2]

And while cotton was obviously still an important aspect of Mobile's trade, with factors and commission merchants scattered downtown, the port had diversified. Lumber, timber, coal, cotton, and cotton-seed oil were the biggest exports, while fruit (particularly bananas), sisal grass, coffee, mahogany, asphalt, and manganese and sulfur ores were key imports. Goods funneled into and out of the city by river and rail, though increasingly by rail, and local boosters rejoiced in a far-flung trade network that stretched from the north Alabama coal fields to the Midwest to Europe and Latin America. As these men adjusted their vests and checked their cravats preparatory to

Dry dock, circa 1895. Whether rickety wooden affairs, like those pictured here, or giant steel structures, dry docks have been a constant riverside. Courtesy of the History Museum of Mobile.

going aboard the *Hartford* to welcome Captain Reeder and his crew officially, they surely took great pride in how far their city had come since the war. The population, stagnant for decades, had begun to grow again and was north of forty thousand souls. The tiny mule-drawn trolleys of Victorian Mobile had given way to commodious electric cars, and many residents enjoyed reliable and labor-saving gas and electrical service. Several streets were paved, with more soon to follow. Handsome businesses, stores, residences, and churches dotted the town. The overall spiritual tone was Catholic, but there were increasing numbers of Protestants as well as small but important Reform and Orthodox Jewish congregations. Slavery was a thing of the past, but black residents were relegated to a different kind of second-class status. Within their restricted sphere, however, they had developed a robust local culture and economy centered along Davis Avenue, northwest of downtown, where black-owned businesses included groceries, hair-cutting establishments, hardware stores, drugstores, restaurants, and three funeral homes.[3]

But by far the most remarkable thing about turn-of-the-century Mobile, the very thing that made the *Hartford*'s visit possible in the first place, not to mention all the trade, was the vastly improved ship channel. In welcoming the vessel to town the *Mobile Register* made due note of it. "The advance in the depth of the port is well shown," the paper bragged in its June 5 edition, "by the fact that the 2,000 ton *Hartford* with all her armaments, stores and ballast came up to the city yesterday, without any knowledge of passing a bar of any sort." Indeed, since the war the channel had been dredged to thirteen, then seventeen, and finally twenty-four feet all the way from Mobile Point to Chickasaw Creek, allowing big vessels like the *Hartford,* which drew seventeen feet, to reach the city's wharves directly and unhindered, eliminating the tortuous and time-consuming Spanish River detour. Gone too were the Lower Fleet, the lighters, and the constant groundings on and about the Dog River and Choctaw Bars as well as at the north end of Blakeley Island. As Captain Reeder awaited his welcoming delegation on deck, sunlight flashing off his abundant gold braid, he could not have known just how hard won Mobile's deep modern channel and harbor were. Nor is it likely that anyone informed him of it. That was thirty years before, when the Civil War's dreadful wounds had yet to heal and old foes that should have united to reinvigorate the seaport instead clashed over how best to achieve the result, costing valuable time, money, and energy.[4] It had been an extraordinary collision of ideas, with both sides claiming to hold the scientific high ground, and resulted in a sustained debate over what kind of harbor Mobile would have and how best to maintain it.

To dredge or to scour? That had been the contentious question, and its origins dated to before the war. In November 1852 a U. S. Army engineer named William H. Chase issued an official report in which he analyzed the condition of Mobile's harbor, as well as the various methods of possibly improving it. That it needed improving no one doubted. Even the lighter draft boats capable of crossing the bars experienced difficulties getting to the city wharves. As one New England captain wrote home on April 17, 1840, "This is a very tedious place to load and ship, it takes much time and expense." A dozen years later the U.S. government provided detailed sailing instructions for navigating the bay and getting to the city, and they were complex. Once vessels neared Choctaw Light, the directions included compass settings and references that allowed little room for error: "from Wreck Stake (the Northernmost of the three) steer N. ½ W. for Turn Stake, haul close around it when Tucker's and Fowler's Stakes are in range, and steer N.W. by W. ¾ W. keeping this range astern, until you get near the Choctaw Point Shore, at the entrance of Mobile River, then haul up to the Northward keeping the Mobile side of the river close aboard."[5] Even with favorable winds and a skilled pilot aboard, grounding was always a real possibility.

In his report Chase noted earlier efforts at dredging and estimated the rate of silting in the cut at about an inch a year. More than a foot of depth had been lost since the last significant work in 1839, a serious situation that demanded redress if the city was to remain economically viable. "Besides dredging," Chase wrote, "there are two other methods suggested for deepening these channels: that of harrowing the bottom, and exposing the material thereof to be carried off by the ebb tidal current; and that of jettees, to be extended from Pinto's Island on one side, and from Choctaw Point on the other side." Both of these alternatives, he believed, were unsatisfactory. While he recognized that harrowing worked where there was a faster current, it "would not answer here" because of the weak tide. Conversely, jetties would be expensive and provide "no adequate assurance of permanent benefit." Chase opined that "alluvium would soon be formed around the mouth of the jettee in a much shorter time than the advocates of the scheme imagine." He admitted that more study was needed to be certain, and that it might be advantageous to close off the Spanish River in order to increase the Mobile's main current, but in the meantime dredging "is assumed to be the best means to be applied."[6]

Good engineer that he was, Chase then provided a detailed breakdown of the resources, material and financial, that dredging required. In order to deepen the cut through Choctaw Bar to 12.5 feet over the course of 940 yards at 100 yards width, he calculated "there must be excavated 868,929 yards of mud." This immense figure amounted to less than 3 feet in additional depth over that stretch, but those extra feet were critical. In order to do the work Chase called for "1 dredging machine and hull capable of discharging 3,800 cubic yards of earth per day, complete in all its parts, with steam-engine, cabin, anchors, cables, boats, &c." This would cost a whopping $16,000 if ordered new. To man and run the dredge he recommended a superintendent, a mate, an engineer, a blacksmith, six deckhands, two firemen, a servant, a dozen men for the hoppers, and two cords of wood daily. All of these men's pay and the wood costs amounted to $60 a day, or $21,900 a year. There were ways to save money, and to that end Chase suggested renting "an excavator recently received here, in private hands" for $400 a month. When not in use, the machines and hoppers could be "laid up in some place above the city of Mobile, under cover from the weather and preserved from injury, at a small annual expense, involving the pay of a faithful and intelligent keeper." The overall goal was a worthy one, Chase concluded, which would "give to commerce great advantages" as well as enhance national defense by allowing "war-steamers . . . of considerable size" to seek resupply or refuge at the city. He recommended that a recent $50,000 congressional appropriation for the harbor be bolstered by another $25,000 to "effect this improvement and secure the attendant advantages."[7]

While Chase's report wended its way through the federal bureaucracy, a local engineer inserted himself into the discussion, convincing restless merchants and boosters that he had a superior plan. Albert Stein was a force to be reckoned with. Born in 1785 in Düsseldorf, Germany, he had trained as a hydraulic engineer and served with Napoleon. In 1816 he immigrated to the United States and established an impressive reputation working with various cities on big-budget projects including surveys, canals, and waterworks. While in New Orleans, he suggested that the issue of silting at the Mississippi River's mouth be eliminated by constructing a series of jetties to close off the extra outlets and channel the river's prodigious current, thereby sweeping and sustaining a clean and deep channel into the gulf. The idea was not adopted until some years later when James Eads employed it. Though it proved correct there, Stein's enthusiasm for scouring was all wrong for the mouth of the Mobile River where the current is weaker and there is no steep fall-off into deep water as at the mouth of the Mississippi. He moved to Alabama's port city in 1840, where he established Stein Water Company and set about supplying the community with reliable fresh drinking water. In order to do this he used a series of pumps and wheels to pipe water from Three Mile Creek, a source of drinking water since colonial times, to a spot west of downtown, where it was stored in a reservoir. Here the water was filtered through rock and gravel, which trapped the sediment. Stein then used the fifteen-foot fall in elevation between the reservoir and downtown to convey as many four hundred thousand gallons of clean water through hollowed cypress logs and some cast-iron pipes every twenty-four hours. This was more than enough potable water for the growing town.[8]

Stein's interest in his chosen field went beyond mere business obligations. In short, he appears to have lived and breathed his subject and was an energetic pamphleteer. After his death in 1874 the local press admired his skill and talent but lamented his lack of tolerance toward contrary opinion. "An ardent lover of truth himself," his obituary stated, "he had but little forbearance toward error, or toward ignorance." And woe betide any who opposed his wisdom. "His scorn of a conceited adversary was unqualified," the paper explained, "and he would scarcely condescend to argue with opposition, even though it might be plausible." Unfortunately for Stein, at least after the Civil War it was not simply enough to state the facts as he judged them. People had to be brought along, and Stein's posture "created antagonism," the paper wrote, and "greatly diminished his influence upon his contemporaries." Not surprisingly, "Old Stein," as he was familiarly known, "often compared himself to Cassandra." A posthumous portrait painted almost a decade after his death depicts a formidable-looking elderly man clad in a black coat and cravat with wavy white hair, steady eyes, prominent nose, and downturned mouth. When once set on an idea, there would be no turning him.[9]

Not long after Chase's report recommending dredging was printed, Stein argued that scouring the Mobile's mouth made much more sense. As his obituary later noted, "he advocated the system of cooperation with Nature" and therefore "was a consistent adversary of the use of the dredge." Despite his difficult personality, Stein had a considerable professional stature before the war, and about 1853 a group of Mobile businessmen, unwilling to wait for federal action, engaged him to study the problem and effect solutions. They paid twenty-five-thousand dollars out of their own pockets for the work, and over the next two years Stein began implementing his plan and detailed it along with his reasoning in a pamphlet written for the merchants, an article for *DeBow's Review,* and a letter to the local chamber of commerce. All of these documents said more or less the same thing at different lengths, the article being an extract from the pamphlet and the letter condensing the facts and figures. Stein's writing style was forceful, a little pedantic, and absolutely focused on the topic at hand.[10]

Stein studied the river thoroughly from the southern end of Twelve Mile Island to Choctaw Point, leaning over gunwales to take depth soundings, measuring water velocity, and mapping the course and shape of the existing channel. He was not a river man in the sense that Timothy Meaher was, who had learned the stream by hard experience, or a Creole who paddled the upper swamps daily checking traps, pulling fish out of the muddy water and knowing what each puff of wind or swirling eddy portended.

He was, rather, a scientist and an engineer with a wide knowledge of hydraulic principles and successful achievements from the Tidewater to the Mississippi. He was determined to acquire the data that would prove his theory correct. He made several drawings to illustrate his findings, but unfortunately these have been lost. Nonetheless, considering his references to them they must have been beautiful to behold—big sheets depicting the river's course with different colors indicating mid-channel, depth lines, wharves, and so forth; cross-sections of the channel carefully showing the angles and slopes; and attendant measurements and notes around the margins. One can easily imagine Stein dressed in black frock coat and all seriousness, spreading these out before the merchants and explaining his findings. They can only have been impressed.[11]

According to Stein, the "evils consequent on the present condition of the Mobile River" were several. They included "the sinuosity of the channel, the want of uniformity in its breadth, and the many branches or outlets, which draw off the greater portion of the water from the main channel." The Spanish River and Pinto Pass were the culprits on the last issue, and Stein had the numbers to prove it. He had measured the river flow and depths at various points during December 1854, and the results were astonishing. At half ebb the river ran at forty-four thousand cubic feet per second (CFS) just above the Spanish River and was twenty-five feet deep. Below the Spanish River the flow decreased to twenty thousand CFS and the depth to fifteen feet. Below Pinto Pass the flow further decreased to ten thousand CFS and the depth to ten feet. "From these calculations," Stein proudly wrote, "it will appear that by those two outlets the waters of the Mobile River are reduced in quantity by 34,000 cubic feet per second." The decreasing depths at each point made his point resoundingly. A weaker current meant a shallower channel. "Can anything be more conclusive?" he asked. "Is any thing more necessary? Can any argument be stronger than these facts?" Stein declared that if local businessmen preferred a deep-water port with all the attendant advantages, ameliorative measures had to be taken at once. Otherwise, he ominously predicted, the town's prospects would "sink to the level of a flat-boat trade."[12]

The proposed solutions included straightening the channel and regulating it, blocking off the Spanish River and Pinto Pass or at least partially reducing their influence, and establishing a strict wharf line downtown to prevent encroachment on the channel by private individuals, which brought shifts in current and undesired shoaling. With the money at his command, Stein made a good start on these goals. As he told the merchants in one of his reports, "By the plan, you will observe that provision is made to contract the bed of the River and straighten the fair-way, by works constructed on the left bank of the River a short distance above One Mile Creek." These works consisted "of piles driven into the bed of the River with alternate layers of brush-wood and brick-bats or ballast stones laid between." These primitive jetties were in three sections, ranging from 120 feet to 400 feet long. Similar works were placed at the Spanish River and across Pinto Pass, where a 116-foot gap was left for small craft. All told, more than one thousand piles were driven into the muddy bottom and tons of rubbish used as infill. It was an ambitious civil-engineering project with no federal involvement, and when the money ran out, progress stopped.[13]

The efficacy of these works would not be determined before the war. The problem for Stein's theory, of course, was that once the Mobile River's current entered the bay, it spread out and lost velocity, which caused all that mud, sand, and vegetative matter to settle onto bars and shoals, as at Choctaw Point and Dog River. Neither the Mobile's current, even channelized as Stein envisioned, nor the inflowing and ebb tides provided enough power to sustain a deep-water channel from river mouth to gulf. As Stein's project stalled, other efforts to develop the harbor proceeded, including contracts to dredge the channel between Choctaw Point and the Lower Fleet using federal funds and the establishment of a Board of Harbor Commissioners by the state of Alabama in 1860. This body was "given power and authority to cause a channel, at least three hundred feet wide, to be opened and kept open" from city to gulf "of such depth, not less than fifteen feet at low-water." This channel was to be dredged, but the onset of sectional hostilities rendered the board impotent before it could properly begin work and eclipsed the debate over the best method of deepening the channel for years.[14]

In the months after the war, the Union navy worked the upper bay and delta, sweeping for torpedoes and removing wrecks, pilings, and obstructions in order to restore safe navigation. Years of defensive efforts by Confederate authorities concurrent with the wartime suspension of harbor improvements had left things in a mess, and though the navy made progress, the task was too great for swift completion. To begin with, Dog River Bar had shoaled to eight feet and Choctaw Bar to five and a half, and only an expensive dredging project or effective scouring, as Stein continued to advocate, would rectify these deficiencies. Then there were all the torpedoes, a real menace, and the obstructions. In February 1866 Brevet Colonel W. E. Merrill, a Union engineer, issued a thorough report on the harbor's condition and his cost estimates for putting things right. Merrill surveyed all of the area waterways along with Colonel von Scheliha and some of the men who actually "drove the piles." The former Confederates were cooperative and even eager to help, but they lacked detailed plans and were forced to work from memory. If the obstructions and pilings did not interfere with navigation, Merrill ignored them, but thousands would have to be removed. "I find that they were always driven from 11 to 16 feet below the bottom," he reported, "with butts downward." One workman told Merrill he had labored almost two weeks just to open a 40-foot gap, and that each pile's "calculated resistance to being drawn out was 36,000 pounds." The man further informed the engineer that "he broke a chain calculated to stand a tension of 38,000 pounds in drawing one." Merrill figured the cost at $6 a pile and the total number of piles to be nearly 10,000. Similarly, he thought the wrecks of the *Huntsville* and *Tuscaloosa,* sunken in the Mobile near the Spanish River split, would be "very difficult to raise" but given their salvage value were worth the effort, an estimated cost of $10,000. As for the other wrecks and obstructions, he considered that the "only practicable method seems to be to blow the vessels to fragments by large charges of powder." Ten thousand pounds of black powder would more than suffice, at 35 cents a pound. Merrill's overall figure for cleaning up the harbor amounted to $91,208. He did not include a figure for removing torpedoes, which he recommended be left to the naval authorities, who had the expertise and equipment to address the problem. None of this work addressed the depth of the bars, of course, but it was absolutely necessary if the harbor was to be at all usable or safe for even the smallest craft.[15]

A few intrepid visitors still managed to sail or steam into Mobile during the war's immediate aftermath, and they encountered both ruin and beauty. An English scientist marveled at the defenses as his vessel headed up the bay. "As we neared Mobile the stupendous works of the Confederates appeared on either side," he wrote, "consisting of piles, sunken ships, and even earthwork forts, supported on piling." In stark contrast to antebellum days, the city was in "a depressed state" and presented "a wretched out-at-elbows appearance." Once he was in town, however, he admired the post office and Bienville Square, "laid out in grass, and shaded by trees." Ohio journalist Whitelaw Reid arrived not long after the magazine explosion and noted the waterfront's "tumble-down" appearance. "Planks had been torn up for squares along the levee to make firewood," he reported, "and the bare sleepers were rotting from exposure; elsewhere the decayed planks rattled ominously under carriage wheels, and disclosed here and there ugly holes that might prove dangerous to unwary walkers." Most of the shops and warehouses were closed, and there was little evidence of commerce. The only vessels in sight were a few transports and "portions of Farragut's famous fleet" anchored "in the stream." Blue-clad soldiers were everywhere downtown, the "shrubbery was as glorious as ever," and lovely "country villas still lined the shell-road, which was once the glory of Mobile."[16]

Life in Reconstruction Mobile was frustrating, exciting, and turbulent in varying degrees for most people of whatever race and class. Many rural ex-slaves crowded the town, seeking opportunity. They thrilled to the sight of black Union troops, armed and bivouacked at Choctaw Point, and took menial jobs as laborers if they could find them. Those with some skills had better prospects and joined groups like the all-black Draymen's Association, which advocated for equal and fair treatment in the job market. As for most white residents, they positively rankled at the sight of the former slaves milling about public places. After a particularly large gathering in Bienville Square on July 4, 1865, a writer for the *Mobile Daily News* sneered, "Quashie had his time yesterday, to his own liking, and with none to make him afraid." No one dared intervene, the reporter grumbled, due to a "detachment of their likes with loaded muskets and glittering bayonets to prevent 'impertinent white folks' from going between the wind and their nobility." The depressed economy only exacerbated the already unsettled social situation, and the following years would bring much political agitation, organization, and at least one serious riot downtown. The local agent for a large Philadelphia ironworks vented to a friend: "The times here and all over the South are in a bad fix. Business paralised, the people afraid to Say there souls are there own, the whole country ruled by a pack of thieving officials holding their positions by fraud, negro rule and bayonets."[17]

Meanwhile businessmen and public officials knew that the city's future depended upon trade, and that meant reopening the harbor and getting the railroads back up and running. On February 16, 1867, the General Assembly of Alabama passed "An Act for the improvement of the river, bay, and harbor of Mobile," establishing a Board of Harbor Commissioners and authorizing it to issue bonds in the amount of one million dollars. This was essentially a reconstitution of the defunct 1860 board. The new entity, variously called the Alabama Harbor Board, the State Harbor Board, and simply the Harbor Board, consisted of the president of the court of county commissioners for Mobile County, the presidents of the Bank of Mobile and the Mobile Chamber of Commerce, and "one citizen of the county of Mobile." The act authorized the new board "to receive such lands and apply them or the proceeds of them to the improvement, cleaning out, deepening, and widening of the river, harbor, and bay of Mobile, or any part thereof." The board could "assess the dues or tolls to be collected on vessels or water-crafts" to fund the work. To help the board implement its program, the city formed a River and Harbor Committee, which on December 10 recommended that a harbor and bay ordinance be passed to issue the necessary bonds as authorized by the General Assembly. The members of this committee took note of the prewar work by Stein but were skeptical of the results and opined that "the dredge alone can accomplish the work and can never be entirely dispensed with." Stein would have something to say about this, of course, and by the early 1870s local efforts would include both dredging and scouring.[18]

The goal of improving Mobile's harbor and ship channel got a major boost in 1870, when after years of postwar inaction Congress appropriated fifty thousand dollars, the first such injection of federal largesse since the 1850s. Major C. B. Reese, the officer in charge of the local corps of engineers office, laid out a series of proposals for spending these funds that included dredging out a channel three hundred feet wide and thirteen feet deep "at mean low tide" right across both bars and out to the gulf, and thoroughly surveying and removing the remaining piles and obstructions to allow generous passages through these works. Fully cognizant of Stein's influence, he recommended that the issue of "confining the current of the river in any way, with a view of producing a useful effect from scouring," be left "in abeyance" until future study could determine its utility. John Grant, who had extensive antebellum experience working area waterways, was quickly hired to begin the dredging at fifty cents a cubic yard. But even as things seemed to be moving at last, troubling battle lines were shaping up over the issue. Stein was fuming and lobbied the State Harbor Board hard, and in 1871 that body hired the ex-Confederate general Braxton Bragg as its engineer. Bragg was famously argumentative but in perfect accord with Stein, and the two would make a powerful team. Increasing their influence was the fact that many Mobilians had no love for the federal government, and its prime contractor on the dredge, John Grant, was a

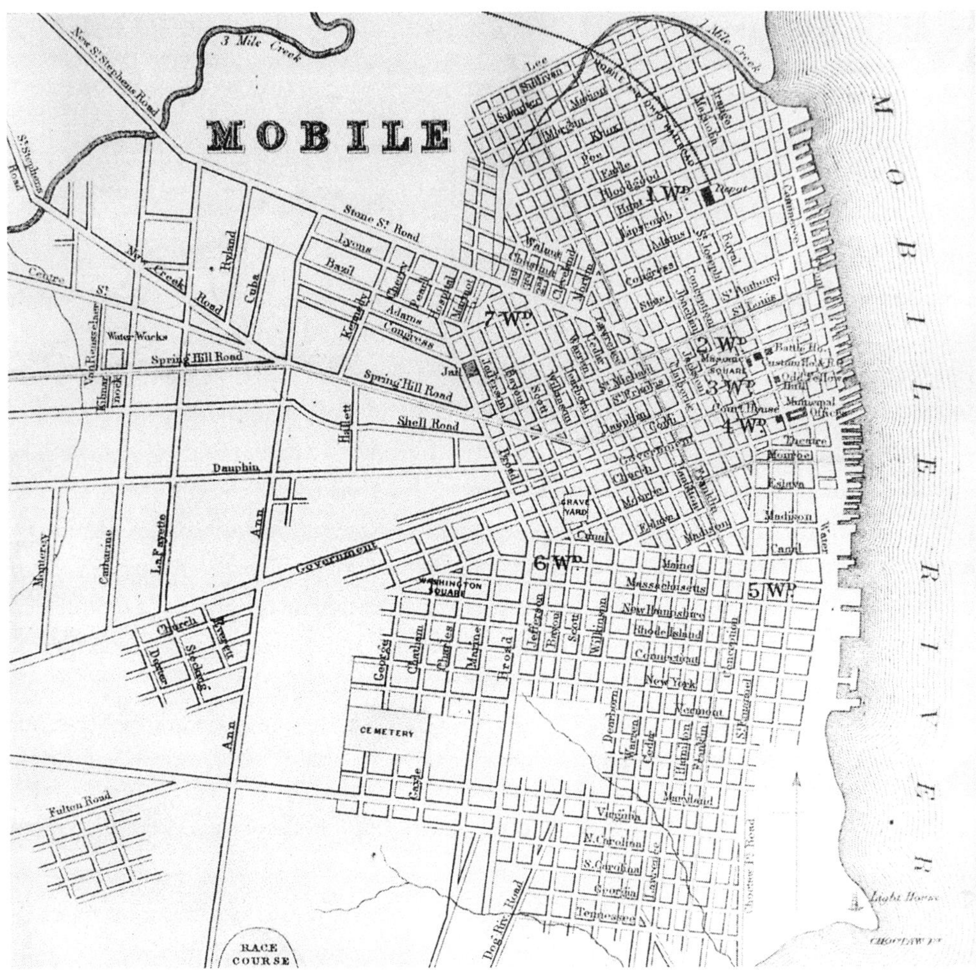

Mobile map, 1874, by Augustus Mitchell. This map was drawn before the finger wharves and slips were eliminated. Courtesy Library of Congress.

well-known Union sympathizer during the war. To further complicate matters, Major Reese died of yellow fever, and his successor, Colonel J. H. Simpson, was a no-nonsense officer with little tolerance for what he perceived as wrong-headed private endeavors like scouring. A major confrontation was only a matter of time.[19]

But at first there was an olive branch. Once Simpson took office, Bragg wrote him a letter promising that the State Harbor Board's plans would not conflict with those of the federal government. As 1871 advanced, both entities pursued their work, warily keeping an eye on each other. The board's efforts involved removing old wrecks along the riverfront, some dredging at Dog River Bar, filling in the old slips along the waterfront and providing a solid linear bulkhead and, in continued pursuit of Stein's scouring theory, the construction of jetties at Choctaw Point, the south end of Pinto Island,

and up at the Spanish River. Because this proceeded in piecemeal fashion, Simpson was not immediately aware of all the elements, nor did he object to what he initially observed. Wreck removal was fine and helpful, as was the dredging on Dog River Bar. Eliminating the old finger wharves and bulkheading the waterfront were likewise desirable goals for all concerned. In a letter to the State Harbor Board on June 12, 1871, Bragg articulated his reasons for this profound change, and Simpson would have agreed with every word. "The considerations in favor of a solid quay and continuous bulk-head along the whole city front are numerous and weighty," Bragg wrote. "Such a structure would remove the many interruptions to a free and easy flow of the river current along the whole city front, prevent the formation of eddies, by which deposits are now made, and secure a rapid removal, by the force of the current, of the vast quantity of offensive matter which now accrues with their use, but undoubtedly proves detrimental to the public health." This changeover from multiple wharves to a solid quay represented a dramatic shift in how Mobilians used and related to their waterfront. Ever since the old King's Wharf of colonial days, locals had been extending wooden piers out into the stream, creating what Bragg called "cess-pools of filth, nausea, and disease." A long marginal quay also made good economic sense, as it could more easily accommodate the oceangoing ships that Mobilians hoped to attract. City maps illustrate this change most dramatically, and by 1891 none of the old wharves remained along the busiest sections of waterfront.[20]

The State Harbor Board was proud of Bragg's progress and in early July 1871 sponsored a waterborne tour led by Bragg and Stein, who offered running commentary on the work. Among those aboard the small steamer *Annie* were Percy Walker, a local physician and lawyer, a former Know-Nothing candidate for Congress, and the chair of the State Harbor Board; other board members; the city engineer; several civil engineers; John Grant, the Corps's chosen contractor; the Mobile County probate judge; Admiral Buchanan; General James Slaughter, Bragg's assistant; lawyers; businessmen; and the press. Attendance was heavily weighted by former Confederate brass, and conspicuously absent were any federal officers. Grant was the only unequivocal voice for dredging among the entire party. The *Annie* steamed up to One Mile Creek and then slowly chugged back downstream along the city front, where the party could see how the numerous finger wharves encroached upon the channel, impeding and diverting its free flow "into lateral outlets." Below Choctaw Point and at Pinto Island, unsightly marsh and driftwood hedged the river and, as Bragg pointed out, only threatened to expand if not swept clear. South of the river's mouth, the *Annie* approached a series of obstructions, where the guests observed a diver "clad in submarine armor" placing black-powder charges in tin canisters to blow open a passage. The men clapped after each explosion as "a little volcano of water and mud" announced an obstacle gone. At noon the *Annie*'s captain informed them that "another explosion was to take place in the lower cabin." As champagne corks popped, Bragg and Stein described their plans, and then Grant outlined what the corps intended. By mid-afternoon the

Wharf scene, from *Harper's Weekly,* July 16, 1887. The waterfront has been converted to a bulkheaded marginal quay. From Mobile Municipal Archives.

tour was over, and those aboard repaired to the Gulf City Hotel for speeches and more champagne.[21]

Simpson was ill in the autumn of 1871, but when he returned to his duties in November, he became alarmed at some of what Bragg and the State Harbor Board were doing. Most objectionable to him were several long jetties, ranging from 1,400 to 4,000 feet, then under construction at the Spanish River, Pinto Island, and Choctaw Point. In a strongly worded complaint to his superiors in Washington, Simpson declared that it was "impossible to anticipate the alterations that would result from so important a change as the throwing of the greater part of the waters of Spanish River into Mobile River." While admitting that Bragg's efforts would probably scour out and deepen the harbor immediately in front of the city, Simpson was adamant that the former Rebel had "lost sight" of the fact that a faster current would inevitably slow down once it hit the broader waters of the bay, dropping its load of silt and debris. Not only would this simply move the problem to another place, but it stood seriously to interfere with the corps's dredging efforts. For his part Bragg was openly dismissive of dredging. As he explained in a long letter to the State Harbor Board, "These dredging experiments have been so often made, and have so often failed, that I must confess to little faith in them, and shall be unwilling, at any time, to resort to them, except as adjuncts to more enduring works."[22]

Clearly this situation could no longer continue, and in response to Simpson's letter the federal government ordered a board of engineers to assemble in Mobile to thoroughly study the matter and issue a report. The panel convened in early February 1872 and consisted of Simpson and two other army engineers from outside the area. Testimony would be taken from Bragg, members of the State Harbor Board, and area watermen. The recording secretary was Captain A. N. Damrell, a Massachusetts native, West Point graduate, and, like almost everyone else involved in the controversy, a Civil War veteran. The first meeting took place on February 3, and, according to Simpson, the members "continued in session from day to day, examining maps of the river and bay of Mobile, and projecting plans for their improvement, and such reports of boards and of officers of the Corps of Engineers as were at hand, and visiting the localities of interest connected with the projected plans of improvement."[23]

Any outdoor excursions cannot have been pleasant. That winter was one of the coldest in memory, and frigid north winds made area waterways pure misery for boatmen. There was a heavy snowfall on January 25, and exuberant urchins and dockside idlers engaged in snowball fights up and down Water Street. Cold drizzle, rain, and sleet continued into the second week of February, and columns of smoke issued from every chimney in town. Even as army engineers, steamboat captains, and State Harbor Board members bundled into and out of the official panel's meetings, the scouring-versus-dredging debate spilled into the public realm. Beginning on Saturday, February 10, a series of six long letters titled "Mobile Harbor: What shall we do with it?" ran in the *Mobile Register* authored by one "Bahia." Given the overall tone and degree of technical knowledge exhibited in these letters, Bahia can only have been Stein, then well into his eighties. The newspaper took a neutral stance in presenting them, simply hoping for "some immediate and practical steps towards relief."[24]

"It would be a waste of words to argue the vast importance, to this city and the region of country commercially connected with it, of the preservation and improvement of the Harbor of Mobile," Bahia wrote in his first letter. "To Mobile itself; to the rich country watered by the Alabama, the Tombigbee, and their tributaries; and to the eastern and southeastern parts of Mississippi, the subject is one of paramount interest." As Bahia saw it, at issue was the best method of maximizing the port's effectiveness so all concerned would benefit. "If the writer can fling a single ray of light, however feeble, upon the subject," he explained, "if he can call attention to any forgotten truth, or remove any prevailing error, the effort will not have been thrown away." It is not surprising that the futility of "subaqueous excavations" was what Bahia wanted to highlight. "The trouble is that, easy as it is for man to dig the trench, Nature has a like and a fatal facility in filling it again." Bahia hammered his point in letter after letter, concluding at the end of his fourth missive, "What I know—what any man of ordinary practical intelligence may know for himself—is, that, viewed in the light of common sense, any plan for opening, and keeping open, a navigable channel through Mobile Bay by means of the dredge, is a stupendous absurdity." No, scouring was the answer. "Its details may be varied or modified," he concluded in this extraordinary series, "but its general wisdom will prevail, as certainly as the waters flow downward from the everlasting hills to the unfathomable seas."[25]

Within days of Bahia's series, John Grant riposted with four long letters to the editor. Despite his wartime Union sympathies, Grant's familiarity with area waters was undisputed, as he had been working dredges all around the bay and gulf for almost forty years. His series, "Harbor Improvement," was gathered together and published as a pamphlet entitled *In Answer to Bahia* that spring. His purpose in entering the public realm, Grant explained, was to correct what he saw as Bahia's many errors. "I am in favor of the greatest freedom of speech and of the pen," he wrote, "and yet I must be permitted to say what I think that before a person undertakes to write upon a subject in which the whole community are interested, he should avail himself of all the means within his reach to make himself acquainted with the subject about which he attempts to enlighten others." Clearly, Grant continued, "'Bahia' has not thought it necessary to give himself any trouble about investigating the facts in relation to the matters treated of in his articles. They look to me more like the ideas of another, clothed in the dress of 'Bahia,' than the outpourings of knowledge from the brain of the writer." There can be no doubt that Grant thought Bahia was Stein or at least someone essentially taking dictation from "the great hydraulic engineer." Grant thoroughly sketched earlier efforts at dredging and scouring the channel, including the antebellum attempt at the latter funded by local merchants. Like Simpson, Grant recognized that once the confined current left "those artificial works" that Stein and Bragg had been working on "and found room to expand in the open bay it would loose its transporting power, drop the materials with which it might be loaded, and thus form a new bar." Dredging during the 1820s and 1830s, in contrast, had effectively opened cuts in the bay that had held their depth for twenty years. By Grant's lights, these were not theoretical conclusions. Both dredging and scouring had been attempted, and the results proved the superiority of the former method.[26]

The power did not reside with Stein, Grant, or the public, however, but with the army engineers convened downtown. By February 14 they had seen and heard enough and issued their report, even as Bahia's letters were appearing. Their conclusions were careful and balanced and even favored some of the State Harbor Board's work. Predictably, they affirmed plans to remove obstacles and wrecks. They also agreed with blocking Pinto Pass and even with constructing jetties at Choctaw Point, though they wanted the latter to be shorter than the State Harbor Board intended. Removal of the finger wharves and filling slips was agreed upon, as was their replacement by a solid bulkhead. The panel was adamantly opposed to the jetties at the Spanish River, however. "Any large increase in the flow of Mobile River will probably move Choctaw Bar farther toward the bay," the report stated, "and result in injury to the works now in progress." As to whether the channel should be dredged or scoured, the panel admitted that the former method was expensive and of necessity more or less continual, but in the end it was far preferable. Finally, the report encouraged the State Harbor Board to work closely with the corps of engineers in going forward. But ultimate authority would rest with the latter body.[27]

Simpson was highly satisfied and thought the matter resolved. But to his consternation, when he opened the March 16 edition of the *Mobile Register*, he encountered an ad soliciting bids "for repairing and extending two jetties at the head of Spanish River," signed by Bragg. In a blue fury Simpson fired off a letter to Percy Walker, protesting "against the construction of any such works by your board." Not a little perplexed, Walker immediately replied: "Your note seems to have been written under the impression that this board had approved of said work after being informed of the report by the board of engineers recently convened in this city. Permit me to disabuse your mind of this impression." Walker said that the State Harbor Board would "speedily" meet and offer an official response. On March 21 he reported that they had met and affirmed that they had no desire "to carry out any scheme of improvement not sanctioned by the authorities of the United States." They stood ready to assist in any manner Simpson desired. Simpson pronounced himself "gratified with the receipt of this resolution" and predicted that it would "be productive of the happiest results." As a bone to the State Harbor Board, he requested that they continue removing wrecks and obstructions.[28]

Why Bragg ran the ad is a mystery. It could have been placed before the panel met and for some reason not printed until after the report was issued. But knowing Bragg's contrary nature, it is not unreasonable to assume he was pushing his luck, just as he had during the war, with the usual dismal results. Nor did Stein accept the panel's report. As late as May of 1873 he was still publishing letters and pamphlets critical of dredging and the "ignorant" and "incompetent" federal engineers. It is doubtful that anyone else was even paying attention to the fussy old man at that point. That same year the Alabama legislature disbanded the State Harbor Board, and the U.S. Army Corps of Engineers held undisputed sway over area waterways, as it continues to do to this day. Disgusted, Bragg moved to Galveston. He died in 1874 and is buried in Mobile's Magnolia Cemetery. Stein passed away the same year. Colonel Simpson was promoted to head the corps's St. Louis office, and Captain Damrell became head of the Mobile District.[29]

Once again the federal government, with superior resources and manpower, had forced Mobile to bend to its will. As the new officer in charge of improving the channel, Damrell was scorned by some. With his trim Vandyke and double-breasted blue coat with brass buttons and epaulets, he was the very picture of military authority and efficiency. Utilizing an unprecedented flow of money—Congress appropriated more than four hundred thousand dollars for the harbor from 1870 to 1875—Damrell awarded numerous dredging contracts to Grant and others in a sustained project to open a channel thirteen feet deep and from two hundred to three hundred feet wide. In 1873 alone 163,269 cubic yards of mud, silt, sand, and clay were gouged out of the bay bottom and deposited onto scows, barges, and flats for disposal. While businessmen and merchants anxiously followed the progress, hopeful that at last Mobile would have a deep water seaport, more cynically minded citizens referred to the project as "Damrell's Ditch."[30]

By the summer of 1873 Damrell was able to judge the effectiveness of Bragg's jetties, and the verdict was yet another blow for the ex-Confederate's and Stein's scouring theory. Damrell reported that "the usual winter freshet in Mobile River" had indeed been strengthened and channeled by the jetties, deepening the harbor along Pinto Island, but had formed a new sandbar off the end of the works and was rapidly filling in the dredged channel across Choctaw Bar. This was just as Chase, Simpson, and Grant had predicted. Damrell proceeded to reopen a gap through Pinto Pass and ripped out most of the jetties in order to correct the situation. The importance and effectiveness of his dredging work showed in the port's improving numbers. More than one million dollars in tariff revenue was collected in 1873, 213 vessels carrying 88,206 tons of cargo arrived, and 195 vessels carrying 88,200 tons cleared out. The total value of exports was more than twelve million dollars. Throughout the late nineteenth century Damrell's focus was unwavering, and the channel's depths increased with each federal appropriation. By the end of Damrell's tenure in 1896, the channel stood at 23 feet deep all the way up to Chickasaw Creek and was an impressive 280 feet wide. A trade publication boasted: "Full rigged ships and ocean steamers now come sailing up the bay and cast out their lines to the pier-heads. Business houses, the wharf lessees and owners rejoice." Upon his death in 1909 Damrell was firm in locals' affections. The *Mobile Register* admiringly wrote that he was "popular with all who knew him" and had "lived to see the city prosper and grow greatly in population."[31]

In addition to the rehabilitation of Mobile's harbor, various interests pursued better rail service and upstate water access. This effort proved to be a double-edged sword, as the South's rapidly expanding railroad network meant that cities like Montgomery could efficiently and economically ship their cotton to other points, ignoring the water transport that had been so vital during the antebellum period. The effect on the Port City's theretofore healthy cotton exports was profound, and by 1880 barely two hundred thousand bales were funneled through, a fraction of the earlier impressive totals. Still and all, local businessmen worked hard to maximize rail's possibilities, knowing that a successful seaport needed good partnerships. On September 7, 1869, the city passed an ordinance that allowed the New Orleans, Mobile & Chattanooga Railroad Company "the right to lay a single track, with the necessary sidings and turnouts, from the northern boundary of its depot . . . northerly through Commerce Street thence northerly with tracks to connect other roads." Soon work gangs were busy "taking up the stone pavement on Commerce Street, and laying down crossties and iron rails on the same." Rails were also laid on Front Street, and waterfront merchants enjoyed the convenience of trackside service. This stimulated a construction boom along Commerce Street, "a noble commercial avenue," and new brick warehouses, a cotton exchange, and the chamber of commerce and other offices quickly arose. Just as important, the speed of loading and unloading ships was now significantly accelerated.[32]

Besides the new tracks laid by the New Orleans line, larger railroad companies such as the Mobile & Ohio and the Louisville & Nashville strengthened their reach into and out of town, and by 1881 the latter road had penetrated Alabama's rich mineral belt and given the Port City a direct link with the vibrant new steel town of Birmingham. The M & O, thoroughly wrecked during the war, reestablished its line, which again soon stretched from the heart of the Mississippi Valley to the Gulf Coast. These restored and expanded connections opened new markets to excited Mobilians, especially in timber and coal, both of which would become dominant products at the port. And in an effort to solidify their upstate reach, locals succeeded in lobbying state and federal officials for improvements to the Alabama and Tombigbee River systems, including snag removal, dredging, and lock and dam construction. All of these efforts consumed much time, money, and energy. Slow as progress no doubt sometimes seemed to impatient local businessmen, their city's economy steadily diversified and grew.[33]

As Mobile's welcoming delegation clambered aboard the *Hartford,* taking in her towering masts, polished and oiled modern weaponry, and nattily attired crew, they no doubt heartily greeted Captain Reeder and proudly pointed out their bustling waterfront. All the old acrimony and battles were now in the past. The war was over and the dredging—scouring arguments and fraught experimentation, too. Big ships came and went every day, sweating longshoremen loaded and offloaded timber, coal, bananas, cigars, coffee, and a hundred other products, and strings of railroad cars clacked up and down Commerce Street. Not since King Cotton's antebellum heyday had things looked so good for the two-hundred-year-old river city.

8

Modern Port, Beleaguered River

It was the evening of November 24, 1906, and the Hoo-Hoos were on parade in downtown Mobile. After massing in front of the newly erected Cawthon Hotel, an elegant six-story building on the west side of Bienville Square, they proceeded east and south three blocks toward the turreted German Relief Hall on Conti Street. According to one observer, the event "was a unique one" and made downtown look "as if Mardi Gras had come during November." The parade was led by a "burlesque drum corps novelly dressed with coats turned inside out." Next came a trick mule and clown, then a Shetland pony pulling a cart with a 270-pound Hoo-Hoo attired in drag, costumed members of the order, a cage containing "the Wild Man captured at Frascati Stealing Cars," another cage containing Hoo-Hoo candidates "costumed as hayseed farmers," more members in file, and finally yet another cage with more candidates and "a performing monkey." After a raucous procession, the Hoo-Hoos pushed into the German Relief Hall where the candidates were formally inducted, and then all returned nosily and joyfully to the Cawthon for "a splendid menu."[1]

The Hoo-Hoo was a fraternal order of lumbermen founded in Arkansas some fifteen years earlier. The unusual name derived from contemporary slang. Anything described as Hoo-Hoo was sui generis and just a little over the top. The group's routines and rituals were rife with the kind of puckish silliness so beloved of early-twentieth-century male clubs, but fundamentally the order provided a valuable network for its members. Among those taking part in the high-hearted doings at Mobile were the machinery manager of Turner Supply Company, the cashier for the Bay Shore Lumber Company, Star Lumber Company's owner, the Chicago Lumber & Coal Company's assistant manager, a lumber buyer for Planiol and Cagiga of Havana, and the traffic manager for the Mobile, Jackson & Kansas City Railroad. Well might they cavort. After decades of struggle and poverty, Mobile at last seemed to be entering a new era of prosperity. Grand buildings were popping up everywhere. Besides the Cawthon and

Rooftop harbor view, 1896, looking south. Perhaps a worker was so beguiled by the prospect that he left his hammer behind. T. E. Armistead Collection. Courtesy of the Doy Leale McCall Rare Book and Manuscript Library, University of South Alabama.

German Relief Hall, there was the Bienville Hotel, a six-story pile on the square's north side; the Battle House Hotel just under construction on Royal Street with its breathtaking lobby, romantic whispering arch, and Trellis Room; the classically inspired First National Bank on St. Francis Street; the Mobile & Ohio Railroad Station on the north end of town, with its red-tiled dome and Plateresque carvings; the ten-story Van Antwerp Building at Dauphin and Royal, Mobile's first skyscraper; and lining live-oak-canopied Government Street, the architect-designed mansions of the new merchant princes, many of them lumbermen.[2]

The city's industrial and commercial situation was impressive, especially in the realm of forest products. Lumber was king now. The improved rail networks traversed what had theretofore been vast unexploited piney woods, and lumber and turpentine camps sprouted all across Mississippi, Alabama, Georgia, and the Florida panhandle. There were more than thirty sawmills in the immediate Mobile area with a daily capacity of 4.15 million feet, and the whine of big blades and the smell of sawdust were constants. One amazed Yankee visitor cried, "Here they plank their gutters with finer woods than we finish our $5,000 dwellings with." Piles of logs, barrels of rosin, and towering stacks of boards, shingles, and staves edged the waterfront, especially around the mouths of Three Mile and Chickasaw Creeks. In 1910 a report cited these creeks as advantages to Mobile, and not just for the sawmills and lumberyards. "The time will undoubtedly come when the value of these creeks will be appreciated as additional water front and as communications penetrating deeply into the heart of the manufacturing and commercial city that may be expected to grow upon their banks," the report stated. This was prescient, but for the present the area was dominated by lumber. Four- and five-masted schooners and square-rigged barks, brigs, and ships regularly loaded up with this wooden treasure and headed out into the gulf, their stained sails billowing in the wind. Such vessels were a common sight well into the 1930s. One couple thrilled to the view as their train approached town from the north, skirting the riverfront. When the cars cleared the delta's tree line, the horizon opened, and they beheld a "beautiful procession of large schooners from the Mexican Gulf and Caribbean Sea" riding at anchor "in the center of the yellow stream, their spars and masts rimmed magnificently with the crisp winter sunlight." The reason for these tall ships' enduring utility may be gleaned from some typical cargos. In June of 1913, for example, the Spanish bark *Lorenze* sailed for Valencia with 904,270 feet of yellow-pine lumber; the American schooner *Doris* carried 333,592 feet of yellow-pine lumber for Guayabal; and a Scottish brig headed out for Glasgow with 153,095 feet of sawn pitch-pine lumber, 40,137 oak staves, 95 ash logs, and 66 poplar logs.[3]

The Port City trafficked in more than woods, of course, and there was plenty of shipping activity south of the creeks. On March 25, 1911, the *Mobile Register* detailed the previous day's "particularly active" waterfront. Near one of the Mobile & Ohio's piers there were "all sorts of things going on," and at the Louisville & Nashville's wharves "fruit steamers were unloading cargoes of bananas." Further south at the municipal wharf, "two bay boats were lying." Also visible were the "motor-boat *Myrtle*" taking on "freight for Baldwin County points," the stern-wheeler *Quill* loading freight, a Spanish steamship loading cotton at the foot of St. Anthony Street, a British vessel unloading, a pile driver hammering away at the Dauphin Street wharf, and a dredge at work midriver. Besides timber, lumber, and cotton, the railroads trundled in all kinds of other products to be exported. In January 1926 a typical sampling of these items included glassware, shoes, pump parts, tractors, lavatories, stoves, woven wire fence, baking powder, feed, beans, butter, and apples. Mobile and Alabama were thoroughly webbed into an international trade network that would have been the envy of merchants a century earlier.[4]

Shipbuilding was another aspect of Mobile's waterfront economy. This industry had always existed locally to some degree, but during the second decade of the twentieth century two major developments greatly increased its importance—the founding of the Alabama Dry Dock and Shipbuilding Company (ADDSCO) in 1916 and of a company village and shipyard on Chickasaw Creek the following year. Both of these enterprises quickly grew into significant waterfront endeavors and brought in thousands of men and women. One became a semi-independent community on Pinto Island and the other a bona fide city with a town hall, public library, parks, stores, sewage-treatment

Steamer *John Quill.* This boat ran the Tombigbee River from 1907 to 1929.
Courtesy of the History Museum of Mobile.

plant, police force, and fire department. Both radically transformed not only the area economy but also the way the riverfront looked.

ADDSCO was established by D. R. Dunlap and his cousin George H. Dunlap when they bought and integrated several operations, including Alabama Iron Works, Mobile Marine Ways, and Ollinger and Bruce Dry Dock Company. Shortly thereafter they added the old Gulf City Boiler Works to the mix and set about marketing themselves as a one-stop maritime repair facility. With the outbreak of World War I business boomed, and four thousand people were at work, many of them on Pinto Island where the company had several large dry docks. Welders, electricians, and engineers labored hard, but the war ended before the yard could have much of a role in the Allied victory. During the early 1920s all of ADDSCO's operations were transferred to Pinto Island. Big slips were dug out and the dredge spoil dumped to enlarge the island and raise it above flood levels. A ten-thousand-ton dry dock, warehouses, offices, sheds, machine shops, and water towers were erected, and by 1925 an observer standing on the west bank would have marveled at the changes across the river. Long simply a marshy spot with few residents and no prospects, Pinto Island had become a major shipbuilding and repair facility easily reached from the gulf. Quite simply, it boosted Mobile to another level and was one of the most important marine operations on the coast.[5]

World War I proved the catalyst for the City of Chickasaw when Tennessee Coal and Iron Company bought 13,500 swampy acres for a company town and shipyard. Located about five miles north of the Mobile's mouth and up Chickasaw Creek a bit, the site was hardly inviting. But utilizing twenty million dollars in federal funds, TCI formed three companies, Chickasaw Shipbuilding and Car Company, Chickasaw Utilities Company, and the Chickasaw Land Company, in order to develop the town and build ships for the war. The endeavor was staggering in its scope and complexity and was realized remarkably quickly. Dykes and pumps were employed to drain the swamps and heavy equipment and dredges used to scoop out deep slips into the creek bank. Paved streets, hundreds of houses, and fully equipped shipbuilding facilities arose on the spot. By 1918 there were five thousand people living in the village and working on concrete and steel vessels. Chickasaw was no grim industrial array of plain soulless boxes but rather a charming collection of mostly Craftsman-style cottages arranged facing one another on blocks provided with tree- and shrub-lined interior sidewalks. The shipyard had only completed one vessel by the time the war ended, but it continued afterward fabricating commercial vessels. A total of fourteen were constructed

Launching SS *Selma City,* April 2, 1921, at Chickasaw. Courtesy of the History Museum of Mobile.

and launched from May 1920 to September 1921 alone. These launchings were festive community occasions. Politicians, executives, dignitaries, citizens, and children all clad in their Sunday best jammed the ways and cheered the awesome spectacle of a big ship sliding into the water with a mighty metallic groan and a huge splash.[6]

Mobile's stature as an international port increased further with the formation of the Waterman Steamship Corporation in 1919. John B. Waterman was a native New Orleanian who moved to Mobile in 1902 as manager for a British steamship company. He was active in local civic and social affairs, and his résumé included numerous leadership positions and board memberships, from the Mobile Cotton Exchange, Mobile Rivers and Harbors Committee, and Mobile Chamber of Commerce to the Athelstan Club and the Country Club of Mobile. He was nothing if not alert to new business opportunities, and shortly after World War I he joined with Walter D. Bellingrath and C. W. Hemstead to form the Waterman Steamship Corporation. They started modestly enough, with one leased vessel, and steadily grew with shrewd alliances and acquisitions. Benefitting from a national effort to strengthen the American Merchant Marine, the company got more ships, and by the late 1920s its network included Tampa, Key West, Miami, Puerto Rico, and the West Indies. In 1924 it organized Ryan Stevedoring, which became a successful subsidiary, and on the eve of World War II another of its subsidiaries, Gulf Shipbuilding Corporation, bought the Chickasaw yard and a chunk of the town as well. By 1950 Waterman had more than 125 ships sailing the world and was headquartered in a handsome downtown Mobile skyscraper designed by Texas architect Paul Cret's firm. For years the Waterman Company was one of Mobile's most respected corporate citizens, and it is still recalled with great affection by many locals.[7]

These changes and improvements were certainly encouraging, if not astonishing, but all was not well with the Port of Mobile. Businessmen and politicians disliked the confused medley of waterfront owners, some of whom, the railroads especially, had other interests and loyalties. This translated into higher wharf fees and multiple charges that some felt disadvantaged Mobile in comparison with other gulf ports. Furthermore, what with the river and rail improvements upstate, Mobile's port organization, aging facilities, and crowded old wharves were not conducive to exploiting the new opportunities. Then there was frustration with the driftwood and numerous logs that floated in the channel, creating a hazard for small craft and ship propellers. Even though there were laws against floating logs onto the river unless they were attached to a raft, plenty got lost or broke free, absorbed water, and became dangerous sinkers and sawyers. Combined with trees that were eroded or knocked into the stream, this lost wood made the mouths of One Mile and Three Mile Creeks, as well as the Mobile & Ohio's slips further down, cluttered and unsightly. But the log-choked creek mouths were not the only eyesore to the north. Despite being on the city's doorstep, the bank between these two creeks was a pestilential swampy wasteland, just as it had been since colonial times. Known as Farmer's Island, named and misspelled for Major Farmar who once owned it, this tract was densely covered by cane and palmetto. The only evident

Sawmill at One Mile Creek. Erik Overbey Collection. Courtesy of the Doy Leale McCall Rare Book and Manuscript Library, University of South Alabama.

improvements were the Louisville & Nashville's tracks and Western Union's telegraph line that punched into town through there. A primitive road covered in sawdust followed the telegraph poles. Worrisome fees, overburdened wharves, untapped upstate opportunities, floating timber, and unimproved swamp were all negatives, but just as troubling was the ship channel, once again deemed inadequate. Though the channel had been dredged to twenty-nine feet by World War I ships kept getting bigger, requiring wider and deeper ditches to maneuver. As one advocate stated in December 1925, the "history of Mobile shows that the vessels have followed Channel improvements as fast as made." Continuing federal appropriations helped, but something more coordinated and encompassing was needed if Mobile was to remain competitive.[8]

In a letter to the Mobile City Commission dated October 6, 1916, one local booster enumerated the "great questions which we must now consider." First, he wrote, "the necessity of additional wharf and dock facilities at Mobile; second, the point of location; third, the character of construction; and fourth, the methods of financing and the volume of traffic which can be reasonably expected to seek the use of these additional facilities." Because local interests and funding sources alone were unequal to the scope of such a project, a state-owned port facility seemed to be the perfect answer. But the earliest efforts to establish it were fraught. The Alabama constitution did not allow the legislature to spend monies on internal improvements, and pleas from Mobile that it be amended to correct this situation were rejected. Complicating matters, World War I distracted public officials and depressed world trade. Progress finally seemed possible in 1919 when Congress enacted the Rivers and Harbors Appropriation Bill. This bill stated that because ports were so vital to trade and national security, every town located on a harbor or navigable waterway should have at least one public terminal "constructed, owned, and regulated by municipality or other public agency." The secretary of war was authorized to withhold federal funds from locales where the facilities were deemed inadequate. Mobile had long had a municipal wharf at the foot of Dauphin Street, of course, a length of bulkheaded river frontage where the bay boats and steamboats called, but this was hardly a modern operation. On any given day down there, the scenes were not dissimilar from those of antebellum days—wooden planks, chuffing steamboats, and bales of cotton and piles of cordage heaped under the sun or in primitive metal sheds.[9]

Nothing lights a fire under recalcitrant state governments faster than the threat of losing federal funds, and the Alabama legislature quickly proposed the necessary amendment. Birmingham industrial interests were fully behind it, but rural voters turned it down, worried, as ever, that they would be taxed for benefits they would never realize. Undaunted, the amendment's advocates launched an aggressive statewide education campaign to highlight the importance of a modern seaport to everyone in Alabama. This effort did the trick, and on a second go in 1922 the amendment passed easily. It cleared the way for Alabama to "engage in the work of internal improvement, of promoting, developing, constructing, maintaining, and operating all harbors or seaports within the State or its jurisdiction" to the tune of ten million dollars. The following year the legislature passed an enabling act which established a State Docks Commission authorized to build, operate, and maintain "wharves, piers, docks, quays, grain elevators, cotton compresses, warehouses and other water and rail terminals, and other structures and facilities."[10]

With a three-member commission and an initial five-million-dollar bond issue in place, the grand endeavor was set to begin. But who best to lead? The commission's first choice was retired army general William L. Sibert, a native Alabamian and skilled engineer who had worked on the Panama Canal and led the army's chemical warfare program. Sibert cut a dashing and distinguished figure with his military bearing, silvered hair parted on the side, trim mustache, and round wire-frame glasses. As he later wrote in an article for the *Atlanta Constitution,* he was comfortably ensconced at "a farm that I had bought near Bowling Green, Ky." and probably blissfully unaware of the complicated maneuvering going on in his home state. Amid pleasant rolling fields and stands of hardwoods, he busied himself with "a good pack of fox hounds and some saddle horses and was starting to enjoy life after 40 years of strenuous labor." One can imagine his mixed emotions when a delegation called and urged him to accept the challenge of developing a modern deep-water port in Mobile, Alabama. Clear-eyed realist that he was, he was foremost concerned that petty political rivalries would make the job exasperating, if not impossible. Alabama governor William W. Brandon assured him that "the work would be kept entirely out of politics" and that he "would be given an absolutely free hand in prosecuting the work." Based upon these assurances, Sibert accepted.[11]

As to exactly where the docks would be built, Farmer's Island presented the most attractive locale. It was largely undeveloped, and its negatives were believed to be realistically manageable. Sibert toured the site with various politicians and businessmen and quickly sketched his master plan. One Mile Creek, on the parcel's southern end, was to be rerouted through a "diversion channel a little more than one mile long" so that its waters would empty into Three Mile Creek. This new canal was to be dug "wide enough and deep enough for barge navigation" and, it was hoped, would offer enticing opportunities to further industry. Dredge spoil from the canal and a series of 350-foot-wide, 35-foot-deep angled slips riverside—more than 15 million cubic yards' worth—would be used to raise the level of the island 7 feet, giving the docks an elevation of 11 feet above sea level, safe from all but the most catastrophic storm surges. The Louisville & Nashville's tracks had to be shifted almost half a mile west, off the site, and a new railroad bridge provided at Three Mile Creek. Last, several sawmills needed to be relocated.[12]

Throughout 1925, 1926, and 1927 a workforce that variously included puttee-clad engineers, surveyors, and chain men; starch-collared lawyers, clerks, and accountants; short-bobbed "girl Fridays"; denim-shirted steam-shovel and dredge operators; bare-chested pile drivers and ditch diggers; hard-hat divers; khaki-trousered tugboat pilots, deckhands, and masons; roadster-capped carpenters; and common laborers both white and black pushed forward the ambitious scheme. Through merciless sun, freezing north winds, and torrential rain the work never abated. The theretofore swampy island was now a seething construction zone. By the middle of 1926 the five-million-dollar bond was spent, and the legislature quickly authorized another. Once the L & N's tracks and sawmills were removed, the industrial canal and slips dug, and the land raised, several big new piers were constructed between the slips. These piers were monstrous concrete affairs that would have amazed the cotton factors and steamboat captains of old. Each was 1,600 feet long and 560 feet wide and featured a 42-foot apron around paired 180-foot-wide structural steel sheds. The sheds were secured by dozens of 20-foot-wide, 12-foot-high rolling steel doors, as well as concrete interior fire walls. Three sets of triple-slotted railroad tracks ran out the piers, one set along each side and another between the sheds. These tracks maximized efficiency. On the dockside runs the front track was to "allow the handling of material with the ship's tackle to or from an open-top car"; the middle track was for handling box cars; and the interior track was a passing line to allow for continual service to multiple freighters berthed alongside. Switches allowed cars to be easily shifted and moved wherever needed.[13]

Alabama State Docks Commission tour. Bigwigs traverse Farmer's Island aboard a flat car. Erik Overby Collection. Courtesy of the Doy Leale McCall Rare Book and Manuscript Library, University of South Alabama.

June 25, 1928, was dedication day. Appropriately enough, Sibert emceed the ceremony, which took place on Pier A in Transit Shed 4. Dozens of dignitaries attended, including Governor Bibb Graves; former Governor William W. Brandon; Senator Hugo Black; Congressman John McDuffie; W. R. Cole, president of the Louisville & Nashville Railroad; Mobile city commissioner Harry T. Hartwell; and A. Lane Cricher, U. S. assistant chief of transportation. Backgrounded by half a dozen ships in "gala attire," Sibert was fairly bursting with pride. "There is nothing that brings quite the satisfaction to the builder," he declared, "as to see structures emerge from the dream through the drawings and blueprints and stand forth realities, ready and useful for man." Governor Graves, the keynote speaker, gave a colorful and entertaining address, in which he made no bones about the significance of the occasion. "We are here opening Alabama's doors to the world," he stated, "not for our benefit alone, but for the benefit of mankind. This is a turning point in the commercial history of Alabama." The dignitaries, numerous out-of-state guests, and thousands of excited ordinary Mobilians then toured the new docks. Everyone was filled with praise and admiration. The vice president of the Atlanta Chamber of Commerce intoned, "Mobile is facing one of the greatest opportunities in its history and I extend the congratulations of Atlanta and her people." The general manager of the Southern Bell Telephone Company, headquartered in Birmingham, announced that "Mobile will benefit not only from the natural increase of tonnage that will come with the opening of the docks, but will be placed in a position to attract big industries here, which need imported raw materials with which to work." And in confirmation of the last point, a representative of the Chicago Chamber of Commerce said that "Chicago, Illinois and the middle west will co-operate in every way in helping to build up the tonnage figures of your port."[14]

From that day forward the Alabama State Docks would only grow and expand its facilities and networks. Surveying the prospects in 1934, John Waterman was confident of this future success. "With coordinated effort of the various interests involved in foreign commerce," he wrote, "namely, the shippers and receivers of cargo in the gulf and in the interior; the ocean steamship services, American and foreign to all parts of the world; and finally, the cooperated coordinated efforts of all the terminal facilities at Mobile, the success of this port cannot be questioned." In 1937 a federal report tabulated Mobile's waterfront assets: "55 piers and wharves with a total berthing space of 46,542 lineal feet, bunkering facilities for both coal and fuel oil, and adequate vessel repair plants." In addition to the Alabama State Docks, the old municipal wharf was still in operation as well as the Turner Terminal, the Alabama Dry Dock and Shipbuilding

Aerial view, Alabama State Docks, 1950. History Museum of Mobile Collection. Courtesy of the Doy Leale McCall Rare Book and Manuscript Library, University of South Alabama.

Company slips, and the Mobile & Ohio piers. The latest big project was the construction of a cold storage plant with a capacity of five hundred thousand cubic feet, and other industrial concerns were locating along the canal. Significant new enterprises at the port included International Paper, Aluminum Ore Company, and Standard Oil Company. Seventeen different steamship lines served Mobile, and a barge line linked it with the interior. Waterborne commerce totaled 3,916,061 tons in 1936, a 95 percent increase over the previous four years. What would Iberville and Bienville have said![15]

Besides port developments during the 1920s and 1930s, two big-budget transportation projects profoundly impacted the Mobile River and how ordinary citizens related to it. Since time immemorial, people travelling east–west along the Gulf Coast had been forced to cross the upper bay by boat or take a long looping land detour around the delta. Even after the Federal Road and railroads penetrated the area, travelers still had to resort to ferries for parts of the route and often experienced frustrating delays. By the 1920s automobiles were common, and better jobs and leisure time meant that ordinary Americans were free to travel long distances. Florida reaped a tourism bonanza during the 1920s, and Mobile's leaders were eager to take advantage of this new phenomenon. In concert with boosters in other cities from Jacksonville, Florida, to San Diego, California, they began working toward their piece of a transcontinental highway. Led by John T. Cochrane, president of the Alabama, Tennessee and Northern Railroad and of the Mobile Chamber of Commerce, the Mobile Bay Bridge Company proposed a ten-mile causeway with multiple bridges that would at last provide a durable and efficient link to Baldwin County. The project was to be financed by the sale of twenty-five million dollars in bonds and paid off by tolls. The first contracts were awarded in 1926, and the entire project completed by the spring of the following year. Besides concrete road laid across the lower delta islands and fixed-span bridges at the Apalachee and Blakeley Rivers, the causeway featured two lift bridges, one over the Tensaw/Spanish mouth and the other over the Mobile. The latter span was located between Three Mile and Chickasaw Creeks so as not to interfere with the heavy ship traffic at the Alabama State Docks. The causeway was officially dedicated on June 14, 1927, with Governor Bibb Graves once again basking in a major achievement for his state. The Mobile River lift bridge was named for Cochrane and initially required a modest toll. Rates were one dollar each for cars, two dollars for large trucks, and ten cents for pedestrians. By 1940 more than a million vehicles a year were using the bridge. The bridge did not age out until the 1980s, and it was replaced in 1991 by a spectacular soaring cable-stayed bridge that became an icon after 2005's Hurricane Katrina wedged an oil-drilling platform beneath its road deck.[16]

The causeway eliminated the wooden bay boats, but because the Cochrane Bridge required an almost four-mile jog north to complete the route, Mobilians dreamed of an even more direct way to motor over the river. Happily, the Great Depression provided the solution in the form of the Works Progress Administration. Some suggested another lift span bridge at Government Street, but this idea was rejected because, being

Cochrane Bridge, 1983. Erected in 1927, the bridge was replaced about a decade after this photograph was taken. Azalea City News Collection. Courtesy of the Doy Leale McCall Rare Book and Manuscript Library, University of South Alabama.

south of the Alabama State Docks, constant interruptions and delays would result. A tunnel looked to be a better option, and with four million dollars of financing in place, construction got under way. By any measure this was an exciting and innovative project, and Mobilians were fascinated. Rather than bore under the riverbed, contractors dredged a trench from the foot of Government Street to Blakeley Island. ADDSCO, the Alabama Dry Dock and Shipbuilding Company, located conveniently close to the site, got the contract to build seven steel tubes, which were floated over the trench, slowly lined with reinforced concrete and sunk in place. The joints were sealed with steel collars and rubber gaskets, and the interior joints welded so that all was watertight. The construction statistics were staggering: 200,000 yards of soil excavated for the entrances, 700,000 yards of river mud dredged, 29,000 yards of concrete poured, and 1,700 tons of structural steel and 800 tons of reinforcing steel used. The finished tunnel was 3,389 feet long, 1,147 feet of it beneath the actual river, and drivers utilized a two-lane, 21-foot-wide road with a maximum grade of 6 percent and 13 feet of headroom. Officials hastened to reassure those worried about massive cargo vessels just over their heads. The tunnel top's maximum depth at mean high water was 47 feet, well below the deepest-draft ships, and even if one sank, the tunnel could support "such gargantuan weight several times multiplied." For those anxious about poisonous fumes in the tube, three large blower fans with a capacity of 548,000 cubic feet per minute and a ventilator shaft built on Blakeley Island were capable of completely circulating the air every two minutes. The tube was officially named the Bankhead Tunnel in honor of former a U. S. senator and congressman from Alabama, John Hollis Bankhead, who had been a champion of river and harbor improvements until his death in 1920.[17]

Opening day, February 20, 1941, was cold and drizzly, but thousands of people turned out for the chance to, as the *Register* put it, "go under the Mobile River for the first time." At a signal from the mayor, police removed two wooden sawhorses, and the crowd surged forward. Boy Scouts helped keep people from either end to their proper lanes. Among the first through were a toddler in a "perambulator" and his mother who, the newspaper reported, "wore an 'I'll-never-look-at-another-tunnel-as-long-as-I-live' expression." There was also a youngster on roller skates who "had a dandy time until the half-way mark was reached." Throngs of teenagers laughed and jostled, and one man without pants and a "not-long-enough raincoat" was surrounded by a clutch of grinning friends, the result "of a lost bet that the tunnel would never open." It took most people about twelve minutes to walk the distance one way. By 10:00 p.m. police cleared the remaining pedestrians and opened the tube to traffic. A toll plaza at the east end collected fees until the 1970s, when passage became free. One of the most notable people ever to travel the tunnel was the Alabama actress Tallulah Bankhead, Senator Bankhead's granddaughter. She was brought to Mobile by Congressman Frank Boykin to appear in a play at Murphy High School. The story goes that after the play, Miss Bankhead hired a cab and hurtled through the tunnel waving a Confederate flag and whooping and hollering. Throughout her long life she gave Bankhead Tunnel postcards as souvenirs to fans.[18]

The same year that the tunnel opened, war came to the river once again. Mobile would be profoundly altered by the experience, doubling in population and changing from a pocketed, exotic, European-flavored big town to a fully modern city. When the Japanese bombed Pearl Harbor, about eighty thousand people lived in Alabama's seaport. But unlike the situation during the Civil War, when Confederate authorities had limited resources for their cause, the city already had key assets in place. ADDSCO at one end of the harbor and Gulf Ship Building at the other were both functioning modern shipyards, and the Alcoa alumina plant riverside was operational. And thanks to the efforts of Congressman Boykin, a large army-air-corps supply depot and air field was then under construction at Brookley Field, just south of town. With the onset of war and a flurry of high-dollar defense projects, Mobile boomed.[19]

Both ADDSCO and Gulf Shipbuilding scored major contracts and quickly expanded their facilities and hired more workers. Tens of thousands of people flooded into town seeking work and were hired as soon as they arrived. The novelist John Dos Passos visited Mobile early in the war and penned one of the most colorful descriptions of local types since antebellum times: "Soldiers, sailors, stout women with bundled up babies, lanky backwoodsmen with hats tipped over their brows and a cheek full of

Gulf Shipbuilding aerial view, 1939. These slips were dredged on Chickasaw Creek. Courtesy of the History Museum of Mobile.

chewing tobacco, hatless young men in light-colored shirts open at the neck, . . . cigar-smoking stocky men in business suits in pastel shades, girls in bright dresses with hair carefully piled up on their heads and highheeled shoes and blooded fingernails, . . . negroes in flap jackets and pegtop pants and little felt hats with turned up brims." The town was fairly bursting at the seams. On the outskirts Dos Passos discovered "acres and acres raw with new building, open fields skinned to the bare clay, elevations gashed with muddy roads and gnawed out by the powershovels and bulldozers." Cheap houses went up by the hundreds, and still there were not enough. People jammed into anything and everything they could find, and in some sections the city looked more like a refugee camp. "The schools are too full of children. The restaurants too full of eaters," Dos Passos declared. Men slept in "hot beds" for eight hours and then vacated them for the next exhausted shift worker. "It was seven days a week," one of them recalled. "Twelve hour days, five days a week. Ten hours on Saturday. On Sunday, when you only worked eight hours, you felt you'd had a week off."[20]

The stresses on Mobile's staid social structure were irritating to long-time residents. One grumbled about the influx of "riffraff." Others, in reference to the rural Southern origins of many of the workers, where textile mills were common, called them "lint heads." One teacher sneered that "these are the lowest type of poor whites, these workers flocking in from the backwoods. They prefer to live in shacks and go barefoot. Give them a good home and they wouldn't know what to do with it." But some rather liked the opportunities presented by the situation. One Minnesota soldier had his eye on the "country girls" who now found themselves in a new place with good jobs. Picking them up "didn't take much sophistication," he quipped. "If you said, 'Would you like a drink?' that would be enough. And then, if you were lucky, you'd get a taxicab and you'd go out to their dreadful little flat among the little houses."[21]

Besides poor white persons, large numbers of black people came seeking war work as well, and many found it. By 1944 ADDSCO employed almost seven thousand black workers out of a total force of thirty thousand. Among them were Herbert Aaron, father of future baseball great Hank Aaron, and nineteen-year-old John Gray. Aaron worked as a boilermaker's assistant, while Gray was a carpenter's helper, earning sixty-five cents an hour. Skilled jobs were initially denied to black seekers, and federal-government pressure that they be given more opportunity in the shipyards did not sit well with white laborers. "It's a thing you just have to go easy on," one white worker warned Dos Passos. "Ain't a white man in the South'll stand for it. Mister, you tell your friends up North that this ain't no time to rock the boat." Attempts to force the issue in the spring of 1943 led to serious riots on Pinto Island, but that story is for a later chapter.[22]

Despite the stresses and strains, the war work went furiously ahead. ADDSCO added new ways and improved its speed and efficiency. In the early days of 1942 the company took 250 days to build a Liberty ship, but by late 1944 ADDSCO was sending them sliding into the river in less than seventy days. Up at Chickasaw, almost twelve thousand workers were building destroyers and minesweepers, but the launches were no longer gala occasions. Men and women kept up their tasks all around the ways while a small workers' band played the national anthem. Multiple crews worked on multiple hulls at both yards, and the glare of welding torches flickered day and night. The overall production of these shipyards was staggering. By war's end ADDSCO had built 102 tankers and twenty Liberty ships and had repaired almost three thousand vessels, some of them battle-damaged. Gulf Shipbuilding could boast twenty-nine minesweepers, thirty tankers, seven destroyers, and a landing dock.[23]

Alcoa also contributed significantly to the Allied effort. Opened just a few years before the war, the company's bauxite refinery sat on a seventy-five-acre parcel leased from the state docks. All during the war, freighters brought in the ore to be refined into alumina, which was then shipped to smelters in North Carolina to be converted to aluminum, a vital war metal. During the refining process the raw bauxite, a soft reddish rock, was ground and mixed with caustic soda and then run through precipitation tanks and kilns. By 1943 the facility was producing more than 1.5 million pounds of alumina a day, more than 30 percent of the U. S. output. But the business was not without risk and cost. On May 6, 1942, the *Alcoa Puritan,* a bauxite freighter en route from Trinidad to Mobile, was targeted by a German U-boat some one hundred miles out from Mobile Bay. The first torpedo sped just below the vessel's stern as the freighter's captain desperately put on speed and a zigzag course. The submarine surfaced and gave chase, all the while pummeling the merchant ship with rounds from its deck gun.

Ferry Alabama, January 1935. Black and white workers file aboard on opposite sides. Erik Overbey Collection. Courtesy of the Doy Leale McCall Rare Book and Manuscript Library, University of South Alabama.

Alcoa Puritan took hit after hit until the captain ordered her abandoned. The U-boat finished her with another torpedo, and the hapless crew abandoned ship and was eventually rescued by a Coast Guard cutter out of Mobile. Incredibly, only two men were wounded in the attack.[24]

Real evidence that there was a shooting war on was thus not hard to come by in the Port City. Several torpedoed vessels limped into harbor for repair during the early 1940s and were the object of much curiosity. Fears of U-boat attacks on the city itself were unfounded, but blackouts along the beaches were ordered to reduce the chances of ships being silhouetted by lights ashore. Nighttime ball games were suspended, cars within five hundred yards of the shore told to use parking lights only, and flounder giggers with lanterns subjected to chastisement by mounted patrols. The army placed several large searchlights at Fort Morgan and mounted two 155-mm guns to help guard the entrance to the bay. But the few U-boats stayed well out in the gulf and by 1944 were gone. Nonetheless, rumors that a U-boat managed to get into Mobile Bay or that German spies had been landed in Baldwin County found receptive ears and are still heard to this day, but there is no evidence of either.[25]

As victory approached, the shipyards began laying off employees by the thousands. Many left town, others stayed, and the city's population settled at almost two hundred thousand. Gulf Shipbuilding suspended operations, but ADDSCO remained in business with a vastly reduced workforce, and in 1949 the company purchased the government's interest in the land and assets developed during the war. Besides a fair chunk of Pinto Island, these assets included a bridge over Pinto Pass, warehouses, shops, the plant hospital, roads and railroad tracks, cranes, barges, derricks, and machine tools. The company remained in business through the late 1980s, mostly doing repair work. It finally closed in 1988, costing four hundred workers their jobs.[26]

The end of hostilities meant surplus warships, and Congressman Frank Boykin, indefatigable as ever, lobbied the War Shipping Administration and the U. S. Maritime Commission to consider mothballing some of them in the Mobile River. While not as exciting or job-rich an endeavor as shipbuilding, mothballing did require personnel and an ongoing federal commitment to maintain the fleet minimally in case war broke out again and the ships had to be put back into service. Within months of peace more than thirty Liberty ships and tankers were moored side by side and end on end at the southern tip of Twelve Mile Island. They presented an eerie sight and were the subject of much interest around the country. On August 31, 1946, the *Pittsburgh Post-Gazette* ran a large aerial photograph under headline "Ghost Fleet Keeps Growing in Mobile River." Eventually a channel was dredged across to link with the Tensaw River, and many ships were transferred there. Over the years the ghost ships were sold to foreign nations or for scrap, and by 1973 the last of them were towed out into the gulf and sunk for fishing reefs.[27]

After the war Mobile's business and political class continued to depend on the river for their economic future. "We have our port and we propose to make the most of it" was how a writer for *Fortune* magazine put the prevailing mood. This was hardly an irresponsible position. In 1946 Mobile ranked as one of the nation's top ten seaports, ahead of Los Angeles and San Francisco. In an effort to solidify this ranking, if not better it, advocates began pushing for what they called the Tenn-Tom Waterway, a proposed series of canals, locks, and dams that would connect the Tombigbee and Tennessee Rivers, thereby linking Mobile directly by water with the Midwest. The idea was an old one, dating back to the colonial French, but during the prosperous post–World War II years it finally appeared achievable. The 1946 Rivers and Harbors Act laid the necessary policy groundwork, and then Congressman Boykin began relentlessly beating the drum. Variously referring to the proposed waterway as "the greatest thing under the shining sun" and "the greatest proposition this side of heaven," Boykin confidently predicted that it would make Mobile "the biggest port in America." Environmentalists feared a catastrophe, and government watchdogs worried about massive spending for dubious freight targets. Nonetheless, by 1970, thanks to the efforts of Alabama senator John Sparkman, Alabama congressman Jack Edwards, and Mississippi senator John C. Stennis, the funding was finally in place. President Richard Nixon traveled to Mobile on May 25 of the following year to celebrate the beginning of construction. The visit was certainly good politics for Nixon, giving him a chance to get out of overcooked Washington and tout economic progress in the conservative South. The speechifying took place at the state docks. Standing on a platform in front of a large ship, Nixon was flanked by Alabama governor George Wallace, dazzling in a white suit, and the governor's wife, Cornelia. Numerous other elected officials from five different states, as well as business and professional elites, were in the audience. As he took the podium, Nixon surely was on guard, for he knew that the popular Alabama governor was a potential opposing candidate, but the throngs of onlookers detected no tension. In his remarks the chief executive extolled the Tenn-Tom's expected benefits. "What does a project like this mean?" he asked. "Well, it means a lot to this city because it means that this port, already a great port, will now have a waterway that will connect it with the Ohio, and with the Missouri, and the Mississippi, but it means, therefore, that there will be more traffic coming in through the port of Mobile."[28]

The Tenn-Tom Waterway was to become the most expensive project in the history of the U. S. Army Corps of Engineers. The final price tag, to the degree that it could even be accurately determined, was nearly two billion dollars. By the time it was dedicated in 1985, the waterway included 10 locks, each 600 feet long and 110 feet wide; a series of slack lakes; and, of course, the storied Tombigbee River itself, thoroughly tamed by all the engineering. Tens of thousands of people turned out for the dedication ceremonies, held in Columbus, Mississippi, and Mobile. The predictions were rosy. The corps claimed twenty-seven million tons would be shipped down the waterway in its first year alone. Unfortunately, the project was to be more of a boondoggle than an economic windfall. An anemic five million tons of cargo, mostly timber and coal, threaded the waterway its first year, and as late at 2009 this total had barely doubled. As far as Midwestern shippers were concerned, the mile-wide mighty Mississippi with its awesome current was a more attractive highway than the narrow Tenn-Tom with all its locks. The waterway's host states did reap some benefit from barge companies running their empties upstream—less fuel cost than in the Mississippi—and from recreational boaters. But sadly, the environmentalists' fears seemed to have been confirmed in the havoc wrought to the river's natural flow cycle by all the locks and dams. Boykin's own son mused years later: "I have some reservations about it. Anytime the Corps of Engineers gets hold of something, they create problems."[29]

The corps was also active on the other half of the Mobile River Basin, dredging the Alabama, removing snags, and building locks and dams. The goal there was a year-round, nine-foot-deep channel the length of the river that could sustain barge traffic. By 1972 the Robert F. Henry Lock and Dam complex was completed in Autauga County, upstream from Selma. This project delivered hydroelectric power, effective flood control, and a recreational bonanza. But the huge commercial benefits promised from increased barge traffic did not materialize. Just as on the Tenn-Tom, on the Alabama the tonnage figures were low. The best year was 1986, when 4.1 million tons moved, but by

2000 the total was a pitiful 100,000. Environmentalists decried the disruption of the river's natural flow cycle and worried about the effect of a big paper mill at Claiborne.[30]

Meanwhile down in Mobile, high-dollar improvements in and around the harbor radically altered the old riverfront and further enhanced transportation and commerce. Perhaps the most profound change came with federally funded urban renewal in the 1960s and 1970s, when all of the historic brick warehouses, cotton presses, and office buildings along Front, Commerce, and Water Streets were leveled. The area was already mostly deserted what with the recent economic changes and the development of the state docks just to the north. One observer called it "a snaggle-toothed array of vacant buildings and parking lots." But to preservationists it was a wonderland of mid- to late-nineteenth-century commercial architecture rich in elegant design and superior building materials including marble, granite, cast iron, and huge heart-pine sills and joists. Nonetheless, block after block of these treasures fell into clouds of rubble and masonry dust. An antebellum Mobilian fast-forwarded to the foot of Government Street would have been completely disoriented. Water Street was now a four-lane "boulevard-parkway entrance to downtown" where drivers could enjoy "a curving panorama of clean-lined and green-set buildings." South of Government Street, where densely populated residential neighborhoods had long existed, acres of houses, streets, and trees were removed for the new Municipal Auditorium and its enormous parking lots. Sweeping into town along the bay shore, the concrete lanes and grass medians of Interstate 10 obliterated whole swaths of the old city, and in the Texas Street and Davis Avenue communities hundreds of substandard but historic houses were demolished and replaced with utilitarian brick boxes. No one in power objected to any of this, and the few preservationists could only mourn the loss of so much character. Unfortunately for Mobile, this drastic redevelopment robbed it of a distinctive historic ambiance that cities such as Savannah, Georgia, and New Orleans later showed could be turned into tourist gold and world fame. As one local architect quipped, "We now have excellent access to a place we no longer want to go."[31]

For those just passing through, the construction of Interstates 10 and 65 provided two more convenient places to cross the Mobile River. Interstate 10 is a transcontinental highway that stretches between Los Angeles, California, and Jacksonville, Florida. In Alabama it spans the head of Mobile Bay, gracefully curving over the old causeway at one point. Completion of this leg presented significant engineering challenges. The decision was made to build another tunnel under the Mobile River, with the road ascending to an elevated viaduct bridge 7.5 miles long connecting with Baldwin County at Spanish Fort. ADDSCO got the contract to build the tunnel, and from 1969 to 1973 Pinto Island bustled. The construction methodology had not changed much since the Bankhead Tunnel was built thirty years earlier. The tunnel, or actually tunnels, since twin tubes were required to accommodate the interstate's two lanes each way, was built in massive sections. Each section held portions of both tubes. These were then floated out into the river and sunk into a dredged trench just south of the Bankhead

Tunnel. The joints were sealed with concrete and rubber and the tubes pumped dry. Now that interstate traffic could get under the Mobile River, it had to get over the bay. Rather than one bridge, engineers proposed two, each two lanes wide and one way, which were not completed until 1978. These improvements were officially named the George C. Wallace Tunnel and the Jubilee Parkway, but locals persist in calling them the New Tunnel and the Bayway. Together these projects made Baldwin County's bucolic Eastern Shore accessible in minutes and stimulated a suburban boom in Spanish Fort, Daphne, and Fairhope.[32]

Interstate 65 is a north–south highway linking Gary, Indiana, and Mobile. Construction began in the mid-1960s, and sections of the road rapidly came into service. But just as Mobile Bay had to be conquered before I-10 could be completed, the Mobile River Delta lay between I-65's roadbed and its successful terminus. From 1978 to 1980 engineers and construction crews labored in the swamps with pile drivers, tugs, derricks, barges, and tons of concrete and steel. By the time they were finished the new bridge was one of the longest in the nation at just over six miles, and its parallel tied arches became one of south Alabama's most iconic landmarks. From its high point 125 feet above the Mobile River proper, travelers can see vast swamps and brown streams to either side, a few smokestacks, and Mobile's downtown skyscrapers on the far horizon. The span was officially named the General W. K. Wilson Jr. Bridge for a local corps of engineers officer who had championed a bridge compatible with marine traffic. Still ignoring formal designations, locals call it the Dolly Parton Bridge for obvious reasons.[33]

Two other big-budget highway projects involving the Mobile River unfolded during the late twentieth and early twenty-first centuries. One was forced into a more community friendly redesign in 1988, while the other remains the subject of ongoing study and debate. In the mid-1980s highway planners proposed a seventeen-foot raised connector to link I-65 and I-10 on Mobile's east side. The road was to run right along the riverfront the entire six miles. The project had vocal supporters, including the editor of the *Mobile Register* at the time, but preservationists worried about historic landmarks such as the Gulf, Mobile & Ohio Railroad Terminal (1908) and the old city hall (1857) being compromised as well as the city's time-honored river access impaired or denied. A lawsuit was brought against the project by the Coalition Against a Raised Expressway, a group made up of, among others, Downtown Mobile Unlimited, the Mobile Historic Development Commission, the Historic Mobile Preservation Society, and the National Trust for Historic Preservation. Eventually the suit wound up at the Eleventh Circuit Court of Appeals, which ruled that the proposed connector would indeed constitute an adverse effect. The court found, in part, that "the raised highway would impact on the protected sites by impairing the view. The highway would cut off the city hall's view of the river and the docks. Conversely, it would reduce the view from the river of the city hall's architecture." Furthermore, seen from the river, "the highway would replace the view of downtown with the sight of the seventeen foot concrete pillars holding up the freeway. In addition, the dirt and debris from an elevated freeway would lessen the beauty of the architecture itself." In order to mitigate these effects, the raised highway was dropped to grade at the north end of downtown, alongside the Gulf, Mobile & Ohio Terminal. Traffic then used Water Street to traverse the riverfront and loop into the Wallace Tunnel from an on ramp. Preservationists were jubilant and rightly so. The decision was a major victory after years of punishing disappointment, and it shaped the riverfront's destiny for years to come. With the raised highway defeated, recreational, cultural, and business developments along the river became attractive propositions. During the next two decades the construction and opening of the Mobile Convention Center, Cooper Riverside Park, the Alabama Cruise Terminal, Gulf Coast Exploreum Science Center, the History Museum of Mobile, and the Gulfquest National Maritime Museum of the Gulf of Mexico all proved the wisdom of those who had argued for open and easy waterfront access. Perhaps no legal decision since *Pollard v. Hagan* in 1844 (the Equal Footing Doctrine) was so important for Mobilians and their relationship to the river at their doorstep.[34]

Preservationists and downtown advocates were unable to rest on this accomplishment for long, however. They were soon appalled to learn that a huge new bridge was being planned to cross the Mobile River somewhere downtown or close to it. By the mid-1990s the Gulf Coast's growing population and economy placed more traffic on I-10 than ever before, and the Wallace Tunnel developed into a major bottleneck. The tunnel's eastern entrance with its badly designed hard curve did not help matters. Wrecks and slowdowns were always common occurrences there, but by the 1990s the delays were happening almost daily. To relieve the pressure and allow for future traffic, federal and state engineers called for "construction of a six-lane, cable-stayed bridge with 190 feet of vertical clearance over the Mobile River navigation channel." At that height a Saturn V rocket with its escape tower attached could be fitted beneath the road deck. Compounding the scale, the deck's support pylons were to be almost five hundred feet tall and brightly lit at night. The George C. Wallace Tunnel would remain in use, becoming a downtown spur, but through traffic would use the bridge. To accommodate the increased interstate traffic volume and speed, the Jubilee Parkway itself was to be widened "by two lanes (to the inside) resulting in a total of eight lanes." The projected cost for all of this was in the hundreds of millions and increased each year. There was no question of not building the bridge; the only issue was where to put it. Numerous locations were hashed out in a series of public meetings and conferences that went on for years. Preservationists and maritime interests preferred a northerly route, near the Cochrane Bridge or even utilizing it, which was far enough away from downtown and the docks to be considered acceptable. Eventually three more southerly routes emerged as the most likely, any of which represented a significant change coming for the river and the skyline. Projections showing the bridge as it would appear from various spots in town were breathtaking evidence that it was likely to become Mobile's defining feature, rather like Tampa Bay's Sunshine Skyway Bridge. The best that preservationists could hope for was an interesting design, anything but a given. On April 7, 2000, the Mobile Historic Development Commission passed a resolution in opposition, stating in part that "the location of the proposed bridge would have a serious and deleterious effect on the development of Mobile's historic waterfront, its downtown, and the neighborhoods in the vicinity of this bridge." Local attorney Palmer Hamilton voiced many historic district residents' opinion when he observed that "millions have been spent to redevelop the waterfront, and we shouldn't throw that investment away." But there were supporters as well. Jimmy Lyons, director of the Alabama State Port Authority, wrote: "Of the three routes under consideration, the one just south of the cruise terminal seems to have the least impact. I hope the project can move forward soon as it is desperately needed." U. S. senator Jeff Sessions expressed a cautious, noncommittal position as he watched the debate unfold. "Much care and much discussion should be given to this important decision," he suggested. As late as 2013 the matter was still unsettled, and the down economy precluded an immediate high-dollar federal highway project in any case. Most people expect the bridge to be constructed eventually. If so, it will hardly be the first or the last major change the Mobile River has seen.[35]

The late twentieth and early twenty-first centuries also brought important new developments at the port. In 1971 the state legislature cleared the way for a new sixteen-million-dollar coal facility at McDuffie Island. Eventually consisting of three berths, as well as rail dumps, stackers, and barge unloaders, McDuffie Coal Terminal greatly boosted Mobile's importance as a coal exporter. During 2012 almost fourteen million tons passed through the port. Just to the north and west of McDuffie Island, on Choctaw Point, the state docks began construction of a vast container and intermodal facility in the early 2000s where it had previously had a bulk cargo handling operation. Memories of the swampy, driftwood-strewn area were long gone by then. The latest improvements to the 380-acre site included a two-berth slip dredged to forty-five feet, four large gantry cranes, a paved staging area, roads, and railroads. In 2009 almost ninety thousand containers moved through the terminal, and by 2011 this figure increased 40 percent. With so many features and assets in place, the port's overall 2012 statistics were impressive, eloquent confirmation that all the long and difficult efforts to improve the harbor had been worth it. Portwide vessel calls stood at 1,222, tonnage through the main docks was 25.2 million, more than 196,000 containers were handled, and tens of thousands of railroad cars loaded or unloaded. Imports included coal, aluminum, steel, copper, lumber, wood pulp, veneers, paper, cement, and chemicals, while among the exports were coal, lumber, laminate, paper, iron, steel, frozen poultry, soybeans, and chemicals. The port's national ranking of twelfth by tonnage is only a little below what it was immediately after World War II. But perhaps the most remarkable recent development has been its ability to handle the gigantic new Post-Panamax ships, those vessels too large to fit in the Panama Canal. These behemoths now routinely call at the Choctaw Point and McDuffie terminals where they take on loads that would have exceeded the capacities of every ship combined in the Lower Fleet 175 years ago.[36]

Mobile harbor dredging, 1988. Courtesy of the Alabama State Port Authority.

Besides the state docks' latest additions, numerous other large-scale developments during the early 2000s in the harbor and upstream further insured the river's enduring significance. These included BAE Southeast Shipyard, located on Pinto Island, with piers, dry docks, heavy lift barges, cranes, welding stations, pipe shop, and storage facilities; ThyssenKrupp's steel slab terminal at the southern tip of Pinto Island, with its giant gantry cranes and magnetic lifting gear, and upstream at Calvert (on the Tombigbee opposite Nannahubba Island), its five-billion-dollar rolling mill and river port; Austal USA's shipbuilding facility on Blakeley Island across from the convention center, where a multibillion dollar series of U. S. government contracts to fabricate and launch trimmaran littoral combat ships, transports, and ferries has rivaled if not yet exceeded ADDSCO's and Gulf Shipbuilding's important legacies; and, last, a 72-million-dollar, 3.5-million-ton vertical lift railroad bridge at the river's 14-mile mark that replaced an 80-year-old pivot bridge. Taken together, these extraordinary projects promise to be transformative for the city and the region, but the full story of their development and achievements will have to await the pen of a later historian.[37]

A century of construction projects, dredging, and industrial development put formidable stresses on area waterways. The Mobile River was never a clear purling stream, of course—an eighteenth-century British surgeon noted its "innumerable impurities"—but as human activity increased on its banks, it only got dirtier. The

French directed their "*conduit des latrines*" directly into the river, and the Americans did the same thing until the middle of the twentieth century. When the river was in flood, raw sewage backed through these pipes and onto the downtown streets, where it mingled with animal waste and rubbish in the open gutters. In 1913 one writer enumerated ten sewage pipes emptying into the river but confidently declared that "up to the present time the amount of waste has not been in sufficient quantity to noticeably defile the river." He was probably right. As long as the city's population remained relatively small and industrial development minimal, and there were no dams to impede the flow, the river could easily cleanse itself.[38]

Matters became acute during the 1920s through the 1950s, however. Increasing pressure on the river and little to no environmental regulation combined to seriously foul the air and water. Besides continued sewage problems, storm-water runoff, and large ships dumping bilge water into the harbor and bay, there were plants such as Alcoa and International Paper (IP) busily making their products and discarding their waste. Alcoa piped its bauxite residue under the river and into ugly red and green tailings ponds on Blakeley Island. Paper mills like IP had been around Mobile for some time and were notable for their sulfurlike stink. Some locals complained; others just shrugged their shoulders. The mills brought jobs, and, as the *Mobile Register* somewhat creepily put it, "To those who were saved by this timely help in time of need during the late Depression, the paper mill fumes were 'sweet as the smell of a dead enemy.'"[39]

During the 1950s and 1960s major industries started building plants upstream along the Highway 43 corridor. Foremost among these was Alabama Power's Barry Steam Plant, situated in Bucks, just to the north of the Ellicott Stone. Dedicated on September 21, 1956, this 35-million-dollar facility represented a massive construction project. One million cubic yards of soil were moved, 7,500 piles driven to a depth of 55 feet, 18 million-plus pounds of structural steel used, two 11-story boilers erected, 65,000 cubic yards of concrete poured, and 10 million pounds of rebar utilized. But the defining feature, visible for great distances, was a 175-foot-tall brick chimney, 20 feet in diameter at the top. In order to generate power, the plant burned coal, which was unloaded from barges riverside with a 400-cubic-foot bucket. The coal was then either bunkered or placed on a conveyor belt that dumped it into chutes. After being ground into fine powder, the coal was ignited to boil water, which produced steam to spin massive turbines and generate electricity. At full pitch the plant burned 195 tons of coal an hour, over one million tons in a year, and its turbines required 300,000 gallons of water a minute for cooling. The water was pumped in from the river through enormous concrete pipes and then released downstream, where it raised the river's temperature almost 20 degrees. In exchange for this prodigious consumption, Barry had a generating capacity of 475,000 kilowatts. The operation grew in subsequent years, with buildings, two more stacks, and even greater power-generating ability. But the environmental costs were sobering. Coal ash, sulfur dioxide, and mercury were among the nasty byproducts. Mercury is of special concern to coastal dwellers, because it contaminates fish and the people that consume them. Adverse health effects include neurological problems and fertility issues. But even as more stringent environmental regulations were put into place later in the century, Barry remained a big polluter. The plant reduced its mercury emissions by nearly one-third in 2008 but still produced enough to make it, as the *Register* reported, "one of the nation's leading emitters of the dangerous metal." The situation appeared to be improving by 2011, however, when the plant began switching to cheaper and cleaner-burning natural gas, in part because of stricter pollution regulations.[40]

The chemical pollution produced by modern industries is not so easily cleansed by the environment, even after the source shuts down. A perfect case in point is the defunct Stauffer Chemical Company plant at LeMoyne, located south of Chastang. Opening in the 1950s, Stauffer started by producing carbon disulfide, a compound commonly used to make rayon, cellophane, and pesticides. In 1964 the plant added chlorine and caustic soda to the list. It dumped its mercury-tainted waste directly into the waters of Cold Creek, which then emptied into the Mobile River. Incredibly, the procedure was legal until 1975. The company also used a landfill on the edge of the swampy land between it and the river. For years it buried fifty-five-gallon drums filled with organics, solvents, heavy metals, acids, and bases here, then covered all with a vinyl top, soil, and grass. Finally, the site was fenced. Predictably, this witch's brew leaked into the groundwater, which meant it was getting into residents' wells and into the river, too. Tests by the Environmental Protection Agency indicated lead, chromium, cadmium, chloroform, and carbon tetrachloride. The area was listed as a Superfund cleanup site in 1984. Superfund sites qualify for federal funds to help clean them and are so designated because they "have the most potential for posing long-term health or environmental hazards." The EPA's work at Cold Creek is ongoing and involves targeting two twenty-five-acre areas where the contamination is worst.[41]

Up and down the river the environmental damage was sobering in extent and severity. A 1982 report stated that "the lower Mobile River, Chickasaw Creek, Three Mile Creek, and portions of Mobile Bay are most subject to toxic wastes in coastal Alabama." Extensive fish kills in the 1970s and later also indicated periodic sewage and high nutrient-waste incursions into area streams. This depleted oxygen in the water and led to the fish kills. Despite construction of a wastewater treatment plant on McDuffie Island in 1957, where all the old downtown pipes were rerouted, and several others since elsewhere, there continued to be periodic line breaks, spills, and overflows. According to the 1982 report, "sections of Three Mile Creek, Hog Bayou, Eslava Creek, Chickasaw Creek, Mobile River and other areas have very low levels of dissolved oxygen caused by organics from industrial, municipal, and agricultural wastes and are so polluted that they are unsightly and malodorous." It is not surprising that by 1996 the Mobile River ranked among the top twenty worst-polluted streams in the nation.[42]

Those frequenting area waterways could personally attest to the evidence of this despoliation. One old-timer who grew up on Blakeley Island during the 1940s remarked fifty years later that "the water is browner than it was." He also sadly described the "cans and bottles and trash in the water now." Some of this rubbish washed into the river after hard rains; the rest was tossed by thoughtless boaters. As for the island itself, tank farms, an oil terminal, dredge dikes, tailings ponds, and shipyards have long obliterated the paradise that once lay at Mobile's eastern border. In 1969 a reporter interviewed some men at a fish camp on Three Mile Creek about their perceptions. "Pollution has sort of messed up the water," one of them said, "except for a good way up the creek. There's no vegetation in the creek bottom anymore." Gone too were the black bear and wildcats and any thought of swimming. "Nobody swims here anymore."[43]

Environmentalists have done the best that they could in a state where economic development at any cost has too often been the mantra. Perhaps their grandest achievement came in 1969, when they blocked Mobil Oil's attempt to drill in the lower bay. Oil is one of the most feared pollutants in coastal communities, which can suffer catastrophic economic damage to fisheries. The issue was successfully delayed in court until 1978, when Mobil put up a fifty-five-million-dollar bond and was allowed to drill one well. The company had to agree to a "no dump" policy for drilling muds, cuttings, and sewage, which instead had to be barged to shore for proper disposal. A Mobil spokesman called the rules "the most stringent by any state." Natural gas was found, and the promised royalties enthralled state solons who wanted to fill depleted government coffers. Gas rigs now stand in lower Mobile Bay, but thanks to the still active bond, environmental damage has been negligible. Forty-one years later, the 2010 BP oil spill luridly demonstrated the most extreme dangers in drilling for gas and oil, but despite fears to the contrary, very little oil got into Mobile Bay during that incident. The gulf beaches were fouled on several occasions, and there was a diesel reek in the air as far north as Mobile some days. Ships coming up the channel had to have their hulls cleaned before they got into the harbor, and slicks and patches of oil were spotted here and there, but the upper bay and rivers stayed free of it. This is not the case after smaller spills in the harbor itself, which sometimes happen. In the autumn of 2011, for example, workers overfilled an asphalt facility's oil-storage tank on Blakeley Island, and 275,000 gallons were released. Absorbent pads and booms were immediately put in place, but the damage was done. Even worse, heavy rains associated with Tropical Storm Lee washed the oil into the river, where it lapped onto seawalls, pilings, and even the walls of the convention center.[44]

In later days several state and local environmental groups have worked hard throughout the Mobile River Basin, and industry has become more cooperative. One of the most effective and visible of these players, Mobile Baykeeper, is a nonprofit focused on "clean air, clean water, and healthy communities." Through public education campaigns and reviews of permit applications by area industry impacting the watershed, Baykeeper has kept an informed eye on local pollution issues. Recently the organization joined a coalition of government groups and concerned citizens to clean up Three Mile

Creek and develop it into park and kayak trail for city residents. When told of the plans, one resident nursing a cane pole remarked that "it may be good for the kids, so they can have something to do out here instead of being out on the street. It's good for the young and the old."[45]

Despite the history of pollution on the river, some people began to take an optimistic view toward the close of the twentieth century. Tom Kelly, a retired woodlands manager for Scott Paper Company and an enthusiastic turkey hunter, set a reporter straight in a 1998 interview. "A lot of people like to say things are going to ruin, everything's polluted, we're losing wetlands," he said. "Every one of those statements was true in 1920, 1930. But it's not 1920 now. Back then, you could drain, fill anything you wanted to, and nobody would say a word. Now you can't do that." Likewise, David Cooper, an executive with the Cooper/T. Smith Corporation, which has extensive waterfront interests, declared in a 2012 interview that "the Mobile River is cleaner than it's ever been in my lifetime." A recent EPA report on local water quality backs him up. Though the Mobile River is still considered "impaired" because of the ongoing mercury issues, its ranking is significantly better on other fronts. The water-quality assessments for recreation, industrial and agricultural use, and the propagation of fish and wildlife are all ranked "good."[46]

While things may be improving compared to the bad old days, it is hard to imagine that the much abused Mobile River will ever again be like it was when the Indians paddled its length, Bienville first built a city on its bank, or Bartram pushed his canoe into the awe-inspiring cypress swamps. There are too many people now, with too many needs. But if a good balance can be maintained between development and environmental integrity that will be success of a sort.

Part 2

Currents

9

"Everything down there's big enough to kill you."

Work. It's been the great constant in the human history of the Mobile River. From the first people to arrive in the area thousands of years ago to those who live there today, work and the Mobile River have been almost synonymous. We cannot know how the first Indians thought about their ceaseless efforts to sustain life on this stretch of coast. They lived in a world of abundant resources, and hunting, fishing, trapping, light farming, fashioning dugouts, cooking, and simple crafts occupied their days. Did they have some special word for the effort and time these things required, what we would call work? Alas, we will never know. Certainly the Indians of the Pensacola Chiefdom made a distinction. Centered on Bottle Creek, their society was rigidly stratified with chiefs, priests, nobles, warriors, and slaves. The most fortunate dwelled atop the earthen mounds, their every need catered to by scurrying menials. The amount of labor needed to build those mounds, to erect shelters, to till the maize, beans, and squash, and to make everything from awls to elaborate turkey-feather capes was prodigious.

With the arrival of the Europeans in the sixteenth century, work meant backbreaking toil on both water and land. The ships and lighter craft that plied area waters had to be sailed, rowed, towed, and regularly careened, caulked, and repaired. Trees were cut down for masts, hulls patched where holed by sawyers, and sails resewn where ripped. But mostly there were hours of rowing and paddling. The shallow waters and long distances between important points, like the almost sixty miles between Dauphin Island and Twenty-Seven Mile Bluff, meant that sailors and soldiers were always at the oars, backs bent, hands callused, sweat streaking their faces. As soon as possible, slaves, first Indians and later Africans, were substituted for this mind-numbing labor, but the sailors' and soldiers' lives did not get any easier. Everyone in the colonial era struggled just to survive. Some of the tasks were the same as those the ancient Indians had performed, especially hunting, fishing, and trapping, but now these activities were bound up with trade and broader economic ambitions dictated from distant shores. Other tasks were new: brick making, building forts, mounting cannon on ramparts, repairing flintlock muskets, selling wine, fashioning iron hoops to contain barrel staves, setting roof tiles, embroidering handkerchiefs, and a thousand other activities.

The nineteenth-century river was defined by cotton and all the multifarious jobs associated with it. From hoeing a few plants in the delta to wrestling the bales aboard steamboats, pressing and warehousing it on the city wharves, and screwing it into the holds of big ships, cotton was a labor-intensive commodity. But now there was an associated realm of office work needed to support the business. Lawyers, clerks, accountants, insurance agents, factors, commission merchants, and distant mill owners all had a part and a purpose. The Civil War diverted people into the exhausting and ultimately futile endeavor of defending their bay and rivers. Driving piles, shoveling earth, building ironclads, and rolling bandages occupied men and women, black and white. Peace meant reopening the harbor and federal help in pulling piles and disarming torpedoes. By the late nineteenth century lumber had supplanted cotton, and vast log rafts choked the river while whining mills threw out mountains of sawdust at the mouths of One and Three Mile Creeks. The early twentieth century brought bananas, and their smell permeated the air riverside. World Wars I and II witnessed shipbuilding on a truly herculean scale and entire communities devoted to the enterprise. Massive transportation projects defined the mid- to late-twentieth century, with bridges, tunnels, and better port facilities. Acres of concrete replaced marshy banks and warped wooden wharves.

In the early twenty-first century, activities such as shipbuilding and cargo handling are just as important as ever, though the associated technologies would stagger the imaginations of old-time practitioners. Whereas early shipwrights used to sally into the delta swamps and eyeball the timber for likely parts, modern naval architects now sit in comfortable cushioned chairs in air-conditioned offices eyeing computer screens and ordering by phone, fax, or e-mail. The nineteenth-century draftsman had to know how to roll his pencil between smudged fingers as he drew the outline of a hull in order to keep the line of even thickness, but his modern counterpart taps a key to run a consistent line into infinity, his free hand dipping into a bag of Cheetos. Some jobs are the same, some are different. But just as much as ever, the Mobile River is about work, and the prosperity of the city at its mouth depends upon the diversity of men and women whose working lives unfold on its brown waters and beside its low banks.

Many of the tasks associated with the Mobile River have already been detailed in previous chapters. In this chapter we examine in more detail certain work that has either been a constant through the centuries or of especial color and significance. The jobs fall into several categories: watermen, meaning the harbormaster, bar pilots, sailors, deckhands, and fishermen; dockworkers, meaning stevedores and longshoremen; shipbuilders; lumbermen; those in the fruit trade; and last, those independent spirits

ADDSCO diver. Of all the people who have worked the river, none have been on such intimate terms with it as the divers who are occasionally called to slip beneath its waters. Courtesy of the History Museum of Mobile.

who live off the grid in the swamps and even on the city's doorstep, the river rats, squatters, and hermits who make do by their wits and cunning.

The steamboat captains may have been the lords of the Mobile River, but the harbormaster was God, and his is still a pretty important position. As waterborne commerce increased during the early nineteenth century, Mobile's harbor became more and more crowded. If confusion, collisions, and general chaos were to be avoided, some authority was needed quickly. In 1818 the Alabama Territorial Legislature established an office of harbormaster and three port wardens, and four years later the Alabama General Assembly passed an "Act for the Government of the Port and Harbour of Mobile." By this legislation a five-person board of port wardens was appointed, with one of them chosen as harbormaster. This individual took an oath, and kept an office with a clerk riverside. His duties and powers were absolute. They included designating and licensing the bar pilots, having say-so over where ships were berthed and when they could be moved and how, and inspecting vessels and cargo in port. Any ship's captain who refused the harbormaster faced a fifty-dollar fine. Compensation included a share of the pilotage fees and three cents a ton for cargo "of every ship or vessel that may enter the port of Mobile and load, unload, or make fast to any of the wharves within the limits of said city." Other powers were added or adjusted over time, including reporting free black seamen in port and turning them over to the sheriff until their ship left, regulating ballast disposal, and numbering the wharves. Authority over the bar pilots was removed in 1848, when the latter were transferred to the Commissioners of Pilotage of the Bay and Harbour of Mobile.[1]

Today the harbormaster is appointed by the director of the Alabama State Port Authority. As of this writing, the post is held by retired Coast Guard captain Terry Gilbreath. "Most of my job is administrative and regulatory," he explained in a 2013 telephone interview. "I'm the go-to man for any of the federal agencies." This means he is in constant contact with the Coast Guard and U.S. Army Corps of Engineers on matters large and small, from routine navigation and dredging to oil spills and accidents. Like his nineteenth-century predecessors, Captain Gilbreath collects port fees and makes sure the ship traffic flows smoothly. When more than one ship is standing off the sea buoy waiting to enter Mobile Bay, it is his call which enters first. Cruise ships and container ships, "which are on tight schedules," are given first priority. Because the channel is narrow, it is critical that vessels have plenty of room. The Post-Panamax ships, sometimes drawing 45 feet fully loaded and boasting 170 foot beams, "sniff the bottom all the way in and hog the 400-foot-wide channel." This situation would create a serious problem for a busier port, and it is hardly desirable for Mobile. Among Gilbreath's priorities is working to get the channel widened to 550 feet south of McDuffie Island. Today, as ever, a wider, deeper channel is the Holy Grail for those responsible for port development and regulation.[2]

Actually getting ships from gulf to harbor and back out falls to the bar pilots, an elite team with a proud history stretching back to the colonial French settlers. The *Shipmaster's Assistant and Commercial Digest* in 1857 clearly detailed the duties and responsibilities of pilots. According to the *Digest,* they were to "conduct any ship or vessel into a road or harbor, over bars or sand, or through intricate and dangerous channels." Furthermore, "after a pilot is taken on board, the master has no longer any command of the ship till she is safe in the harbor." As such, the pilot was liable for any accident or damage resulting from his "ignorance or negligence." With its shifting shoals, shallow waters, and multiple entrance options, Mobile Bay has always been difficult and potentially hazardous for larger vessels. Recognizing this, the king of France appointed one Simon Coussot as the first Mobile Bay bar pilot in 1711. Throughout the colonial era, shipping was sporadic, sometimes agonizingly so. During the British period Samuel Carr was the pilot, and he lived a lonely existence on Dauphin Island, waiting for sails. He mostly had the island to himself, but he cut down so many trees and killed so many cows that he was moved over to Mobile Point, where a house was built for him.[3]

During the nineteenth century more than a dozen pilots occupied a little village near Fort Morgan known as Pilot Town. Here they idled, fished, swam, and played with their eighteen-foot yawls to the accompaniment of booming surf. One antebellum visitor to Pilot Town reported a "likely widow's kind of public-house" where he hung out with the pilots and drank rum while puffing Havana cigars. When a sail was spotted, however, all thought of leisure vanished, and the pilots raced one another out to the vessel, the winner getting the job. Competition was fierce and with good reason. Pilotage fees were calculated by how much water a vessel drew. Those drawing under ten feet were $2.50 a foot; ten to twelve feet, $2.75 a foot; twelve to fourteen feet, $3 a foot; and so on. This was an era when a common laborer might make a dollar a day. Because so many deeper-draft vessels had to anchor among the Lower Fleet, the pilots divided themselves into two groups, one guiding ships there, the other steering the lighter-draft boats all the way up to the city. This system would persist until the 1890s, when Damrell's Ditch opened downtown's wharves to big ships. Pilot Town was destroyed in the hurricane of 1906 and never rebuilt. After that the pilots made do with simpler quarters and kept a schooner offshore where they awaited ships in week-long shifts.[4]

Something of that era's flavor may be discerned from the experience of Captain Joe Ollinger, who worked as an apprentice "on the bar" during the 1940s. Ollinger is heir to a distinguished family maritime tradition. His forbears owned shipyards and dry docks in northwest Florida and Mobile, including a six-thousand-ton wooden dry dock on Pinto Island. Young Ollinger graduated from Murphy High School in 1943, went on to the Citadel, and then joined the Merchant Marine Corps. Duty with the bar pilots had its attractions for a young man, but the time spent waiting for ships offshore was wearing. On these shifts Ollinger lived aboard the schooner *Alabama* with two cooks, two launchmen, a mate, and an engineer. The men relieved the tedium with card games, practical jokes, and storytelling. Rough water meant sea sickness for everyone, and any greenhorn who claimed to be immune "hadn't been in the proper situation," Ollinger asserted. When a ship approached, she made a lee, and the pilot closed with her in a motor launch and then climbed a rope ladder up her steep sides. Sometimes he would board vessels in heaving seas and lashing rain at 2:00 a.m. The climb was dangerous, and pilots faced the very real possibilities of falling into the briny deep or being crushed against a steel hull. Ollinger recalled only one pilot lost to a fall, and, incredibly, the rope ladder is still the preferred method of boarding to this day. Once the pilot was safely aboard the vessel, it was four hours to town. "We put toothpicks in our eyes to stay awake," Ollinger laughed when recalling the long predawn rides to port. Among his favorite vessels were the "little fruiters, small and very handy" steamships that regularly ran up from Central and South America. After guiding these ships to the fruit docks he usually got a big stalk of bananas as special thanks.[5]

Mobile's modern bar pilots now command technology that Ollinger and his mates could not even imagine—no more whistles and flashlights in port like only a few decades ago. They continually shuttle up and down the bay in large air-conditioned SUV's in constant radio contact with dispatchers and one another. They own a handsome new brick headquarters in one of downtown's historic districts, complete with bedrooms and a well-stocked kitchen, and a Dauphin Island station equipped with two fast motor launches. According to bar pilot Patrick Wilson, there are now fourteen of them to manage the roughly 250 ships a month that sail into and out of the "big/small port" of Mobile. But despite the technological improvements, there are still dangers aplenty, especially in the harbor with its traffic and currents. "You must respect that river, it will get you in trouble," said pilot Kirk Barrett in a 2013 magazine article. The importance of having a good pilot aboard was graphically demonstrated in 2005, when the *Nordic Svenita,* carrying twenty-one million gallons of crude oil to the Shell refinery upriver, suffered an engine fire and lost power midstream. As the crippled fifty-thousand-ton vessel drifted toward the west bank, her captain moved to drop her twin five-ton anchors and arrest the drift—standard procedure. Pilot Pete Burns quickly intervened, warning the captain that the ship was sitting directly atop the Wallace tunnels. Had those heavy anchors plummeted more than fifty feet rattling out chain, the damage and loss of life might have been significant. But how to arrest the ship? Burns quickly got two big tugs alongside, which successfully stayed a catastrophe. "There were people working in the shipyards and in the convention center," Burns later recalled of the frightening moment, "and guys mowing the grass in Cooper Riverside Park that never had a clue what was going on. The people of the Mobile area just don't realize—the entire state doesn't realize—what happens in Mobile, in the harbor."[6]

There are those who know a good bit about the harbor besides the pilots and the harbormaster, however, and they are the deckhands, dredge operators, sailors, and fishermen who spend at least part of their working days amid its maritime bustle. Vincent George, now an employee with the City of Mobile, recently recalled his youth as a tugboat deckhand in local waters with something close to amazement at the experience. George became a deckhand "when I turned 17" and worked for a small family-owned company during the early 1980s. His boat was a big 3500-horsepower oceangoing tug that helped dock large ships. When not under way, it berthed at the foot of Dauphin Street. The boat had a captain, an engineer, and two deckhands. George quickly learned that the captain was to be obeyed at all times or else. When ordered to throw some garbage overboard, George kept the trash on deck and disposed of it later in a dumpster on the dock. "I didn't want to litter our bay," he explained, but when the captain found out he gave the youngster a good "ass-chewin'" for disobeying orders. The issue was not whether or not it was okay to litter but the need to bend unquestioningly to the captain's authority. "They were strict. They gave an order they expected it to be followed." As for the work itself, it included constant "chippin' 'n paintin,'" galley scut work, and the more exciting task of shepherding big vessels into port. Often George's tug met ships out at the farewell buoy, twelve miles south of Dauphin Island. "The scariest time was when you first butted the ship," he said. The vessel's suction would grab the tug when it was still about a dozen feet away and quickly draw it against the steel hull. "The captains really knew their stuff," George declared. From the sea buoy it was three hours to town. The secret to the job was to let the "ship and the ropes do the work," but even then the dangers were numerous and forbidding. "Everything down there's big enough to kill you," George asserted. A large ship gliding along may look graceful, but there are serious mass and momentum in play, and collisions can have frightening consequences. Even a minor bump into a concrete bulkhead will send concrete dust and debris exploding into the air. Other dangers included snapped lines, which could sting like a rubber band breaking or "cut you in half." When the tug was holding a ship in place dockside, its propellers roiling the river water, big logs could be sucked into the screws, badly damaging or crippling them. The deckhands had to prowl the gunwales with long poles and stave them off whenever they bobbed into view. As if the work itself was not difficult enough, weather conditions were often less than ideal. Wind and rain simply had to be endured, and George swore that in winter "it was 10 degrees colder on the river than in town."[7]

Talk of winter caused George to recall vividly the night when he had a brush with a very different kind of waterfront worker. While getting ready to head out and meet a ship coming into port, he noticed another tug at the foot of Government Street powering up as well. Before it pulled away four women scampered on board in the fluorescent-lit chill. They were prostitutes from the Club Royal on Royal Street, who had convinced the other boat's captain to ferry them out to drum up some business with the incoming sailors. Later, as the tugs pushed the ship, George could hear the "ladies" shouting at the crew and telling them where to come find them. Back at the dock he went over to the other boat's wheelhouse and talked to the girls, who were huddling with their hot coffee, reluctant to sally out into the cold. There was much discussion among them about the ship and not a little grumbling that it was a Greek vessel. "I hate fuckin' Greeks," one of them complained. "They like to fuck you up the ass!"[8]

Such lurid scenes and language have ever been part of wide-eyed youths' coming-of-age on the Mobile River. George values his time there and the life lessons learned. He also appreciates the special perks that sometimes came his way. These included gifts of booze by thoughtful captains, invitations to dine with foreign crews—the Germans always had good beer—and once a meal aboard a Chinese ship at Mardi Gras, which also happened to be the Chinese New Year. He learned a lot about grain, bananas, and coal, the most frequent cargoes he encountered, and once hauled aboard waterlogged bales of pot abandoned offshore by some smuggler. George's personal horizons expanded greatly, and he became a wiser and more curious person. "Docking those ships from all over the world instilled a desire to go to those places," he concluded, a desire that has led to a lifetime of travel and enrichment.[9]

For bona fide salt-water sailors, time on the Mobile River was a brief episode in much grander voyages. But their colorful and routine presence in Alabama's only seaport served to fire the imaginations of local boys such as George, some of whom determined to seek a little adventure. In the spring of 1922, for example, three "salt-aspiring youths" at Spring Hill College decided to put to sea until school started up again in the fall. They haunted the docks downtown until finding berths on the SS *Colthraps*, a fast World War I–era ship bound for LeHarve with phosphate rock and lumber. "We left at about 5 a.m.," Thomas Fox, one of the students, wrote for the campus newspaper

Lone sailor from aloft, photographed in 1939. Even in port, the sea-faring life meant toil. Courtesy of David Newell.

several months later. Progress was slow at first due to "the narrowness of the channel and a schooner in front of us." But even as Fox and his companions watched the channel lights gliding past, they realized they at last were "going to sea." Under way, the crew worked from 6:00 a.m. to 8:00 a.m. and then took breakfast. Fox expected poor fare but was pleasantly surprised to find it "really luxurious." His enthusiasm for the chow might be explained in part by the fact that his appetite was more robust after two hours of labor on a rolling deck than it would have been at a peaceful school cafeteria. The onboard tasks mostly consisted of "chipping or scraping rust off, and then painting the decks." But the students discovered the constant exposure to sun and weather to be more than they had bargained for, and Fox was badly sunburned through his shirt. After their arrival in Europe, the young men visited Paris by train, and then sailed back to the United States with a load of coal. They were in class again at the beginning of term, a very different kind of education under their belts.[10]

In addition to deckhands and sailors, fishermen have plied Mobile's waterways since time immemorial. Since World War II commercial fishermen have mostly congregated closer to the gulf at Bayou La Batre and Bon Secour, and one only sees the occasional recreational angler in the harbor, where his small skiff is frighteningly dwarfed by the ship, tug, and barge traffic. Then there are the downtown residents and country people who cast their lines from the railing at Cooper Riverside Park and a hundred other spots up and down the stream, hoping to catch a little supper. But during the late nineteenth and early twentieth centuries the Mobile River was home to a fleet of oyster boats and fishing smacks that regularly sallied down the bay or into the gulf and returned their bounty to dockside dealers such as Star Fish & Oyster Company, with its packing sheds, warehouse, condensers, and ice machine.

According to an 1881 report on the Alabama fishery, these boats were "rather cheaply and roughly built," weighing from three and twenty tons and drawing from two to three feet. Many were rigged as schooners and sloops and had a reputation for speed and maneuverability. "They are arranged so as to have as much deck and hold room as possible for the oysters," the report stated; "therefore their cabins are small and uncomfortable." Crews usually consisted of only two or three men on the oyster boats and up to ten on the larger fishing smacks. The total number of vessels in the fleet was listed at 62, and 250 men were employed in manning them. The annual oyster production stood at more than 100,000 bushels, valued at $44,950. The smacks concentrated on fish, especially red snapper, and typically brought in from 100 to 1,000 pounds of fish per boat. When not at work, the boats were gathered in a slip at the foot of Eslava Street, flanked by Mobile Fish & Oyster Company on the north and Arrow Fish & Oyster Company on the south.[11]

The men who operated these boats were a hardy and independent lot. An 1887 government study described them as mostly of southern European stock, with only a few black individuals. According to the report's author, they generally chose to live in the city, and "when not broken down by dissipation, live to a considerable age." Their women were not so lucky—"worn out in early life" and usually dead by age fifty. Many fisherman never married and preferred to spend their off hours carousing "and in the 'lock-up.'" Most were illiterate and uneducated, though their children attended school, and a better future was predicted for them. As for these families' spiritual life, "nearly all who profess any religion are Catholics."[12]

Life aboard these boats, as later recalled by one of the men's sons, was "hard, long, demanding, and dangerous." Elmo B. Ziebach wrote a series of stories inspired by his father's history, and in them he detailed many of the fishermen's routines and activities. "Most of the fishing was for red snapper and grouper on the coral reefs off the coast of Mexico," he wrote. "The smacks would be out three weeks and in dock one week. The crew got a percentage of the catch as their pay." The elder Ziebach made his first trip in 1925, and as he told his son, "the crew, to entertain themselves I guess, took great delight in playing tricks on the new kid on board. They thought it was amusing for me to find a fish in my bunk or to see me try to put on my pants with the legs tied in knots." Most of the ten-man crew ranged in age from twenty to fifty, and, like the bar pilots, they "played cards and slept for entertainment."[13] The oystermen stuck closer to home in their work, tonging the reefs in the lower bay until their holds were filled.

When the smacks and oyster boats returned with their catches, the dockside warehouses that served them went into high gear. In 1881 the oyster industry in Mobile was estimated to support more than one hundred families, "chiefly of colored persons," who cracked open the shells to supply the restaurants and eateries that so glowingly advertised their product. Typically, the oyster-boat crews simply dumped their catch in a big pile in the middle of the warehouse, where it was surrounded by a crowd of "negroes and creoles of the worst character," flashing six-inch steel knives. "Still they are very expert at opening oysters," an observer conceded, "and often make fair wages." The men, and too frequently children, held each oyster in their left hand, "lower shell down and lips outward," and deftly pried it open, tossed away the upper shell and severed the meaty oyster from the lower shell in "one stroke." The oysters and the liquor were dropped into a bucket, where they were later tallied to determine the shuckers' pay. Twenty cents a gallon was the going rate. The men were closely supervised, since they preferred to discard smaller oysters as not worth the effort to open. Once shucked, the oysters were iced, canned, and shipped.[14]

There was also bigger cargo coming and going dockside, and it required its own class of laborers. These were the stevedores and longshoremen, whose heirs still pursue their noble trade. The term *stevedore* dates to the eighteenth century and derives from the Spanish *estibador,* meaning "one who packs" or "stuffs." *Longshoreman* was originally a nineteenth-century Canadian usage, referring to men who worked "along-the-shore." In Mobile the terms have been used somewhat loosely over the years, but by the mid-twentieth century stevedores were the contractors who supplied work gangs composed of longshoremen to load and unload ships.[15]

Efficiently and safely handling bulky, heavy cargo has always been critical to Mobile's maritime economy. As already noted, nineteenth-century dockworkers' skill at managing cotton was the subject of much admiration and comment by well-traveled and knowledgeable observers. By the early twentieth century the port had diversified considerably, and though cotton was still an important commodity, numerous other items ranging from lumber, coal, bauxite, and steel pipe to bananas, oil, and molasses

Longshoreman, circa 1960. Courtesy of the Alabama State Port Authority.

required attention. In 1922 a section of a U.S. War Department publication examined Mobile's waterfront assets and capabilities at length and devoted considerable space to labor practices and cargo-handling methods. "Ships are brought alongside of piers or wharves and the general cargoes are unloaded by means of ship's tackle or by hand direct to cars or transit sheds," this section of the report began. "All unloading is done by stevedores." Usually, it continued, the men "work one gang to the hatch, each gang consisting of 20 men for general cargo and 5 men for cotton." Agents or "tally clerks" stood nearby to check the totals and compare them to the bill of lading.[16]

Everything about the process was stringently defined. The hours, wages, and techniques had been carefully, painfully, and sometimes violently negotiated between the various parties over many decades. The stevedores were all white, but dockside labor consisted of both white and black longshoremen, who were represented by the International Longshoremen's Association. Black longshoremen had formed their own Colored Longshoreman's Benevolent Association as early as 1894 and in 1910 had ten local associations of their own. They had historically been confined to the least-skilled tasks but through their unions were able to improve their situation by 1900, especially relating to cotton and timber cargoes. Work hours for all races were from 7:00 a.m. to noon and from 1:00 p.m. to 4:00 p.m. every weekday. Holidays included New Year's Day, Mardi Gras, July 4, Labor Day, Armistice Day, Thanksgiving, and Christmas. Of course, ships sometimes arrived at strange hours, requiring night shifts. In these cases a midnight "lunch hour" was prescribed. In 1922 wages for white longshormen were 55 cents an hour and 82.5 cents an hour overtime. Black workers earned less. Foremen got an extra 10 cents an hour for their trouble. Vessels and cargoes had specific personnel complements assigned. For example, when timber needed unloading from a steamer, fifteen men were required, a foreman, four holders, one swinger, one hooker-on, and eight winchmen. Sailing ships with timber required ten winchmen, one swinger, one hooker-on, four holders, and a foreman. The workers were responsible for showing up with the proper equipment, which in 1922 meant "slings, ropes, hooks, trucks, conveyors, and save-alls [large bins]." For their part the shippers had to "furnish and maintain in good order the necessary steam winches capable of lifting 3 gross tons in single gear," as well as all the "blocks, ropes for falls, dunnage, hatch tents, gangways, and necessary light where work is to be performed at night."[17]

Modern conveniences unknown to their earlier brethren certainly made the longshoremen's jobs easier, but even under the best circumstances theirs was still a dangerous profession. Exposure to wind, sun, and rain was a given, and after several years on the docks these men had deeply tanned and weathered countenances. Falls, scrapes, and accidents were common, ranging from minor and laughable to life-threatening. Those who dealt with logs could tell the scariest stories. Wrestling expansive timber rafts and heaving up the logs required getting into water up to their waists, where snakes sometimes lurked. Nursing chain-bound log bundles onto railroad cars sometimes meant disaster if the load shifted or broke loose. "I have seen as many as three men get covered up at once and smashed to pieces," one stevedore grimly recalled in 1919. Nonetheless, the longshoremen's skills were legendary. As one of their number declared in a 1963 interview, they knew "what to do with lift machines, ship winches and cargo rigging gear. Mobile longshoremen know what a crowbar does and how rollers work, and they get the job done and give a full day's work for a full day's pay."[18]

Today there are almost a dozen stevedoring firms in Mobile. Two in particular have long been prominent in the city's maritime history. Ryan-Walsh Stevedoring, a subsidiary of SSA (Stevedoring Services of America) Marine, is the oldest, with a pedigree stretching back to the chaotic end of the Civil War. Richard Walsh, a pilot before hostilities, established a stevedoring outfit as soon as the guns stopped shooting. He was successful, and the enterprise prospered as the port was improved. Still going strong in 1974, the company merged with Ryan Stevedoring Inc., a firm that had been founded somewhat later than Walsh's, and subsequently owned by Waterman until the 1950s. In 1977 Ryan-Walsh Stevedoring built a handsome new headquarters on North Royal Street, and in 1995 it was absorbed by SSA Marine.[19]

Cooper/T. Smith Corporation traces its origins to the legendary river man Angus Cooper. Cooper grew up in central Baldwin County, where he and his brothers worked on their family's resin plantation. Angus Cooper was tasked with hauling the valuable barrels of amber product over to Mobile. He was fascinated by the big ships and bustling wharves and convinced his father to let him sign on as a tally clerk. He helped pick men for work gangs, sometimes rousting them out of waterfront dives. According to his grandson David, he soon learned which ones were the best workers. Some of these later became decades-long loyal employees. Cooper rented a house in town and rode the trolley down to the docks every morning. His "office" was a table at a riverside eatery, where he sat every afternoon with a pistol in front of him, paying his men in heavy silver dollars. David Cooper remembers him as "dapper" but "tough as nails; he looked like he came out of the pages of *GQ* magazine, but he knew how to handle men, and it was all about manpower in those days. He kept brass knuckles in his coat pocket and would descend into the hold of a ship to fight out a dispute with the men." Given this raw talent, Cooper soon moved up to become a superintendent for the Munson Line, and in 1908 he started a stevedoring firm in New Orleans with Munson and Alcoa as his first customers. Cooper shifted his headquarters to Mobile in 1934 and his son, Ervin, helped him solidify the business end. According to David, Angus Cooper lacked a formal education but appreciated the importance of a good "numbers guy." Ervin Cooper got a college degree at Tulane and honed his business acumen by working a stint for a New York steamship firm. David Cooper began helping the family enterprise as a youngster, doing menial tasks like "sweeping out." Today David Cooper and his brother Angus II manage a sophisticated global operation that would have stunned old Angus. In 1983 they merged with the largest and oldest New Orleans stevedoring firm, T. Smith, and today Cooper/T. Smith Corporation has tugs, push boats, wood chip facilities, dockside assets, and even restaurants from Virginia to California and Mobile to Mexico. Still headquartered in Alabama's port city, the firm is proud of its enduring ties to the Mobile River. In honor of their father's passion "about the working waterfront" and the belief that residents should know about it, David and Angus Cooper II helped establish Cooper Riverside Park in the early 1990s. One of the park's features is an elegant cast-iron bench with a sculpture of Ervin Cooper seated facing the river. "My father wanted the common man to enjoy the working waterfront," David explained. "People can sit next to him on the bench and do so."[20]

Ryan-Walsh, Cooper/T. Smith, and their competitors pride themselves on their diverse capabilities and efficiency in handling all kinds of cargoes, from forest products and break bulk to containers. Visitors to Mobile's waterfront, especially those from inland locales, marvel at the sight of giant container ships, their decks stacked with orange, blue, red, white, and green metal boxes. Nudged into dock by powerful tugboats, these vessels are positioned directly under towering container cranes. Operated by an individual perched in a little cabin attached to the crane's trolley, high above the busy harbor, these contraptions mechanically pluck the containers off the deck and deposit them on the dock or directly onto flatcars or truck trailers. Filled with anything and everything from athletic shoes and toilet tissue to antiques, these units are then delivered far and wide. Containerized shipping ranks as one of the most revolutionary developments of the twentieth century, and it was the brainchild of an innovative entrepreneur who knew Mobile's waterfront well.

Malcolm McLean was a North Carolina-born farmer's son who pumped gas during the Great Depression. Hard-working and frugal—a reporter once called him "aggressive, dynamic"—he saved up $120 and bought a truck, which he used to haul dirt, produce, and other items for the poor farmers around his hometown. From these modest beginnings he built up a large and successful trucking business. McLean's famous innovation unfolded by degrees over time, but perhaps the seminal moment came in 1937 when he was delivering a load of cotton bales from North Carolina to a ship berthed at the docks at Hoboken, New Jersey. "I had to wait most of the day to deliver the bales, sitting there in my truck, watching stevedores load other cargo," he later recalled. "It struck me that I was looking at a lot of wasted time and money. I watched them take each crate off the truck and slip it into a sling, which would then lift the crate into the hold of the ship." The first step toward containerization came when McLean inaugurated the concept of piggyback, roll-on/roll-off truck service for ships. This technique already existed with railroad cars, and McLean had been impressed by it. But he took the concept further and decided to use trucks alone. This meant that drivers could quickly deposit their trailers and cargo directly onto "trailer ships" and hook up to them and unload them with equal ease at their destinations. But McLean chafed at the wasted weight and space. Why not have the cargo in a detachable box, he thought, which could be easily lifted off the trailer and loaded or removed from a deck and simply eased onto a waiting truck? In 1955 McLean bought the old Waterman Steamship Corporation, then a subsidiary of the Pan-Atlantic Steamship Company, and acquired his Mobile connection. From his new coastal Alabama foothold McLean set about perfecting his idea. This meant utilizing heavy steel containers for the cargo, which could survive rough ocean voyages. Furthermore, the containers needed to be standardized so they could be easily stacked and unstacked and, not to be forgotten, fitted safely and legally onto truck trailers, meeting height clearances and weight limits for the highways they would traverse. McLean worked for years to get other seaports to accept the idea and make the necessary investments in equipment and infrastructure to handle the containers. Needless to say, he succeeded brilliantly and sold his affectionately named SeaLand Industries to R. J. Reynolds in 1969 for $160 million.[21]

While Mobile's business, professional, and political leadership extols McLean's achievement, ordinary citizens do not find containerized shipping particularly sexy. Far more to the fore in their imaginations, to the degree that anything to do with the waterfront is in their heads at all, are the storied old banana docks, obliterated in the early 1990s for the new downtown convention center. There was an outcry when the docks' forlorn remnants were demolished, and for years a popular west Mobile seafood restaurant called itself the Banana Docks Café. The heyday of Mobile's banana trade was decades past by this time, of course, but many ordinary people had heard stories from parents and grandparents for whom the banana docks was an unforgettable place. In his oral biography as told to Katherine Clark, *Milking the Moon,* Mobile writer and Renaissance man Eugene Walter recalled the docks as something of a whiff from the nineteenth century. Walter's uncle owned an import-export house down on Water Street, a "wonderful place with old-fashioned—like in Dickens—high desks with high stools where the clerks were scratching with pens in big ledgers." Railroad cars arrived out front to load or unload fruit and produce, while at the wharf "freighters pulled in from the Caribe."

In a column for the *Atlanta Journal and Constitution,* native Mobilian Celestine Sibley remembered the smells. "Smells are evocative," she wrote. "I never smell a banana that I'm not taken back to my childhood in Mobile, Ala., and the free fruit you could collect down by the dock and the railroad where they were offloading great, green-gold stems of fruit and hefting them into freight cars—usually to the accompaniment of a lusty work song." Poet Julian Rayford's strongest memory was of the almost musical racket that accompanied the bananas' unloading: "Ching-ching-ching of the tabulating machines / The hum and click and the roll and the bumpity thumpity clanking of the conveyors / The chanting of the checkers and the steady hum of men toting bananas, and occasionally a fragment of song."[22]

The personality most closely associated with Mobile's fruit trade is Sam "the Banana Man" Zemurray, a Russian Jew who arrived around 1895. Mobile had imported bananas since at least the 1820s, but the trade was erratic and the results often disappointing with overripe loads. Eager to stabilize the situation, the chamber of commerce offered prize money for any company that could sustain the fruit trade for a full year. The possibilities of doing this improved during the 1880s and 1890s when American firms began amassing vast banana plantations in Costa Rica, Cuba, Honduras, Nicaragua, and Panama. In 1899 the United Fruit Company swallowed up the smaller outfits and came to dominate the trade. Its white-hulled little steamers were ubiquitous in the gulf ports and helped fill Americans' growing enthusiasm for fruit in their diet. Zemurray sensed an opportunity to help get the product into the hands of hungry consumers and started with fifty dollars' worth of "ripes and turnings" that he was able to sell quickly before they spoiled. Within three years Zemurray had parlayed his modest

Officers line the rail of a Norwegian fruiter, circa 1895.
Courtesy of the History Museum of Mobile.

initial investment into one hundred thousand dollars in the bank. Early twentieth-century Mobile port records track his meteoric success—336,000 bunches sold in 1903, 574,500 in 1904, and 408,900 in 1905. Zemurray then invested in a steamship company, opened a New Orleans operation, and soon enough was beating out the United Fruit Company in acquiring Latin American banana plantations. By 1932 he had outmaneuvered the Boston firm's polished businessmen and acquired control of the company itself. He would run United Fruit for two decades.[23]

In Mobile the banana docks' most distinguishing feature was the towering electric-powered conveyors, enclosed in protective wood clapboarding. According to a 1934 publication, these were "a continual source of interest to tourists and Mobile riverfront visitors." Situated at the foot of Dauphin Street, the conveyors were flanked by long open-sided sheds. The United Fruit Company leased the land from the Mobile & Ohio Railroad. When a fruiter arrived, she berthed alongside the conveyors, which had arms that could extend over the ship's hold. Laborers descended into her hull and loaded the fruit stems onto the canvas belt. The work was hot and sweaty, and sometimes big spiders or little monkeys were discovered down in the bananas. Once the conveyors got the stems to the sheds, black and sometimes Hispanic workers hoisted them onto their backs and carried them to refrigerator cars. Along the way the bananas were weighed, marked, and monitored for quality by various checkers.[24]

Just like bananas and cotton, the lumber industry involved heavy harbor activity, especially at the mouths of One and Three Mile Creeks. But to a degree far exceeding the other trades, it also impacted the deep delta swamps and multiple spots along the Mobile River's upper reaches. Bananas arrived from the south and were shipped aboard railroad cars, and cotton simply passed down the river to the wharves where it was processed and shipped out. But logging meant timber cruisers, swampers, sawyers, ox drivers, raftmen, cooks, and inspectors scattered throughout south Alabama and along even smaller bayous and streams. Logs were harvested from the woods and swamps,

Worker, Mobile banana docks, 1937. Arthur Rothstein photographed this weary Latin American on a chilly afternoon. Courtesy of the History Museum of Mobile.

Sawmill advertisement. From *Mobile City Directory,* 1884.

dragged to the riverside, tied into timber rafts, and then floated out, with the heavier logs supported on so-called gunboats, primitive pontoons with an attached frame supplied by the mills. Once the logs arrived at the mills, they were drawn out of the water and sawn into valuable lumber for export.[25]

The forest-product industry's peak was probably during the 1930s, when trucks became an important part of the equation, but it had been at least a piece of the bay area's economic picture since colonial times. In 1750 the commander of Fort Tombecbe engaged some Choctaw warriors to cut down cedar trees and build a sixty-by-twenty-five-foot raft. The frame was positioned two miles south of the fort on the Tombigbee's west bank, and during the course of the summer it was filled with cut logs. With the following spring's freshets, the commander and four men mounted the big raft and rode it downstream. The ungainly contraption drew twelve feet of water, but it drifted along "without let or hindrance, carrying before it every obstacle (even bending large trees under it all the way to Mobile)." From logs like these residents built houses and ships and fashioned practical things such as barrel staves. A skilled gang of a few men could produce five hundred staves a day, cutting logs into the proper lengths, splitting, riving, and shaving them into the desired shape. During antebellum times sawmills began springing up all around the city. John J. Deshon had one as early as 1823. Twelve years later he boasted an eighty-horsepower steam engine, which powered a total of thirty-six saws. Deshon's mill turned out twenty thousand board feet of lumber a day as well as thousands of laths and shingles. During the late nineteenth and early twentieth centuries, as already noted, Mobile's lumber production reached high levels. In 1887 lumber exports stood at almost thirty million board feet. Shingle production was seventy-five million, nearly doubled from just three years previous. As the trade embraced mechanization during the mid-twentieth century, logs ceased to be floated downstream. Trucks could then grind deep into the woods along rutted, muddy roads to get at the cut timber. During the 1980s logs were airlifted out of the delta by helicopter, and travelers over the Dolly Parton Bridge could see the odd round gaps left in the tree canopy by this activity.[26]

Working for the logging and lumber outfits during the early twentieth century meant a wild and dangerous life. Some men relished being in the swamps for days at a time, away from their town troubles. Others were surprised by unanticipated turns. In the summer of 1911 John McMillan, the general manager of Mobile's Bacon-Underwood veneer plant, was checking timber in the swamp when he found himself confronted by a black bear. According to a newspaper account, "Mr. McMillan felt disposed to go on counting trees, and let the bear go his way, but, as was later discovered, the bear had just lost a paw in a bear trap and was not inclined to compromise, being in a bearish temper." All McMillan had on hand was a shotgun loaded with birdshot. "He fired one barrel of this small shot into the face of Mr. Bear," the paper reported, "and being so near, the load knocked the bear down." McMillan then closed the distance and fired three more shells, killing the "very thin, apparently almost famished" animal. Likewise, the timber inspectors who were required to scamper across the floating log rafts sometimes met with ill-tempered cottonmouths sheltering in the logs. In their efforts to accurately measure the logs these inspectors had to keep moving lest the rafts start sinking. In the woods and in the mills the dangers were more obvious—falling trees and big spinning blades. The earliest logging truck drivers operated their vehicles bouncing atop a seat cushion fixed to the chassis with the cab removed. Most companies believed these protective shells would be knocked loose during the work anyway. Their exposed situation suited the drivers, who could see better and leap away from danger without impediment. Logging and lumber mills were and are their own worlds, with distinctive traditions and terms. *Go-devils, grabs, jumpbutts, bum boats, canthooks, spike poles,* and *binders* make up but the smallest sampling of a rich specialized vocabulary once heard all up and down the Mobile River.[27]

Shipbuilding and repair are also long established activities on the river. Ever since Iberville ordered a forty-ton flat-bottomed pinnace in 1702 to better navigate shallow local waters, the Mobile River's advantages to this kind of work have been obvious—plentiful good timber close by, abundant naval stores, numerous convenient locales for launching and testing vessels, and easy access to blue water. Down the decades there have been multiple shipbuilding and repair businesses concentrated in the harbor, including J. M. and T. Meaher, the Confederate naval yard, Henderson Shipbuilding

Shipbuilding. Hulls propped on ways have long been a common sight riverside. Courtesy of the History Museum of Mobile.

Company, Ollinger, Bruce Dry Dock Company, Harrison Brothers Rollerway and Spar Yard, Bender Shipbuilding & Repair Company, ADDSCO, and Gulf Shipbuilding, and, most recently, Austal USA, BAE Systems Southeast Shipyards, and Signal Ship Repair.

The nature of shipbuilding and repair work has varied with the times. In the eighteenth and nineteenth centuries skilled shipwrights were worth their weight in gold and enjoyed certain rights and protections that would have been the envy of other trades. In the winter of 1840, for example, the Alabama General Assembly passed an "Act for the relief and protection of Ship-Carpenters, Ship-Joiners and others in the City and County of Mobile." These tradesmen were empowered to place liens on "all articles or work put up, made or repaired by them, in any ship, ship-yard, dock-yard within said city or country . . . until paid." If the work was not paid, they were allowed to auction it off for the value of the lien and pocket the money. The skill these men brought to their craft was legendary. Joe Ollinger had the privilege of knowing the last of them in the 1940s. Ted Meloney rented a dry dock at Choctaw Point and kept the bar pilot's schooner *Alabama* shipshape. More than sixty years later, Ollinger is still awed by Meloney's depth of lore and knowledge, especially his ability to eyeball standing timber and accurately calculate its suitability to particular jobs.[28] In the twentieth century welders emerged as the definitive shipyard workers. ADDSCO and Gulf

Shipbuilding employed thousands, many of them women and, later, black workers. In February 1944 there were two thousand females at ADDSCO alone, most welders but a smattering of firemen and riggers as well. In a 2013 newspaper interview Zaddie Johnson recalled her life as a wartime welder. Born near Gadsden in 1918, she grew up in a sharecropping family and ran away to get married at age seventeen. Shortly after the war started she and her husband moved to Mobile so he could find work at the docks. Attracted by the opportunity and money at the shipyards, she joined her husband in the workforce, initially tacking the welds for the welders. "I had never seen a welding machine in my life," she said. "Ever chance I got, I would start practicing. It wasn't long till I got on a welding crew." The work was hard, but she and the other women developed a good rapport and reveled in calling each other by their last names. "I didn't know anybody by their first name," she recalled. This was new social territory for everybody, and a nine-member Women's Counseling Service made it their duty to "keep the girl workers happy, healthy, and on the job." Black workers' advancement into skilled shipyard jobs came much harder, but that story is for the next chapter.[29]

Of all the different types of men and women who have labored along the Mobile River, among the most intriguing are those independent souls who follow their own lights and patch together a living by odd jobs, hunting, fishing, and ingenuity. One can regularly see their little ramshackle houseboats roped to delta stream banks or their improvised shacks and trailers perched on stilts far from any road. Of their 1930s predecessors one old-time delta hand wrote that "the swamp provided for these residents. They needed few clothes, paid no rent or taxes, raised their own tobacco, and used few medicines. Peas were dried and threshed by being beaten in sacks. Okra, corn, beans, collards, and cushaws [squash]—which could be kept all winter—were grown in season." Their meat came from deer, coon, possum, and turtles, and they bartered for salt, sugar, and other commodities from passing tugboat crews. Among the most unusual of this lot was Pete Bernard Jr., a Wisconsin-born man who moved to Mobile in 1910. He worked various shipyard jobs and ran a café. In 1958, after the deaths of his wife and his son, he moved onto the remains of Battery McIntosh, or Goat Island, as some locals called it. Here he fashioned three one-room shacks, one for sleeping, one for cooking, and the last for guests. "Everyone has a hobby," he told an interviewer, "and mine is living here, fishing when I please, and giving people a place to stay when they are stranded." He only came into town for his monthly pension check and a few supplies, and to attend Mass. In 1966, at the ripe old age of ninety-seven, Bernard, or the Hermit of Goat Island, was run over and killed by a car at Eslava and St. Emanuel Streets downtown.[30]

Even closer to the city people found a way to lead semi-independent lives. In the summer of 2011 retired SEC championship coach Vince Dooley attempted to find the remains of his mother and uncle's Blakeley Island homestead. A frequent visitor to the island, he vividly remembered their lives there. "They would come pick us up in a little motorized launch at the foot of Eslava Street," he told a reporter. "They raised cattle and farmed vegetables . . . , and sold the occasional alligator skin." There was no running water in the house so they caught rainwater off the roof, nor was there any electricity. "Light a candle or a lamp," he said of the nights, "then stay up half an hour after it got dark. It was a tradition that every Saturday night, the family would all go over to the Spanish River and bathe." Dooley remembered a nearly pristine environment in Polecat Bay, where the water was clear and sea grass waved on the bottom. He and the reporter found the old family place, an overgrown pile of bricks and a few rusted relics. Even as recently as 2013 one family was holding on at Pinto Island, their shacks perched beside the mostly in-filled Pinto Pass. A little wood wharf extended over the water. Ray Hamblin, forty-eight, talked to a newspaper reporter in 1996 about his family's life on the island and their desire simply to be left alone. Hamblin admitted that they were squatters, but by all appearances they were comfortably ensconced, and the land's corporate owners said they had no plans to evict. Occasionally family members had taken various restaurant or shipyard jobs in the area and hunted rabbits or fished the river. The family had electricity and air conditioning but no television. Modern visitors to the island's booming high-tech shipyards sometimes do a double take at the sight of the Hamblins' little compound in such an incongruous location. But its presence is testimony to the dogged determination of the human spirit to hold its own in Mobile's unpredictable coastal environment.[31]

10

Pleasure and Peril

The Mobile River is mostly about work, but it has also been and occasionally still is a place of recreation and pleasure. In the past casual boaters, racers in community regattas, and even swimmers were not at all uncommon. Early-twentieth-century photographs depict brightly bedecked sailboats crowded with ladies in white dresses and leghorn hats, accompanied by their gallant gentlemen, all incongruously backgrounded by the grubby wharves, tall ships, and steamers. Such sights are long gone, though enthusiastic kayakers may sometimes be seen in the harbor. Fishermen regularly use the river as a highway to their delta honey holes, and during the annual alligator season, nocturnal hunters ghost along its banks hoping to spot a big 'un. But at no time, past or present, has anyone with their wits about them ever made the mistake of not respecting the river as a potentially dangerous place. Since colonial days violence has been a near constant riverside, and accident, fire, and flood have all had their impact. Then there are the hurricanes that spin up out of the gulf and slam into the coast with frightening surges and howling winds, wreaking havoc for hundreds of square miles. The Mobile River has seen its share of hurricaines across time, and maritime interests and area residents all know that any given year could bring the killer storm that will forever after serve as demarcation and reference point.

But first the pleasure. Holidays were often marked by festive boat races in the harbor. On New Year's Day 1839 the *Mobile Daily Commercial Register* reported one such occasion. "The wharves and vessels and their rigging were crowded with spectators," the paper recounted. "The river was alive with glancing craft of all shapes and sizes and various speed." Seventy years later, only days before Christmas, excited Mobilians once again thronged the waterfront to watch a power-boat race. The boats were far different from the elegant little yawls and schooners that still dotted the bay and harbor. These were long thin vessels with awnings or cabins and internal combustion engines capable of up to thirty mph. The January 1909 issue of *Power Boat* enthused that "Mobile is one of the live towns in the South when it comes to power boating, and the Mobile Yacht Club under Commodore Barry Lyons has done much to encourage the sport." The bay was praised for its protection from the gulf, but the Mobile River was singled out as "a splendid place for holding straight-away speed boat races." Just as during the mid-nineteenth century when crowds thrilled to steamboat contests, the new technology exhibited by speed boats provided spectacular entertainment value riverside.[1]

Other kinds of diversion were available on the river from time to time, including, incredibly enough, a bona fide circus. In the winter of 1853 Spalding & Rogers' Floating Circus Palace tied up to the local wharves and attracted as many people "to see the structure itself, as to witness the excellent performances that are conducted within its walls by the enterprising managers." Built at Cincinnati in 1851 and subsequently towed up and down Southern rivers, this contraption was essentially a big arena plopped on a barge. "It is not a sham built affair," *Gleason's Pictorial Drawing-Room Companion* assured its readers on February 19, 1853, "but it is really very finely fitted, and perfect in every respect." The exterior looked like a big wooden box with two tiers of windows and was enlivened by enormous fluttering flags. Once inside, visitors no doubt gawked at the accommodations. "The 'dress-circle,' as it is termed, consists of eleven hundred cane-bottom arm-chairs, each numbered to correspond to the ticket issued," *Gleason's* continued, and the more exclusive "family circle" included five hundred "cushioned settees." For those who could not afford either the dress or family circle, there were the cheap seats, nine hundred hard-bottomed chairs in the upper galleries. But whether situated in a cushioned settee or a hard-bottomed chair, one and all were swept away by the shows, which included displays of horsemanship and animal tricks. Chimes provided musical accompaniment to the performances. The interior was lighted by gas jets and heated by hot water pipes. Besides the amphitheater, there were offices, dressing rooms, green rooms, halls, saloons, and a stable. *Gleason's* did not exaggerate when it concluded that "taken altogether it is a most curious, original and interesting affair, and we have therefore selected it as something that would interest our readers."[2]

Floating circus or no, adventurous boys have always found the river irresistible, though it is much harder to get to along the city front these days with all the heavy industry and modern security measures. It was easier to access in the past but was not the kind of place any careful parent wanted a child to frequent. As Rayford wrote in *Cottonmouth*, "You never saw one of the boys from a better family lounging down there around the river. If a kid hung out around the wharf, he was called a tough kid. Many a kid had the hell whaled out of him for playing around that river." But happily for some boys, they lived close enough to the stream for it to be, if not their playground, at least their front yard. Hudson McDonald was one such youth, who spent his first eleven years at the mouth of Three Mile Creek. During the 1930s and 1940s, McDonald's father was a swing-bridge tender for the railroad span over the creek. The family's house was perched right beside the tracks, on the northern bank. "It was a grey frame house which consisted of a kitchen, dining room (serving as a second bedroom), a living room and one bedroom," McDonald recalled in his 2010 autobiography. A wraparound gallery faced east and south, providing good views of both the river and the creek. When McDonald was six his father gave him a little cypress skiff with a 2.5-horsepower kicker. "I was allowed to travel from the Mobile River to Conception Street on Three Mile Creek," he fondly remembered, "and told never to enter into the river because the Aluminum Corporation of America (ALCOA) had huge ships docking at the entrance to the creek." This incredible freedom meant that young McDonald could putter up and down Three Mile Creek and contemplate enormous ships, hulking locomotives, and heavy steel bridges far more closely than most modern parents would permit. But, being a boy, he could not resist the allure of the main channel. "On two occasions I was caught going out into the river to ride the waves," he wrote. "The waves were taking the boat up and down, but I never could figure out how my father was detecting this. When I would get back to our dock at the railroad bridge he would be waiting at the wharf with a strap in his hand and give me a beating. I'd say to myself, 'Oh, how did he know I was out in the river?'" As it turned out, some black men fishing nearby had seen him and told his father. McDonald's immaturity got him into yet another pickle when he attempted to dart under the railroad bridge at high tide, with precious little vertical clearance. Believing he could duck just in time to scoot under, he gunned the engine and crouched down. Unfortunately, the future engineer had not factored in the engine's height, and its top banged into a girder, nearly ripping out the boat's stern. This meant another whipping. Despite his brushes with disaster, McDonald survived his childhood and went on to a long and successful career.[3]

Not surprisingly, there are few references to people swimming in the Mobile River for fun. Its depth, muddy currents, sawyers, and frightening critters have always been effective deterrents, although, as we have already seen, some antebellum boys were not afraid to jump in and swim after steamboats. However, there are examples of people choosing the river as a stage to demonstrate their athletic prowess. Among these was Lottie Mayer, a vaudeville actress and "aquatic expert" who, on September 7, 1911, announced her intention to swim from the foot of Dauphin Street down to Frascati, below Choctaw Point. Only days later, inspired by her success, a fireman aboard a South American fruiter "dived from the deck of that vessel," berthed at the foot of Dauphin, and swam all the way out to Battery Gladden Lighthouse and back. His time was a respectable one hour and fifteen minutes. Far safer and, frankly, more pleasant for most were the swimming holes and sandy creek banks well back from the main stream. These often presented shallow, clear, and cool waters where children splashed and families picnicked. During the Great Depression, a swimming pool was excavated on the banks of Conrad Creek at Chastang and lined with brown rocks and concrete. Located hard by St. Peter the Apostle Catholic Church, the pool and a nearby baseball diamond were godsends for the boys of color at the parish orphanage.[4]

Swimming was of no interest to most sailors visiting Mobile; in fact many did not even know how to swim, as the all-too-frequent harbor drownings attest. Nor were the sailors looking for boat races or sightseeing cruises upriver. For them pleasure meant

Swimming pool on Conrad Creek near Chastang, 1951. History Museum of Mobile Collection. Courtesy of the Doy Leale McCall Rare Book and Manuscript Library, University of South Alabama.

the time-honored combination of drinking, gambling, whoring, and fighting. As the official agitation over "whore balls" in 1847 and deckhand Vincent George's vivid 1984 memories of the Club Royal girls demonstrate, this unholy quartet represents one of the great constants riverside. The official records and newspapers during the nineteenth and early twentieth centuries are sprinkled with references to all four, especially toward eliminating prostitution or controlling and confining it to certain districts. On May 27, 1866, the Mayor's Court heard a case involving several "'scrumptious' females with scrambled hair" who had been arrested for lewd behavior and foul language downtown. One of the women, Kate New, "a gushing damsel," admitted that she swore "but didn't use any such words as was attributed to her." The court was unconvinced, and the women were fined and released. By the turn of the twentieth century officials were willing to tolerate prostitution if it did not messily spill into the public realm. In 1903 local bars and brothels published the *Blue Book* in order to help interested patrons find the city's sanctioned "Tenderloin District," or that area "set aside by law for the fast women." Bounded by St. Michael, St. Louis, Lawrence, and Warren Streets downtown, this "Red Light" district was packed with bars, smoke shops, "Ladies Cafés," and whorehouses. The *Blue Book* assured its readers that it offered all the best information for navigating this potentially treacherous terrain. If read carefully, its author declared "you know who is who and the best place to go spend your time and money." The various houses, with their madams, telephone numbers, and the girls' names, were listed on page after page. Among the hot spots were the Mansion of Aching Hearts, presided over by Blanch Williams at 405 St. Louis Street, and the Palace of Palms, overseen by Madam Ruby Lee at 554 St. Michael Street. The guide also helpfully listed the woman's race, white, black, or octoroon. Madam Rosa Lee ran an establishment with four girls of the last classification, among them Lorie Dreyfus and Lizzie Alexander. Local tolerance disappeared during World War I, when it was worried such a district would have a deleterious effect on the troops moving through port. But prostitution was never wholly to be stamped out. Eugene Walter recalled the madams during the 1930s in his oral biography, with Katherine Clark. "The fat ladies, the ample ladies who were mistresses, were strange combinations of mother superior, mother, grandmother, doctor, nurse, female notary," he remembered. "They knew everybody's little perversions." Even today, determined sailors or anyone else, for that matter, can find sexual adventure easily enough somewhere downtown.[5]

When not in tiny rooms earning their money or recovering from their labors, prostitutes haunted the waterfront bars and dives trolling for customers or just vacantly nursing drinks. These establishments were routinely host to liquor-fueled mischief. One prohibition reformer in 1909 singled out lower Conti Street as a zone rife with "bar rooms and tough places" where "no lady of my family would go unescorted by a man and no man of my acquaintance would take a lady if he could help it." Conditions there were so bad, he claimed, that neither the sheriff nor a U.S. marshal would arrest a sailor without a guaranteed fee of five dollars per head, "as they frequently had trouble." Eugene Walter knew these kinds of places and described one in his 1954 novel *The Untidy Pilgrim.* "The streets are dark in the waterfront section," he wrote, "the old buildings gloomy and beetle-browed—that gloom of empty upper stories, wharf rats, the eternal waterfront sensation of departures amidst hustle bustle, and returns to things familiar for one moment strangely seen. Down by the wharves there are coffee-joints and beer-joints full of noise, pouring yellow light into the street. . . . " His character enters the Bluebird Lunch Room and encounters a typical assemblage of types—"Spanish-ish or Italian-ish sailors" with gold earrings, "chubby whores," and a piano player "tiddlyfingering a muted version of 'Wanta get something straight between us.'"[6]

Waterfront vice might have promised pleasure, but most of those tasting its proffered delights experienced disappointment at best or violence at worst. Even for those who did not partake, life on or near the water was fraught with peril. Places such as Spanish Alley and Monkey Wrench Corner were notorious among merchant seaman around the world, the former during the nineteenth century and the latter during the twentieth. Criminals were forever busy, and an innocent man might easily lose his purse or his life for being in the wrong place at the wrong time. As Rayford wrote, "Many a man had a knife slipped into him, or his head bashed in, in Spanish Alley." And if the threat of physical violence was not enough to give one pause, the regular occurrence of accidents ranging from boiler explosions, sinkings, collisions, and fires was. Life on the river is dangerous, always has been, and probably always will be.[7]

The historical roster of violence and mishaps on the river is a long and depressing one. During the eighteenth century everyday life could be brutal and was sometimes made worse by those in power. Such a case occurred in 1757 with several Swiss soldiers stationed on Cat Island, off what is today the Mississippi coast. These unfortunates were consistently abused by their French commander who made them semislaves. When they protested, he had them stripped and tied to trees, where the mosquitoes tormented them. Finally goaded beyond endurance and having received no official relief from their complaints up the chain of command, the men shot their commander and threw his body in the sea. In their euphoria they liberated a prisoner named Beaudrot who had also suffered at the commander's hand. Beaudrot subsequently guided the mutineers deep into the interior, but they were eventually caught and imprisoned at Mobile. After a quick trial all were condemned to death. The sentence was carried out in front of the gates of Fort Condé for everyone to see. Beaudrot's ghastly fate was to be broken on the wheel. Soldiers lashed him to a large upended wagon wheel, and a burly prisoner methodically smashed his limbs, torso, and head with a heavy mallet. Afterward Beaudrot's body was pitched into the river. The fate of the Swiss soldiers was equally grim—they were pushed down into long wooden boxes and sawn in half. Public reaction to this horrific justice was mostly shock. Beaudrot was thought innocent because people believed he had been compelled to act as guide for the Swiss.[8]

During the nineteenth century public execution meant hanging, but given the frequency of crime it hardly appears to have been a deterrent. One visitor to Mobile during the 1840s was stunned by the freewheeling chaos riverside. "From dark to dawn, lawlessness stalked abroad rampant in Mobile," he wrote. "Gangs of drunken boatmen, sailors, and reckless adventurers, staggered through the streets, making night hideous with obscene songs and loud oaths, hunting for the next dramshop or a fight, both of which were conveniently at hand. The imbecile police were utterly powerless, and could not in the least prevent the full-deck fights which were constantly going forward." Less spectacular but more common were the isolated incidents involving only a few individuals. There are dozens of cases of disorderly conduct and "acting in a most riotous manner" scattered through the Mayor's Court record and local newspapers. On the evening of April 6, 1822, for example, the court record details a fracas down by the wharves. A city policeman spotted a man attempting to board a barge with "a large stick in his hand," and "a negro on board the boat would not let him." Two other white men materialized out of the gloom, one of them with a dirk, and all three assaulted the black man. During the scuffle he was stabbed. The white men were arrested, charged, fined, ordered to "keep the peace," and released on six months' probation. Sometimes witnesses gave conflicting testimony. On November 29, 1821, Stephen Chandler was arrested and charged with "abusive conduct." One witness said that Chandler had approached John Sarage, who was peacefully resting with his dray beside a steamboat, and "ordered him off." When Sarage refused, Chandler kicked him in the face. Yet the boat's captain testified that the dray was in Chandler's way, and when he asked politely that it be removed Sarage "called him a damned rascal and collared him." Unable to determine where the blame lay, the court ordered the parties to shake hands and share the court costs. Occasionally, but rarely, police were able to prevent trouble from escalating into a fight. On August 26, 1859, a mate aboard the schooner *Potomac* pressed charges against two seamen aboard the bark *Pilgrim.* According to the mate, the men "asked him to come to the wharf and get whipped." He declined, and the sailors began loudly "cursing him." This brought the police, the sailors' arrest, fines, and a bond of "$100 for good behavior."[9]

Violence occurred upriver as well, though not nearly as frequently as in town due to the sparser population. When it did occur it was just as swift and bloody. Such was the case at Twenty-One Mile Bluff in the summer of 1858, and race complicated the outcome. According to a sixteen-year-old witness named Lawrence Gregory, he was sitting at the landing under a large oak tree on the morning of August 1 when he heard a black woman screaming and "the sound of blows, like that of a whip." Then Gregory saw a man named William Dupree, carrying a gun, run for the cabins where the screaming originated, some twenty yards from the river. When he neared the cabins, Dupree fired, and a man named Smith ran out and headed toward Dupree. The latter fired again, killing Smith. Gregory swore that he had not seen any arms on Smith but that when he returned with help, a stick, a whip, and a knife were beside the body and the body had been moved several feet. Not surprisingly, it was learned that there was prior history between Dupree and Smith, especially regarding stealing chickens. Smith had a reputation as a mean drunk and had been threatening Dupree and those on his place for weeks. Hoping to bolster his defense, Dupree "offered three witnesses," the children of the black woman, who was named Clara. The court noted that Clara "was a mulatto" and her children "appeared to be white." In fact, Clara's grandmother was none other than Jane Seymour, the Creole widow of Simon Andre who had offered Andrew Jackson lodgings on his 1814 downriver voyage. Unmoved by this distinguished lineage, the court refused any testimony by Clara or her children. Shamefully, they were ruled "incompetent witnesses" because of their mixed ancestry. Of the children the court declared: "Their father, maternal grandfather, and great-grandfather were white men. Their great-grandmother was the child of a mulatto, by a negress." But white forebears were not enough, because prior to the great-grandfather, "the ancestors of both sexes were either negroes, or of mixed blood." The law was clear: any mixed ancestry "to the third generation" meant one could not testify. Fortunately for Dupree, he was able to produce white witnesses who could confirm Smith's drinking and threats, and the case was dismissed.[10]

As the foregoing case demonstrates, people of color were at a distinct disadvantage along the river for most of its history, before and after slavery. And because the Mobile was a working river, labor issues were often the source of their troubles. Any attempt to better their lot or claim privileges was likely to be met with open hostility. Strikebreaking was especially hazardous. In the winter of 1912, for example, the white crew of a Norwegian steamship walked off the job, and black sailors were hired to replace them. While the vessel lay at anchor midriver, the white seamen worked out an agreement with the captain and were rehired. When the black hires then demanded "a month's salary on the ground that they had been regularly signed and could not be discharged," the white sailors set upon them with cudgels and fists. After being transported to the wharves, the black men angrily complained to an official and showed him "swollen lips, bruised hands, and discolored optics as evidence of their maltreatment." An unsympathetic crowd gathered to jeer, and their complaints went nowhere. Black longshoremen were just as disrespected as black sailors, and only a year later, several thousand walked off the job and demanded half of the port's skilled work as well as better wages and overtime work. Outraged, white longshoremen struck as well, and angry rhetoric flew back and forth. Amid police harassment and press hysteria, the black longshoremen still managed to negotiate a share of the timber work and a wage increase of five cents an hour. It was not much, but it was something.[11]

Because of compromises and uneasy truces, racial tensions mostly simmered along the waterfront until World War II, when a full-scale riot rocked ADDSCO's Pinto Island yards. White resentment was the cause. On the evening of May 24, in response to an order from President Franklin D. Roosevelt's Committee on Fair Employment Practice, ADDSCO upgraded twelve black men to welders, and they successfully worked their 11:00 p.m. to 7:00 a.m. shift alongside white coworkers without incident. But the following morning rumors began flying around the yard, among them the claim that a white woman had been murdered by one of the black welders. Whether or not the rioters believed there had been a murder, the specter of black social equality was more than enough provocation to them, and they angrily gathered at the ways. With cries of "We gotta get every one of them Niggers off this island" and "No nigger is goin' to join iron in these yards," thousands of white workers grabbed steel pipes, bricks, and whatever else lay at hand. Trapped, hundreds of terrified black workers had no choice but to run through the mob in an attempt to reach the ferry and safety in the city. Some white individuals tried to protect black workers and got clobbered for their efforts. By all accounts the rioters were young hotheads, and many of them were women. As one New York newspaper wryly commented, the females "did a good job in upholding Southern tradition, sharing with their white comrades in the chase." Fortunately, no one was killed, but numerous black workers suffered cuts, bruises, and lumps on the head. In a telegram to Thurgood Marshall, then chief counsel for the NAACP, local civil rights activist John LeFlore reported that he had visited the victims in hospital and interviewed them about what had happened. He called the attack "well organized" and urged that the federal government "take a firm stand in dealing with those responsible for the trouble and also afford complete protection to colored workers in all capacities." By the time LeFlore sent his telegram, six hundred troops from nearby Brookley Field had already restored order and posted an illuminated sign that read "United States troops are here to protect government property and to see that there is no interference with the war effort."[12]

In the riot's aftermath cooler heads were horrified, and the city's elite attributed the violence to the upcountry rustics who had flooded into town for shipyard jobs. Afraid for their lives, thousands of black workers refused to return to Pinto Island, and some white workers, upset by the violence, decided to quit as well. ADDSCO's production plummeted 50 percent, and the press pleaded for calm and a return to normalcy lest the war effort be compromised. As far as an editorial in the *Mobile Register* was concerned, the trouble had been sparked "by indiscreet mingling of white and negro workers," and the writer insisted that only a policy of "complete segregation" stood any chance of working. A group of black ministers urged "our people to return to work" and fervently prayed that the day would soon come "when all men will recognize God as our Father, Christ as their Redeemer, and man as their brother." In the end ADDSCO set up a fully segregated yard, which allowed black laborers to return to work, including to skilled jobs, without further trouble.[13]

There were, of course, lots of ways to get into trouble on the river that had nothing to do with race. The river is an unstinting equal-opportunity hazard if there ever was one. Accidents of various kinds were (and remain) all too frequent. In his account of a trip upriver in 1759, the French captain Bossu described a precarious but rather comical situation. While inching upstream during high water one night, his boat suddenly became "hemmed in by the branches of a tree that was set under water." Trapped, he and his men could do nothing but wait "in this disagreeable situation" until dawn. By then the river had fallen, and Bossu lamented, "I found myself now quite in the air in my boat." Several Mobile Indians comforted him with the observation that the incoming tide would refloat the little craft, which soon enough it did. Less amusing were the sudden unexpected situations that ended with a person thrashing in the water. At about nine o'clock on a winter's evening in 1860, a Mr. Myers had a berth on the steamboat *Yorktown* and was attempting to board. According to a newspaper report on the incident, Myers was blinded by the torch blazing at the boat's bow and when he stepped off the wharf, rather than encountering the deck, he plunged into the river. A quick-thinking bystander was able to get him out, but the newspaper warned anyone visiting the wharves to be "careful of their steps, the various lights and shadows in that quarter being very deceptive." Not everyone was as lucky as Myers. On December 11, 1909, Sidney Hoskins, an eighteen-year-old British seaman, drowned off the Louisville & Nashville Wharf in broad daylight. According to the ship's captain, "Sidney was standing on a barge tallying pieces of timber being hoisted aboard the vessel. The stevedore was rushing the men and they were working as fast as they could. A sling load of the timber swung to one side and knocked the boy into the water." The captain guessed that young Hoskins had been injured by the blow, "for if he ever came to the surface no one saw him." And then there were those bizarre occasions when even grizzled river men could only shake their heads at the wonder of it all. Such occurred on June 8, 1909, when one Carl Carlson, a sailor aboard a schooner in port, "encountered a horse swimming in the Mobile River near the vessel." Carlson and his mates were able to man a boat quickly and guide the animal back to the bank. "The horse is thought to have walked overboard in the vicinity of Texas Street," the newspaper reported. "Carlson brought the horse to the police station where it awaits an owner. It is a fine black animal, with white stocking on the left hind foot, and blind in both eyes."[14]

Mishaps involving river traffic were far scarier and more consequential to larger numbers of people. To begin with vessels weighing many tons and under way were potential weapons of mass destruction if they were damaged or lost control. The horrifying results of nineteenth-century steamboat boiler explosions and fires have already been examined, but many other things could go wrong—collision, sinking, grounding, mechanical failure, load shifts—the list was endless. Something of the danger and difficulty of river navigation and the consequences of not getting it right may be appreciated by the 1884 case of the *Mary Ida* and the *Maggie Burke.* The nocturnal smashup between these two vessels led to lawsuits and ultimately gave one of the Mobile River's tight hairpin turns its colorful name—Mary Ida Point.

It happened on January 19 between the hours of 10:00 and 11:00 p.m. By all accounts it was a fine night, clear and starlit with a steady north wind. The steamboat *Mary Ida,* J. W. McDowell master, was descending the river with three barges in tow. Her cargo consisted of cotton seed and lumber. Just below Chastang Bluff, heading into the river's narrowest section and tightest bends, the *Ida* collided with the ascending steamboat *Maggie Burke,* captained by veteran river man Owen Finnegan. The vessels were within twenty feet of the east bank when they hit. The *Ida* smashed into the *Burke* at an angle and then swung out into the center of the stream, her tows tracing a crazy circle in her wake. Badly holed and taking on water, the *Ida* heeled over and sank in fifty-six feet of water. Her crew and passengers were rescued by the *Burke,* which returned to Mobile with the news.[15]

In the aftermath the owners of the respective boats sued one another, each claiming "negligence, want of skill, recklessness, and improper conduct" of the other's officers and crew. The case went to the Alabama District Court, where the lawyers argued their respective points of view. The court first had to decide which vessel had the right of way and so which was at fault. According to maritime law at the time, "Where steamers are approaching each other from opposite directions, the signals for passing shall be one blast of the steam-whistle to pass to the right, and two blasts of the steam-whistle to pass to the left." The ascending pilot was usually to be the first to indicate his preference, but if the descending pilot believed the preference dangerous, he could indicate with his whistle how he wished to pass and was due the right of way. According to Captain McDowell, he spotted the *Burke* coming upstream and blew two blasts, indicating his wish to pass to the left, or east. The *Burke* responded, with one blast, indicating that she disagreed, but whether or not she responded promptly enough was the source of some disagreement. The *Ida* countered with two blasts, the *Burke* with one again, and then they collided. The court noted that "the *Burke* came up the river in the usual place where it is navigated by ascending steamers, and below that point hugging the west shore, and was, consequently, under the false point, which obstructed the view, and this was doubtless the reason why the boats approached so near to each other before the signals were exchanged." In river parlance "false point" referred to land that jutted into the stream but did not alter the current. Such is the feature that came to be called Mary Ida Point. The boats would have been invisible to each other from opposite sides of this tree-covered bend, though actually quite close. Crewmen did indicate that they could see smoke from each other's vessel as they approached, however. The *Burke*'s master claimed that he did not accept the *Ida*'s signal because he was running from the west bank to the east bank and thus obeying the navigation rule that "ascending boats run the points to evade as much as possible the force of the current, while descending boats follow the current in the middle of the river around the bends." Once he was committed to his course, he claimed, he could not alter it without risking a collision. The *Ida* was better able to change course. But, the court wanted to know, if the *Burke* could not change course, why did she not at least back her engines? When her engineer was asked what the engines were doing at the time, he answered, "I *think* they were backing." In the end the court decided that both vessels were at fault, but that the *Burke* owned the greater share. The loss was apportioned "in the ration of one-fourth against the *Ida* and three-fourths against the *Burke*." The case showed just how fraught river navigation could be. The Mobile was an unforgiving environment, and even experienced hands got into trouble.[16]

Collisions were not confined to tight bends at night, either. One case occurred at 7:15 a.m., January 20, 1900, right out in the harbor, just opposite One Mile Creek. The tugboat *Captain Sam* was puffing upstream "against a strong wind and current" with a heavy barge in tow. The cargo was fifty-five thousand feet of timber and lumber. Just below, the tugboat *Hero* was also ascending and gaining fast. There were numerous witnesses to what happened next, as there were several stevedores aboard the barge and dockworkers up and down the wharves. The *Hero* carried a three-man crew of pilot, engineer, and fireman, but none of them was posted as a lookout. Later, the *Hero*'s survivors claimed they had not seen the barge, which at the time of the collision was 250 feet behind the *Captain Sam* on a taut hawser. The *Hero* got ahead of the barge but was too close, and the men aboard the *Captain Sam* yelled, "Look out, the barge is coming!" Their warning came too late, and the barge rammed the *Hero*, knocking her over and dragging her under. As the vessel tipped, her captain broke out the pilothouse window, cutting his hand, and kicked out into the chilly river. The engineer, Robert Davidson, and the black fireman, Luke Robinson, jumped free from the deck. Immediately the

Captain Sam cut her tow and backed to render aid. Her crew threw out a line and life preservers. Davidson, who could not swim, was helped in the water by Robinson, but when the latter felt his strength giving, he told Davidson to let him loose. "Davidson made a few more futile strokes," the newspaper reported, "and soon sank. Twice did he sink and was finally seen no more." A determined effort to recover the body failed.[17]

Thorough knowledge of navigational procedure and a vigilant crew are important on the water, but even these are no protection from the dreaded deadheads, sinkers, and sawyers that plague river traffic. No vessel, large or small, is immune. In an article for *Mobile Bay* magazine in 2012, local writer and delta aficionado Watt Key described the dangers of submerged logs and driftwood to small craft, particularly at night. "The only way to see these is with handheld spotlights," he explained, "but by the time you recognize them, it's usually too late. Boats flip, have their bottoms torn out, and their engines ripped off." Key's greatest fear was getting thrown out of the boat. "Assuming that I don't hit my head on anything as I eject," he wrote, "I'll be stranded in a place where nightmares can come true. I was told as a boy always to keep my bootlaces untied in the boat." It was hard to decide which was more terrifying in such a circumstance—to be adrift in open water with dangerous eddies and currents or struggling through mud and head high marsh grass surrounded by alligators and cottonmouths "with heads as big as my fist." Rather than give in to anxiety or fear, Key, like most experienced swamp rats, admitted that he simply chose to race ahead "playing the odds." One can never predict where deadheads are likely to be, and running at night is always a gamble "in the river's favor."[18]

Nor is a bigger boat any guarantee of safety where deadheads are concerned, as is graphically illustrated by the case of the *Nettie Quill* in the spring of 1902. The *Quill* departed Mobile's wharves on the evening of May 13 with Captain John Quill in the pilothouse. Her cargo was a one-hundred-thousand-pound locomotive sitting atop a barge lashed to her side. The weather was good, winds were light, and the moon brightly illuminated the river's dark waters. Shortly after the boat got underway, Captain Quill retired for supper and turned the helm over to his mate, a man named Campbell. Just south of Twelve Mile Island, Campbell suddenly spotted a sawyer bobbing some two feet out of the water directly ahead. Later measurement showed the obstacle to be a forty-foot sawn log, butt down and two feet in diameter at the small end. Unable to do anything but frantically sound the alarm, Campbell braced for impact. The log rammed into the barge, making a large hole. As water rapidly flooded in, the barge began to tip and the *Nettie Quill*'s roustabouts sensibly feared that the heavy locomotive would flip the steamboat. They hurriedly cut the lines and let cargo and barge plummet to the bottom, where they likely rest still beneath who knows how many feet of river mud.[19]

Thanks to no small measure of good luck and quick action by their crews, disasters like those involving the *Mary Ida, Maggie Burke,* and *Nettie Quill* were free from loss of life. But on the morning of September 22, 1993, there was no such fortune at

Bayou Canot, north of Twelve Mile Island, when an inadequately trained push boat pilot slammed into a bridge abutment, causing one of the nation's worst rail disasters up to that time. The terrible chain of events began at around 2:45 a.m. when the pilot of the boat *Mauvilla,* pushing three barges, became disoriented in heavy fog. Unable to interpret his radar, he steered the vessel out of the Mobile's main channel and into Bayou Canot, which though a big and deep stream is not navigable for barges. Running blind, the *Mauvilla* then rammed its lead barge into the steel-and-timber railroad swing bridge, built in 1909. Thinking he had perhaps run aground, the pilot was unaware that his vessel had hit a bridge abutment and knocked its track significantly out of line. But because the rails were only kinked and not broken, the bridge block approach signals on the main track remained green, and no trains could know of any trouble ahead.[20]

Meanwhile, Amtrack's *Sunset Limited,* en route from Los Angeles to Miami with 220 people aboard, was hurtling north out of Mobile, parallel to the dark and mysterious delta to its east. At around 2:53 a.m., only minutes after the collision in the bayou, the train roared onto the bridge, hit the kink, and flew off the rails. The three locomotives, the baggage and dormitory cars, and two of the six passenger cars knifed into the muddy bank or into the water, while another passenger car hung precariously over the now completely destroyed span. The engines' diesel tanks ruptured, and fuel leaked into the water. Two of the engines caught fire, as did the baggage and dormitory cars. No one aboard knew what had happened, only that their world was now one of chaos, water, fire, smoke, and terror. "It was very murky and misty, and too dark to see," passenger Simon Grant told a *Mobile Register* reporter shortly afterward. Luckily for Grant, his car was still on the tracks. Not so that of twenty-one-year-old Joseph Boniface, who said: "All of a sudden all I saw was orange flame and sparks. We had to go into the water and swim to shore." Passenger Tim Palmer, twenty-three, of London, England, said that he had been asleep before the wreck. "Suddenly the train started bumping tremendously," he recalled. "We were shaking up and down. Then splash—we were in the water." Susan Healy, twenty-one, no doubt voiced the thoughts of many when she told the reporter, "I thought we had come to the end." She escaped when the man in front of her broke out a window. "Once he did that we just held our breaths until we floated to the top. Then we had to swim away because the train was on fire in the water."[21]

Due to the wreck's remote location and the heavy fog, first responders had difficulty getting to the scene. CSX officials called 911 at 3:08 a.m., but the first coast guardsmen did not arrive for more than two hours. In the meantime a motley assortment of work boats and pleasure craft was converging on the scene. By 5:15 a.m. two EMTs aboard a rescue chopper were hovering over the bridge remains trying to assess the situation. "It was pitch black," one of them remembered, "and the floodlights from my copter and from the tugboat limited the field of view." In an act of incredible skill and bravery the pilot eased the chopper down onto a barge. Slowly emergency management officials began to establish some order, placing the dead along the edge of one of the barges and covering them, treating the dazed and injured, and directing rescue divers into the submerged cars to look for survivors. "It was all dark water, all bad current," one of the divers declared. Once divers realized there were no air pockets below and likely no survivors either, they switched to recovery mode, using guide lines to inch down into the wreckage. "Our reaction was to get the job done," one of them said, "but not to endanger any more lives." All along, boats and choppers kept bringing more help. Among those ferried to the site were Mobile mayor Mike Dow and Alabama governor Jim Folsom Jr. "It was not a pretty sight," Folsom told the press. "It was the most terrible sight I've ever seen. This is without question the worst transportation disaster in this state's history."[22]

By daylight officials were finally getting the upper hand. A staging area and command center were established underneath the towering Cochrane/Africatown USA Bridge. Amtrack was able to run another engine and a car up to the scene in order to ferry the survivors back to the staging area, where a waiting fleet of ambulances whisked them to local hospitals. Mobile churches and private citizens also responded to the crisis, donating blankets and clothing to passengers who had only the wet, diesel-soaked shirts on their backs, bringing food, counseling those who had lost loved ones, and giving blood. The final tally of victims stood at 47 dead, most of whom drowned, and 103 injured. Fortunately, only a few of the injured required hospital admission. It was a bizarre twist to be sure; people were either killed or they were alright. In a 1994 report the National Transportation Safety Board issued a blizzard of recommendations to multiple agencies—Amtrack, the U.S. Coast Guard, the Association of American Railroads, and Warrior & Gulf Navigation Company, the *Mauvilla*'s owner. Perhaps the most important recommendation concerned better radar training for towboat operators, followed closely by improved railroad-bridge monitoring and inspections to identify vulnerable spans.[23]

There were few if any witnesses to the *Sunset Limited* wreck except those directly involved. Not so those disasters that unfolded in the harbor on the doorstep of thousands. Among the most memorable of these in recent history was the April 2013 wild ride of the Carnival cruise ship *Triumph*. This nine-hundred-foot leviathan had been towed into the Port of Mobile on Valentine's Day after a crippling engine fire at sea. Onboard, thousands of passengers had endured the proverbial vacation from hell with no power and raw sewage sloshing in the hallways. Millions of television viewers around the world were able to follow the drama of powerful tugs shepherding the *Triumph* up Mobile Bay, thanks to live television coverage from multiple networks, including CNN and Fox News. After the passengers were safely transferred to buses and returned home, *Triumph* was shifted across the river to BAE Shipyard on Pinto Island, where it was to undergo months of repairs and renovations. And there the vessel lay, a new fixture on the downtown skyline, until a freak thunderstorm on April 3 lashed the area. Sustained hurricane-force winds whipped over the city and caught *Triumph* like a big sail. Hawsers snapped, and at least one bollard was ripped from its setting as the huge vessel broke free with hundreds of helpless workmen and crew aboard. The event's violence also knocked a guard shack and two shore workers into the river, one of whom drowned. Freed from its moorings, *Triumph* careened across the river like a battering ram and smashed into a large ship secured on the opposite side, damaging both vessels. Afterward *Triumph* drifted menacingly for hours until tugboats got her under control again. During the next few days, Mobile residents and commuters gawked at the twenty-foot gash wrapping the *Triumph*'s stern, scuffs along her hull, and dangling electrical cables and ropes. While regretting the loss of life, some locals smirked that the ship's engine fire in the gulf and crazy river ride were richly deserved payback to Carnival for summarily abandoning Mobile two years earlier, leaving citizens with an empty and as yet unpaid-for state-of-the-art cruise facility.[24]

Human beings face risks in every age and every place. Nonetheless, the residents of the Mobile basin have had to contend with certain perils that were especially acute and threatened even those living well back from the water. Over time these dangers have included disease, fire, and tropical weather. The central Gulf Coast's summer climate certainly contributed to the first of these, and eighteenth-century residents knew it. As the Dutch engineer and surveyor Bernard Romans observed then of the summers, "The atmosphere is, during this season, so burning hot, that undoubtedly very sudden rarefactions of the humours are often experienced, which cause such abundant perspiration, that water, as soon as drank, penetrates the open pores, so that the human skin seems to be comparable to a wet spunge." Those who were lucky enough to own plantations upstream could retreat during the worst months, "there to enjoy a freer circulation of the less putrified air." This also benefited those left behind, who were then "less crowded together." But whether one lived in town or to the north, the list of diseases likely to strike was sobering. "Fevers are the first of the summer diseases," Romans informed his readers, and they were often violent and fatal. These typically manifested themselves "about the latter end of July, and in August, and continue throughout September, and part of October, just the season succeeding our greatest rains and most violent heats." Yellow fever, as already noted, was the most dreaded of these. In order to protect themselves Mobilians were advised to take cold baths, "wear garlic and camphire in the pockets," eat "highly seasoned food," keep their feet dry, and above all avoid the night air, when "poisonous effluvia" was believed to be most prevalent. As for those who took sick, the treatments were grim and ineffective, ranging from bitter potions of magnolia root to blisters and "copious bleedings." Other common diseases included "dropsies, consumptions, hemorrhoidal and habitual fluxes, relaxed and bilious habits of the body, ruptures, worm-fevers, and among blacks the leprosy, elephantiasis and body yaws." The last affliction, still encountered among the poor in tropical regions, is a bacterial infection that causes painful skin lesions. And as if all of that was not scary enough, simply walking around during the summer could lead to what the French called *un coup de soleil,* or sunstroke. The preventive measure there was funny, but perhaps helpful—"a clean piece of writing paper" inserted between hat and head "to ward off the attacks."[25]

Ever since the *Pélican* arrived in 1704 carrying yellow fever, ships from foreign shores were known to be a potential health hazard. During the nineteenth century suspect vessels were routinely quarantined in the lower bay, as the *Florida* was after her daring dash from Cuba. In the early twentieth century the United Fruit Company was allowed to unload its bananas straight away but required immediately thereafter to fumigate them in railroad cars. Workers plugged each car's vents and burned seven pounds of sulphur for three hours to eliminate any tropical nastiness. By the 1920s measures to protect the public health from imported trouble became much more sophisticated when Alabama congressman John McDuffie introduced a bill to establish a quarantine station on what was then called Sand Island (renamed McDuffie Island in 1951).[26]

This was an ideal choice for such a facility. It was close to downtown and convenient to resources and services yet also isolated, and traffic onto or off the island was easily restricted. Construction got under way, and the station opened in 1927. It eventually consisted of twelve buildings—a hospital, detention facilities for passengers and crew, disinfecting and laundry facilities, officers' quarters, carpenter shop, paint shop, and fumigant storeroom. Whenever a foreign ship arrived in port, public-health officers from the station left their little wharf aboard a motor launch and boarded the vessel. If any passengers or crew were found to have one of seven diseases—cholera, yellow fever, smallpox, plague, typhus, anthrax, or leprosy—they and their ship had to go into immediate quarantine. While no doubt frustrated and anxious to get on with their travels, passengers and crew had pretty good accommodations on the island, complete with recreational opportunities and a library. Meanwhile their ship was searched from stem to stern by station employees wearing protective masks, and any stowaways were rousted into the sunlight. Once it was certain that no one was aboard, deadly fumigants were spread throughout the vessel and left for an eight-hour period. The station operated until 1950, when medical and sanitary improvements negated its usefulness and it closed. Several of the well-built brick structures stood into the 1990s, elegant fossils of another era and easily visible from downtown before they were demolished for a one-hundred-million-dollar iron-ore-processing plant.[27]

Another important health facility anchored the river's northern end from 1900 until its 2012 closure. This was Searcy Hospital, a state-owned psychiatric facility at Mount Vernon's old federal arsenal. After the Civil War the federal government resumed control of the arsenal and renamed it Mount Vernon Barracks. During the late 1880s and early 1890s Apache Indians captured in the Southwest, including the famed Geronimo, were held there. Shortly after the Indians were transferred to Texas and Oklahoma in 1894, the Mount Vernon Barracks was abandoned, and on March 1 of the following year it was deeded to the state of Alabama. In 1900 the Alabama General Assembly approved converting the installation into a mental hospital and two years later appropriated twenty-five thousand dollars to make the necessary changes. The new facility was to accommodate black patients only and was meant to relieve overcrowding at Bryce Hospital in Tuscaloosa. But due to several years of abandonment and neglect, some of the barracks buildings showed serious rot and deterioration. Teams of workmen spent almost two years making repairs and built a new kitchen, laundry, and heating and lighting plant. By 1902, renamed Mount Vernon Hospital, the facility was at last ready for its patients and staff.[28]

They came en masse by special train from Tuscaloosa—318 patients and 25 employees, including the state's superintendent for insane asylums, Dr. James T. Searcy. The journey took place without incident, and in a subsequent interview with the *Mobile Register,* Dr. Searcy proudly recounted it. He remarked that the patients were tranquil during the trip and fascinated by being on a train. "They were like children out upon a holiday excursion," he told the reporter. He attributed the lack of scenes or trouble to the fact that his patients had been "well trained to obey." He then reverted to deeply held racial assumptions with which few, if any, of his readers in turn-of-the-century Alabama would have disagreed. "We find the negroes very tractable," he explained. "They easily learn what we want them to do." The reporter noted that the patients at Mount Vernon would be kept occupied working in the laundry and on the large farm outside the walls. As at Tuscaloosa, he reassured readers, "kindly discipline and suggestion are relied upon to keep the patients in order and encourage them to physical exercise."[29]

Upon Dr. Searcy's retirement in 1919, the hospital was renamed in his honor. Despite the upgraded facilities, state funding, and a professionally trained staff, the hospital's black patients fared poorly over the years. In 1906 a pellagra epidemic swept through their ranks, and dozens died. Pellagra is an awful condition that results from certain vitamin deficiencies in the diet. Patients suffer skin lesions, diarrhea, and increasing dementia. The condition was widespread throughout the South during the early twentieth century among poor white and black persons, but for an epidemic to hit a concentrated population under the state of Alabama's care was nothing short of a public health crisis, not to mention an embarrassment. Dr. Searcy's assistant and son, Dr. George H. Searcy, inspected the patients' diet and sent a cornmeal sample to Tuskegee for analysis. Tests found that the cornmeal was made of "moldy grain and contained rather large quantities of a variety of bacteria and fungi." The cure was simple enough given this information—a more varied diet that avoided contaminated corn—and the importance of the Mount Vernon study to poor Southerners in general was hugely significant. According to tradition, Dr. George Washington Carver of Tuskegee sent samples of peanut oil to help treat the hospital's victims. Still, the fact that the patients' diet had been so poor in the first place indicated a serious lack of quality care at the segregated institution, and more than sixty years later overall conditions remained subpar. Despite intense pressures to desegregate Searcy Hospital during the late 1960s, the State resisted. In 1967 an outside inspection team was disgusted by what it found.

Services were deemed "horrible," with only five doctors on staff, four of them foreign and unlicensed. The administrator, Dr. Harry S. Rowe, superintendent since 1946, was described as "elderly, obviously not conversant with modern psychiatry and seemed to be running a southern plantation." A visit to the dirty wards and their howling patients left the inspectors shaken, and in their report they likened the experience to a scene out of Kafka. Despite these abject conditions it took another two years of judicial action and federal pressure before Searcy Hospital finally desegregated. Patients of all races were served in much improved circumstances until the hospital closed in 2012, as mental-health care continued its shift toward community-based treatment.[30]

While the majority of the Mobile Bay area's residents were mercifully free from mental illness and pellagra, fire and storm were not so discriminating in their destruction, and both regularly scourged the river. Nineteenth-century American cities were particularly vulnerable to fire given their concentration of frame buildings and primitive to nonexistent fire codes. Mobile suffered three devastating downtown blazes, in 1827, 1839, and 1890, that destroyed hundreds of buildings and retarded trade. The 1890 conflagration was confined almost solely to the city's riverfront assets and was a topic of dockside conversation long afterward. Widespread destruction from fire was eventually limited by improved construction regulations, waterlines, and a professional fire department. But hurricanes remain dangerous big events, and throughout the city's history they have raked across its landscape with unpredictable regularity, in 1717, 1772, 1893, 1906, 1916, 1926, 1979, and 2005.

The fire of 1827 began during the wee hours Sunday morning, October 21, when flames appeared through the roof of the Mobile Hotel, located on Royal Street just north of Dauphin Street in the heart of the business quarter. Conditions were ripe for a rapid increase: a two-month drought with only one rain shower of note, water in short supply, and a strong northwest wind. Finally, the number of citizens available to fight the fire was much reduced because of the prevailing fear of yellow fever epidemics. According to an account in the *Mobile Commercial Register,* nearby houses "caught with the quickness of powder," and soon all the buildings in the fire's widening path, "whether wooden or brick, fire proof or not, appeared to dissolve at its touch, without any more apparent resistance than if they had been columns of snow." By the time it was over, at least 169 structures "exclusive of warehouses and other back tenements not enumerated" had been destroyed in a nine-block area. The damage riverside was bad: "Water and Commerce streets, both sides; from the north corner of St. Francis street to Government street with but one or two exceptions of temporary buildings, sweeping wharf and everything else in its way." Losses were estimated at one half to one million dollars.[31]

After this experience Mobile's authorities and citizens took numerous practical steps to lessen the risk of another such misfortune. At least eight volunteer fire companies were formed, water reservoirs and a wooden pipe and cast iron hydrant system put into place, frame construction disallowed downtown, brick firewalls required for row buildings, and a property guard created. The last group's task was to move ahead of the flames and rescue furniture, valuables, and personal possessions, place them in a pile, and protect them from "all idle and disorderly persons." Nonetheless, in October 1839 a series of both small and big fires consumed the downtown. At the time arson was suspected, and years later at least two different men claimed the credit.[32]

The worst of the fires were on October 7 and 9. The first started early in the evening in a nondescript shed at Dauphin and Conception Streets and swiftly advanced through the neighboring frame outbuildings and tenements. In a desperate bid to create firebreaks police and militia rousted out panicked inhabitants and blew up their residences with barrels of black powder. In all more than five hundred buildings were burned and hundreds of people made homeless. Unfortunately the city's exhausted firemen and traumatized residents were unable to catch their breath, for two days later another fire began at the Mansion House Hotel at the corner of Conti and Royal and swept over the business district with a roar audible three miles away. When the destruction was over, the local press mourned that "Mobile looks more like a beleaguered town, battered by the cannon of a foreign enemy . . . than a commercial city in a time of peace and abundance."[33]

Though numerous vagrants and other suspicious characters were arrested, the blame was never satisfactorily placed. Several years later an escaped slave said that he had been partly responsible. In an account published in 1843 he claimed that the blazes were part of a terrifying diversion set by Mobile slaves planning to fly for their freedom. Fortunately for the city's already oppressed black population, authorities had no intimation of this at the time. More credible was the tale told by the notorious outlaw James Copeland, who said his gang started the fires as a diversion so they could loot Dauphin Street stores. According to Copeland, his men had infiltrated the city guards, and, on a night when they had the first watch, the burglars slipped into town disguised "with false whiskers, some with a green patch over one eye, and many of them dressed like sailors." Armed with knives and revolvers, they systematically broke into the deserted stores, robbing them and setting the fires as they left. Back-lit by a lurid red glow, the men hauled their plunder down to the river, where they placed it aboard skiffs and a "wood flat" and glided downstream. The gang made its way down the bay, turned into Dog River, and secreted their loot in that stream's upper reaches. Copeland put their take at more than twenty-five thousand dollars and said that it included silver, fine silks, muslins, gold watches, and clothing.[34]

Despite the property loss of these fires, Mobilians were able to recover thanks to their advantage as a seaport and the growing importance of the cotton trade. By 1890 cotton remained a key commodity, along with cottonseed oil and lumber. But the concentration of these kinds of combustibles spelled potential disaster if a fire got started among them, and on Sunday, October 26, that is just what happened. The spark came at the Stewart & Butt shingle plant on One Mile Creek. Conditions were not dissimilar to those of the 1827 and 1839 fires—a dry autumn and gusty winds. Fortunately for

Mobile, however, the wind was out of the northwest rather than from true north, and this helped keep the blaze confined to the immediate riverfront. The first fire alarm sounded at 12:40 p.m., when the blaze had already gotten a good start. Fire companies from all over the city responded, clattering down to the wharves in their shiny service wagons, but, because of the fire's proximity to the river, they could not run their hoses into the stream and had to depend on fireplugs for their water supply. According to a reporter on site, "the fire then looked ugly and dangerous," and it was spreading fast, consuming Goodman's Warehouse at the corner of Commerce and Lipscomb Streets, leaping on to the southward and shooting out over the river. The firemen's greatest concern was for the large tanks of the Standard Oil Company, only six hundred yards from the fire and vulnerable to windblown embers. They hosed down the tanks and, thanks to the favorable northwest gusts, managed to prevent an even greater catastrophe. Something of what might have happened had these caught fire was not hard to imagine. Residents only had to watch the big tank at the Gulf City Oil Mill erupt in "the grandest sight of the fire." An "immense rope of lurid flame" snaked and whipped angrily above the skyline like a malevolent force. Heaps of oily black smoke tumbled across the river and Blakeley Island. More and more people came running to see the spectacle, and firemen desperately began watering down the stacks of cotton bales to prevent their loss.[35]

Meanwhile ordinary citizens and those with interests along the wharves pitched in to try to save what they could or at least limit the disaster. More newspaper reporters converged and were able to document example after example of heroic action by ordinary folk. "Along Commerce Street wagons, carts, drays—in fact vehicles of every description—were hurrying to and fro," one of them wrote, "conveying to places of safety valuables, books, papers and merchandise." Major J. W. Spratley, the auditor for the Mobile & Ohio Railroad, sat on a cart "filled with big ledgers, piles of papers and other valuable documents belonging to the railway." The reporter peered into his "smoke-begrimed face and lachrymose eyes" and understood at once "the gauntlet of smoke and heat and falling debris" that the major had braved. "I have cleaned out everything of value except the furniture," the weary auditor said, "and this is the third cartload." Patrons at Angelo Arata's nearby barroom helped quickly extinguish the falling embers before the roof could ignite. Railroad employees worked tirelessly among the box, flat, and passenger cars standing on the Commerce Street tracks, coupling them to an engine and pulling them "away from the rapacious maw of the firey element." Mr. R. Russell, a railroad lawyer, circulated among the firemen, encouraging them and pouring out liquor from a brown jug. The reporter described him as soaking wet with trouser legs rolled up sooty legs and a felt hat jammed on his head. At Cooley's Press, the Reverend Gardner C. Tucker fought the fire with everything he had. "He says that it was pretty hot work," a reporter wrote. "He was outside the press under the shed upon whose roof there was a constant rattle of falling embers." The reverend stood his ground, and said his task was to keep the fire from catching the nearby woodpile, which might help save the press. "So I prayed to God to give me the strength to stay." Despite his call for divine protection, the good reverend was soon forced to flee for his life and the press was a total loss. On the river itself things were just as chaotic. The steamer *Jewel* was "wrapped in brilliant flames from stem to stern," and the crew of the *Ruth* was working frantically to try and save the vessel, which was tied up in a slip. A dozen men and a tug tried to pull her out, but the wind had blown much of the water from the slip, and with it low tide to boot, the *Ruth* was grounded amidships on a stump. Four crewmen stayed aboard to the last minute and then jumped for their lives onto the tug. One of them, Henry Young, had singed hair and eyebrows. But the most inspirational story was that of Larry McDonald, "the well-known newsboy" who distinguished himself when he raced through the flames and cut loose the steamboats *Lee* and *Tally*, which drifted safely south through the rolling smoke and grounded on Pinto Island. Not content to retreat and rest on his laurels, McDonald spied the tug *Helen* drifting south with a burning flat lashed alongside, and he dove into the river and swam out to them. Cutting free the flat, he then grabbed a loose rope and swam back to shore with it. Once on dry land he reeled in the flat and doused the blaze with bucketsful of river water. Still determined and energetic, he dove into the stream again and performed the same feat on a drifting flat loaded with thirty cotton bales. These he managed to corral at the foot of Government Street. He later got five dollars a bale from the grateful insurance company. True exemplar that he was, however, young McDonald did not hoard the money but instead shared it with his fellow newsies and the blind organ-grinder who encouraged citizens throughout the ordeal with his instrument.[36]

Not since the magazine explosion of 1865 had there been so much devastation on the wharves. Though, thankfully, no one was killed, the property losses were large. Almost seven thousand bales of cotton had been consumed, as well as numerous presses, warehouses, wood yards, small boats and skiffs, and a few large steamers. "The long sweep of river front, clear of any obstructions from the upper Mobile & Ohio wharf down to St. Anthony Street, makes an impression upon the beholder that nothing else equals," the newspaper concluded. "There is nothing left of the wharves and buildings along the waterline except the stumps of piling and here and there a collapsed piece of flooring which reached the water before the flames completed their destructive work." But despite the ruin, there was much to be thankful for. The business core of the city had been spared. Firefighters "from chief to hoseman" had performed like true professionals and the water and plug system had not failed. Only a day later, the *Mobile Register*'s irrepressible editorial staff began to see some positive good. "Now that the firey element has removed the former obstructions," they wrote, "the opening up of Front street from the foot of St. Anthony through to Beauregard street would give as handsome a riverfront as one would wish to see." This, of course, would be even better for traffic and trade. Newspaper editors in neighboring New Orleans were also optimistic about their neighbor's prospects. "We cannot doubt that the brave and enterprising people of the Gulf City will go to work at once with energy," they declared, "to repair their damages and rebuild the structures in which their great industries were housed." The river had been purged once again, but after the smoke cleared energetic boosters found themselves to be strangely excited by it.[37]

It is only right to conclude this list of the Mobile River's woes with hurricanes, a coastal reality long before humans came and probably long after they vanish as well. The Atlantic hurricane season runs from June 1 to November 30 each year, but the most intense storms usually cluster in late August and in September when the tropics are at their hottest. The old-time sailors had a handy proverb that ran "June—too soon, July—stand by, August—you must, September—you'll remember, October—all over." For centuries, before improved technology and communications could adequately warn populations of impending trouble, hurricanes simply made landfall, catching shipping and people off guard and at their most vulnerable. Experienced seaside residents learned to read certain weather signs and watch for changes in animal behavior, and by the seventeenth century mariners knew that a falling barometer meant trouble.[38]

Hurricanes deliver their heaviest punches along the beaches, where frightening storm surges of many feet and the most-intense winds can wreak awesome destruction. Fortunately for Mobile, its location well up the bay tends to mitigate the initial hammer blow, but even weak tropical systems cause difficulty for riverine interests. Every storm is unique, and the angle of approach dictates just how bad things will be. Because cyclones north of the equator spin counterclockwise, their northeast quadrant is the strongest. If a system tracks east of Mobile, the city will be spared the worst effects, but if one hits just to the west, the storm surge will drive directly up the bay and rivers, flooding the downtown up to three or four blocks inland. Romans described the effects of a 1772 storm. Everything in Mobile was "in confusion," he wrote, "vessels, boats, and loggs were drove up into the streets a great distance." Houses near the riverfront were flooded to their roofs, and a schooner smashed into one of these dwellings, utterly obliterating it. Even gardens well back from the shore were burned by the salt-laden winds, and trees toppled all along the coast.[39]

During the colonial era hurricanes could literally alter the course of local history, as happened with the destruction of Tristán de Luna's fleet in 1559 and the silting of Pelican Bay in 1717. During the nineteenth, twentieth, and twenty-first centuries, more-entrenched communities and better resources allowed for faster recovery and less disruption over time. People cleaned up the mess, engineers removed offshore obstructions, dredges corrected any loss of depth in channels and passes, and insurance companies paid out settlements. Warning time steadily improved, and loss of life declined.

Three big storms hit Mobile in close succession from 1893 to 1916 (hurricanes were not named until the 1940s). All were roughly similar in their impact because the city waterfront was essentially the same during those years—a long quay with a few slips, railroads down Front and Commerce Streets, and a plethora of steamboats, sailing ships, lumber mills, and cotton warehouses. The 1906 blow was the worst of the three, a late-September system that hit just west of town and piled a ten-foot surge into upper Mobile Bay. No one who experienced the storm would ever forget it.

Mobilians knew trouble was coming as early as September 22 as the U. S. Weather Bureau tracked a tropical cyclone through the Caribbean. Locally the barometer began to drop, and scudding clouds darkened the sky. On Wednesday September 25 water built up in the bay and was soon lapping the tops of the wharves downtown. By midnight it was too windy to walk with an umbrella, and the barometer bottomed out at 28.84 inches. The winds steadily increased and from 7:00 a.m. Thursday until lunchtime blew at speeds reaching a punishing one hundred miles per hour. The water continued to rise, overtopping the wharves and creeping all the way to Royal Street. A newspaper reporter described Water Street as "a perfect maelstrom," and on Royal one observer looked out over "the angry surface of the swollen river, wave on wave rolling upstream in obedience to the unspent strength of the storm, each wave a lash of white fury." Down at Front and Commerce six feet of water sloshed around the rail cars and flooded businesses and warehouses, pushing barrels and boards and cotton bales around like they were corks. Despite having had plenty of time to prepare, people were in real peril. Sam Jordan, a watchman down at Choctaw Point, was drowned while trying to release mules from a stable. On the east bank two men and a woman were aboard a boat that broke in half, and they quickly boarded a yawl and then got aboard a bay boat. That vessel "came clipping across the river," where the trio jumped off and waded to higher ground. All up and down the harbor boats, barges, tugs, and flats were driven onto the quays, knocked adrift, or smashed and sunk against pilings. At the foot of Dauphin Street the ship *Miranda* was stranded atop the wharf, "locked with an old barge." Down at the foot of Eslava the barquentine *Hornet* was "piled high and dry" along with two fishing smacks and a sloop. The mouths of One and Three Mile Creeks were cluttered with logs, driftwood, and broken vessels, and in town trees were "torn, wounded, savagely uprooted and killed." Roof damage was extensive, and the steeple at the magnificent Greek Revival Christ Episcopal Church was blown down onto the roof, causing it to collapse on the interior.[40]

The most hair-raising adventure undoubtedly belonged to William J. Carver, city editor for the *Mobile Register* who rode the river north in an effort to file his report. All the telegraph lines were down. Anxious to let the outside world know that, though battered, the city and its residents were mostly okay, Carver determined to get a boat ride upriver after dark. But four blocks from the wharves, he found himself wading and was quickly up to his shoulders in dirty water. Pressing onward, he found a tug quayside with only the captain aboard. In short order Carver hired the tug and an engineer and convinced several militiamen to act as crew. Then the motley group cast off. "It was with difficulty that we made headway against the turbulent current, speeding like a raceway and bearing with it logs, trees and debris that threatened to sink us at every throb of the engine," he told *The New York Times.* The scene was enough to make the stoutest river man's heart quail, and the captain muttered, "It is suicide." Logs and wreckage of

Duncan Place, 1906. Located at Government and Royal Streets, this busy block was entirely flooded by a strong hurricane that year. Courtesy of the History Museum of Mobile.

all kinds tumbled and pitched in the frothy stream, plunging below surface and shooting up again several feet into the air. The sturdy little tug was hit again and again but labored on while a bright moon broke through the scudding clouds. Carver's destination was the fourteen-mile railroad bridge, where he hoped the wires would still be working. At 3:00 a.m., incredibly, they made it. While the captain held the boat against the breakwater, Carver and another man clambered onto the girders and broke open the cable box. But the wires were down on the bridge, too, and in yet another rash act, Carver decided to walk the tracks more than two miles to a small settlement on the Baldwin County side. The moon had disappeared, and Carver gingerly crossed the bridge by the faint light of a flickering lantern. As the men jumped from tie to tie, the river roiled just a few feet below them. One misstep meant certain death. Carver eventually walked the tracks four miles, his shoes and feet cut by the railroad-bed gravel, before he reached a lumberman's house. The man gave the intrepid newspaper editor a horse so he could go the ten miles to the larger town of Bay Minette. Even on dry land the journey was difficult, the road frequently barred by large uprooted pines. After four hours of constant detours into swamps and thickets, Carver reached town, where the wires were still operable, and sent his reassuring report singing out of south Alabama.[41]

Total damage in Mobile was figured at fifteen million dollars, and numerous landmark structures were damaged, including the Cawthon and Bienville Hotels, the courthouse, and Christ Church. The riverfront was a complete jumble of broken and beached vessels, logs, soaked cotton bales, wooden roof shingles, lumber, bricks, and rubble. Trees and wires were down all over town, and Old Shell Road washed badly in several spots. But only two people had died, forcefully proving Mobile's advantage compared to burgs closer to the gulf. More than fifty people died at Pensacola, numerous fisherman and residents in southern Mobile County, and dozens more in coastal Mississippi and Louisiana. Only a decade later, after the somewhat less severe 1916 hurricane, Mobilians could be forgiven for thinking they had storm survival and recovery down to a science. Even before that blow fully subsided, repairs were under way by "gangs of men and tugboats." Despite the usual waterfront wreckage, the *Register*'s editor estimated that things would be good as new within a week.[42]

In more recent decades two storms have been most memorable in the Mobile area, Frederic in 1979 and Katrina in 2005. Frederic made landfall just west of Mobile

Storm damage, 1916. Erik Overbey Collection. Courtesy of the Doy Leale McCall Rare Book and Manuscript Library, University of South Alabama.

on the evening of September 12. Winds at Dauphin Island were measured at 145 miles per hour, and by the time the storm rolled over downtown they clocked in at a fierce 130 mph. Frederic was more of a wind event than a flood event for the riverfront. It was something of a dry storm, with a surge in Mobile Bay of eight feet. Though still significant for low-lying areas, this rise was not able to overtop the Alabama State Docks with its eleven-foot elevation. Otherwise, damage was bad all over town. The roof of the Italianate City Hall on South Royal Street was torn off, and thousands of homes were hit by trees and limbs. The city's graceful live oaks were shredded, with leaves and Spanish moss stripped from their branches. Closer to the coast, the Dauphin Island Bridge was destroyed. Frederic was the most expensive storm on record up to that time, causing an estimated two billion dollars in damage. Bay-area residents who had ridden out the hurricane were shaken, but only one person died, and the resulting insurance payments for property losses resulted in a miniboom, transforming the lightly settled gulf beaches into a high-rise condo corridor.[43]

Twenty-six years later Hurricane Katrina was a far more massive storm than Frederic and hit just east of New Orleans. Media attention was riveted by the Mississippi coast's obliteration and the subsequent flooding of the Crescent City, with all the attendant human tragedy played out on television for unbelieving eyes. But conditions on the Alabama coast were almost as dire on a more limited scale. The storm surge in Mobile bay was twelve to fourteen feet, even higher than that of the 1906 hurricane. Houses in south Mobile County were wiped from their foundations, historic homes in the tony Eastern Shore community of Point Clear flooded with several feet of bay water, a Jubilee Parkway onramp washed away, and downtown flooded to Royal Street. Cooper Riverside Park was inundated, with just the top of the Ervin Cooper statue's hat peeking above the flood. Water Street was a white-capped mill race, and there was some damage along the docks where containers broke loose and battered everything in their path. Mobile's most compelling Katrina shot came when a floating dry dock with a large oil-drilling rig aboard broke its moorings and was pushed upstream before finally becoming wedged beneath the Cochrane/Africatown USA Bridge. Engineers were quickly dispatched to the span even while strong winds were still blowing. Fortunately things were not as bad as they might have feared. Several bearing assemblies were damaged, as was some cable insulation, and the road had been shoved some two feet off center. After careful evaluation it was decided to leave two lanes open with weight restrictions. Bridge repairs soon got under way, and the derrick was extracted with only minor damage to its superstructure.[44]

Future storms will certainly come to the Mobile River, and some will bring stronger winds than Frederic and higher surges than Katrina. But as long as people live and work this stream, they will meet the adversity head on and rebuild even better and bigger than before. That is one lesson that local history most definitely teaches.

11

Diverse Legacies

For such a short stream the Mobile holds a surprisingly rich and complex human story. Among the most intriguing chapters are those of the African slaves smuggled by Timothy Meaher and subsequently settled in Plateau, or African Town, as they called it; the Creoles upriver, many of whom were never enslaved; the Apaches imprisoned at Mount Vernon during the late 1880s; and the MOWA Band of Choctaws in northern Mobile and southern Washington Counties (hence the derivation of their name), still struggling for federal recognition. Each of these groups suffered mightily, and the way continues to be difficult for some of them at times. But despite the challenges and obstacles, they have each also managed to carve out their own identities and leave their own legacies.

The story of African Town begins with a ship. She was an unassuming little schooner named the *Clotilda,* and by the time she went up in flames somewhere near Twelve Mile Island in the summer of 1860, only five years after her keel had been laid, she had secured her place in history as the last vessel to land a cargo of slaves in the United States. She was fated to be an unhappy ship. But in the fall of 1855 the *Mobile Daily Advertiser* could only admire the *Clotilda*'s construction and lines at the foot of St. Anthony Street, where she was being rigged. Sleek and handsome, she was a 120-ton two-masted boat 86 feet long and 23 feet in the beam, with a coppered hull, a single deck, and a square stern. "This vessel in model and fastning does great credit to her builder," the paper held, "and affords another evidence of the capacity of our city for successful and economical shipbuilding. She is light and commodious, draws thirty-two inches forward and forty-two inches aft, and is intended for the Texas trade." According to the newspaper she was of "a graceful turn" and would prove "a fast sailer."[1]

Her owner was William Foster, a thirty-something Nova Scotian who had immigrated to Alabama in 1843. He had learned the trade of ship carpenter and employed this skill to good effect in the construction of his new vessel. On January 26, 1856, Foster hopefully launched the *Clotilda* on her maiden voyage to Havana with seventy thousand feet of lumber. Other trips to Cuba and along the United States and Mexican gulf coasts followed, with workaday cargoes of sugar, plantains, beef, bacon, lumber, and salt. Foster employed a master and six crewmen to work the schooner and made a decent enough living. He boarded in a home near Three Mile Creek and was a familiar figure riverside.[2]

Whether or not Foster cursed his association with the *Clotilda* on Sunday, October 23, 1859, is unknown, though soon enough he would. On that day two men, one of them white and the other a slave named Alfred, were fishing from a small skiff. They had moored their craft to a sawyer in the Mobile River opposite the city. It was yet morning, and the two men were enjoying a pleasant day on the water. A light northeast wind riffled the river's surface, and the pair watched their corks while various watercraft passed to and fro. Just to the south, the *Clotilda* was heading into port, all hands taking in sail as she approached her destination. About thirty yards south of the skiff, one of the schooner's crew, hanging out over the bow to pull in the jib-sail, called out "Boat ahead" to his mates. The helmsman immediately put the wheel over, and the *Clotilda* slewed in the stream. Alfred and his companion had of course seen the schooner's approach, and they frantically shouted and waved their paddles to get the crew's attention. Unfortunately they had not been spotted in time, and the *Clotilda* plowed over the skiff at an inexorable four miles an hour. Alfred tumbled into the river, while his companion desperately grabbed onto the schooner's anchor. The crew quickly hauled the white man aboard and launched a boat to search for Alfred, to no avail. Alfred's owner later sued Foster, hoping to recover his slave's $1,500 value, but he failed to prove negligence on the part of Foster or the *Clotilda*'s master or crew. Foster had dodged a bullet, but the court defense had cost him money, and he no doubt rejoiced when Timothy Meaher stepped in shortly thereafter and bought the vessel for thirty-five thousand dollars.[3] The two men already had some association, being co-owners of the *Susan*, recently wrecked by the filibusters. Meaher's interest in the *Clotilda* had nothing to do with her utility in the coastal trade, however. He was playing a far different and more dangerous game than even with his support of the filibusters, and as he began to implement his scheme, the rakish little schooner looked to be perfect for the task.

There are several versions of where Meaher decided upon his plan and exactly what the circumstances were, but his ultimate goal—illegally to import a cargo of black African slaves into Mobile Bay—has never been in doubt. The most common version places the plan's origins aboard the *Roger B. Taney* on an upriver run from Mobile to Selma late in 1859 or early 1860. Meaher and a clutch of men were engaged in a spirited discussion about the desirability and feasibility of importing African slaves and the U.S. Congress's ongoing efforts to eliminate the trade. The United States had outlawed the international slave trade in 1808, and ever since some voices in the South had agitated for reopening it to provide fresh labor. A few smugglers had tried and succeeded in recent years, and though they were later caught, their punishment was minor. Not surprisingly, Meaher was all for the trade, but a Yankee in the group believed anyone attempting to smuggle black persons should be hanged to "scare the rest off." Meaher scoffed: "Nonsense! They'll hang nobody—they'll scare nobody." Another Yankee opined that it would be impossible to import Africans given the prohibitions and the United States Navy. A Louisiana planter disagreed and put down a one-hundred-dollar bet to prove it. Meaher found this irresistible and upped the ante, wagering one thousand dollars that "inside two years I myself can bring a shipful of niggers right into Mobile Bay under the officers' noses." This was bold talk, indeed, but as Meaher's history had already demonstrated, he was not given to bluffing.[4]

Eager to launch his daring gamble, Meaher got right to work, buying the *Clotilda* and engaging Foster as captain, who knew her qualities under sail better than anyone. The men's first priority was to convert the *Clotilda* into a viable slave ship without attracting unwelcome attention. The J. M. and T. Meaher shipyard up Chickasabogue Creek was the perfect place, and the firm's men did the work. The vessel got new taller masts and longer spars to allow her to carry more canvas at sea, both to make good time and to outrun any pursuers. In order to support her captives on the return voyage, large quantities of food and water had to be concealed in the hold—25 barrels of rice, 3 of sugar, 25 of flour, 40 pounds of pork, several barrels of bread and molasses, and 125 barrels of water. Grim tools of the slave trade would also have been loaded—cutlasses and cudgels, whips and chains and restraints. Cheap trade items were also stowed aboard in order to help tempt African slave dealers—trinkets and beads and eighty kegs of bad liquor. These items were really just gimmicky come-ons, however; the sale would be insured by the nine thousand dollars in gold coins that Foster hid in a bulkhead. In order to help conceal the *Clotilda*'s real purpose, Meaher and Foster had her deck stacked with fresh-sawn lumber. This was a fiendishly clever ruse with a practical twist—not only did it make the *Clotilda* look like she was hauling harmless cargo, but it also hid the provisions that were on deck, and on the return voyage it could be hammered into slave beds below deck. The last piece of the plan was the crew, and here no chances were taken. Eleven men were hired aboard, the usual assortment of waterfront toughs (two of them were Rhode Islanders), but they were not told about the real purpose of their voyage.[5]

Foster sailed the *Clotilda* out of Mobile Bay on the night of March 3, 1860. The voyage over took two months and was punctuated by a frightening storm and pursuit by a Portuguese warship. Finally, in early May the *Clotilda* anchored at the port of Ouidah, on the west coast of Africa. This was a notorious slave-trading post, where Foster was able to buy 125 Africans, mostly young Yoruba men and women taken in a raid by the king of Dahomey. By this time the *Clotilda's* crew knew the purpose of their voyage, and they were none too happy about it. Slaving was a distasteful business fraught with peril. Besides the risk of capture and punishment, there was the scary possibility of slave mutiny or revolt during exercise periods on deck. Foster was able to keep his men in line through a mixture of threats and promises of double wages once they returned to the United States.[6]

As the young Africans were herded below the *Clotilda*'s deck and shackled in place, it is doubtful that Foster or his crew thought much about who they might be or what they might be feeling. As far as the white men were concerned, their captives were black savages with no culture or feelings that they were bound to respect. The reality was, of course, very different. Among the slaves was a teenager named Oluae Kossola (also spelled Kazoola), who had grown up learning the customs and traditions of his people, and he had even been initiated into a secret society that acted as something of a regulatory body/police force for the tribe. Another, named Kupollee, had embarked on spiritual training that involved elaborate preparations and rituals. But to the crew of the *Clotilda,* Kupollee's earrings, tattoos, and filed teeth would have simply been evidence of his primitive ways rather than bearers of sacred meaning. That the Africans keenly felt their humiliation and suffered miserably during the middle passage has been amply confirmed by numerous interviews they gave in later life. According to one of the women in the group, identified as Abacky by a writer for *Harper's Monthly Magazine* in a 1906 interview, the captives endured awful heat and thirst in the *Clotilda*'s sweltering hold. "After forty years her eyes were burning," the *Harper's* writer declared, "her soul inexpressibly agitated, at the memory." Overall, her tale of nakedness, being prodded and pushed, lying in her own filth in the hold, and being treated as a commodity "was related in a way that would have melted a stone."[7]

Thirteen days into her return trip, the *Clotilda's* crew let the slaves on deck for light, air, and exercise. In an interview with the Mobile artist Emma Langdon Roche about 1913, Oluae Kossola, or Cudjo Lewis as he had come to be called in Alabama, vividly recalled the experience. "We looka, an' looka, an' looka—nothin' but sky and water. Whar we com' from, we do not know—whar we go, we do not know." Roughly thirty days after the day Oluae Kossola described, on July 7, 1860, the *Clotilda* hove into the Mississippi Sound, anchoring off the southern end of Mobile County. The slaves were buttoned up below lest they be detected by other vessels, but the crew showed them green branches as evidence that land was near.[8]

For his part, Foster was anxious to get his vessel up the Mobile River as fast as possible. United States revenue cutters regularly patrolled the sound and Mobile Bay, and numerous small craft were around whose bored occupants would have been eager to talk to men who had obviously just returned from a long voyage. In order to make the ship less conspicuous Foster had the men take down her masts, dramatically lowering her profile. His next task was to engage a tug to tow the vessel up the bay. Meaher had posted lookouts along the coast, but none of them had yet seen the *Clotilda,* and Foster had to act fast. Unfortunately for him, his men grew increasingly belligerent, demanding their pay at once. Foster was a tough customer, but threats and bluster were no longer enough to keep the men in line. Everyone wanted to be done with Meaher's little adventure as soon as possible. Relenting, the captain went ashore and hired a buggy for Mobile to get their money. He also sent a fast messenger ahead of him to let Meaher know the *Clotilda* had arrived at last.[9]

In an 1893 newspaper interview, complete with the reporter's interpretation of dialect, Timothy Meaher's "house boy" Noah Hart recalled the moment when they got the news. "Ole Marse wuz settin' out on de gallry smokin' wid his heels on de banisters when a man on hoss-back come tearin' up de road." Meaher put down his pipe and scrambled to the bottom of the porch steps in anticipation. "The niggers have come. The niggers are here," the rider excitedly told him. Instantly Meaher sprang into action, riding into town with his brother James to get a tugboat. In the meantime he told Byrnes to get up steam on the *Czar* and have her in readiness at the mouth of the Spanish River. The *Roger B. Taney* was also ordered to be ready to assist.[10]

And so the denouement of Meaher's brash and unholy gamble played out on a Sunday. The tugboat captain was plucked from church, Meaher himself striding down the aisle to whisper in his ear, and in due course the *Billy Jones* was pulling the *Clotilda* up Spanish River as the clock in the watchtower struck 11:00 p.m. All the pieces came together at the head of Twelve Mile Island's dark and looming mass, well north of downtown and screened from easy observation. The *Czar* came alongside the *Clotilda* and a plank was placed between the vessels. The frightened and confused Africans, along with the *Clotilda*'s white crew and Timothy Meaher, hastily transferred onto the *Czar,* and then it quickly pulled away, steaming north up the Mobile. Within a few miles Meaher and the crew boarded the *Roger B. Taney,* which headed on to Montgomery. When they reached the capital Meaher paid the unhappy sailors and put them on a mail train for New York. Each man received seven hundred dollars, the standard fee for a transatlantic voyage, but not the double wages Foster had promised them. Even so, they were alive and had not been arrested, and thus they disappeared into history with their gold.[11]

As for the *Clotilda,* she was left to Foster, and the sooner she was destroyed the better. There could be no question of refitting her for coastal work. To begin with, the evidence of her recent use was inescapable; she reeked of unwashed humanity, urine, vomit, and filth. And so Foster had her towed into Bayou Canot, where he opened her sea cocks and piled her deck with pine knots. She sank and burned simultaneously, flickering her destruction in the black delta night, and slowly settled into the brackish, muddy water. Foster had been a key player in Meaher's scheme, but as he watched the fine schooner slowly die, he must have come to the realization, if he had not already, that the venture was likely to end up costing him far more than he would ever gain.[12]

Foster's economic woes were in a completely different universe from the wrenching changes faced by the *Clotilda*'s African cargo. These unfortunates were ferried upstream aboard the *Czar* to a point along the Mount Vernon Stretch, where they were hustled ashore into thick cane. This was property owned by John Dabney, a Virginia émigré and friend of the Meahers who had agreed to participate in the plan. The Africans were carefully concealed here by James Meaher and a few friends. Noah Hart brought clothes and a few basics, and he was shaken by what he found. "Dat wuz a terrible sight," he recalled in his 1893 interview. "Dey wuz wanderin' around lak crazy pussons—skeered and ebberyting: half naked, an' 'most starved ter der death." The garments were not much—rags and corn sacking—but Oluae Kossola remembered the moment as one of the most significant, when at last they could cover their nakedness and shame.[13]

Events of this magnitude could not stay secret for long, and only a week later the local press registered its approval. "Whoever conducted the affair has our congratulations on his or their success," the *Mobile Daily Advertiser* wrote. Nor did the paper hesitate to make the larger point: "Why should not those who are in want of negro labor import it at a low cost, when they are civilizing and Christianizing a set of barbarians by the same course which redounds to their interest?" The story spread to other papers across the land, but mostly as a simple news report. Timothy Meaher returned to his home several days after dispatching the crew and had a good chuckle over the entire adventure. As Noah Hart related it, Meaher crowed, "I's sho' had er race wid dem niggers. I put them off de ship in de middle ob de night and put em on er steamboat to bring 'em up de ribber, but de Yanks wuz on my track." But he had outwitted them and returned home to tell the tale. As for the slaves, they were parceled out, thirty-two for Timothy Meaher, twenty to Byrnes Meaher, ten to William Foster, and eight to James Meaher (among them Oluae Kossola). The rest went to slave dealers.[14]

But Timothy Meaher and his confederates were not wholly in the clear. The federal government was onto the crime and determined to pursue the matter in the courts. Cases were brought against Timothy Meaher, Byrnes Meaher, John Dabney, and William Foster, the last for failing to pay dues on his "cargo." At least one attempt was made to locate the Africans, but Timothy Meaher again outfoxed the opposition, moving the slaves from the cane to Byrnes Meaher's plantation and delivering free liquor to the searchers. Predictably, they promptly got drunk, and by the time a replacement crew was in place, the Africans were nowhere to be found. Without any evidence of the crime, either slaves or slave ship, the cases against Byrnes Meaher and John Dabney were dismissed, and the onset of civil war eliminated any ongoing legal threats for Timothy Meaher and William Foster. Just as Meaher had boasted when he made his bet aboard the *Roger B. Taney,* no one had been hanged, and no one had been scared.[15]

Slowly the Africans began adjusting to their new lives. Cudjo and some of the other men were put to work on one the Meaher's riverboats, where they were encountered by Russell of the *London Times* early in the war. Others went to work in the firm's shipyard, the lumber mill, and the family's farms and households. Incredibly after all they had endured, the Africans' spirits were not broken. Noah Hart was somewhat in awe of them and considered them powerful men and women. "Dey wuz mo' blacker an' straighter an' larger dan us," he later recalled. He found them quiet and dignified in person, not given to horseplay or shouting, nor would they brook any nonsense from others: "dey wouldn't stand a lick fum white or black." On one occasion, when Byrnes Meaher's overseer attempted to whip an African woman for some infraction, her screams brought the others running. They knocked down the overseer and thrashed him with his own whip.[16]

The end of the war brought the Africans the freedom that had been stolen from them five years before. Cudjo got the news on the river, when he encountered Union soldiers gobbling mulberries at one of the landings. When he asked what was happening, the men told him he was free and could go wherever he wanted. "I sho' appreciate dey free me," Cudjo later told the renowned black folklorist Zora Neale Hurston. Where he most wanted to go, of course, was home to Africa, but that being impossible, downstream he went. Back at Magazine Point the Africans decided to celebrate the event in a special way. They made a drum from a log and some animal skin and beat out their joy, free of any worry that they would be arrested or chastised.[17]

The Africans and Timothy Meaher were now fated to be free neighbors, and, as far as the former were concerned, they were owed something for having been kidnapped and enslaved. Cudjo was chosen from among them all to approach Meaher and make their case. As Cudjo later told Roche, he approached the author of their misery as the white man sat on a log whittling a stick. "Kazoola, what makes you so sad?" he remembered Timothy asking. "I grieve for my home," the African replied. "But you've got a home," Meaher responded. "Captain Tim, how big is Mobile?" "I don't know, I've never been to the four corners." "If you give Kazoola all Mobile, that railroad, and the banks of Mobile, Kazoola does not want them for this is not home." And then he delivered his wish: "Captain Tim, you brought us from our country where we had land and home. You made us slaves. Now we are free, without country, land, or home. Why don't you give us a piece of this land and let us build for ourselves an African Town?" This was a daring gambit to say the least, and Meaher did not react well. He jumped up and cried, "You do not belong to me now!" He was not going to give them anything. But Meaher was nothing if not a businessman and an opportunist, and he did make it clear that he would sell.[18]

So too, as it developed, would some of the other white men in the area, and during the 1870s the Africans steadily bought property around Magazine Point—seven acres in 1870, two acres purchased by Cudjo in 1872, two by Kupollee (now known as Pollee) the same year, and so on among several others. Then the Africans went to work erecting wooden houses with attached gardens and fences. Cudjo put up eight gates around his property as a reminder of home and friends. They called the little community African Town, and soon people far and wide came to know it as a distinctive place. Writers and the curious were moved to visit and learn about its unusual history for themselves. When S. H. M. Byers of *Harper's Monthly* called in 1906, the community looked like an ordinary hardscrabble dirt town. Timothy Meaher was dead by then, and Byers's guide pointed out the burned remains of his house with the bemused comment, "That's all that's left of him." As for African Town, it consisted of "dilapidated cabins" surrounded by "truck-gardens and rose-bushes." Byers's guide told him that even though only a few of the Africans were living at that late date, they still observed "superstitious notions and customs" such as burying their dead in graves filled with oak leaves and annually plunging into the river in order to determine who was still strong enough to swim across. Those too weak "were allowed to drown; their time had come."[19]

Noah Hart acted as a guide for the writer Mary McNeil Scott and a friend in 1893, and on the drive up Telegraph Road cautioned them: "You musn't spec ter see nothin' no-way uncommon, ladies. You know de Affikins lives jes erbout lak Mexican niggers now." As their carriage made its way along a rutted red-dirt road through magnolia, cypress, "black jacks and gopher grass," the "dilapidated fences and unattractive little cabins" came into view. Nonetheless, Scott noted that "each had its little patch of flower garden, its clambering vines and its vegetable garden of potatoes, corn, tobacco and watermelons." At the gate of one garden, they came upon a white-haired woman "hoeing among the melon vines." But when she discerned that they only wanted to study her out of curiosity and not to buy melons, her "dignity was therefore offended," and there was no interview. Somewhat disappointed by their afternoon, the white women finally had some excitement on their return to Mobile, thrilling to the sight of a group of black workmen walking along the road, one of whom displayed prominent tattoos on his bare chest. "In that one second," Scott declared, "we had seen as by a flashlight the depth, the pathos, and the keen reality that lay in the simple tale of 'Affika Town.'"[20]

As these white women had learned, daily life for the Africans during the late nineteenth and early twentieth centuries was not dissimilar to that of their black American neighbors. They worked in the area's mills, lived in frame houses, tended their little gardens, and sold what produce they did not need. Many, but not all, converted to Christianity and attended area churches such as Union Missionary Baptist and Stone Street Baptist. But there were important differences. In the home they still spoke their native tongue. Their perceptions of the world, their identity, their relationships to each other and to outsiders, and their longing for Africa were all grounded in their tribal past. They also governed themselves with a small panel of judges who heard disputes and arbitrated. In order to police the rowdier elements in the community, Cudjo and several friends formed the Hickory Club. They met at a local grocery store and patrolled the community with revolvers and handcuffs, arresting troublemakers and holding them until the sheriff arrived. Despite these efforts, the local press held a jaundiced view of affairs at Magazine Point. In a 1902 report the *Mobile Daily Herald* luridly declared that "pandemonium frequently reigns where the two sexes gather for their weekly orgies."[21]

African Town was never a purely African community, however. While many like Cudjo and Pollee married other Africans, some wed American black persons and started families. As the twentieth century progressed, the original captives passed from the scene, and some of their children chose to leave the region for better opportunity and more tolerance in the North. Pollee died in 1922, having sired fifteen children. By the early 1930s only Cudjo remained, and in his final years he became a local celebrity.

Hurston interviewed him at length in 1928, when he was probably in his eighties, at least, and even shot a forty-three-second silent film of him in his yard. It is a remarkable artifact, the only moving picture of a native African who was brought to these shores as a slave. It shows him throwing out his arms in greeting, acting like he is splitting wood, and then facing the camera hat in hand. His clothes are old and patched, but his vigor and zest for life are clear.[22]

In his last days Cudjo appeared to make peace with the fact that he would never return home. "Cudjo no want to go back," he said sadly. "No fadder, no mudder, no sister, no brudder, no child there to meet Cudjo." Late in the afternoon on Friday, July 26, 1935, he died after a heart attack. The funeral was an event, lasting four hours and featuring ten preachers at the Union Missionary Baptist Church. A few white people were there, including a reporter, who mused that to most white Mobilians this was "just another nigger funeral." The preachers did Cudjo proud, and one of them positively soared. "It ain't shameful to be a colored man," he reassured the faithful. "We've got a lot to be proud of. We've come a long way, from off in Africa where we were free and owned the land, to this country where we were slaves before we could be free again." Cudjo had not left much of an earthly estate, but he did have property. His debts were settled and his property sold. His body was interred in the nearby Plateau Cemetery, where today a tall white marker designates the spot.[23]

During the late twentieth and early twenty-first centuries there were numerous efforts to promote and develop African Town, or Africatown as it came to be called. Unfortunately, the site remained mired in difficult economic circumstances, and the nearby paper mill and looming Cochrane/Africatown USA Bridge were hardly attractive neighbors. Many of the houses were in poor condition, and most did not date from the early years in any case. Successful efforts included preserving and protecting the lone chimney that remained of one of the original slave's homes (the home of Gumpa, or Peter Lee); improving the overgrown cemetery and placing a historic marker there and at the Union Missionary Baptist Church as part of an African American Historic Driving Tour; and sponsoring archaeological digs in the winter of 2010 by a team from the College of William & Mary that had also dug at sites in West Africa associated with the African Town founders. Most recently, on December 4, 2012, much of the original site was placed on the National Register of Historic Places, largely because of the archaeological significance and potential. Numerous descendants of the original residents still live in the area, and there is a great deal of local pride in the history and legacy of those young African men and women enslaved so long ago.[24]

The Africans were not the only people of color with a distinctive heritage trying to make their way near Mobile. There was an older group, the Creoles, that had been in the area for a century before Cudjo and his comrades even landed. Originally the term *Creole* was used in French Louisiana to designate a child of European parents born on American soil. But in local parlance *Creole* came to mean someone with some African ancestry. In the Mobile area Creoles are the racially mixed offspring of early French and

Creole girls at play near Chastang, 1951. History Museum of Mobile Collection. Courtesy of the Doy Leale McCall Rare Book and Manuscript Library, University of South Alabama.

Spanish male settlers and their black female partners, colonial holdovers who historically enjoyed special legal status and owned land, livestock, and even slaves. There are clusters of their descendants all around the bay area, but the nucleus and largest concentration is upriver on those tight hairpin turns at Chastang and Seymour Bluffs.[25]

One of the earliest Creole families there traces its origins to Dr. John Chastang (1739–1813), a New Orleans–born surgeon and planter who settled in the area with his brother Joseph in the mid-1700s. Dr. Chastang's land holdings were extensive and included almost two thousand acres "lying west of the Mobile River, butting and bounding on the south by Grog Hall creek, on the north by Cedar Creek." Life was good but hard along the river, and there were not many white women living in the colony. At some point Dr. Chastang fell in love with one of his brother's black slaves, a woman named Louison, and in 1780 he bought and freed her. They lived together some twenty years and had ten children together. In his last will and testament, recorded in 1805, Dr. Chastang acknowledged their relationship and left Louison his worldly goods, which included the river land, property in Mobile, slaves, cattle, silverware, furniture, and sundry other valuables. Upon his death in 1813 a full inventory of his property revealed just how well off he left Louison. It included two houses, nine slaves, 236 head of cattle, three canoes, cooper's and carpenter's tools, two gold watches, four axes, six silver forks, six spoons, 12 teaspoons, china, crockery, a feather bed, three guns, a case of surgical instruments, and 167 books. And then there were the children, two of whom, Bazile and Zeno, did especially well raising cattle and corn. Zeno lived in a sturdy dog-trot house overlooking the river, tended 350 head of cattle, and like many area residents did a little farming, wood cutting for the steamboats, hunting, and gardening to keep body and soul together. Like his mother, Zeno Chastang was a slaveholder, owning twenty-nine human beings by 1860.[26]

Other families were equally well established. They included the family of Simon Andry, "an interpreter of the Choctaw language" who initially divided his time between town and the bluffs but who by 1797 was mostly in residence upstream. Andry owned almost five hundred acres north of Chastang, which he farmed with his slaves. One of these, a woman named Jane (whom we have already met), became his partner as early as 1782, and they had eight children, all with lovely names, including Romaine, Euphrosine, Maximilian, Maria Judee, and Anastasia. Andry was somewhat reluctant to acknowledge paternity, however; when the children were baptized, their father was listed as unknown. But in the end Andry did want to insure their freedom and publicly recorded their manumission in 1805. Jane outlived Andry and became a woman of substance and some fame, as witnessed by her 1814 offer of hospitality to Andrew Jackson. Another important Creole family descended from the three Dubroca brothers, Maximilian, Hugh, and Hilaire, all of whom had extensive property.[27]

People of color with this kind of independence and stature were clearly at risk when the Spanish folded to the Americans in the early nineteenth century. Desirous of protecting the Creoles' status and condition after the turnover, Spain specifically provided for them by the terms of the Adams-Onis Treaty of 1819, which guaranteed their rights of citizenship. In the early days these protections held up well. In 1822, for example, the Alabama legislature passed a law forbidding any kind of "spirituous liquors" to free black persons and mulattos, excepting those who, "by the treaty between the United States and Spain, became citizens of the United States, or the descendents of any such person." After the Civil War one amazed observer remarked that the Creoles "could stay out as late as they pleased at night, could smoke cigars on the streets, could testify in courts of justice." They also enjoyed officially sanctioned schools. In 1833 the legislature authorized Mobile city officials to educate free Creole children in the area. This advantage was in no way to carry over to non-Creole free black children, however. By 1856 a school for white and Creole children was established at Chastang Bluff, where two of Zeno Chastang's sons served as trustees. A school census that year showed eleven white students in attendance and twenty-six Creoles.[28]

Unfortunately, as the Civil War approached life became more difficult for the Creoles. While many white people saw them as tainted by their "Negro" blood, the Creoles considered themselves to be a separate, privileged caste and resisted identifying with area black residents. As late as 1887 a Catholic bishop reported that the Creoles "kick against the Negro" and that the "antipathy between the Negro and the mulatto is a special difficulty in Alabama and Florida." In a 2012 interview Noel Andry Sr., born in 1952, recalled his grandparents speaking in a French patois and "using the N-word. They were a proud people, tough. They had land." Before the war, of course, many of these families owned slaves, and some of their sons were eager to serve the Confederate cause. In the spring of 1862 one officer assured his higher-ups that he could raise a Creole regiment, "mixed-blooded; all of them free." They were mostly property holders, he continued, and "are as true to the South as the pure white race." As we have already seen, however, such offers were rebuffed.[29]

Throughout their history along the Mobile the Creoles have found faith and solace in the Roman Catholic Church, which has closely ministered to their spiritual and physical needs. In the colonial era services were conducted in area homes, but in 1833 St. Paul Chapel was established at Chastang Bluff. This mission church was taken over by the Jesuits in 1854. Twenty-two years later Bishop John Quinlan of Mobile decided to build a more permanent church. The Chastang and Andry families donated a little more than five acres of land alongside the new railroad. Bishop Quinlan contributed fifty dollars toward construction, and after several years of labor the church was dedicated on Sunday, July 6, 1879. It was a grand affair, advertised by a special advert in the *Mobile Register.* "Grand Excursion!" proclaimed the notice, "to Chastang's Bluff, On board of the new and magnificent passenger steamer *Maggie F. Burke,* Owen Finnegan, Master." The steamer left the Dauphin Street wharf about 8:00 a.m. with almost four hundred aboard. She nosed into the bluff around 11:00 a.m., where the locals were already gathered. The Mobile Fire Department Brass Band escorted one and all from the riverbank to the church for the dedication services. In an account of the proceedings published several days later, the newspaper praised the new sixty-by-thirty-foot building as "a beautiful structure, standing alone in a pine forest about three-quarters of a mile from the river." The Solemn High Mass was celebrated at 1:00 p.m. with Rev. D. Beaudequin S.J., president of Spring Hill College, as the celebrant. The choir "consisted of a number of gentlemen from Mobile, who sang the Mass without the assistance of any musical instrument." Afterward a "fine lunch" was spread out which everyone "enjoyed hugely from the way they made 'grub' scarce."[30]

Today, more than 130 years beyond its dedication, St. Peter the Apostle remains an important landmark on Highway 43. The church fronts the railroad and highway, with a cluster of ancillary buildings, including a parish hall built in 1933. Though the buildings have been covered with asbestos siding, their historic massing and form remain evident, and the church features a handsome round window at the façade set over a delicate entry porch. The parish was never large, but most area residents were of the faith, and St. Peter the Apostle dominated their spiritual calendar. About 1908 there were an estimated two hundred Catholics living at the bluffs, "all more or less related." While St. Peter's is still an active parish, its heyday was at mid-century, when there was a boys' orphanage, a school, a baseball diamond, and the swimming pool on Conrad Creek, now overgrown.[31]

As with most historic communities, the pressures of modern life and development have encroached on Chastang Bluff and its distinctive identity. The railroad and then Highway 43 meant better and faster access from distant points and an escape for offspring seeking more opportunity. A 1946 newspaper article noted that because of these changes the "once almighty river is forgotten except for the families who live close to old homes near its high banks." For them the river, as ever, remained paramount. In his 2012 interview Noel Andry Sr. recalled hunting the bluffs with his father and being rowed across the river by his grandfather in a "double ender." Residents maintained big farm plots on the flat delta land where they grew corn and squash, and they filled out their menu with trapping. Many of the men also logged, storing up wood until high water when it could be floated downstream to the lumber mills.[32]

The railroad brought a new people to the Mobile River in 1887, one unfamiliar with its turbid waters and swampy country. On April 28 of that year, at 8:30 in the morning, a train pulled into Mount Vernon station with 354 Apache Indians aboard. They included men, women, and children, all prisoners of war surrendered in the American Southwest by Geronimo after years of fighting both the United States and the Mexican governments. They had been previously held in Florida hard by the gulf, but the heat and disease there had depleted their numbers and sickened the survivors. Wishing to lower the mortality rate and to improve their situation, the government moved the Apaches to Mount Vernon Barracks. Upon first glance this new place with its higher ground and piney woods was thought to be perfect. A reporter for the *Mobile Register* who visited shortly after the Indians arrived praised the location as "beautiful beyond imagination," with "great and beautiful" trees. The Indians were settled into tents and log-and-frame cabins hastily erected outside the barracks walls. Unfortunately for the Apaches, Mount Vernon quickly proved less than ideal. As one of them later recalled, "We thought anything would be better than [Florida] with its rain, mosquitoes, and malaria, but we were to find out that it was good in comparison with Mt. Vernon Barracks. We didn't know what misery was till they dumped us in those swamps. There was no place to climb or pray. If we wanted to see the sky, we had to climb a tall pine."[33]

The band was discontented enough by the move that when Geronimo himself arrived some months later, not a single Indian met him at the station. When he reached the barracks all of the tents and cabins were tightly shut. Dr. Walter Reed, the post surgeon, recorded the scene: "While he gazed intently a woman emerged from a distant tent to advance slowly and with bowed head. Hesitantly she advanced and then hurried to the chief, threw her arms around his neck, and wept as if her heart would break." The Apaches soon enough warmed to their old leader and began adjusting to their new life. They were given a great deal of freedom. Many of the women gardened, the children "played soldier all the time," and the men worked on the buildings and

Geronimo at Mount Vernon, circa 1890. Courtesy of the Doy Leale McCall Rare Book and Manuscript Library, University of South Alabama.

around the post. Hoping to provide a little incentive, the army approved the men's taking jobs in town or on area farms for wages. In a further attempt to assimilate the men a large group of them was formed into Company I, an infantry outfit with white officers. Results were so encouraging that the commander planned a march downriver to Mobile for a public demonstration.[34]

The march was one of the most unusual and today underappreciated military episodes to unfold along the storied old river. At 5:00 a.m. March 8, 1892, seventy-seven men stepped smartly off government property. They included three white officers, three white sergeants, four Apache corporals, two Apache musicians, and sixty-five Indian privates. Garbed in brown fatigues and kitted out with canteens, haversacks, field belts, rifles, entrenching tools, bedding, and tents, they soon passed through Chastang and rapidly proceeded south, crossing Gunnison Creek just above Twelve Mile Island. Their pace was so fast that their officers decided to slow them down, weaving them back and forth through swamps and timber to accustom them to hard marching. By the end of their first day they had made more than seventeen miles.[35]

The following morning the troops again rose early and approached Mobile over the Sawdust Road. They marched through downtown amid great excitement and pitched their tents at Frascati Park. The press had a field day. "An Indian Invasion" read one bold headline. Not since the Creek Wars, the *Mobile Register* enthused, had there been such a sight. Armed Indians in their very midst! Reporters and citizens watched admiringly as the men executed their various maneuvers during the public exhibition. "The drilling of the men was very good," wrote one newsman, "and they seemed to take a great deal of pride in their individual work in line. The command was somewhat hampered by the crowd, especially the small boy, who was on hand as usual." The citizens pushed so close that the officers ordered several Indians to brandish their rifles and fire into the air. The effect was not to disperse the people, however, but only to thrill them more. Armed Indians were actually shooting! Afterward, many of the Indians pulled liberty in town, freely spending money provided them. Most of them behaved well. Only two missed the curfew, having become drunk, and landed in jail.[36]

Geronimo was more interested in insuring that the Apache children got the equivalent of a white education; that, more than military competency, was the route to assimilation and future success. By 1892 eighty children were attending a one-room school staffed by white teachers. Eager to make sure the kids behaved, Geronimo appointed himself monitor, stalking the room with a stick. Besides attending to discipline, Geronimo had a more personal stake in the school—a son and a granddaughter were enrolled. Overall he was pleased. "We have fine lady teachers," he proudly told an army inspector. "All the children go to their school. I make them. I want them to be white children." Geronimo had fought the United States government with everything he had, but in surrender he was confident that his people would be well treated, and he wanted them to enjoy the fruits of the dominant culture. "I believe white men have kind hearts," he said in the fall of 1894. "They will catch a wild deer in the woods and tame and teach it to feed from their hands and follow their steps. They will take a wild bird from the tree top and make it feed from their lips and come at their voice. We are like the deer and the wild bird. We listen for your voice and we follow your steps."[37]

People were curious to see the Apaches, and excursion trains and boats regularly called at Mount Vernon. Once at "Geronimo's Alabama Camp," tourists freely wandered among the cabins and tents, gawking at the Indians and purchasing various wares and trinkets on display. In a letter to the *New York Times,* one visitor described what he saw. "It would be difficult to find anything more picturesque and interesting than the camp of the Chiricahua Apache Indians now held prisoners of war at Mount Vernon Barracks, Alabama," he opined. "It consists of a hundred or more cabins and a few wigwams, which the older women have been unable to abandon. Geronimo, who foiled our army again and again, is seated in front of his cabin, beading a whip."

Another visitor wrote: "Geronimo has an eye to thrift and can drive a sharp bargain with his bows and arrows, and quivers and canes, and other work, in which he is skillful. He prides himself on his autograph." This particular visitor bought an expensive war bonnet from the chief and gave him a pen to "write his name in the bonnet." Geronimo declined the pen and instead "went out and cut a small, dry twig, which he sharpened to a fine point, and then very slowly, and with much pains-taking, printed his name with the stick dipped in ink."[38]

But there were difficulties at Mount Vernon for the Apaches. They never took to the climate, and their mortality rates remained high. Consumption, various fevers, malaria, and dysentery were among the culprits. Dr. Reed was convinced they needed to be removed to an environment more like that of their native Arizona. Furthermore, they were depressed over the U.S. War Department's transferring more than one hundred children to a special new school in Carlisle, Pennsylvania. Dr. Reed remarked that though this move had been well intended, he questioned its wisdom. "If the Apaches have any redeeming characteristic, it is love for their children." Repeated appeals to government officials had been made over the years by Reed and various experts who had visited Mount Vernon, and at last it was decided to move the Apaches to Fort Sill, Oklahoma. The transfer took place in 1894. The Indians boarded trains for the move, and their cabins were broken down and loaded as well. Unfortunately, the cabins burned while sitting on a siding in New Orleans, but the Indians safely made it to their new home. They had spent seven years beside the Mobile River, but other than as a difficult place filled with unpleasant memories, it never signified for them. Their memory faded, along with the feathered crafts that gathered dust atop white children's mantels in downtown Mobile, but it never completely went away.[39]

Not far from where the Apaches were held there were other Indians living on the fringes of white society. But unlike the Apaches, they were native to the area and thoroughly at home in the muggy air and dense river swamps. Descendants of early Choctaw warriors and women who had held on in south Alabama, they either managed to avoid the early-nineteenth-century removals or, if they were removed, had filtered back home. Some of them mixed with area white and black residents over time, becoming, as one 1992 study termed them, "tri-racial isolates." In the 1910 census a local researcher described them as "composed of Indian, of Spanish, some of them French, some with White, and some with Negro. The prevailing habits are Indian. Called 'Cajun.'" During the early twentieth century they were referred to as either Cajun or Cajan, with the latter term becoming more common. Today *Cajan* is considered a pejorative term and is rarely heard. Beginning in the late 1970s, they dubbed themselves the MOWA Choctaws, and this is the name that currently prevails. The MOWA suffered considerable discrimination and ridicule in the past and even now are struggling with the Bureau of Indian Affairs for federal recognition. Their quest is opposed by the existing federally recognized tribes in the region, the Poarch Creek Indians of Alabama and the Mississippi Choctaws, who run profitable gambling operations.[40]

Scholars trace the MOWAs' origins to the chaotic aftermath of the Creek War. A number of Choctaw Indians sided with the Red Sticks during the conflict, and after the American victory they melted into area swamps and lived as maroons. During the antebellum period they became a common sight in downtown Mobile, where they went to sell firewood, vegetables, and game. When a visitor asked where they lived, one of the men answered: "It does not matter who the swamp belongs to. No one lives on it, nor does any white man ever go into it. It is all marsh or water, except an occasional dry spot of elevated ground. On these little islands we have our houses and live very comfortably and out of the way of the rest of the world." He went on to describe how they hunted ducks in the winter and during the summer moved into the piney woods where it was healthier and "game is very plentiful."[41]

During the late nineteenth and early twentieth centuries, many MOWA men made money logging the delta and running the timber downstream. "Men from different families cut the tall timber," a Choctaw elder named Roosevelt Weaver explained in a 1986 interview. "They 'snaked' the logs to a creek with a team of oxen and rafted the logs together. When the rains came and the creek rose, they climbed on the raft, steered it with 15-foot paddles to keep it in the main stream and out of the woods. My daddy said they always had a tent stretched on the logs, on the front end. That's where they cook and eat going to Mobile." Other common male activities included making turpentine, hunting, fishing, and farming. During the Great Depression and later, quite a few worked for Congressman Frank Boykin, who had extensive interests in northern Mobile County. In a 1960 letter Boykin boasted to a colleague that in his neck of the woods "We have a lot of wild Indians. . . . Well, I still have a lot of them and they work for us. They can see in the dark and they can trail a wounded deer better than some of our trail dogs." While the men were accomplished woodsmen, the women were adroit gardeners and cooks, cultivating collards, mustard greens, potatoes, tomatoes, okra, lettuce, squash, beans, and melons and making mouth-watering gumbo and succotash. The children attended a special "Indian" school and outside the classroom learned their elders' ways.[42]

During the early 1930s the writer and English professor Carl Carmer visited northern Mobile County and devoted several chapters of his book *Stars Fell on Alabama* to the "Cajans." He first encountered them in a country store. "A young man and a girl came in to buy ice cream cones," he wrote. "They were both dark and tall, the man about six feet. Save for their height, they looked like Sicilians. The man's hair was curly, his cheek bones were high, his features were aquiline, and his eyes were large and gray. The girl was of olive complexion and her straight well-formed nose and generous mouth under a wealth of dark brown hair that was braided and caught up at the base of her neck gave her exotic beauty." Carmer asked a companion about the origins of these people and was laughingly told to ask around. He received a variety of salty answers, including that they had "sprung right out'n the ground"; had come from animals, "coons and foxes and such-like"; and were born of pirates that had mixed with women of all backgrounds, "Russian, Spanish, French, English, Nigger." Later Carmer was invited to tour their school house, "a one-room frame structure which its builders had thought to dignify with an ecclesiastical-looking belfry," where he observed "curly-headed boys and girls of olive complexion a number of yellow-haired, blue-eyed blondes—as Nordic in appearance as Dakota Swedes." A teacher merrily told him, "Yellow and black hair often run in the same family." But when Carmer asked a little boy where he came from, the sharp response betrayed defensiveness already bred of hard experience. "From French people that married Indians," the boy said, "and not from any niggers at all."[43]

By the late twentieth century some MOWA members were going away to college and returning to score good jobs at local chemical plants up and down the river. Nonetheless, poverty was an issue for too many of the several thousand tribal members, and in 1980 leaders embarked on a sustained effort to gain federal recognition and, thus, better assistance. Despite recognition by the state of Alabama, the Bureau of Indian Affairs has proven to be a very tough sell, and the politics are dicey. Unfortunately for the MOWAs, their abundance of oral tradition was not enough to convince the bureau of a consistent tribal identification over time. While federal researchers accept the existence of Choctaws in south Alabama after the Creek War and early-nineteenth-century removals, the community's profound late-nineteenth- and early-twentieth-century isolation meant that there was scant written documentation deemed critical for formal recognition. The Bureau of Indian Affairs was looking for government documents that would prove that tribal members descended from more than one ancestor who was a member of a historic tribe. For their part the MOWAs found the federal dismissal of oral tradition extremely frustrating. As member Cedric Sunray put it, "When elder after elder recounts the same story in a relatively similar fashion . . . how can we discount it?"[44]

Federal recognition for the MOWAs has been actively opposed by both the Alabama Creeks and the Mississippi Choctaws. In 1994 Mississippi Choctaw tribal archaeologist Ken Carlton said of the MOWAs that "we do not recognize them as Choctaws or Indians." He went on to describe them as "Cajuns" of predominantly white and black ancestry, with only a little Indian in the mix. In a 2002 interview MOWA chief William "Longhair" Taylor remarked that "it boils down to politics and money." The federal pie is large, but it is limited, and numerous other groups besides the MOWAs are campaigning for tribal recognition. Understandably, those who have already achieved recognition are loath to see their share diminished by the admission of what they consider groups with marginal claims to authentic tribal status. History has been painful for the MOWAs. They have been classified and ostracized in the past as "Cajans" and "a mongrel race," yet their faith in their Indian status remains unshaken. Their struggle will continue, and perhaps one day the politics of official recognition will shift in their favor. Until then their quest remains an open chapter in the Mobile River's long and sometimes dark history.[45]

Epilogue

Elegy for a Small Shipyard

He looks more like a psychologist than a shipyard owner—lightly built with a relaxed, kind countenance fringed by a nimbus of blonde hair. His voice is welcoming and sunny, and he laughs readily. Impressions, as it turns out, do not deceive. William Harrison III in fact trained and worked as a psychologist for several years in Chattanooga before returning home to manage the family business in 1986. Harrison Brothers Dry Dock and Repair, founded in 1895, consists of two small yards on the east bank of the Mobile River, separated by less than a mile—an upper yard for brown-water work and a lower yard for blue-water work (purchased in 1960). Originally situated at the foot of Palmetto Street on the city side and called Harrison Bros. Rollerway and Spar Yard, the operation moved across the river in 1915 where it grew and became an institution. It constitutes one of the oldest, if not the oldest, businesses on the waterfront. Eager to learn more about this bit of local maritime history, I went to meet Bill Harrison at the upper yard on a soft May morning, almost a year to the day, it turned out, after his father, William Harrison Jr., had passed away.

Bill Harrison Jr. was a legend on the Mobile River, and he thoroughly looked and acted the part. Born in August 1919, he was big, raw boned, and ruddy faced with a booming voice. A hellion to work for, he drove his men and himself hard and settled disputes with bluster and fisticuffs. He started working riverside at the tender age of ten—the yard was founded by two of his uncles—sweeping office floors for three cents an hour.[1] As a young teen he dove deep in winter water encased in a hard-hat diving suit to survey a vessel's underside, ruining his eardrums in the process. During World War II he saw his beloved waterfront property confiscated by the United States government for the war effort, and half a century later the state of Alabama threatened to seize the lower yard for an enormous Interstate bridge project. The ensuing confusion and wrangling badly hurt the business. By that time, of course, Bill Harrison III had taken over the yard's affairs, but the elder Harrison still came to work at the crack of dawn each day, monitoring every detail, hopping around barges like an eighteen-year-old deckhand, and lavishing attention on his latest hobby boat, a vintage 1946 tug with beautiful curving lines.[2]

The upper yard was not hard to find, situated just a stone's throw north of the Bankhead Tunnel. I drove through a beat-up chain-link gate into a graveled square enclosure with a scattering of structures and vehicles—a trailer, a small utility building, a rectangular tin workshop, a two-story asbestos-sided gray office building with a lean-to attached, and a few cars and pickup trucks. As I parked and got out of my car, Harrison hurried down the two-story building's steps to greet me. After a warm exchange I followed him back up and into his front office, overlooking the river through a pair of windows.

I had not quite known what kind of operation to expect, but Harrison Brothers had clearly seen better days. The office building was weathered and rough—Harrison said Katrina's surge had come up as high as the second floor—and other than Harrison's own space, deserted. I could see where a secretary's office had been, but the desk was uncluttered and dusty, and the old copier looked little used. Occasionally as we spoke, a river tug would grind by in the stream, wonderfully near, and various open windows and doors admitted delightful cool puffs, likely the last we would experience for many months as the gulf sun approached its summer dominance.

The yard's working end featured three hundred feet of waterfront, every one of them visible from Harrison's windows and every one of them occupied. A long set of badly deteriorated iron-and-timber ways stretched along the north side of the office and terminated at a small slip hedged by narrow wooden piers. The riverbank here was jammed with driftwood, and a rusted work barge with a small crane sat askew in the slip. Immediately north of the slip a derrick barge listed hard by the bank, and off the end of the south pier a large dry dock floated. A gaggle of small work boats and barges huddled closer to shore and two men were doing some kind of topside repair on a modern tug, the *Marathon.* Periodically our conversation was punctuated by their desultory clangs and shouts.

Harrison was reflective and more than willing to tell me how the business had changed during his lifetime. In its heyday the shipyard had employed more than twenty men and confidently owned a niche as a nimble can-do company with multiple capabilities that included two dry docks, underwater work, topside repair, sand blasting, electrical, welding, piping, fabrication, crane service, and a high-tech sounding task called thermal imaging. While the work was hardly glamorous, and famously perilous and rough in the past, Harrison made it clear that things were safer now for shipyard employees than ever. Bloody fist and knife fights were mostly history thanks to background checks and drug tests, and increased regulation had dramatically reduced accidents. "Back in the 80s," he said, "the yard had one hundred injury-lost days a year. Not even one this year." Even so, the average shipyard worker still leads a harsh life. "They work hard all day in all kinds of weather," he said. "It's dangerous. They go home and drink all night. And then they come back the next day and do it all again. It's a country song—the car wrecks, you name it."[3]

Though definitely not that kind of river man, at fifty-eight Harrison was clearly feeling his age—"you're pretty much done as a shipyard worker at 55"—and then he let go a bombshell, telling me that because of multiple pressures he was closing the 117-year-old enterprise. He expected to have that accomplished by the end of the year and was already down to five employees. The phase-out plan included listing all the equipment for sale and leasing the land at the two sites, which other riverfront interests had long eyed hungrily. Calmly, Harrison ticked off the accumulation of terrible ifs that had forced his hand—the '08 recession; the BP oil spill; the consolidation of the barge and towing companies which buy new equipment and depend less on small repairs; competition from newer, larger, and better outfitted shipyards; mind-numbing governmental oversight; and frivolous lawsuits. Thankfully, he sighed, his father had not lived to see this.[4]

To give me a closer look at his dying business, Harrison offered a Cook's tour of the two yards. He started to hand me a hard hat but then dismissed the idea, and we clumped downstairs bareheaded. As we walked out on the south pier he described each piece of equipment and its function. Everything was well used and worn. The little shift tug *Libby* featured a red deck and green pilothouse with wires and rags and ropes scattered about and was secured to the dock by a frayed yellow-and-black hawser. The large dry dock, which Harrison said was older than he was, was painted a faded green with yellow railings but was almost completely rusted within the wing walls. A couple of older men laboring over a small item looked up and spoke as we stepped onto the dry dock. I could feel it swaying slightly in the current, and the towering walls nicely funneled the refreshing river breeze. I had never been on a dry dock before and was fascinated to hear Harrison describe how they work, chambers filling with water and sinking the whole so that a vessel can be maneuvered into position and the chambers pumped out, raising everything into light and air for thorough examination. The wing walls displayed depth measurements in feet, and his father's vintage tug sat perched in the middle on slide blocks.

The upper yard's highlights soon exhausted, Harrison drove me down to the lower yard, which on that day was inactive, and unlocked the gate. He explained how he had dredged it out to improve the depth, but the controversy over the bridge had deterred him from making improvements here for too long. A few trailers and a white pickup were off to one side, and a dry dock and dormitory boat sat idle in the water. Despite the parcel's air of abandonment, its primo location and desirability were readily apparent. To begin with, the views were stunning. Downtown's waterfront assets—the cruise terminal, GulfQuest National Maritime Museum then under construction, Cooper Riverside Park, and the convention center—were all handsomely arrayed across the river. And on Blakeley and Pinto Islands, all around the lower yard where ADDSCO had once dominated, were the booming new waterfront businesses that were investing millions and employing thousands—Austal, ThyssenKrupp, and BAE Southeast Shipyard.

As I stood next to Harrison marveling at all the changes, it struck me that it has ever been thus on the Mobile River. The Indians with their dugout canoes and mounds had given way before the French with their sailing ships and fort. The French had in turn folded to the British, and they to the Spanish in the eighteenth-century game of European musical chairs that played out on these shores. Then the Americans had transformed the stream with warehouses, dredges, steamboats, shipyards, coal terminals, sawmills, and belching industries. Wars had been fought. Disasters and storms had wrought havoc. Men and women untold had perished beneath these waves. Economies and technologies and governments had all come and gone, leaving their relics and legacies. People of all kinds had settled along the river, and some had been brought against their will. Somewhere, roughly a dozen miles north of where I stood, the wreck of the *Clotilda* lay silently in the mud. Timothy Meaher had won his bet, but slavery was done, and now the descendants of those Africans proudly rubbed shoulders with Creoles and white people and Indians and mixtures of all, as well as with a hundred new kinds of immigrants in a sprawling and complicated region that, no matter what, will always owe its essence and future to the ever flowing river at its heart—Mobile!

Abbreviations

HMPS	Historic Mobile Preservation Society
Mass.	Municipal Archives
MHDC	Mobile Historic Development Commission
MPL	Mobile Public Library, Local History and Genealogy Division
PC	Probate Court, Mobile County

Notes

Prologue: Downriver with Cap'n Joe

1. Probate court records indicate Timothy and James Meaher assembling the parcels that would become the Promised Land as early as 1861. See Deed Book 16, 419 (December 17, 1861, 1242 acres), 652 (May 17, 1862, a 611-acre parcel); Deed Book 18, 656 (December 11, 1863, 445 acres); and Deed Book 19, 65 (May 28, 1864, 455 acres), PC, for the earliest purchases. During the Civil War, the brothers paid for some of their parcels with Confederate money. Derivation of the name *Promised Land* from an interview with Joe Meaher, July 19, 2011. The Feast of First Fruits from an e-mail communication to the author from Rabbi Steven Silberman, September 9, 2011.
2. The tour date was July 19, 2011. Joe Meaher's men were Joey Guess and John Harper, the pilot.
3. *Mobile Register*, January 8, 1999. In a special issue about the Mobile delta, a writer for the *Register* noted that "because of these flow manipulations, sections of the rivers near the dams frequently swing from a state of spring flood to summer drought and back again in a matter of hours, often several times each week." Even hundreds of miles downstream "average flows during the high-water winter and spring months are often significantly lower, and average flows during low-flow summer and fall months are much higher."
4. On the alligator, see *Mobile Register*, August 14, 2011. On bull sharks, see ibid., July 22, 2009. Eels have also been reported; see ibid., December 7, 1960, describing a hole in a ship's hull that was found plugged by a river eel.
5. The Environmental Working Group, a lobbying organization, ranked the Mobile as the seventeenth most polluted river in the United States in 1996. See "Dishonorable Discharge: The Fifty Most Polluted Rivers in the Country," http://www.ewg.org/node/20399 (accessed July 21, 2012); see also the *Mobile Register*, September 25, 1997, and January 12, 1999. Fortunately, better environmental regulation and efforts by the public and industry have improved matters in recent years, but no one interviewed for this book expressed a willingness to swim in the river.
6. See the *Mobile Register* article "Woes of a Working Class River," December 20, 1998.
7. On the *Torm Camilla*, see "*Torm Camilla*," http://www.marinetraffic.com/ais/ru/shipdetailsaspx?MMSI=22040200 (accessed July 21, 2012); on *Tai Honesty*, see "*Tai Honesty*," http://www.marinetraffic.com/ais/shipdetails.aspx?mmsi=372506000 (accessed July 21, 2012); for *E. R. Boston*, see "*E. R. Boston*," http://www.marinetraffic.com/ais/shipdetails.aspx?MMSI=636091947 (accessed July 21, 2012); and for *Caesar Helix*, see Hogue, "Caesar Pipelay Vessel Joins Helix ESG Fleet," http://gcaptain.com/caesar-pipelay-vessel-joins-helix?11496 (accessed July 21, 2012).
8. On the CSS *Tennessee*, see von Scheliha, *A Treatise on Coast Defense*, 114; on the *Coronado*, see "Navy Names Combat Ship USS *Coronado*," http:/www.navy.mil/search/display.asp?story__id=43396 (accessed July 21, 2012). A friend of mine told me that an

Austal worker told him that the littoral ships can do up to sixty knots—that is an astonishing sixty-nine miles an hour. When I mentioned this figure to a retired marine colonel he did not bat an eye. All off the record of course!

INTRODUCTION: "A fine, large river"

1. The size of the Mobile basin is thoroughly detailed in "National Water-Quality Assessment Program: Mobile River Basin," http://tn.water.usgs.gov/MOBL/mobl-fact.pdf (accessed September 9, 2012). See also Kammerer, "Largest Rivers in the United States," http://pubs.usgs.gov/of/1987/ofr87–242/ (accessed October 7, 2012).
2. The Mobile basin's constituent streams are described in Hall and Hoyt, *Report of Progress of Stream Measurements,* 127.
3. Jackson, *Rivers of History,* 6. Studies of Mobile such as Thomason, *Mobile: The New History of Alabama's First City;* Higginbotham, *Old Mobile;* Hamilton, *Colonial Mobile;* and Amos, *Cotton City: Urban Development in Antebellum Mobile,* of course cover the Mobile River extensively and are excellent sources, but these either confine themselves to the harbor or are limited in their chronological scope.
4. Owen, *History of Alabama and Dictionary of Alabama Biography,* vol. 2, 1031. The French referred to the Naniabas as "Les gens de la fourche," or "The people of the fork." The tribe was small and eventually absorbed by larger groups.
5. On width and depth, see Goodrum et al., *Rivers of Alabama,* 187. The annual intake at the fork is given in "Wetland and Habitat," http://www.alabamawildlife.org/stewardship/?pageID=54 (accessed September 11, 2012).
6. "Mobile-Tensaw Delta," *Encyclopedia of Alabama,* http://encyclopediaofalabama.org/face/Article.jsp?id=h-1201 (accessed July 20, 2011).
7. The "trembling land" quotation is from Giraud, *A History of French Louisiana,* vol. 1, 63. The "much of it is impassable" quotation is from Walthall, *Prehistoric Indians of the Southeast,* 266. The geographic divisions are in Morse, *The American Gazetteer,* no page numbers, entry for Mobile alphabetized under page headed MOB.
8. Rix, *Incidents of Life in a Southern City,* no page; look for section titled "Mobile River—The Gulf States in the Secession Drama—The First Exultant Gun of the War."
9. Rayford, *Cottonmouth,* 1. Maxwell Perkins edited Rayford's book for publication.
10. Van Doren, *The Travels of William Bartram,* 325–26. See also "William Bartram: 'What a sylvan scene is here!,'" *Mobile Register,* December 20, 1998.
11. Chester, *Transatlantic Sketches,* 223; *Mobile Register,* May 30, 1948. The "Great Magnolia Tree" is mentioned in hundreds of early deeds. The St. Louis Tract was bordered on the east by the Mobile River, the south by Three Mile Creek, the west by the Wolf Ridge hills and the north by Eight Mile Creek.
12. Romans, *A Concise Natural History,* 25 ("enormous size" of the cypress trees), 30 ("extremely dangerous" swamps); Buckingham, *Slave States of America,* vol. 1, 266–67.
13. On seasonal ebb and flow, see "How a Primordial Struggle between the Rivers and the Gulf Forged a Delta," *Mobile Register,* December 20, 1998. The cartographer's words are on the unsigned map *A Draught of the River Mobile,* ca. 1765.
14. "Mobile-Tensaw Delta," *Encyclopedia of Alabama,* www.encyclopediaofalabama.org/face/Article.jsp?id=h-1201 (accessed July 20, 2011).
15. Manatees are not common in the delta, but they are not rare either. See "Manatee and the Fisherman: Angler Gets Big Surprise When He Accidentally Gaffs Tagged 1,600 Pound Creature," *Mobile Register,* September 26, 2009. I have not yet found any historical references to manatees in the Mobile River; their increased presence may be a result of climate change.
16. Van Doren, *The Travels of William Bartram,* 327.
17. Bossu, *Travels through Louisiana,* vol. 1, 280–81.
18. Carter, "William Howard Robertson," 107–8.
19. Cabeza de Vaca, *Relation,* 105–6.
20. Ensor, Wilson, and Hill, *Historic Resources Assessment,* 9.

21. Goodrum et al., *Rivers of Alabama,* 179.
22. On temperatures, see Chadwick and Feminella, "Influence of Salinity and Temperature," 532. On the winter of 1807, see Waselkov, *A Conquering Spirit,* 123. Edmund P. Gaines, the postmaster at Fort Stoddert, reported heavy snows that January and described ice on the Tombigbee, just above the fork, extending out more than one hundred yards from the banks.
23. Rayford, *Seven Poems,* n.p. MPL.
24. Sidney Schell personal interview, April 17, 2012.
25. Rayford, *Cottonmouth,* 7.
26. Land, *Mobile: Her Trade, Commerce and Industries,* 26.
27. Knight and Adams, "A Voyage to the Mobile and Tomeh in 1700," 34.
28. Bossu, *Travels through Louisiana,* vol. 1, 221. Bossu's encounter with the alligator came later. Certainly nothing like that ever happened on the Seine!
29. Hamilton, *Colonial Mobile,* 512.
30. Saxe-Weimar Eisenach, *Travels,* 88.
31. Featherstonaugh, *Excursion through the Slave States,* 144.
32. Gosse, *Letters from Alabama,* 31.
33. Phares, "Huxtry!," 11, for the cub reporter's words. The "sea legs" quotation is from a personal interview with Judith Adams, April 18, 2012.
34. Rayford, *Cottonmouth,* 7.
35. Oldmixon, *Transatlantic Wanderings,* 153.
36. Abraham Ortelius was the Flemish cartographer. His *World Map of 1570* listed Mobile Bay as the *Bahia de Culata,* Spanish for "gunstock bay." See Hamilton, *Colonial Mobile,* 13. On the antebellum traveler, see Ingraham, *The Sunny South,* 502.
37. *The Bachelor's Button,* 44.
38. Giraud, *A History of French Louisiana,* vol. 1, 65–66.
39. For the British captain's words, see Oldmixon, *Transatlantic Wanderings,* 161. On the 2010 incident, see "Oil Spill at 4 Million Gallons; Mobile Bay Protection Plan Stymied by Currents," *Mobile Register,* May 11, 2010.
40. See "Ancient Forest Lies 10 Miles Off the Alabama Coast," *Mobile Register,* September 2, 2012.
41. For sea-level changes, see "How a Primordial Struggle between the Rivers and the Gulf Forged a Delta," *Mobile Register,* December 20, 1998; Ensor, Wilson, and Hill, *Historic Resources Assessment,* 7. On spruce trees, see Williams et al., "Sea-level Rise and Coastal Forests," 10. On megafauna, see "The Ice Age (Pleistocene Epoch)," www.epa.gov/gmpo/edresources/pleistocene.html (accessed September 16, 2012). On the channel's changes, see Smith, *A Field Guide to Mobile Delta Geomorphology,* 1.

Chapter 1: Indian Stream to *Entrada Española*

1. On the Clovis point and the inundation of other likely early evidence, see Ensor, Wilson, and Hill, *Historic Resources Assessment,* 18–19. For a map showing the changing shorelines, see Thomason, *Mobile: The New History of Alabama's First City,* 5.
2. On the Woodland Period, see Ensor, Wilson, and Hill, *Historic Resources Assessment,* 23–24. See also "Woodland Period," *Encyclopedia of Alabama,* http://www.encyclopediaofalabama.org/face/Article.jsp?id=h-1166 (accessed October 29, 2012).
3. Ensor, Wilson, and Hill, *Historic Resources Assessment,* 38–39.
4. On the Chuckfee Bay site, ibid., 44, 46.
5. On the Big Briar Creek site, ibid., 46, 48. For a list of the human bones, 77.
6. Walthall, *Prehistoric Indians of the Southeast,* 185.
7. Galloway, *Choctaw Genesis,* 61–63. Galloway writes that "a sort of Moundville-Bottle Creek axis of peaceful interaction apparently existed, to which the 'domestic' and 'foreign' relationships of the two chiefdoms contributed," 62.
8. "Bottle Creek Site," *Encyclopedia of Alabama,* http://encyclopediaofalabama.org/face/Article.jsp?id=h-1160 (accessed October 30, 2012).
9. Bossu, *Travels through Louisiana,* vol. 1, 222–23. See also Brown, *Bottle Creek,* 196–97.
10. The quotation describing the Indians as "well made" and the physical descriptions are from Romans, *A Concise Natural History,* 82. For the Coosa chief, see Pickett, *History of Alabama,* 29.

11. Hudson, *The Southeastern Indians,* 255–57.
12. Hamilton, *Colonial Mobile,* 8. See also Hudson, *The Southeastern Indians,* 235–36. On injuries reported in the nineteenth century, see Hudson, 409–10.
13. McWilliams, *Fleur de Lys and Calumet,* 91.
14. See Thomason, *Mobile: The New History of Alabama's First City,* 6–7. For Sevier's letter, see Deacon, *Madoc and the Discovery of America,* 186–87.
15. Rea, "Madogwys Forever!," 6. Robert Right Rea was an Auburn University history professor who retired in the early 1990s. During his distinguished career he wrote dozens of books and more than a hundred articles on Gulf Coast history.
16. Weddle, *Spanish Sea,* 100. In Galloway, *Choctaw Genesis,* 79–80, the author posits that Álvarez de Pineda made up his account of gold jewelry to impress the Crown. Soto saw none thirty years later, nor does the archaeology confirm the existence of such jewelry.
17. Hamilton, *Colonial Mobile,* 10–11. See Weddle, *Spanish Sea,* 104–5, on the Mississippi River as Álvarez de Pineda's Río Espíritu Santo. Álvarez de Pineda's map is reproduced in Weddle, 101.
18. Weddle, *Spanish Sea,* 26.
19. Ibid., 188–89.
20. Galloway, *Choctaw Genesis,* 82.
21. See Hamilton, *Colonial Mobile,* 13, which claims that the Spanish came as far north as the Fowl River. On the Teodoro incident, see Galloway, *Choctaw Genesis,* 82, and Weddle, *Spanish Sea,* 193.
22. Cabeza de Vaca, *Relation,* 55.
23. Ibid., 59–60.
24. Galloway, *Choctaw Genesis,* 83.
25. Weddle, *Spanish Sea,* 209–10.
26. On the size of Soto's force, see Hamilton, *Colonial Mobile,* 17; see also Weddle, *Spanish Sea,* 213. The chronicler's statement is in Weddle, 218.
27. Weddle, *Spanish Sea,* 219.
28. On the location of Mobila, see Knight, *The Search for Mabila,* 4, which presents a map showing ten possible locales, and Jackson, *Rivers of History,* 8. There are multiple spellings of *Mobila* and *Tascaluza.* For consistency I have adopted those used by Weddle, a good general source on the *entradas,* in *Spanish Sea,* 218.
29. On the battle and Soto's end, see Weddle, *Spanish Sea,* 219–20, and Knight, *The Search for Mabila,* 15.
30. Jackson, *Rivers of History,* 11.
31. On the colonization plan, see Weddle, *Spanish Sea,* 257–58. On Lavazares's report, see Priestly, *The Luna Papers,* vol. 2, 335.
32. Weddle, *Spanish Sea,* 261. The viceroy's quotation is from Priestly, *The Luna Papers,* vol. 1, l.
33. Weddle, *Spanish Sea,* 268.
34. Priestly, *The Luna Papers,* vol. 1, xlix, l.
35. Ibid., vol. 2, 121, for the quotation; vol. 1, 217, for items lost.
36. On the meaning of *Mobile,* see Swanton, *Early History of the Creek Indians and Their Neighbors,* 160. On the French estimate of the tribe's numbers, ibid.; see also Higginbotham, *The Mobile Indians,* 80. On the trade jargon, see Waselkov and Gums, *Plantation Archaeology,* 16.

Chapter 2: Colonial Days and Ways

1. *Mobile Register,* January 21, 1902.
2. Ibid.
3. Ibid., January 24, 1902.
4. Hamilton, "The Beginnings of French Settlement," 1.
5. Ibid., 12.
6. *Mobile Register,* January 24, 1902.
7. Ibid.
8. Modern surveyors use the Bankhead Tunnel downtown to denote the official mouth of the Mobile River. Measuring from there, the site of Old Mobile is 25.7 miles north. Historically, the mouth was considered to be further south, where the river broadens into the bay at Choctaw Point. See Higginbotham, *Old Mobile,* 45n.
9. On strategy, see Waselkov, *Old Mobile Archaeology,* 3.
10. "LeMoyne Brothers," *Encyclopedia of Alabama,* http://www.encyclopediaofalabama.org/face/Article.jsp?id=h-1102 (accessed November 23, 2012).
11. The quotation regarding the "vessels" is from Higginbotham, *Old Mobile,* 36. On the bones and Pénicaut, see McWilliams, *Fleur*

de Lys and Calumet, 11. On the island name, see "Dauphin Island," *Encyclopedia of Alabama,* http://www.encyclopediaofalabama.org/face/Article.jsp?id=h-3360 (accessed July 13, 2011). The original *e* was later dropped and the island called simply Dauphin, which means dolphin in French. The princess's coat of arms featured this sea animal. Dauphin Street, in contrast, was named for the French prince, as *dauphin* is the masculine form of the word denoting the heir to the throne of France.

12. Knight and Adams, "A Voyage to the Mobile and Tomeh in 1700," 35. See also Higginbotham, *Old Mobile,* 41–42.
13. Knight and Adams, "A Voyage to the Mobile and Tomeh in 1700," 36.
14. On French watercraft, see Surrey, *The Commerce of Louisiana,* 55 and 58 (on canoes); 74 (on Indians and black slaves as rowers); 70 (on brigantines at Old Mobile). See also Hamilton, *Colonial Mobile,* 55 (*chaloupe*); 173 (*bateau*).
15. McWilliams, *Iberville's Gulf Journals,* 162.
16. On the supplies, see Higginbotham, *Old Mobile,* 38–39. On site clearing, see Waselkov, *Old Mobile Archaeology,* 5.
17. Waselkov, *Old Mobile Archaeology,* 6–7. The quotation is from McWilliams, *Fleur de Lys and Calumet,* 59. During the bicentennial celebration a Mobile architect named Cary Butt fell into the powder magazine's old remains and, in an effort to keep from sliding into the river, clawed out several bricks. See Hamilton, *Colonial Mobile,* 566.
18. On the layout, see Waselkov, *Old Mobile Archaeology,* 7–9. See also Giraud, *A History of French Louisiana,* 43, for a map of Mobile with the lot assignments identified in English. On Tonti, see Thomason, *Mobile: The New History,* 18–19.
19. On French and Spanish relations, see Higginbotham, *Old Mobile,* 30–31; 425–27.
20. McWilliams, *Iberville's Gulf Journals,* 167.
21. For quotations from Iberville, see McWilliams, *Iberville's Gulf Journals,* 168–69. On the modern search for the idols, see Waselkov and Gums, *Plantation Archaeology,* 8, and Higginbotham, *The Mobile Indians,* 70. Higginbotham writes that "in the summer of 1964, while in Paris, I attempted to locate these idols without success."
22. Higginbotham, *Old Mobile,* 75–77.
23. Ibid., 108.
24. The Spanish officer's words are quoted in Boyd, Smith, Griffin, *Here They Once Stood,* 43. For Old Mobile houses, see Waselkov, *Old Mobile Archaeology,* 16–18. On gardens, see Romans, *A Concise History,* 115.
25. Hamilton, *Colonial Mobile,* 74.
26. On the census, see Pickett, *History of Alabama,* 172–73; on the soldiers, see Gums, "Earthfast (*Pieux en Terre*) Structures at Old Mobile," 13–14.
27. On factionalism, see Thomason, *Mobile: The New History,* 19.
28. Higginbotham, *Old Mobile,* 132.
29. Ibid., 134.
30. Ibid., 170, 174. Pénicaut is quoted in McWilliams, *Fleur de Lys and Calumet,* 97.
31. Sledge, *Cities of Silence,* 9.
32. Higginbotham, *Old Mobile,* 196–98. According to University of South Alabama archaeologist Gregory Waselkov, the Old Mobile Cemetery has proven difficult to explore. "There is only one clue to its location, the map of the town dating (according to Higginbotham) to 1704–1705 that places it on the western edge of the settlement in a quarter of a town block. The location may be correct, but the county's road crosses and covers most of that area, so we've only been able to test around the edges." As a result neither Tonti nor his iron hand has been located. Gregory Waselkov, e-mail message to the author, December 14, 2012. The quotation expressing the priest's "amazement" is from Waselkov and Gums, *Plantation Archaeology,* 9. On the early family names, see Thomason, *Mobile: The New History,* 20–21.
33. The "continual alarms" quotation is from Giraud, *A History of French Louisiana,* 211. On the buccaneer attack, see Higginbotham, *Old Mobile,* 445–48; on the Alabama Indian raid, see Higginbotham, 383–86.
34. McWilliams, *Fleur de Lys and Calumet,* 130.
35. Hamilton, Craighead, and Wilson, *Bicentennial Celebration of the Founding of Mobile,* 36–37. See also Thomason, *Mobile: The New History,* 24–25.

36. Waselkov and Gums, *Plantation Archaeology,* 26–27. See also Thomason, *Mobile: The New History,* 25. Pénicaut's words are from McWilliams, *Fleurs de Lys and Calumet,* 134.
37. On Pénicaut, see McWilliams, *Fleurs de Lys and Calumet,* 133. Bienville's quotation is in Higginbotham, *Old Mobile,* 464.
38. Hamilton, *Colonial Mobile,* 86–90. The map is between pages 86 and 87. On early streets, see page 91.
39. Ibid., 92.
40. Gayarré, *History of Louisiana,* 126.
41. Hamilton, *Colonial Mobile,* 95–98. Quotation of Pénicaut, 99.
42. Thomason, *Mobile: The New History,* 32–36. On Pénicaut's estimate of the garrison, see McWilliams, *Fleur de Lys and Calumet,* 163. The actual number of troops is reported in Waselkov, e-mail message to the author, December 14, 2012.
43. Hamilton, *Colonial Mobile,* 79 (on Bienville's slaves); 103 (on slave ships).
44. Surrey, *The Commerce of Louisiana,* 239.
45. Waselkov and Gums, *Plantation Archaeology,* 80 (on Twenty-One Mile Bluff), 69 (on slave life).
46. *American State Papers, Public Lands,* vol. 1, 636.
47. For the inventory, see Andrews, *Rochon and Related Families,* 93. On clothing, see Johnson, *British West Florida,* 159.
48. Thomason, *Mobile: The New History,* 32–33.
49. Giraud, *A History of French Louisiana,* vol. 5, 358–60. See also Hamilton, *Colonial Mobile,* 153–54.
50. On the population, see Thomason, *Mobile: The New History,* 38. On Mobile, 1760, see Hamilton, *Colonial Mobile,* 150–53.
51. Thomason, *Mobile: The New History,* 41.
52. Ibid., 42. The "extraordinary man" quotation is from Hamilton, *Colonial Mobile,* 254.
53. Rowland, *Letters and Enclosures,* vol. 1, 19. The quotation describing "this place" is from Thomason, *Mobile: The New History,* 43.
54. Rowland, *Letters and Enclosures,* 11–12.
55. Romans, *A Concise History,* 72. The quotation "fortunate diversion" is from Rowland, *Encyclopedia of Mississippi History,* vol. 1, 302.
56. On the treaty, see Rowland, *Encyclopedia of Mississippi History,* 301. On the Mobiles' disappearance, see Waselkov and Gums, *Plantation Archaeology,* 17; see also Higginbotham, *The Mobile Indians,* 80–82.
57. Thomason, *Mobile: The New History,* 45. The quotation "whipt through the streets" is from Rea and Howard, *The Minutes, Journals and Acts,* 335.
58. On French reaction, see Rea and Howard, *The Minutes, Journals and Acts,* 44. On Rochon, see Andrews, *Rochon and Related Families,* 10–11. Johnstone's quotation is from Hamilton, *Colonial Mobile,* 247. On Romans, see his *Concise History,* 332–33. On population figures, see Usner, *Indians, Settlers and Slaves,* 115.
59. Hamilton, *Colonial Mobile,* 265–67 (Lorimer's report), 268 (Mobile as a "black trifle"); Thomason, *Mobile: The New History,* 46 (Mobile as a "disagreeable and unhealthy place").
60. Usner, *Indians, Settlers and Slaves,* 126–27. On the wine and pearl diving, see Fabel, *Bombast and Broadsides,* 48.
61. On Durnford, see Hamilton, *Colonial Mobile,* 260. On Taitt, see "David Taitt," *Encyclopedia of Alabama,* http://www.encyclopediaofalabama.org/face/Article.jsp?id=h-1538 (accessed July 12, 2013). The quotation is from Romans, *A Concise History,* 332–33.
62. See Hulbert, *The Crown Collection,* map 90 (Mobile Harbour); maps 91–95 (Field Survey of Mobile River). For Pittman's maps, see Hamilton, *Colonial Mobile,* 260–61 (between these pages for Mobile Bay); Gould, *From Fort to Port,* 14 (Plan of Mobile).
63. For details of the Taitt map, see Waselkov and Gums, *Plantation Archaeology,* 63 (upper Mobile River); 84 (Tensa River); and Waselkov, *A Conquering Spirit* (plate 1, showing upper Mobile).
64. On Bartram's Mobile descriptions, see Van Doren, *The Travels of William Bartram,* 324. On Farmar's alleged smuggling, see Fabel, *The Economy,* 138.
65. Marley, *Wars of the Americas,* vol. 2, 449. Gálvez is quoted in Fabel, "Reflection on Mobile's Loyalism," 38.
66. On the artillery, see National Park Service, "18-pounder Revolutionary War Cannon," Fort Moultrie informational sheet, n.d. On the opposing forces, see Hamilton, *Colonial*

Mobile, 312–13; and Thomason, *Mobile: The New History,* 50–51.

67. Beatson, *Naval and Military Memoirs,* 213. See also Hamilton, *Colonial Mobile,* 313–14.
68. Hamilton, *Colonial Mobile,* 315.
69. Thomason, *Mobile: The New History,* 51–52.
70. Ibid., 54 (for the quotation describing Spanish rule); 52 (on Panton, Leslie & Company); 53 (on Fort San Esteban). For more on Panton, Leslie, see Hamilton, *Colonial Mobile,* 352–53.
71. Hamilton, *Colonial Mobile,* 502. See also Gould, *From Fort to Port,* 27; Gums and Shorter, *Archaeology at Mobile's Exploreum,* 74 (reducing "the putrid exhalations") 75.
72. Thomason, *Mobile: The New History,* 58.
73. Ibid., 58.
74. Land Claim of Widow Rochon, Record Book 2, 72, PC. On Louise Fievre Rochon and her holdings, including the loss of her house during the siege, see Shepherd, *Cases Argued and Determined in the Supreme Court of Alabama,* 399–402.

Chapter 3: American Dawn

1. For the population estimate, see Ellicott, *The Journal of Andrew Ellicott,* 237.
2. On the survey appointments and Ellicott, see Matthews, *Andrew Ellicott,* 127–29 (appointments); 7 (Ellicott's birth); 83–105 (D.C. survey); 112–13 (roads and Erie).
3. Register, "Andrew Ellicott's Observations," 26. See also Ellicott, *The Journal of Andrew Ellicott,* 197.
4. Ellicott, *The Journal of Andrew Ellicott,* 201. See also Register, "Andrew Ellicott's Observations," 26.
5. Spies, "A Line of Demarcation," 5. Castor and Pollux in the constellation Gemini were two of Ellicott's target stars.
6. For the portraits, see Matthews, *Andrew Ellicott,* frontispiece (sketch); 164 (miniature). The "excellent likeness" quotation is on 165. The "elegant silk" mosquito curtains, 158; the china bowls, 165. For Freeman's claims, see Wilkinson, *Memoirs,* appendix no. 32, n.p. For Ellicott's opinion of Freeman, see Matthews, *Andrew Ellicott,* 164 (rascal and liar); 160 ("expeld... from the camp"). On Walker's letter, see Claiborne, *Mississippi,* 197–98, the footnote marked by a cross. Whatever went on with Betsy, Ellicott was certainly attentive to his wife during his survey. See Matthews, *Andrew Ellicott,* 164 and 165, for letters in which he addresses her as "My Dearest of all Earthly Beings" and "My Dear Girl." He also sent her gifts, including "two fashionable fans of this country" (165) from New Orleans. As to sexual practices, he did write to his wife that he considered "mens kissing . . . a most abominable custom" (159). The comment was occasioned by a visit from a Spanish official who kissed Ellicott on the cheek.
7. On shooting the delta by firelight, see Ellicott, *The Journal of Andrew Ellicott,* 83–84.
8. On the stone, see Hamilton, *Colonial Mobile,* 354–55. For Ellicott's quotation on the difficulties, and on the 799-foot error, see Spies, "Major Ellicott's Triangulation," 2. The Ellicott Stone is easily visited today, there being a pull-off with a historic marker alongside Highway 43 near the community of Bucks. An unpaved trail across a railroad bed and through the woods a short distance leads to the stone. It is surrounded by a cast-iron fence and covered by a large pavilion placed in 1999 for bicentennial celebrations at the site. The City of Mobile owns the stone and a fifty-foot square patch of land surrounding it. The rest of the area is owned by Alabama Power Company, which patrols the property. Even easier to visit is an exact replica of the stone at the History Museum of Mobile, 111 S. Royal Street, downtown.
9. On West Florida, see Hamilton, *Colonial Mobile,* 356. On the abandonment of Fuerte San Esteban, see Thomason, *Mobile: The New History,* 58. On the need for a new fort at the thirty-first parallel, see Christopher et al., "Archaeological Survey of the Old Federal Road," 60.
10. On Fort Stoddert, see Owen, *History of Alabama,* vol. 2, 1272. On Schaumburgh, see Holmes, "Fort Stoddard," 231. The name of the fort has been spelled in various ways down the years, but *Stoddert* is the correct version.
11. For the quotations, see Holmes, "Fort Stoddard," 235 ("I come on but slowly" and

"Doctor Hogland arrived"); 234 (remedies "for the use of the hospital"); and 239 ("the sickly state of the men").

12. All quotations are from Holmes, "Fort Stoddard," 236, 249, and 250.
13. On broad developments, see Thomason, *Mobile: The New History,* 58–59. On Governor Claiborne and Chambers's complaint, see *American State Papers, Foreign Relations,* vol. 2, 678–79.
14. For Jefferson's words, see Jefferson, *Writings,* 1137 ("all in good time," "In the meanwhile"); Smith, *The Republic of Letters,* vol. 2, 1328 ("We shall enter into"). *Pari passu* is Latin for "on equal footing."
15. Doster, "Early Settlements," 87.
16. See Welborn, "A Traitor in the Wilderness," 15. For the quotation "the gods invite us to glory," see Parton, *The Life and Times of Aaron Burr,* 428.
17. Welborn, "A Traitor in the Wilderness," 16. For Dinsmoor's words, see Owen, "Burr's Conspiracy," 169.
18. On Toulmin, see "Harry Toulmin," *Encyclopedia of Alabama,* http://www.encyclopediaofalabama.org/face/Article.jsp?id=h-3108 (accessed January 5, 2013). For the quotation, see Owen, "Burr's Conspiracy," 171–72.
19. On Burr's appearance and arrest, see Stumpf, "The Arrest of Aaron Burr," 119–20. On Burr's exchange with Gaines, see Pickett, *History of Alabama,* 493.
20. Pickett, *History of Alabama,* 494. On the Spanish officer, see Stumpf, "The Arrest of Aaron Burr," 122.
21. On Burr's departure from the fort, see Parton, *The Life and Times of Aaron Burr,* 448–49. For Toulmin's letter to Madison, see Owen, "Burr's Conspiracy," 175. For Burr's words, see Welborn, "A Traitor in the Wilderness," 19.
22. On the Kempers, see Waselkov, *A Conquering Spirit,* 62. For Kennedy's letter, see "West Florida, Its Attempt on Mobile," 701; for Toulmin on Kemper, see page 702. For the officer on Kennedy, see Clark and Guice, *The Old Southwest,* 57. For Kemper on Toulmin, see Clark and Guice, 59. The personal anxiety suffered by Judge Toulmin during this episode may be inferred by the fact that one daughter was married to Gaines; another to one of General Wilkinson's sons; and a son to one of James Caller's daughters. None of these tangled connections seems to have prejudiced his official duties in the least. See Clark and Guice, *The Old Southwest,* 62.
23. On the Spanish offer, see "West Florida, Its Attempt on Mobile," 703. On the expedition, see Pickett, *History of Alabama,* 508.
24. Pickett, *History of Alabama,* 509.
25. Ibid., 508–9.
26. Christopher et al., "Archaeological Survey of the Old Federal Road," 67. For the quotation, see the *Mobile Centinel,* May 30, 1811.
27. Waselkov, *A Conquering Spirit,* 29 (on the origin of Federal Road), 59 (on travel time for the mail). The route of the Federal Road through south Alabama roughly parallels that of Interstate 65 today.
28. Christopher et al., "Archaeological Survey of the Old Federal Road," 63.
29. Hamilton, *Colonial Mobile,* 404–7.
30. Thomason, *Mobile: The New History,* 61.
31. Pickett, *History of Alabama,* 516. See also, Hamilton, *Colonial Mobile,* 410–15.
32. For the inventory, see Wilkinson, *Memoirs,* 514–15. For Wilkinson's words, see Hamilton, *Colonial Mobile,* 415.
33. For Jackson as "Sharp Knife," see Buchanan, *Jackson's Way,* 297. For his remarks in the *Clarion,* see Waselkov, *A Conquering Spirit,* 97.
34. Buchanan, *Jackson's Way,* 217–18.
35. On the fort, see Waselkov, *A Conquering Spirit,* 117–18. On the attack, ibid., 127–29.
36. Ibid., 136 (quotations of Toulmin), 142. Toulmin described the events fully in a letter that was widely reprinted in the newspapers of the day. For example, see *Baltimore Weekly Register,* October 16, 1813.
37. Waselkov, *A Conquering Spirit,* 134 (survivors of the Fort Mims massacre); 141 (property loss); 149–52 (burials).
38. On the Canoe Fight, see Pickett, *History of Alabama,* 563–66; and Buchanan, *Jackson's Way,* 253–57.
39. Waselkov, *A Conquering Spirit,* 173 (on Weatherford); 204 (on the treaty).
40. Hamilton, *Colonial Mobile,* 428.
41. On army life and clothing, see Braund, *Tohopeka,* 242. On the Springfield musket, see Turner, *The War of 1812,* 133. For the quotation describing the surgeon's report, see Buchanan, *Jackson's Way,* 308.

42. Hamilton and Owen, "Topographical Notes," 173 (for quotations); Hamilton, *Colonial Mobile*, 428.
43. Buchanan, *Jackson's Way*, 302–55 (on the war); Coker, "How General Jackson Learned of British Plans," 92–93 (on Innerarity). Cynical readers might wonder whether James Innerarity was crying because of his fears for his adopted homeland, or, good Scotsman that he was, of what the war would do to business.
44. Buchanan, *Jackson's Way*, 306–07.
45. Ibid.
46. Ibid. See also Pickett, *A History of Alabama*, 609–11; 436 (on the second attack on Bowyer and the end of war).
47. Hamilton, *Colonial Mobile*, 449–41. For taxes and town limits see, Toulmin, *A Digest*, 781.
48. Amos, *Cotton City*, 4–5. Mississippi achieved statehood in 1817, Alabama in 1819.
49. Ibid., 6. On the demolition of Charlotte, see Hamilton, *Colonial Mobile*, 478–79.
50. Erickson, *Mobile's Legal Legacy*, 43–45. See also Hamilton, *Colonial Mobile*, 473. The quotation citing danger to the health of the city is from *Memorial of the Mayor and Aldermen*, 4.
51. On the wharves, see Gould, *From Fort to Port*, 39; and Hamilton, *Colonial Mobile*, 445. On the commodes, see "Interesting Transcriptions from the City Documents," 1820–1911, 236. On the Fish Market, ibid., 1823–1844, 3–5.
52. *Mobile Commercial Register*, February 7, 1822. See also Gould, *From Fort to Port*, 39 (quotation describing Commerce Street), and *The Bachelor's Button*, 44 (the traveler's observation, "One entire street").
53. On city's use of gunwales, see "Interesting Transcriptions from the City Documents," 1820–1911, 200.
54. On steamboats, see Hamilton, *Colonial Mobile*, 471–72. On federal investment, see New South Associates, *From Alluvium to Commerce*, 59.

Chapter 4: Calliope Song

1. For the passengers, see "Manifest of the U.S. Mail Steamer *Southern*, May 17, 1842," Mass. On the varieties of Mobile's people, see Shippee, ed., *Bishop Whipple's Southern Diary*, 87–88.
2. Meriwether, ed., "'A Southern Traveler's Diary,'" 136–37 (clergyman's words); Koch, *Journey through a Part of North America*, 109 (German paleontologist's words); "Interesting Transcriptions from the City Documents," 1820–1911, 485 (grand-jury findings).
3. Shippee, *Bishop Whipple's Southern Diary*, 87 ("lazy, laughing singing negroes"); Oldmixon, *Transatlantic Wanderings*, 153 ("hackney carriages" at the waterfront); *Mobile Daily Advertiser*, September 27, 1860 (on the piles of cotton bales); Meriwether, "A Southern Traveler's Diary," 136 (Mobile as "a city of cotton"); Amos, *Cotton City*, xiii (cotton "has made Mobile"); Phillips, *Plantation and Frontier Documents*, 286 ("Look which way," "I must have heard").
4. Rothman, *Flush Times and Fever Dreams*, 3–6; 5 (on "a new El Dorado").
5. Ibid., 3–4. On Mobile numbers, see Amos, *Cotton City*, 21.
6. Amos, *Cotton City*, 22; 23 (on Mobile exports and imports). The story illustrating the imbalance was one I heard my grandmother tell at table. See also *DeBow's Review* 9 (December 1860): 654–60 for lists of items exported and imported.
7. Jackson, *Rivers of History*, 60–62; Neville, *Directory of Steam* (see the appendix "River Landings in Alabama"); Mellown, "Steamboat Travel in Early Alabama," 6 (quotations of Olmstead).
8. Amos, *Cotton City*, 28–29. For Goodman's ad, see New South Associates, *From Alluvium to Commerce*, 110–11.
9. McGehee, "Ask McGehee," 92–93 (on the "English Channel"); Beadle, *The American Lawyer*, 61–63 (on the contracts); Amos, *Cotton City*, 40–41 (on insurance).
10. Hunt, "Cotton Warehouses," 266.
11. New South Associates, *From Alluvium to Commerce*, 118–19 (on the presses); Hunt, "Cotton Warehouses," 266 (quotation reporting the captains' opinion).
12. Erskine, *Twenty Years Before the Mast*, 296–98.
13. Amos, *Cotton City*, 92 (on free labor); Walton and Grimm, *Windjammers*, 61 (the song). There are numerous variations of "Roll the

Cotton Down," but almost all of them mention Mobile. See also Bone, *Capstan Bars*, 84. White sailors heard black workers singing it on the wharves of Mobile and New Orleans and adopted it as a capstan shanty sung around the world into the late nineteenth century.

14. Buckingham, *The Slaves States of America*, vol. 1, 282–83; Oldmixon, *Transatlantic Wanderings*, 155; Bremer, *The Homes of the New World*, vol. 2, 217. The best overall architectural history of Mobile is Gould, *From Fort to Port.* See also Sledge, *The Pillared City*, which presents a thorough exploration of the city's Greek Revival movement.
15. Amos, *Cotton City*, 64–65. Something of Mobile's continuing fame as a social capital is highlighted by the joke that in Birmingham strangers are asked what their business is; in Montgomery who their people are; and in Mobile what they will be drinking.
16. Ibid., 65–67; see also Davidson, *The Living Writers*, 329 (on Madame LeVert's guests and quoting Washington Irving). LeVert's account of her journeys was published by the Mobile firm of S. H. Goetzel in two volumes and was titled *Souvenirs of Travel.* A first edition of this treasure is one of the most prized books in my personal library.
17. Amos, *Cotton City*, 46–47 (*Tribune* quotation); Delaney, *Remember Mobile*, 140 (Ludlow's theater), 184 (list of players).
18. Morris, *Wanderings of a Vagabond*, 461–62 (quotations of O'Connor). O'Connor used the pseudonym John Morris as editor for his book. "Interesting Transcriptions from the City Documents," 1820–1911, 28–29 (on the "whore balls"). On the failure to clean up vice, see Amos, *Cotton City*, 149–50. As late as 1986, while walking to work one morning I encountered the ragged end of an all-nighter among merchant seamen and prostitutes as they spilled out of a Royal Street bar.
19. Thomason, *Mobile: The New History*, 146 (on the depth over Choctaw Bar).
20. *Laws of the United States Relating to the Improvement of Rivers and Harbors*, vol. 1, 35 (on federal improvements). Congress specified the money "for the purpose of removing the obstructions and deepening the harbour of Mobile"; Prelini, *Dredges and Dredging*, 4 (on the grapple dredge); 3–4 (on the ladder dredge); *Annual Report of the Chief of Engineers*, 1886, 1184 (on progress by 1831). The last source includes a recounting of the history of dredging efforts in Mobile going back to the first appropriation in 1826.
21. Lyell, *A Second Visit*, 85 ("prodigious quantity of drift timber"); Harris, "On the Climate and Fevers," 684 (on the area as "a cypress swamp"); Power, *Impressions of America*, 162–63.
22. *Annual Report of the Chief of Engineers*, 1886, 1184 (on the width of the cut); Newman, "A Brief History of Choctaw Point Lighthouse," n.p.; Oldmixon, *Transatlantic Wanderings*, 159–60. The lighthouse cost $6,500 to build. See also "Lighthouses of Alabama," *Encyclopedia of Alabama*, http://www.encyclopediaofalabama.org/face/Article.jsp?id=h-2564 (accessed February 2, 2013).
23. Amos, *Cotton City*, 26.
24. Oldmixon, *Transatlantic Wanderings*, 152. See also Ingraham, *The Sunny South*, 502–4. The latter is an odd work, purported to be the journal of a Yankee governess, edited by Rev. J. H. Ingraham. In reality it is a novel entirely written by Ingraham, but it is based on actual travels and is quite convincing in the female voice.
25. Lloyd, *Lloyd's Steamboat Directory*, 272 (on Mobile boats, tonnage, and names); Patterson, *The Great American Steamboat Race*, 93 (tonnage comparisons by city).
26. Mellown, "Steamboat Travel in Early Alabama," 4; Hunter, *Steamboats on the Western Rivers*, 84 (the joke "to run on dew").
27. Buckingham, *The Slave States of America*, vol. 1, 262–63; Vestal, *The Missouri*, 46 ("crusted, rusted, busted"); Lyell, *A Second Visit to the United States*, 46.
28. *Mobile Daily Advertiser*, July 14, 1860 (on the *James Battle*); see also Jackson, *Rivers of History*, 164; Gosse, *Letters from Alabama*, 30. Mobile's daily newspaper merged, was bought out, and changed names multiple times throughout history. In this book, its various antebellum names—*Mobile Commercial Register, Mobile Daily Advertiser*, and *Mobile Daily Register* are all used as appropriate until late 1861, when the *Mobile Daily Advertiser* merged with the *Mobile Daily Register.*

References to the newspaper from late 1861 onward are all simplified to *Mobile Register* in text and notes. Despite multiple name changes after 1861, *Register* has always been on the masthead somewhere. Two Civil War era papers—the *Mobile Daily News* and the *Mobile Evening News*, as well as the *Mobile Tribune* and *Mobile Daily Herald* somewhat later, were independent, short-lived operations and those names have been preserved to connote them as separate enterprises.

29. Diouf, *Dreams of Africa in Alabama*, 93–94.
30. New South Associates, *From Alluvium to Commerce*, 114, 119 (support services); *Mobile Daily Advertiser*, May 9, 1856.
31. Russell, *My Diary North and South*, 266 (description of Timothy Meaher); Diouf, *Dreams of Africa in Alabama*, 8–10.
32. *Clarke County Democrat*, June 12, 1890. See also Diouf, *Dreams of Africa in Alabama*, 9.
33. *Mobile Register*, February 10, 1885 (James Meaher's obituary); Robertson, *The Slave Ship Clotilda*, 24–25 (Meaher's Hummock); see also Deed Book N.S. 16, p. 373, PC (quit claim deed by Bank of Mobile to Meahers for 1300 acres between "Chickasaw Bogue Creek" and Three Mile Creek); Diouf, *Dreams of Africa in Alabama*, 10–11 (businesses, Timothy Meaher's slave ownership); O'Meagher, *Some Historical Notices*, 177 ("Jim and Tim"), 178 (quotation describing Abby Meaher).
34. Amos, *Cotton City*, 22 (on Cox, Brainard & Company); Gould, *Fifty Years on the Mississippi*, 621 (quoting Owen Finnegan "I landed in Mobile," "a large and profitable trade"); *Mobile Register*, March 2, 1909 (Finnegan's obituary); "Steamboat Bill of Facts" (Finnegan as a captain who could "kick up dust"); Neville, *Ante-Bellum Floating Palaces*, 62–63 ("his name . . . a household word"). Finnegan's memory still looms large along the Mobile River, as I discovered when touring Chastang Bluff in the summer of 2012. My four guides were showing me a badly crumbled old brick tomb hard by the riverbank that had no name on it. They believed it had to be Finnegan's grave, but I later learned that he is not buried there.
35. Neville, *Ante-Bellum Floating Palaces*, 5–6 (on Otis); 3 (on Cloudis); 2 (on Cox); 4 (the story of the bereaved mother).
36. *Mobile Register*, November 11, 1914.
37. Neville, *Ante-Bellum Floating Palaces*, 7–9. Foster became a judge and wrote his steamboat stories for the *Wilcox Banner* in 1904. They were collected and reprinted by Neville in 1960. In toto they constitute a valuable firsthand account of antebellum river life.
38. *Mobile Register*, August 11, 1859.
39. Aiken, *Digest of the Laws of the State of Alabama*, 79; *Mobile Commercial Register*, March 14, 1836.
40. *Mobile Commercial Register*, March 14, 1836. See also Lloyd, *Lloyd's Steamboat Directory*, 74–75.
41. *Mobile Commercial Register*, March 15, 1836.
42. *Alabama Planter*, January 30, 1847. See also Lloyd, *Lloyd's Steamboat Directory*, 156.
43. *Alabama Planter*, February 2, 1847.
44. Jackson, *Rivers of History*, 87–97 (on the *Orline St. John*); Ward, *The Tombigbee River*, 69–92 (on the *Eliza Battle*). See also Windham, *13 Alabama Ghosts and Jeffrey*, 47–54 (the *Eliza Battle* chapter).
45. Amos, *Cotton City*, 196–204. In 1858 the Mobile & Ohio brought in more than 152,000 bales of cotton and 73,000 passengers.
46. Scroggs, *Filibusters and Financiers*, 345 (on Walker as the "grey-eyed man of destiny"); 373–75 (the *Susan* episode). See also Diouf, *Dreams of Africa in Alabama*, 23.
47. Scroggs, *Filibusters and Financiers*, 376; *Mobile Daily Advertiser*, January 4, 1859.
48. Amos, *Cotton City*, 235–36.

Chapter 5: Rebel River

1. Frost, *The Rebellion in the United States*, 91–92 (describing the reaction to secession); Cumming, *Gleanings*, 20–21; Amos, *Cotton City*, 236–37 (on the reaction and the state convention).
2. Silverstone, *Civil War Navies*, 43–44 (on the *Crusader*); U. S. War Department, *War of the Rebellion: Official Records of the Union and Confederate Navies*, vol. 4, p. 5 (hereinafter cited as *ORN;* all references are to series 1 unless otherwise noted) (*Crusader* ordered to Mobile); Maffitt, *The Life and Services of John Newland Maffitt*, 30 (describing Maffitt as "a son of Neptune"); see also Shingleton, *High Seas Confederate*, 7, 20 (on Maffitt's career).

3. Maffitt, *The Life and Services of John Newland Maffitt,* 215–16.
4. McMillan, *The Alabama Confederate Reader,* 22–23; Childress, "Mount Vernon Barracks," 126.
5. Goodheart, "Caught Sleeping," *New York Times,* January 3, 2011. See also the *New Orleans Bee,* January 8, 1861.
6. Goodheart, "Caught Sleeping," *New York Times,* January 3, 2011; U.S. War Department, *War of the Rebellion: Official Records of the Union and Confederate Armies,* vol. 1, p. 327 (hereinafter cited as *Oreg.;* all references are to series 1 unless otherwise noted) (quoting Reno's excuse); *New Orleans Bee,* January 8, 1861; *New York Times,* January 18, 1861.
7. McMillan, *The Alabama Confederate Reader,* 23 (quoting Moore's letter to Buchanan); on the Alabama militiaman, see South, "January 4, 1861," http://www.7score10years.com/index.php/south/81-south/143-january-4-1861-two-federal-forts-seized (accessed March 2, 2013).
8. Tenney, *The Military and Naval History of the Rebellion,* 9–10.
9. Bergeron, *Confederate Mobile,* 10 (quotation describing "stout, serviceable gray" uniforms); *Mobile Daily Advertiser,* April 24, 1861.
10. Russell, *My Diary North and South,* 184–89. The mid-nineteenth century was a racist age, and the n-word was used with great frequency among all classes, but one is tempted to label Meaher's brand of racism as particularly virulent. Whether or not this was actually the case—there are plenty of other appalling examples of racist thinking by numerous individuals at the time, not to mention heinous crimes such as rapes and beatings inflicted on black persons, neither of which there is any evidence of Meaher's having committed—he bent his considerable resources and channeled his formidable energies into directly spreading and supporting slavery at every opportunity.
11. Ibid., 273–75.
12. Bergeron, *Confederate Mobile,* 3 (on Mobile's population); 14–15 (on the rail connections).
13. *City of Mobile Directory,* 1859, 1861. See also Amos, *Cotton City,* 212. On Park and Lyons, see Chaffin, *The H. L.* Hunley, 86–88.
14. Bergeron, *Confederate Mobile,* 8 (quoting Governor Moore that "Mobile must be defended"); Russell, *My Diary North and South,* 279–80; Cumming, *Gleanings,* 32.
15. Fornell, "Mobile during the Blockade," 29 (on the state legislature's 1862 resolve); Bergeron, *Confederate Mobile,* 31–32; Delaney, *Confederate Mobile,* 99 (quoting the letter to Major Leadbetter).
16. Bergeron, *Confederate Mobile,* 18–29 (on Confederate departments and commanders); 61 (on the upriver forts). See also Schell, "The Confederate Fortifications at Fort Stoddert," 1–2.
17. Von Scheliha, *A Treatise on Coast Defense,* 191–92.
18. Ibid., 192–93; Irion, *Archaeological Testing of the Confederate Obstructions,* 12 (quoting the Union engineer's remark); 9 (on the drawing of the trapezoid); Bergeron, *Confederate Mobile,* 128 (on the sinking of the *Selma*).
19. Perry, *Infernal Machines,* 38 (on the torpedoes); O'Brien, *Mobile, 1865,* 167 (the torpedoes as charged "beer casks"); Perry, *Infernal Machines,* 188 (the toll of the torpedo warfare and the quotation of Thatcher).
20. Bergeron, *Confederate Mobile,* 64–66 (all batteries); Trickey, Holmes, and Clute, "Archaeological and Historical Investigations at Pinto Battery," 40 (locales); 46–47 (construction, deserter accounts).
21. Bergeron, *Confederate Mobile,* 70–71 (on name changes for the batteries); Trickey, Holmes, and Clute, "Archaeological and Historical Investigations at Pinto Battery," 49, 52 (on the extra work to improve the batteries and quotations of von Scheliha).
22. Bergeron, *Confederate Mobile,* 109–11, 159 (for the quotation beginning "It would be a novel sight"), 114 (on the "Forrest Negroes"); *Oreg.,* vol. 26, p. 503 (quoting von Scheliha); *Oreg.,* vol. 8, p. 153 (quoting Howard).
23. Bergeron, *Confederate Mobile,* 33 (Buchanan chosen commander); 35–38 (on Union sway in the gulf and Admiral Farragut); Symonds, *Confederate Admiral,* 192 (quoting Farragut on Buchanan: "bag him").
24. *ORN,* vol. 22, p. 134 (on Mobile's naval yard and assets); Bergeron, *Confederate Mobile,* 33–34, 70 (describing the vessels and where they were built); "Selma Ordnance and Naval

Foundry," *Encyclopedia of Alabama*, http://www.encyclopediaofalabama.org/face/Article.jsp?id=h-2331 (accessed March 7, 2013); Symonds, *Confederate Admiral*, 190 (the *Nashville* as a "tremendous monster").

25. Delaney, *Confederate Mobile*, 122 (on where the vessels were built); Bergeron, *Confederate Mobile*, 33 (the vessels themselves); *Mobile Register*, February 14, 1862 (*Gaines* launch); March 12, 1862 (the procession).
26. *Mobile Register*, March 12, 1862 (on the gunboat fund); March 10, 1862 (on the editor's tour); Bergeron, *Confederate Mobile*, 126–27; Still, "The Confederate States Navy at Mobile," 129n8 (quoting the *Morgan* officer).
27. Still, *Iron Afloat*, 80 (on the *Baltic*); see also Bergeron, *Confederate Mobile*, 34, 70.
28. Still, "The Confederate States Navy at Mobile," 134 (quoting Buchanan: "I have neither . . ."); Symonds, *Confederate Admiral*, 182 (on drills); O'Brien, *Mobile, 1865*, 164 (quoting the *Morgan* officer: "To call the *Morgan*'s crew sailors . . ."); Symonds, *Confederate Admiral*, 183 (quoting Buchanan: "There are on board . . ."); 182 (on uniforms); O'Brien, *Mobile, 1865*, 164 (quoting an officer: the men "never were backward").
29. Trickey, Holmes, and Clute, "Archaeological and Historical Investigations at Pinto Battery," 54–57 (on life at Gladden); 55 (on the New Year's Eve celebration); Still, *Iron Afloat*, 200 (quoting the Rebel webfoot, "We are in four watches," and on the shipboard ball); 54 (on the church services).
30. Saltus and Schell, *The* CSS Huntsville *and* CSS Tuscaloosa, 13–16; *Mobile Evening News*, August 10, 1863.
31. Still, "The Confederate States Navy at Mobile," 133 (on the *Tennessee's* launch).
32. Symonds, *Confederate Admiral*, 191 (on the construction of the *Tennessee*); Friend, *West Wind, Flood Tide*, 42–44 (description of the *Tennessee* and quoting Cumming); Symonds, *Confederate Admiral*, 200 (the crew as "hard characters").
33. *New York Times*, March 9, 1865; Corsan, *Two Months in the Confederate States*, 51–52.
34. *Oreg.*, vol. 2, p. 197 (act for the "enrollment of the 'Creole Guards'"); 941 (Maury's plea); Bergeron, *Confederate Mobile*, 106 (quoting Seddon); 113–14 (von Scheliha's proposal).
35. Bergeron, *Confederate Mobile*, 138–39 (on Farragut's fleet); Trickey, Holmes, and Clute, "Archaeological and Historical Investigations at Pinto Battery," 55 (quoting the Battery Gladden officer).

Chapter 6: Rebel Defeat

1. South Carolina Geographic Alliance, "The *Hunley*," 17. See also Schell, "Submarine Weapons," 164–65.
2. Chaffin, *The* H. L. Hunley, 18–19 (on Hunley); 39–40 (on McClintock and Watson); 74–76 (regarding the letter of marque).
3. Ibid., 87–88, 148. On the Park and Lyons Machine Shop, see also O'Brien, "Where Was the *Hunley* Built?," 38.
4. Chaffin, *The* H. L. Hunley, 90–92 (on the *American Diver*); see also Wills, "The *H. L. Hunley* in Historical Context," http://www.history.navy.mil/branches/org12–7b.htm (accessed April 1, 2013).
5. Chaffin, *The* H. L. Hunley, 93, 96–97.
6. Ibid., 100–102.
7. O'Brien, "Where Was the *Hunley* Built?," 32–33 (on the Seamen's Bethel and the little boy); Chaffin, *The* H. L. Hunley, 111 (quoting the Rebel deserter).
8. Alexander, "Thrilling Chapter," 165; Schell, "Submarine Weapons," 175 (Alexander's sketch); Chaffin, *The* H. L. Hunley, 107–8 (construction); 232 (appearance and design).
9. Chaffin, *The H. L.* Hunley, 108–9, 232–33.
10. O'Brien, "Where Was the *Hunley* Built?," 33 (getting the vessel out of the bethel); Chaffin, *The H. L. Hunley*, 112–13 (on the river tests and quoting Buchanan); 117 (quoting the army lieutenant); Bak, *The CSS* Hunley, 53 (on the July 31 test). Bak's title is an error; the *Hunley* was never officially a Confederate states vessel and never had the CSS prefix.
11. *ORN*, vol. 21, pp. 902–3 (quoting Jones); 748 (spy).
12. O'Brien, *Mobile, 1865*, 162–63 (on the *St. Patrick* and the attack); *ORN*, vol. 22, pp. 267–69 (quoting Maury and his superior). See also Schell, "Submarine Weapons," 179–80, and Perry, *Infernal Machines*, 183–84.
13. Bergeron, *Confederate Mobile*, 101–2.
14. Ibid., 115; *Mobile Register*, August 8, 1862; Sexton, *A Southern Woman of Letters*, 100–101

(on Evans); Arnold, *The Denbigh's Civilian Imports,* 49 (on the liquor).

15. Bergeron, *Confederate Mobile,* 116 (on the *Denbigh* as "the mail-packet"); Powell, Cordon, and Arnold, *Civil War Blockade Runners,* 14 (describing the *Denbigh*); Wise, *Lifeline of the Confederacy,* 305 (describing the *Heroine*); *ORN,* vol. 20, p. 753 (on the *Grey Jacket*).
16. Bergeron, *Confederate Mobile,* 115–16; McKenna, *British Ships in the Confederate Navy,* 237 (quoting Farragut).
17. Bergeron, *Confederate Mobile,* 118–19; Maffitt, *The Life and Services of John Newland Maffitt,* 252–55 (quotations).
18. Maffitt, *The Life and Services of John Newland Maffitt,* 256 (quoting Buchanan); 261 (on adulation for Maffitt); Shingleton, *High Seas Confederate,* 52 (the *Oneida* captain's "great mortification," Welles's downfall).
19. Ibid., 266 (on Buchanan's suggestion); 267–69 (on the run out). Light House Island refers to the Sand Island Lighthouse, built in 1838 on a sandy island several miles off Fort Morgan. The lighthouse was destroyed in 1863, and a new one built in the 1870s that still stands, though it is no longer in use. The island has been eroded and its original four hundred acres reduced to a small mound of rocks and riprap surrounding the lighthouse base. Bergeron, *Confederate Mobile,* 118 (quoting Porter); Shingleton, *High Seas Confederate,* 54 (quoting Semmes).
20. *ORN,* vol. 20, pp. 752–53 (on pursuit and capture of the *Grey Jacket*); Wallace, *Cases Argued and Adjudged in The Supreme Court,* 343 (on the *Grey Jacket*'s cargo).
21. Wallace, *Cases Argued and Adjudged in The Supreme Court,* 343–44.
22. Ibid., 344–46.
23. *ORN,* vol. 21, p. 934 (on commissioning the *Tennessee*); Rix, *Incidents of Life in a Southern City,* 3.
24. *ORN,* vol. 21, pp. 934–35; Rix, *Incidents of Life in a Southern City,* 3.
25. *ORN,* vol. 21, pp. 935; Still, *Iron Afloat,* 201 (quoting Buchanan).
26. Symonds, *Confederate Admiral,* 202 (quoting Buchanan); Friend, *West Wind, Flood Tide,* 168 (quoting Farragut). The closest I have ever come to any living memory of the battle occurred decades ago, when I met an old man who, when he was a youth, had known an old man, who as a boy had been tonging oysters with his father just north and east of Fort Morgan on that August morning. At the sound of the first gun, the father declared, "They're shootin' boy! We'd better get home!"
27. Friend, *West Wind, Flood Tide,* 165–67; 168 (quotations).
28. Ibid., 171 (on the first shot); ix (Farragut on the "most desperate" battle); Hearn, *Admiral David Glasgow Farragut,* 263 ("Damn the torpedoes . . .").
29. Ibid, 184–85 (on the girls); O'Brien, *Mobile, 1865,* 17.
30. Hearn, *Admiral David Glasgow Farragut,* 272–80 (on the battle); Rix, *Incidents of Life in a Southern City,* 3 ("musket wad or popgun pellet" quotation); Hearn, *Admiral David Glasgow Farragut,* 282 (the *Manhattan*'s shot); 287 (on the casualties).
31. Friend, *West Wind, Flood Tide,* 231; *Mobile Register,* June 5, 1902 (the *Morgan*'s captain as a "timid man"; the "*Morgan* going to town").
32. *Mobile Register,* June 5, 1902 ("a regular conflagration of gunpowder"); Friend, *West Wind, Flood Tide,* 233 (on the *Morgan*'s run); *Mobile Register,* June 5, 1902 (the *Morgan* with "colors flying").
33. Trickey, Holmes, and Clute, "Archaeological and Historical Investigations at Pinto Battery," 54 (on Maury's preparations); Bergeron, *Confederate Mobile,* 153 (on Farrand); 102 (on impressing the steamers).
34. Hearn, *Admiral David Glasgow Farragut,* 297 (Farragut's letter to his wife); Trickey et al., "Archaeological and Historical Investigations at Pinto Battery," 54 (quoting Mumford's diary); *ORN,* vol. 21, p. 787 (on the *Chickasaw*); Rix, *Incidents of Life in a Southern City,* 17 (on the *Morgan*'s "bark"); von Scheliha, *A Treatise on Coast Defense,* 157 (Farragut to Welles); Bergeron, *Confederate Mobile,* 156 (quoting Rix on Farragut's fleet and the "Green Mountain Range").
35. Hearn, *Admiral David Glasgow Farragut,* 301–3.
36. O'Brien, *Mobile, 1865,* 31 (on Canby); 34 (Canby's strategy); 169 (the fleet); Gratwick, *Mainers in the Civil War,* 58–59 (on Thatcher).
37. Bergeron, *Confederate Mobile,* 174 (on Maury's strength); 170 (the commander's aversion to

"strenuous" service); O'Brien, *Mobile, 1865,* 44–45 (on Gibson); 53 (Gibson to his men: "dig"); 83–85 (on Liddell); 68 (on Blakeley's strength); 69 (Blakeley as a "pretty village").

38. Trickey, Holmes, and Clute, "Archaeological and Historical Investigations at Pinto Battery," 58–59 (on Mumford); O'Brien, *Mobile, 1865,* 147 (the Union line as "one blaze"); Rix, *Incidents of Life in a Southern City,* 18 (on the houses shaking).
39. Waterman, "Afloat, Afield, Afloat," 25–26.
40. *Mobile Register,* November 1, 1914 (quotations of Cox); Rix, *Incidents of Life in a Southern City,* 18 (quotations of Rix); O'Brien, *Mobile, 1865,* 180 (on the evacuation and the quotation describing the "Pell-mell scramble").
41. Trickey, Holmes, and Clute, "Archaeological and Historical Investigations at Pinto Battery," 60 (on Mumford); O'Brien, *Mobile, 1865,* 202 (casualties); 199 (black troops); 233 (quoting Grant).
42. Trickey, Holmes, and Clute, "Archaeological and Historical Investigations at Pinto Battery," 60–61 (on Mumford); Bergeron, *Confederate Mobile,* 190 (on the evacuation).
43. Rix, *Incidents of Life in a Southern City,* 19–22.
44. *ORN,* vol. 21, pp. 92–94 (on the surrender); *Mobile Register,* November 1, 1914 (Cox); Porter, *The Naval History of the Civil War,* 782 (on the mayor's response).
45. *Mobile Register,* November 1, 1914 (on the appearance of the troops); Delaney, *Confederate Mobile,* 320 (quoting the letter of a disgusted Southerner); Bergeron, *Confederate Mobile,* 191 (quoting Cox); Rix, *Incidents of Life in a Southern City,* 23.
46. *ORN,* vol. 22, pp. 95–96 (on spoils); Bergeron, *Confederate Mobile,* 192 (quoting the newspaper reporter); Cumming, *Gleanings,* 257, 259.
47. *ORN,* vol. 22, pp. 95–96 (on clearing torpedoes); 96 (on the losses); O'Brien, *Mobile, 1865,* 170 (quoting the *Ida* sailor); *ORN,* vol. 22, pp. 130–32 (reports of torpedo damage).
48. Rix, *Incidents of Life in a Southern City,* 24.
49. O'Brien, *Mobile, 1865,* 209–14.
50. Waterman, "Afloat, Afield, Afloat," 24–25; Cameron, "The Battles Opposite Mobile," 306–8.
51. Cameron, "The Battles Opposite Mobile," 307.
52. Smith, *The People's City,* 212–13 (in Demopolis); Cameron, "The Battles Opposite Mobile," 308.
53. O'Brien, *Mobile, 1865,* 217–19.
54. Waterman, "Afield, Afloat, Afield," 27; Scharf, *History of the Confederate States Navy,* 596 (on the parole); *ORN,* vol. 22, p. 180 (on the surrender); Cameron, "The Battles Opposite Mobile," 308 (on the surrender), 307 (Cameron spots Sam again).
55. *ORN,* vol. 22, pp. 225–29 (reports on the vessels); Diouf, *Dreams of Africa in Alabama,* 166–67 (on Meaher).
56. Bailey, "Mobile's Tragedy," 41–42.
57. Ibid., 42 (quoting Hamilton); 43–45 (on the damage); Delaney, *Confederate Mobile,* 340 (the scene at the Battle House); *ORN,* vol. 22, pp. 200–201 (on the *Cowslip*'s actions).
58. *New York World,* June 5, 1865 ("Not a warehouse . . . left standing"); Bailey, "Mobile's Tragedy," 46–47.
59. Bailey, "Mobile's Tragedy," 44 (quotations), 48 (property losses).

Chapter 7: "Mobile Harbor: What shall we do with it?"

1. The *Hartford*'s visit is detailed in the *Mobile Register,* June 4, 1902. There are at least twenty-seven versions of Farragut's famous command. Given the noise and confusion of battle, his exact words were uncertain.
2. For Fort Morgan's "frowning ramparts," ibid. On the waterfront, see Joint Rivers and Harbor Committee. *Report of Sub-Committee on Harbor Improvement,* 7; and Sanborn Fire Insurance Map, 1904, plates 1–4, 7, 9, 10, 12, 89.
3. Thomason, *Mobile: The New History,* 155 (population); 158–59 (imports, exports); 160–61 (services); 166 (black Mobile). See also "Mobile," *The Encyclopedia Britannica,* vol. 18, New York: The Encyclopeida Britannica Company, 1911: 635-36.
4. *Mobile Register,* June 5, 1902. See also *The Encyclopedia Britannica 1911,* vol. 18, p. 636 (channel depth).
5. Report, in *Message from the President,* 521–27 (Chase's report); Captain Winsor to Magouin & Son, April 17, 1840, Delano/Magouin Papers ("a very tedious place"); Bache,

Preliminary Sketch of Mobile Bay (sailing instructions).

6. Report, in *Message from the President,* 522–23.
7. Ibid., 524–27.
8. "Albert Stein: Pioneer of City Water Supply," 18 (jetties idea); 20–21 (Mobile waterworks); see also O'Brien, "Albert Stein," *Encyclopedia of Alabama,* http://www.encyclopediaofalabama.org/face/Article.jsp?id=h-3056 (accessed June 7, 2013).
9. *Mobile Register,* September 20, 1874 (Stein's obituary). The Stein portrait hangs in the History Museum of Mobile. The artist is unknown.
10. Ibid. (quotation from Stein's obituary); Weber, "Mobile Harbor," 14 (on the twenty-five-thousand-dollar payment).
11. Stein, *Report on the Improvement of the Mobile River and Bay,* 11.
12. Ibid., 7 (quotation describing the "evils" of the Mobile River's condition); 6, 8 (on the issues); 16 (the measurements).
13. Ibid., 11–13.
14. *Mobile Register,* July 11, 1860 (on the dredging contract); *Acts of the Seventh Biennial Session of the General Assembly of Alabama,* 535–46 (the Board of Harbor Commissioners).
15. Weber, "Mobile Harbor," 13 (on shoaling); Merrill, "Report on the Present Condition of the Harbor of Mobile," 52–55.
16. Chester, *Transatlantic Sketches,* 221 (quoting the English scientist); Reid, *After the War,* 205. Like several other visitors to Mobile, Reid referred to "levees" downtown. However, because of the delta, downtown never had built-up levees like New Orleans, and visitors' use of the term simply meant the immediate waterfront.
17. *Mobile Daily News,* July 6, 1865; Diard Ironwork Ledgers, vol. 1, p. 235 ("The times . . . are in a bad fix").
18. Otto, *Cases Argued and Adjudged in the Supreme Court,* 692 (on the Alabama Harbor Board); "Interesting Transcriptions from the City Documents," 1820–1911, 267–69.
19. First National Bank, *Highlights of 100 Years in Mobile,* 16–17 (on Reese's proposals). See also Weber, "Mobile Harbor," 14.
20. Simpson, "Annual Report, 1872," 576 (Bragg to Simpson, State Harbor Board plans); 606–7 (Bragg to State Harbor Board); New South Associates, *From Alluvium to Commerce,* 173 (on maps and the elimination of old wharves).
21. *Mobile Register,* July 12, 1871.
22. Simpson, "Annual Report, 1872," 576 (quoting Simpson's complaint); 602 (Bragg on dredging).
23. Ibid., 576 (on the board of engineers); 577 (quoting Simpson).
24. *Mobile Register,* January 26–February 10, 1872 (on the winter weather); February 10–18, 1872 (Bahia's series). On the probable identity of Bahia, see Weber, "Mobile Harbor," 14. Bragg could have also been Bahia, but given Stein's training and long history of pamphleteering, he is the more likely candidate. No one ever publicly claimed to be Bahia.
25. *Mobile Register,* February 10, 1872 ("It would be a waste of words to argue"; "If the writer can fling a single ray of light"); February 13, 1872 ("subaqueous excavations"); February 15, 1872 ("The trouble is"; "What I know"); February 18, 1872 ("Its details may be varied").
26. Grant, *Improvement of the Harbor, Bay and River of Mobile,* 2–3; *Mobile Register,* February 24, 1872 (Stein as "the great hydraulic engineer"; describing the current departed from "those artificial works").
27. Simpson, "Annual Report, 1872," 590–97 (engineers' panel report).
28. Ibid., 578–80.
29. Stein, *Brief Notes on the Report of the Board of U.S. Engineers,* 7 (the federal engineers as "ignorant"); Weber, "Mobile Harbor," 16 (abolition of the State Harbor Board); Davis, *A History of the Mobile District,* 42.
30. Davis, *A History of the Mobile District,* 45 (appropriations); Damrell, "Annual Report, 1873," 692 (material dredged); Davis, "Damrell's Ditch," 25 (local scorn of Damrell).
31. Damrell, "Annual Report, 1873," 693 (reporting on "the usual winter freshet"); 694 (port statistics); Davis, *A History of the Mobile District,* 45 (increasing channel depths); Land, *Mobile: Her Trade, Commerce and Industries,* 2 ("Full rigged ships and ocean steamers"); *Mobile Register,* June 27, 1909 (obituary).
32. McLaurin and Thomason, *Mobile: The Life and Times of a Great Southern City,* 80 (cotton exports); "Memorandum of Research

Regarding CSX Main Line," 5 (1869 ordinance); Jones, *Reports of Cases Argued,* 415 (work gangs); Reynolds, *Sketches of Mobile,* 22 ("a noble commercial avenue").

33. McLaurin and Thomason, *Mobile: The Life and Times of a Great Southern City,* 78–79.

Chapter 8: Modern Port, Beleaguered River

1. "Big Time Down in Mobile," 18. Frascati was a public park situated on the bay south of Choctaw Point. Founded in 1867, it was a popular resort for white Mobilians until the hurricane of 1893 destroyed it. Afterward the site was called Frascati Shops and was used by railroads for maintenance of rolling stock. Hence the reference to the "Wild Man . . . Stealing Cars." For an excellent history of the park, see the blog "Climbing the Branches of My Family Tree," by Susan Thomas, http://climbingthebranches.blogspot.com/2011/10/saturdays-structures-frascati-park.html (accessed July 4, 2013). The dishes the Hoo-Hoos enjoyed at their banquet are not named in the article, but an example of the Cawthon's fare may be gleaned from a 1912 menu that lists crab-flake cocktail in bell peppers, tenderloin of trout, filet mignon with mushrooms, duchess potatoes, green peas, asparagus tips, ice cream, and cake. See "M.E.B.A. No. 14," 34.
2. On Hoo-Hoo history, see "Concatenated Order of Hoo-Hoo," *Encyclopedia of Arkansas History & Culture,* http://www.encyclopediaofarkansas.net/encyclopedia/entry-detail.aspx?entryID=1199&type=Category&item=Organizations+and+Civic+Leaders (accessed July 4, 2013). On early twentieth century Mobile architecture, see Gould, *From Fort to Port,* 234–47.
3. McLaurin and Thomason, *Mobile: The Life and Times of a Great Southern City,* 81 (lumber capacity); Morrison, *Mobile: The New South,* 57 (quoting the Yankee visitor); Jervey, "Report to the Joint Rivers and Harbor Committee of Mobile," 1910 (the creeks as advantages); Cram and Cram, *Old Seaport Towns,* 268 (on the visiting couple's experience); *Lumber Trade Journal,* July 1, 1913, 12 (on the tall ships' cargoes). My father watched lumber schooners in the bay and gulf during his youth and intrigued me with stories of these memories when I was growing up.
4. *Mobile Register,* March 25, 1911 (activity on the waterfront). The newspaper did not specify whether the steamboat was the *John Quill* or the *Nettie Quill.* Named for a steamboat captain and his wife, both boats were active on local waterways at the time. The *Nettie Quill* was moved over to New Orleans in 1914, and the *John Quill* sank just south of Twelve Mile Island in 1929. See Ward, *The Tombigbee River Steamboats,* especially chapter 10, which lists the steamboats that plied the Tombigbee and Mobile Rivers. On exports, see *Mobile Register,* January 26, 1926.
5. "The ADDSCO Story," 9–12. See also "Alabama Dry Dock and Shipbuilding Company," *Encyclopedia of Alabama,* http://www.encyclopediaofalabama.org/face/Article.jsp?id=h-1475 (accessed July 4, 2013), and "New Floating Dry Dock Built at Mobile," 216. There is a wonderful aerial sketch of the island on p. 214.
6. "Mobile's Rich Tradition," 28–29 (describing Chickasaw). See also "Mobile's Piers in the Bridge to France," 1185. The Chickasaw Shipyard Village Historic District was placed on the National Register of Historic Places in 2004.
7. Thomason, *Mobile: The New History,* 185 (on Waterman Steamship Corporation). See also "Building an Essential Trade Route," 3. The Mobile Rivers and Harbors Committee that Waterman served on was formed by the state legislature in the 1880s and did not bear relationship to the State Harbor Board of 1867. Its organization and charge were nearly identical, however. Waterman sat on the committee because he was president of the chamber of commerce at that time, and the slot went with the office. See Owen, *History of Alabama and Dictionary of Alabama Biography,* vol. 2, 1030.
8. "Statement before U.S. Engineers," December 21, 1925 (driftwood and logs in the channel); Glennon, "State Docks Site," 12–13 (on Farmer's Island). Farmer's Island was only just an island, being separated from the mainland by a narrow branch feeding into One Mile Creek. The sawdust road evolved into Telegraph Road, or Highway 43.

9. A. G. Ward to the Mobile City Commission, October 6, 1916 (letter); McLaurin and Thomason, *Mobile: The Life and Times of a Great Southern City*, 110 (early efforts toward a state-owned port facility; Rivers and Harbors Appropriation Bill).
10. Glennon, "State Docks Site," 1. See also "Alabama State Docks Celebrates 40th Anniversary," 17–18.
11. *Atlanta Constitution*, December 11, 1927. See also "Alabama State Docks Celebrates 40th Anniversary," 18.
12. *Atlanta Constitution*, December 11, 1927. See also "Alabama State Docks Celebrates 40th Anniversary," 19.
13. *Mobile Register*, May 13, 1928. See also Davis, "Work Starts on Port Development," 1024–25, for detailed descriptions of the piers, sheds, and other facilities.
14. *Mobile Register*, June 26, 1928 (all quotations). See also "Alabama State Docks Celebrates 40th Anniversary," 21.
15. Waterman, "Mobile's Port Record," November 28, 1934; Board of Engineers for Rivers and Harbors, *Port Series No. 3*, pp. 5, 7, 158 (1930s port facts). It is interesting that during the Alabama State Docks dedication no one wondered what Mobile's early French founders would have thought about all the progress. Bienville in particular had a keen interest in linking with streams and regions to the north.
16. McLaurin and Thomason, *Mobile: The Life and Times of a Great Southern City*, 111–12. See also Thomason, *Mobile: The New History*, 186–87.
17. Thomason, *Mobile: The New History*, 187–89 (construction of the Bankhead Tunnel); *Mobile Register*, February 2, 1941 (statistics).
18. *Mobile Register*, February 2, 1941 (on the tunnel's opening day); Higginbotham, *Mobile: City by the Bay*, 235 (Tallulah Bankhead story). See Walter, *Milking the Moon*, 65 (on postcards as souvenirs). Boykin was a notorious womanizer, but one suspects that Tallulah Bankhead more than held her own with him.
19. Thomason, *Mobile: The New History*, 211 (population of Mobile); Ward, *The War*, 88 (Mobile's key assets).
20. Ward, *The War*, 88, 94.
21. McLaurin and Thomason, *Mobile: The Life and Times of a Great City*, 127 (on the influx of "riffraff"; workers as "the lowest type of poor whites"); Ward, *The War*, 95.
22. Thomason, *Mobile: The New History*, 218 (on Herbert Aaron); Ward, *The War*, 95–96 (on John Gray; quoting the white laborer).
23. "Mobile's Rich Tradition," 30–31; see also Thomas, "The Mobile Homefront," 57 (ship production).
24. Thomason, *Mobile: The New History*, 186 (on Alcoa); *Mobile Register*, June 25, 2013 (Alcoa production); Thomason, *Mobile: The New History*, 235 (on the U-boat attack).
25. Before he enlisted, my father recalled seeing a British freighter in Mobile with a hole in her hull big enough to drive a truck through. Thomason, *Mobile: The New History*, 236–37 (on the blackouts). The Alabama-born writer Mark Childress wrote a 1989 novel *V for Victor* (Knopf), about a Nazi submarine in Mobile Bay. In reality, of course, the bay is so shallow that a World War II Nazi submarine would have been forced to travel on the surface and probably stick to the ship channel. There was no chance of this happening in wartime.
26. Thomason, *Mobile: The New History*, 244 (on the layoffs); *Mobile Register*, February 3, 1949 (assets purchased by ADDSCO); "Alabama Dry Dock and Shipbuilding Company (ADDSO)," *Encyclopedia of Alabama*, http://www.encyclopediaofalabama.org/face/Article.jsp?id=h-1475 (accessed July 10, 2013).
27. Thomason, *Mobile: The New History*, 244; *Pittsburgh Post-Gazette*, August 31, 1946; *Mobile Register*, November 24, 2006 (move to Tensaw River, disposal of ghost ships). During a Baldwin County historic building survey in 1985, I happened upon the abandoned Ghost Fleet infrastructure—concrete piers extending into the Tensaw River, gutted and graffiti-marred ancillary buildings and an overgrown parking area. It was reached by a long road and was deserted and slightly spooky.
28. Thomason, *Mobile: The New History*, 277 (*Fortune* magazine quotation); 281 (port ranking); 300 (the Tenn-Tom Waterway);

Mobile Register, December 16, 17, 2001 (quoting Boykin); General Services Administration, *Public Papers of the Presidents*, 659 (Nixon's remarks).

29. "Tenn-Tom Waterway," 14 (on the locks); *Mobile Register*, December 16, 17, 2001. See also, "Tennessee-Tombigbee Waterway," *Encyclopedia of Alabama*, http://www.encyclopediaofalabama.org/face/Article.jsp?id=h-2365 (accessed July 13, 2013).
30. Jackson, *Rivers of History*, 219.
31. McGehee, "Ask McGehee," 92 (quotations); Thomason, *Mobile: The New History*, 294–95 (on urban renewal); Nicholas Holmes Jr., e-mail to the author, July 11, 2013.
32. Thomason, *Mobile: The New History*, 292, 300 (tunnel and parkway improvements); 318 (suburban development).
33. "About General W. K. Wilson Bridge," https://www.facebook.com/pages/General-WK-Wilson-Jr-Bridge/112866822060298 (accessed July 13, 2013).
34. "Coalition against a Raised Expressway," http://law.justia.com/cases/federal/appellate-courts/F2/835/803/296813/ (accessed July 13, 2013). My first years as an architectural historian with the Mobile Historic Development Commission coincided with this battle, and I observed much of it firsthand. My grandmother was a determined opponent of the "One two ten," as she referred to the highway's I-210 designation. Today the raised portion north of downtown is called I-165. Despite the hopes of those who campaigned for an exit in Prichard, one of Alabama's poorest cities, the road has had little economic impact there.
35. Alabama Department of Transportation, "Environmental Assessment," 5 (plans); Appendix A-1 (MHDC resolution); Drago, "Bridging the Divide," http://www.mobilebaytimes.com/bridge.html (accessed July 13, 2013).
36. McLaurin and Thomason, *Mobile: The Life and Times of a Great Southern City*, 139 (on the McDuffie Coal Terminal); "Port of Mobile," *Encyclopedia of Alabama*, http://www.encyclopediaofalabama.org/face/Article.jsp?id=h-3196 (accessed July 13, 2013) (Choctaw Point Terminal); "Mobile Gets First Post Panamax Ship Call," http://article.wn.com/view/2012/06/04/Mobile__Gets_First__PostPanamax__Ship__Call/#/related__news (accessed July 13, 2013).
37. "Southeast Shipyards Mobile," http://www.thisismyshipyard.com/your-locations/southeast-shipyards-mobile/ (accessed July 13, 2013) (BAE); "Welcome to the World of ThyssenKrupp Steel," http://www.thyssenkruppsteelusa.com/ (accessed July 13, 2013); "Austal USA shipbuilding," http://www.austal.com/us/home.aspx (accessed July 13, 2013); *Mobile Register*, October 28, 2011 (railroad bridge).
38. Alverson, *History of the Water Supply*, 12 (British surgeon's observation); Gould, *From Fort to Port*, 8 (see map); Alsobrook, "Alabama's Port City," 15 (on sewage backing up); *Professional Memoirs*, 16 (quotation describing the state of the river).
39. *Mobile Register*, July 15, 1938 (quotation).
40. Ibid., September 21, 1956 (Barry Steam Plant statistics); January 12, 1999 (rise in water temperature); March 18, 2010 (continued mercury emissions); February 19, 2012 (switch to natural gas).
41. Ibid., May 20, 2001; "Stauffer Chemical Co. (Cold Creek Plant)," http://www.epa.gov/region4/superfund/sites/npl/alabama/stacocreal.html (accessed July 14, 2013).
42. Friend, *Alabama Coastal Region Ecological Characterization*, 118–19; "MAWSS Facilities," http://www.mawss.com/facilities2.html (accessed July 14, 2013) (sewage treatment plants); "Dishonorable Discharge: The Fifty Most Polluted Rivers in the Country," http://www.ewg.org/research/dishonorable-discharge/50-most-polluted-rivers-country (accessed July 14, 2013).
43. *Mobile Register*, December 20, 1998 (on Blakeley Island); December 11, 1969 (describing Three Mile Creek).
44. Thomason, *Mobile: The New History*, 307 (on Mobil Oil); Wade, Plater, and Kelley, *History of Coastal Alabama Natural Gas Exploration*, 5–6 (on the drilling permit; quotation describing the rules); *Mobile Register*, September 7, 2011.
45. Mobile Baykeeper website, http://www.mobilebaykeeper.org/ (accessed July 14,

2013); *Mobile Register,* September 7, 2009 (Three Mile Creek).

46. *Mobile Register,* December 20, 1998 (quoting Kelly); David Cooper, personal interview, September 27, 2012; recent EPA report, "Watershed Assessment, Tracking and Environmental Results," http://iaspub.epa.gov/tmdl__waters10/attains__waterbody.control?p__list__id=AL03160204-0505-100&p__state=Ala.&p__cycle=2010 (2010 EPA report).

Chapter 9: "Everything down there's big enough to kill you"

1. Pickens, *Acts Passed at the Fourth Annual Session of the General Assembly of the State of Alabama,* 106–12, 109 (quoting the 1822 General Assembly act); Mansfield, "An Onerous and Unnecessary Burden," 15 (on reporting free black men); *The Charter and Code of Ordinances of the City of Mobile,* 1889, 190 (regulating ballast disposal); 191 (numbering the wharves); "State Pilotage Commission," http://www.archives.state.al.us/officials/rdans/pilotage.html#__1__12 (accessed August 3, 2013) (transfer of pilots).
2. Terry Gilbreath, personal interview, August 1, 2013.
3. Blunt, *Shipmaster's Assistant,* 59 (on pilot duties); Hamilton, *Colonial Mobile,* 80, 259 (colonial pilots).
4. *Mobile Register,* March 19, 2000 (on Pilot Town); Oldmixon, *Transatlantic Wanderings,* 161 (the Pilot Town "public-house"); Blunt, *Shipmaster's Assistant,* 488 (pilotage fees).
5. Joe Ollinger, personal interview, January 10, 2013.
6. Patrick Wilson, personal interview, September 10. 2012; Reynolds, "Safeguarding a Perilous Harbor," 20 (quoting pilot Kirk Barrett); *Mobile Register,* August 6, 2006 (the *Nordic Svenita* incident).
7. Vincent George, personal interview, September 7, 2012.
8. Ibid. I not so fondly recall the old Club Royal and the sometimes revolting scenes that would spill onto the sidewalk there. One morning as I was walking to work, a drunken sailor and a black prostitute staggered out of the bar, laughing uncontrollably and animatedly blowing snot from their nostrils for entertainment.
9. Ibid.
10. Fox, "My Experiences as a Sailor," 5–6.
11. Goode, *The History and Present Condition of the Fishery Industries,* 196 (on boats and oyster production); United States Commission of Fish and Fisheries, *Report of the Commissioner for 1885,* 286 (on the catches of fish).
12. Goode, *The Fisheries and Fishery Industries of the United States,* 27.
13. Ziebach, *The Second Head of Chocalata,* 32–33.
14. Goode, *The History and Present Condition of the Fishery Industries,* 196.
15. Cresswell, *Oxford Dictionary of Word Origins,* 421 (*stevedore*); Almond, *Dictionary of Word Origins,* 155 (*longshoreman*).
16. Board of Engineers, *Port Series No. 3,* 1922, p. 35.
17. Voogd, *Race Riots and Resistance,* 71 (on the Colored Longshoreman's Benevolent Association); Woodrum, "'The Past Has Taught Us a Lesson,'" 101–2 (black workers' situation in 1900); 123 (black local unions); Board of Engineers, *Port Series No. 3,* 1922, pp. 36–37 (work hours and wages); 41–42 (men, tools).
18. Woodrum, "'The Past Has Taught Us a Lesson,'" 101 (dangers working with logs); "A Full Day's Work," 12 (1963 quotations).
19. McLaurin and Thomason, *Mobile: The Life and Times of a Great Southern City,* 182–83.
20. David Cooper, e-mail to the author, September 27, 2012 (on Angus Cooper's early days); McLaurin and Thomason, *Mobile: The Life and Times of a Great Southern City,* 163 (firm history); David Cooper, personal interview, September 27, 2012 (all quotations).
21. *Mobile Register,* July 13, 1956 (McLean as "aggressive"); Mayo and Nohria, *In Their Time,* 203 (Quoting McLean: "I had to wait"), 204–7.
22. Walter, *Milking the Moon,* 10; *Atlanta Journal and Constitution,* July 6, 1992; Terkel, *And They All Sang,* 269 (quoting Rayford).
23. New South Associates, *From Alluvium to Commerce,* 153–57 (on Mobile's banana trade); 156 (Zemurray's sales); McCann, *An American Company,* 18 (Zemurray's first investment).

24. "Efficient Service to Tropics," 3; New South Associates, *From Alluvium to Commerce*, 157 (unloading the bananas).
25. Smith, *Gone to the Swamp*, 262 (on the gunboats).
26. Ibid., 22 (lumber industry peak); Romans, *A Concise Natural History*, 211–12 (early cedar raft); 182 (production of barrel staves); Eisterhold, "Mobile: Lumber Center," 89 (Deshon); Morrison, *Mobile: The New South*, 47 (1887 production); Edwards, *Proceedings*, 229 (helicopter logging).
27. *Mobile Register*, November 21, 1911 (bear episode); Smith, *Gone to the Swamp*, 25 (snakes and other perils); 253–73 (logging glossary).
28. McKinstry, *Code of Ordinances*, 350–51; Joe Ollinger, personal interview, January 10, 2013.
29. Harrison, "Riveters," 43 (women welders); *Mobile Register*, July 13, 2013 (Zaddie Johnson); Harrison, "Riveters," 43 (Women's Counseling Service).
30. Smith, *Gone to the Swamp*, 12–13; "Goat Island," 5.
31. *Mobile Register*, August 28, 2011, and May 14, 2012 (Dooley); April 16, 1996 (Hamblins).

CHAPTER 10: Pleasure and Peril

1. *Mobile Daily Commercial Register*, January 2, 1839; *Mobile Register*, December 21, 1909 (report on *Power Boat* magazine article).
2. *Circus Scrap Book*, 19–20 (reprints *Gleason's*). See also McLaurin and Thomason, *Mobile: The Life and Times of a Great Southern City*, 46.
3. Rayford, *Cottonmouth*, 6; McDonald, *One Man's Message*, 27–28 (house); 30–31 (incidents on the water).
4. *Mobile Register*, September 7, 11, 1911 (Miss Lottie Mayer); Noel Andry Sr., personal interview, June 20, 2012 (Chastang swimming pool).
5. *Mobile Register*, May 27, 1866; *Blue Book*, 2 (quotation); 15 (Mansion of Aching Hearts); 17 (Palace of Palms); 33 (Madam Rosa Lee); Walter, *Milking the Moon*, 7–8. By the late twentieth century downtown gay bars became popular sites for sexual assignations. Among the most visible was the Golden Rod, at the corner of Conti and Joachim, gone many years now. When I first arrived in Mobile in 1985, my grandmother and I would go to dinner at Rousso's on Royal Street, and afterward she wanted me to drive her by the Club Royal and up Conti so she could watch the action on the sidewalks and profess mock horror at the various racial and sexual combinations gathered there. After one or two such tours, my interest in Mobile vice was pretty well satiated. It all struck me as sad more than anything else—desperate, lonely, hurting people looking for love.
6. Alsobrook, "Alabama's Port City," 314 (lower Conti Street); Walter, *The Untidy Pilgrim*, 83–84.
7. Rayford, *Cottmouth*, 6 (Spanish Alley); 7 (quotation); Joe Ollinger, personal interview, January 10, 2013 (Monkey Wrench Corner). I grew up hearing stories about Monkey Wrench Corner at the dinner table.
8. Pickett, *History of Alabama*, 360–63. See also Bossu, *Travels*, 324–25.
9. Morris, *Wanderings of a Vagabond*, 462 (1840s visitor); "Interesting Transcriptions from the City Documents," 1820-1911, 46 (stick incident); "Interesting Transcriptions from the Mayor's Court," November 29, 1821, n.p. (Chandler and Sarage); *Mobile Daily Advertiser*, August 26, 1859 (sailors cursing the mate).
10. Shepherd, *Cases Argued and Determined in the Supreme Court of Alabama*, 1859, 381–87.
11. *Mobile Register*, January 20, 1912; Woodrum, "The Past Has Taught Us a Lesson," 131–34 (black longshoremen).
12. Nelson, "Organized Labor," 952, 978–79 (riot); Bernstein, "The Story of a Race Riot" (quotations); LeFlore to Marshall, telegram, May 27, 1943; *Mobile Register*, May 26, 1943 (sign posted by federal troops).
13. *Mobile Register*, May 26, 28, 1943 (black ministers' group; editorial); Thomas, "The Mobile Homefront," 71 (creation of a segregated yard).
14. Bossu, *Travels*, 227; *Mobile Daily Advertiser*, January 20, 1860 (Myers); *Mobile Register*, December 11, 1909 (Hoskins); June 8, 1909 (the blind horse).
15. Desty, *The Federal Reporter*, vols. 19–20, pp. 741–42.

16. Ibid., 743–47.
17. Ibid., vol. 115, pp. 1001–3; *Mobile Register,* January 21, 1900 (quotations).
18. Key, "A Camp Man," 76–77.
19. Desty, *The Federal Reporter,* vol. 123, pp. 667–71.
20. U. S. National Transportation Safety Board, "Railroad Marine Accident Report," http://www.ntsb.gov/investigations/summary/rar9401.htm (accessed September 2, 2013).
21. Ibid; *Mobile Register,* September 22, 1993 (quoting Grant and Boniface); September 23 (quoting Palmer and Healy).
22. U.S. National Transportation Safety Board, "Railroad Marine Accident Report," http://www.ntsb.gov/investigations/summary/rar9401.htm (accessed September 2, 2013) (event times); *Mobile Register,* September 23, 1993 (quoting EMT and diver); September 22 (governor's comments).
23. U.S. National Transportation Safety Board, "Railroad Marine Accident Report," http://www.ntsb.gov/investigations/summary/rar9401.htm (accessed September 2, 2013).
24. *Mobile Register,* February 14 and April 3, 2013.
25. Romans, *A Concise Natural History,* 14 (the heat causing "abundant perspiration"); 10–11 (fleeing to plantations upriver); 230, 238 (fevers); 239 (preventative measures); 249 (other diseases); 247 (sunstroke).
26. *Public Health Reports,* 1872 (fumingation of bananas); "The Capitol Eye," 11 (quarantine station established).
27. *Mobile Register,* January 18, 1948 (buildings and operation); *Birmingham News,* December 24, 1995 (demolition).
28. Bemis, "Mount Vernon Arsenal/Searcy Hospital Complex," 10–11.
29. *Mobile Register,* May 28, 1902.
30. Kremer, *George Washington Carver,* 82 (pellagra); Smith, *Health Care Divided,* 150 (1967 report); Bemis "Mount Vernon Arsenal/Searcy Hospital Complex," 10–11 (describing Dr. Rowe).
31. *Mobile Commercial Register,* October 27, 1827. See also Sledge, *The Pillared City,* 26–27.
32. Gould, *From Fort to Port,* 77; "Interesting Transcriptions," 1820–1911, 473 (quotation).
33. *Mobile Commercial Register,* October 18, 1839. See also Sledge, *The Pillared City,* 78–81.
34. *Mobile Register and Journal,* June 1, 1843 (escaped slave's account); Pitts, *Life and Confessions,* 38–41 (Copeland's gang). See also Sledge, *The Pillared City,* 80–81.
35. McSwain, "Fire Hazards," 600 (start of the October 1890 fire; quotations mentioning the "grandest sight" and the "immense rope" of flame); *Mobile Register,* October 28, 1890 (the fire as "ugly and dangerous").
36. *Mobile Register,* October 28, 1890.
37. Ibid. October 28, 29, 1890. *New Orleans Picayune,* October 30, 1890. It is surprising that, given its spectacular nature and the huge number of witnesses, the 1890 fire is one of Mobile's least appreciated and remembered disasters. There are no known photographs of the devastation, and it is never referenced in modern conversation to the degree that the earlier fires and hurricanes of 1906 and 1916 are. It may lie in that odd limbo between widely known historical events, such as the 1827 and 1839 fires, and living memory, like those of many Mobilians' grandparents who vividly recalled the early-twentieth-century hurricanes. The 1890 event has been little written about and took place a bit too early to be in the memory cone of modern families.
38. Schwartz, *Hurricanes,* 60. There are several variations of this proverb; I have provided the one I most often heard in my youth.
39. Romans, *A Concise Natural History,* 5.
40. First National Bank of Mobile, *Highlights of 100 Years in Mobile,* 67–69; *Mobile Register,* September 28, 29, 1906 (all quotations).
41. *New York Times,* September 29, 1906.
42. First National Bank of Mobile, *Highlights of 100 Years,* 68; *Mobile Register,* July 7, 1916 (describing the "gangs of men and tugboats").
43. Thomason, *Mobile: The New History,* 301.
44. Curtis, *Hurricane Katrina,* 87–88; Bill Wilson, "Bridge Stands Up to Katrina," http://www.roadsbridges.com/bridge-stands-katrina (accessed September 8, 2013).

Chapter 11: Diverse Legacies

1. *Mobile Daily Advertiser,* October 17, 1855; *Clotilda* registration, April 19, 1855 History Museum of Mobile.

2. Diouf, *Dreams of Africa in Alabama,* 23 (Foster); for cargoes, see National Archives at Atlanta, "The *Clotilda:* A Finding Aid," http://www.archives.gov/atlanta/finding-aids/clotilda.pdf (accessed October 9, 2013).
3. Shepherd, *Cases Argued and Determined in the Supreme Court of Alabama,* 77–80; Diouf, *Dreams of Africa in Alabama,* 24 (Meaher buys schooner).
4. Ibid., 20–21.
5. Ibid., 24–25 (transformation of the *Clotilda*); 26–27 (crew). See also Robertson, *The Slave Ship Clotilda,* 31 (fitting out the ship).
6. Robertson, *The Slave Ship Clotilda,* 27–28.
7. Ibid., 43 (Kazoola); 44–45 (Kupollee); Byers, "The Last Slave Ship," 43 (Abacky).
8. Roche, *Historic Sketches,* 89 (quotation); 91 (green branches).
9. Diouf, *Dreams of Africa in Alabama,* 72–73.
10. *Mobile Register,* August 6, 1893 (Noah); Diouf, *Dreams of Africa in Alabama,* 73.
11. Diouf, *Dreams of Africa in Alabama,* 73–74.
12. Ibid., 75. For years, the *Clotilda*'s ribbing was visible at low tide, and Emma Langdon Roche even provided a picture of the wreck in her book, *Historic Sketches of the South.* During the late twentieth century several efforts were made to locate the wreck, and one study noted several promising anomalies in Bayou Canot. Foster himself said he towed the vessel into Canot, and Roche says so as well, though she misspells the name. The *Clotilda* will not be easy to identify even if found, given the profusion of historic wrecks up and down the river and its tributaries. See Krivor, "Remote-sensing Investigations," 23; Roche, *Historic Sketches,* 97 (she places it at the mouth of "Bayou Corne").
13. Diouf, *Dreams of Africa in Alabama,* 76–77; *Mobile Register,* August 6, 1893 (quoting Hart).
14. Diouf, *Dreams of Africa in Alabama,* 78 (press reports); 82 (slaves parceled out); *Mobile Register,* August 6, 1893 (Hart describing Timothy Meaher's joy).
15. Diouf, *Dreams of Africa in Alabama,* 86–87.
16. Ibid., 100; *Mobile Register,* August 6, 1893 (quoting Hart).
17. Diouf, *Dreams of Africa in Alabama,* 124–25.
18. Roche, *Historic Sketches,* 115–16.
19. Diouf, *Dreams of Africa in Alabama,* 155–56 (land purchases); Byers, "The Last Slave Ship," 742–43 (description of African Town and residents' customs).
20. *Mobile Register,* August 6, 1893.
21. Diouf, *Dreams of Africa in Alabama,* 181 (differences in ways of life); Alsobrook, "Alabama's Port City," 156–58 (Hickory Club).
22. Diouf, *Dreams of Africa in Alabama,* 225.
23. Ibid., 230.
24. Ibid., 237 (the surviving chimney); "Africatown Listed," http://www.nuzzapp.com/2012/12/18/africatown-listed-on-historic-place-registry/ (accessed October 12, 2013). During my career with the Mobile Historic Development Commission I have been involved with several of these efforts, and I recount them here based on memory.
25. Fitzgerald, *Urban Emancipation,* 10–11. Fitzgerald rightly notes the differences and occasional confusion surrounding the usage of the word *Creole* in Louisiana and Mobile. See also Gould, "In Defense of Their Creole Culture," 32–33.
26. Nordmann, "Free Negroes," 4–5, 7; Munson, "Chastang Family Reunion," Chastang vertical file, MPL (full inventory).
27. Nordmann, "Free Negroes," 9–10 (Andry family); 13 (Dubroca family).
28. Gould, "In Defense of Their Creole Culture," 40–42; Fitzgerald, *Urban Emancipation,* 12 (quotation); Chastang, *St. Peter the Apostle Church,* 43 (schools).
29. Chastang, *St. Peter the Apostle Church,* 46–47 (quoting the Catholic bishop); Noel Andry Sr., personal interview, June 20, 2012; *Oreg.,* vol. 1, p. 1088 (offer to raise troops).
30. Chastang, *St. Peter the Apostle Church,* 47–8, 51 (founding of the church); *Mobile Register,* June 29, 1879 (dedication advert); July 9, 1879 (account of the dedication).
31. Nolan, *A History of the Archdiocese,* 140–41 (parish); Carroll, *A Catholic History,* 339–40 (quotation).
32. *Mobile Register,* February 3, 1946; Noel Andry Sr., personal interview, June 20, 2012.
33. Bemis, "Mount Vernon Arsenal," 9; Skinner, *The Apache Rock Crumbles,* 239 (*Mobile Register* reporter); Turner, *Wise Women,* 81 (quotation detailing misery at Mount Vernon).

34. Utley, *Geronimo*, 235–36, 244 (quotations); Debo, *Geronimo*, 349 (tasks); Skinner, *The Apache Rock Crumbles*, 328 (Company I). Post surgeon Reed later became well known for his efforts to discover the cause of yellow fever.
35. Skinner, *The Apache Rock Crumbles*, 328.
36. Ibid., 330–31.
37. Debo, *Geronimo*, 341 (school); "The Removal of the Apaches," 198 (quotation).
38. Skinner, *The Apache Rock Crumbles*, 239 (quoting the *New York Times*); Debo, *Geronimo*, 353 (purchase of the bonnet).
39. Reed, "Geronimo and His Warriors," 233; Bemis, "Mount Vernon Arsenal," 10 (move to Oklahoma).
40. Matte, "Extinction by Reclassification," 164 ("tri-racial" designation); 200 (1910 census); 204 (opposition to tribal recognition).
41. Ibid., 171–72; Waselkov and Gums, *Plantation Archaeology*, 57–58n175 (quotation).
42. Matte, "Extinction by Reclassification," 181 (quotation describing logging); 188 (quoting Boykin).
43. Carmer, *Stars*, 257 (at the store); 262 (quoting the boy).
44. Ibid., 196–98, 199 (quotation).
45. *Tuscaloosa News*, November 25, 1994 (Carlton quotation); *Ocala Star Ban*ner, December 1, 2002 (Taylor quotation); Murphy, "The Cajans of Mobile County, Ala.," 1 ("mongrel race").

Epilogue

1. *Mobile Register*, May 3, 2011.
2. William Harrison III, personal interview, May 1, 2012.
3. Ibid.
4. Ibid.

Bibliography

Archival Sources

"Albert Stein: Pioneer of City Water Supply." Unpublished manuscript, n.d. Mass.

Bache, A. D. Preliminary Sketch of Mobile Bay, U. S. Coast Survey, 1852. Mass.

City of Mobile Directories, 1859–1861. Mass.

Deed Books. PC.

Delano/Magouin Papers.

Diard Ironwork Ledgers. 2 vols. HMPS.

Glennon, John. "State Docks, Early History of the Alabama State Docks," 5 pages. Mobile Harbor and Shipping (Docks) I, Vertical file. MPL.

"Interesting Transcriptions from the City Documents of the City of Mobile." Vols. for 1820–1911, 1823–1844. Prepared from original data by the Municipal and Court Records Project of the Works Progress Administration, 1939. Mass.

Jervey, Henry. "Report to the Joint Rivers and Harbor Committee of Mobile." 1910. MPL.

Land Claim of the Widow Rochon. Record Book 2, October 22, 1792. PC.

"Manifest of the U.S. Mail Steamer *Southern*, May 17, 1842." Box 18005, envelope 7, folder 1, document #270. Mass.

Rayford, Julian Lee. *Seven Poems.* Privately printed chapbook, 1931. MPL.

Schell, Sidney. "The Confederate Fortifications at Fort Stoddert (Mt. Vernon, Alabama), December 15, 1994." MHDC.

"Statement before U.S. Engineers in Connection with Necessity for a Deeper Channel and a Wider Harbor at Mobile, Alabama." Letter dated December 21, 1925. Mobile Harbor and Shipping (Docks) I, Vertical File. MPL.

Ward, A. G., to City Commission, October 6, 1916. Mobile Harbor and Shipping (Docks) 1, Vertical file. MPL.

Waterman, John B. "Mobile's Port Record, November 28, 1934." Mobile Harbor and Shipping (Docks) I, Vertical File. MPL.

Maps

A Draught of the River Mobile, ca. 1765. National Archives, Kew, England.

Sanborn Fire Insurance Map, 1904. MHDC.

Newspapers

Alabama Planter, 1847.

Atlanta Constitution, 1927.

Atlanta Journal and Constitution, 1992.

Baltimore Weekly Register, 1813.

Birmingham News, 1995.

Clarke County Democrat, 1890.

Mobile Centinel, 1811.

Mobile Commercial Register, 1822–1836.

Mobile Daily Advertiser, 1855–1861.

Mobile Daily Commercial Register, 1839.

Mobile Daily News, 1865.

Mobile Evening News, 1863.

Mobile Register, 1861–2012.

Mobile Register and Journal, 1843.

New Orleans Bee, 1861.

New York Times, 1861–2011.

New York World, 1865.

Ocala Star Banner, 2002.

Pittsburgh Post-Gazette, 1946.

Tuscaloosa News, 1994.

Books, Articles, and Other Sources

"The ADDSCO Story." *Port of Mobile* (April 1969): 9–15.

Aiken, John G. *Digest of the Laws of the State of Alabama: Containing All the Statutes of a Public and General Nature, in Force at the Close of the Session of the General Assembly, in January, 1833*. Philadelphia: Alexander Towar, 1833.

Acts of the Seventh Biennial Session of the General Assembly of Alabama Held in the City of Montgomery, Commencing on the Second Monday in November 1859 . Montgomery: Shorter & Reed, 1860.

Alabama Department of Transportation. *Environmental Assessment for the I-10 Mobile River Bridge and Bayway*. Montgomery, 2003.

"Alabama State Docks Celebrates 40th Anniversary." *Port of Mobile* (June 1968): 14–25.

Alexander, W. A. "Thrilling Chapter in the History of the Confederate States Navy: Work of Submarine Boats." *Southern Historical Society Papers* 30 (January-December 1902): 164–74.

Almond, Jordan. *Dictionary of Word Origins: A History of the Words, Expressions, and Clichés We Use*. New York: Kensington, 1985.

Alsobrook, David. "Alabama's Port City: Mobile during the Progressive Era, 1896–1917." Ph.D. diss., Auburn University, 1982.

Alverson, Roy M. *History of Water Supply of the Mobile Area, Alabama*. Tuscaloosa: University of Alabama, 1973.

American State Papers: Documents of the Congress of the United States in Relation to the Public Lands. Vol. 1 (1789–1809). Washington: Duff Green, 1834.

American State Papers, Foreign Relations. Vol. 2. Washington: Gales and Seaton, 1832.

Amos, Harriet. *Cotton City: Urban Development in Antebellum Mobile*. Tuscaloosa: University of Alabama Press, 1985.

Andrews, Johnnie. *Rochon and Related Families*. Mobile: Bienville Historical Society, 1992.

Annual Report of the Chief of Engineers United States Army, to the Secretary of War for the Year 1886. Washington: Government Printing Office, 1886.

Arnold, J. Barto, III. *The* Denbigh's *Civilian Imports: Customs Records of a Civil War Blockade Runner between Mobile and Havana*. College Station, Tex.: Institute of Nautical Archaeology, 2011.

The Bachelor's Button. 1 (January 1837): 42–45.

Bailey, Mrs. Hugh C. "Mobile's Tragedy: The Great Magazine Explosion of 1865." *Alabama Review* 21 (January 1968): 40–52.

Bak, Richard. *The CSS* Hunley: *The Greatest Undersea Adventure of the Civil War*. Dallas: Taylor Publishing, 1999.

Beadle, Delos W. *The American Lawyer and Businessman's Form Book*. New York: Ensign, Bridgman and Fanning, 1855.

Beatson, Robert. *Naval and Military Memoirs of Great Britain from 1727 to 1783*. Vol. 6 London: Longman, Hurst, Rees and Orme, 1804.

Bemis, Devereaux. "Mount Vernon Arsenal/Searcy Hospital Complex." National Register of Historic Places Nomination Form. 1987. MHDC.

Bergeron, Arthur W., Jr. *Confederate Mobile*. Baton Rouge: Louisiana State University Press, 1991.

Bernstein, Victor H. "The Story of a Race Riot: Women Joined Men In Clubbing and Stoning Negro Ship Workers." *PM*, May 31, 1943.

"Big Time Down in Mobile." *Bulletin* 13 (December 1906): 18.

Blue Book, 1903. Doy Leale McCall Rare Book and Manuscript Library, University of South Alabama.

Blunt, Joseph. *Shipmaster's Assistant and Commercial Digest*. New York: E. & G. W. Blunt, 1857.

Board of Engineers for Rivers and Harbors. *Port Series No. 3: The Ports of Mobile, ALA., and Pensacola, FLA. Part I-The Port of Mobile, ALA*. Washington, D.C.: United States Government Printing Office, 1938.

———. *Port Series No. 3: The Ports of Mobile, Alabama and Pensacola, Florida*. Washington, D.C.: United States Government Printing Office, 1922.

Bone, David William. *Capstan Bars*. Edinburgh: The Porpoise Press, 1931.

Bossu, Jean Bernard. *Travels through that Part of North America Formerly Called Louisiana*. 2 vols. London: T. Davies, 1771.

Boyd, Mark Frederick, Hale G. Smith, and John W. Griffin. *Here They Once Stood: The Tragic End of the Apalachee Missions*. Gainesville: University Press of Florida, 1951.

Braund, Kathryn E. Holland, ed. *Tohopeka: Rethinking the Creek War and the War of 1812*.

Tuscaloosa: University of Alabama Press, 2012.

Bremer, Fredrika. *The Homes of the New World: Impressions of America.* 2 vols. New York: Harper, 1854.

Brown, Ian W. *Bottle Creek: A Pensacola Culture Site in South Alabama.* Tuscaloosa: University of Alabama Press, 2003.

Buchanan, John. *Jackson's Way: Andrew Jackson and the People of the Western Waters.* New York: John Wiley & Sons, 2001.

Buckingham, J. S. *The Slave States of America.* 2 vols. London: Fisher, Son, 1842.

"Building an Essential Trade Route." *Port of Mobile Bulletin* 6 (September 1, 1933): 3–4.

Byers, S.H.M. "The Last Slave Ship." *Harper's Monthly Magazine* 113 (June 1906): 742–46.

Cabeza de Vaca, Álvar Núñez. *Relation of Álvar Núñez Cabeza de Vaca.* Edited by Buckingham Smith. New York, 1871.

Cameron, William Lochiel. "The Battles Opposite Mobile." *Confederate Veteran* 23 (July 1915): 305–8.

"Capitol Eye." *Congressional Digest* (October 1921–September 1922). Washington, D. C.: Government Printing Office, 1923.

Carmer, Carl. *Stars Fell on Alabama.* New York: Farrar and Rinehart, 1934.

Carroll, Austin. *A Catholic History of Alabama and the Floridas.* New York: P. J. Kennedy & Sons, 1908.

Carter, Kit C. "William Howard Robertson: His Early Years on the Gulf Coast, 1804–1808." *Gulf Coast Historical Review* 8 (Fall 1992): 105–13.

Chadwick, Michael A., and Jack W. Feminella. "Influence of Salinity and Temperature on the Growth and Production of a Freshwater Mayfly in the Lower Mobile River, Alabama." *Limnology and Oceanography* 46 (May 2001): 532–42.

Chaffin, Tom. *The* H. L. Hunley: *The Secret Hope of the Confederacy.* New York: Hill and Wang, 2008.

The Charter and Code of Ordinances of the City of Mobile, 1889. Mobile: George Matzinger, 1889.

Chastang, Richard. *St. Peter the Apostle Church: From the Origin of St. Paul's Chapel to the Departure of Fr. Sabino Grossi.* Mobile: STA Publications, 1994.

Chester, Greville John. *Transatlantic Sketches in the West Indies, South America, Canada, and the United States.* London: Smith, Elder, 1869.

Childress, David T. "Mount Vernon Barracks: The Blue, The Gray, and The Red." *Alabama Review* 42 (April 1989): 125–35.

Christopher, Raven M. and Gregory A. Waselkov. *An Archaeological Survey of the Old Federal Road in Alabama.* Mobile: University of South Alabama Center for Archaeological Studies, 2012.

Circus Scrap Book 13 (January 1932): 19–20.

Claiborne, J. F. H. *Mississippi as a Province, Territory and State with Biographical Notices of Eminent Citizens.* Vol. 1. Jackson: Power & Barksdale, 1880.

Clark, Thomas D., and John D. W. Guice. *The Old Southwest, 1795–1830.* Norman: University of Oklahoma Press, 1995.

Coker, William S. "How General Jackson Learned of the British Plans Before the Battle of New Orleans." *Gulf Coast Historical Review* 3 (Fall 1987): 85–95.

Corsan, W. C. *Two Months in the Confederate States: An Englishman's Travels through the South.* Baton Rouge: Louisiana State University Press, 1996.

Cram, Mildred, and Allan Cram. *Old Seaport Towns of the South.* New York: Dodd, Mead, 1917.

Cresswell, Julia. *Oxford Dictionary of Word Origins.* New York: Oxford, 2002.

Cumming, Kate. *Gleanings from Southland: Sketches of Life and Manners of the People of the South before, during and after the War of Secession, with Extracts from the Author's Journal.* Birmingham: Roberts and Son, 1895.

Curtis, Stephen A. *Hurricane Katrina Damage Assessment: Louisiana, Alabama and Mississippi Ports and Coasts.* Reston, Va.: American Society of Civil Engineers, 2007.

Damrell, A. N. "Annual Report of Captain A. M. Damrell, Corps of Engineers, for the Fiscal Year Ending June 30, 1873." In *Annual Report of the Chief of Engineers to the Secretary of War for the Year 1872,* 691–94. Washington, D.C.: Government Printing Office, 1873.

Davidson, James Wood. *The Living Writers of the South.* New York: Carleton, 1869.

Davis, A. C. "Work Starts on Port Development." *Engineering News Record* 8 (June 1925): 1024–25.

Davis, Virgil S. "Damrell's Ditch." *Alabama Heritage* (Summer 1994): 25.

———. *A History of the Mobile District U. S. Army Corps of Engineers, 1815–1971.* Mobile: South

Atlantic Division Corps of Engineers, U. S. Army, 1975.

Deacon, Richard. *Madoc and the Discovery of America.* New York: George Braziller, 1966.

Debo, Angie. *Geronimo: The Man, His Time, His Place.* Norman, Okla.: University of Oklahoma Press, 1976.

Delaney, Caldwell. *Confederate Mobile.* Mobile: Haunted Book Shop, 1971.

———. *A Mobile Sextet.* Mobile: Haunted Book Shop, 1981.

———. *Remember Mobile.* Mobile: Gill Printing, 1948.

Desty, Robert. *The Federal Reporter,* vols. 19–20. St. Paul: West Publishing Co., 1884.

Diouf, Sylviane A. *Dreams of Africa in Alabama: The Slave Ship* Clotilda *and the Story of the Last Africans Brought to America.* New York: Oxford University Press, 2007.

Doster, James F. "Early Settlements on the Tombigbee and Tensaw Rivers." *Alabama Review* 12 (April 1959): 83–94.

Edwards, M. Boyd. *Proceedings of the Eighth Biennial Southern Silvicultural Research Conference.* Asheville, N.C.: U.S. Forest Service, 1995.

Eisterhold, John A. "Mobile: Lumber Center of the Gulf Coast." *Alabama Review* 24 (April 1973): 83–104.

"Efficient Service to Tropics by United Fruit Company Steamers." *Port of Mobile Bulletin* 7 (April 1, 1935): 3.

Ellicott, Andrew. *The Journal of Andrew Ellicott.* Philadelphia: William Fry, 1814.

Ensor, H. Blaine, Eugene Wilson, and M. Cassandra Hill. *Historic Resources Assessment, Tennessee-Tombigbee Waterway Wildlife Mitigation Project Mobile and Tensaw River Deltas, Alabama.* Tuscaloosa: Panamerican Consultants, 1993.

Erikson, Benjamin. *Mobile's Legal Legacy: Three Hundred Years of Law in the Port City.* Mobile: Mobile Bar Association, 2008.

Erskine, Charles. *Twenty Years Before the Mast.* Philadelphia: George W. Jacobs and Co., 1896.

Fabel, Robin F. A. *Bombast and Broadsides: The Lives of George Johnstone.* Tuscaloosa: University of Alabama Press, 1987.

———. *The Economy of British West Florida,* 1763–1783. Tuscaloosa : University of Alabama Press, 2002.

———. "Reflection on Mobile's Loyalism in the American Revolution." *Gulf South Historical Review* 19 (Fall 2003): 31–45.

Featherstonaugh, George W. *Excursion through the Slave States.* New York: Harper, 1844.

First National Bank. *Highlights of 100 Years in Mobile.* Mobile: First National Bank, 1965.

Fitzgerald, Michael. *Urban Emancipation: Popular Politics in Reconstruction Mobile, 1860–1890.* Baton Rouge: Louisiana State University Press, 2002.

Fornell, Earl W. "Mobile during the Blockade." *Alabama Historical Quarterly* 23 (Spring 1961): 29–43.

Fox, Thomas H. "My Experiences as a Sailor." *Springhillian* 25 (March 1923): 5–9.

Friend, Jack. *Alabama Coastal Region Ecological Characterization, Vol. 3, A Socioeconomic Study.* Washington, D. C.: Fish and Wildlife Service, 1982.

———. *West Wind, Flood Tide: The Battle of Mobile Bay.* Annapolis: Naval Institute Press, 2004.

Frost, Mrs. J. Blakeslee. *The Rebellion in the United States; or The War of 1861.* Hartford: Mrs. J. Blakeslee Frost, 1862.

"A Full Day's Work for a Full Day's Pay." *Port of Mobile News* 36 (November 1963): 12.

Galloway, Patricia. *Choctaw Genesis, 1500–1700.* Lincoln: University of Nebraska Press, 1995.

Gayarré, Charles. *History of Louisiana.* New York: William J. Widdleton, 1867.

General Services Administration. *Public Papers of the Presidents of the United States.* Washington, D.C.: Government Printing Office, 1999.

Giraud, Marcel. *A History of French Louisiana.* Vol. 1, *The Reign of Louis XIV, 1698–1715.* Translated by Joseph C. Lambert. Baton Rouge: Louisiana State University Press, 1974.

———. *A History of French Louisiana.* Vol. 5, *The Company of the Indies, 1723–1731.* Translated by Brian Pearce. Baton Rouge: Louisiana State University Press, 1991.

Girdler, L. Tracy. *An Antebellum Life at Sea: Featuring the Journal of Sarah Jane Girdler Kept Aboard the Clipper Ship 'Robert H. Dixey' from America to Russia and Europe, January 1857–December 1858.* Montgomery: Black Belt Press, 1997.

Glennon, John. "State Docks Site Was Chosen for Rice Field," *Port of Mobile News* (December 1939): 12–13.

"Goat Island: Defender of Mobile and Home for Hermit." *Six Flags Reporter* (September 1977): 5.

Goode, G. Brown. *The Fisheries and Fishery*

Industries of the United States: Section IV: The Fishermen of the United States. Washington, D.C.: Government Printing Office, 1887.

———. *The History and Present Condition of the Fishery Industries.* Washington, D.C.: Government Printing Office, 1881.

Goodheart, Adam. "Caught Sleeping." *New York Times,* January 3, 2011.

Goodrum, John C., et al., eds. *Rivers of Alabama.* Huntsville: Strode Publishers, 1968.

Gosse, Philip Henry. *Letters from Alabama.* London: Morgan & Chase, 1859.

Gould, Elizabeth. *From Fort to Port: An Architectural History of Mobile, Alabama, 1711–1918.* Tuscaloosa: University of Alabama Press, 1988.

Gould, E. W. *Fifty Years on the Mississippi; or Gould's History of River Navigation.* St. Louis: Nixon-Jones Printing, 1889.

Gould, Virginia. "In Defense of Their Creole Culture: The Free Creoles of Color of New Orleans, Mobile and Pensacola." *Gulf Coast Historical Review* 9 (Fall 1993): 26–46.

Grant, John. *Improvement of the Harbor, Bay and River of Mobile, In Answer to Bahia.* Mobile: Henry Farrow, 1872.

Gratwick, Harry. *Mainers in the Civil War.* Charleston, S.C.: The History Press, 2011.

Gums, Bonnie L. "Earthfast (*Pieux en Terre*) Structures at Old Mobile." *Historical Archaeology* 36, no. 1 (2002): 13–25.

———, and George Shorter. *Archaeology at Mobile's Exploreum: Discovering the Buried Past.* Mobile: University of South Alabama Center for Archaeological Studies, 1998.

Hall, M. R., and John C. Hoyt. *Report of Progress of Stream Measurements for the Calendar Year 1904. Part IV—Santee, Savannah, Ogeechee, and Atlamaha Rivers and Eastern Gulf of Mexico Drainages.* Washington, D. C.: Government Printing Office, 1905.

Hamilton, Peter Joseph. "The Beginnings of French Settlement of the Mississippi Valley." *Gulf States Historical Magazine* 1 (July 1902): 1–12.

———. *Colonial Mobile.* Boston: Houghton, 1910.

———, Erwin Craighead, and W. K. P. Wilson. *Bicentennial Celebration May 26–28, 1911 of the Founding of Mobile by Jean Baptiste De Bienville 1711.* Mobile: Commercial Printing, 1912.

Hamilton, Peter Joseph, and Thomas M. Owen, eds. "Topographical Notes and Observations on the Alabama River, August 1814 by Major Howell Tatum." Vol. 2, 130-177. *Transactions of the Alabama Historical Society, 1897–1898.* Tuscaloosa: Alabama Historical Society. 1898.

Harris, Dr. J. G. "On the Climate and Fevers of the Southwestern, Southern Atlantic, and Gulf States." Part I. *DeBow's Review* 26 (June 1859): 679–91.

Harrison, Patricia G. "Riveters, Volunteers and WACS: Women in Mobile during WW II." *Gulf Coast Historical Review* 1 (Spring 1986): 33–54.

Hearn, Chester G. *Admiral David Glasgow Farragut: The Civil War Years.* Annapolis: Naval Institute Press, 1998.

Higginbotham, Jay. *Mobile: City by the Bay.* 1968. Reprint, Mobile: Mobile Jr. Chamber of Commerce, 2000.

———. *The Mobile Indians.* Mobile: Sir Key's Printing, 1966.

———. *Old Mobile: Fort Louis de la Louisiane, 1702–1711.* Mobile: Museum of the City of Mobile, 1977.

Holmes, Jack D. L., ed. "Fort Stoddard in 1799: Seven Letters of Captain Bartholomew Schaumburgh." *Alabama Review* 26 (Fall/Winter 1964): 231–51.

Hudson, Charles. *The Southeastern Indians.* Knoxville: University of Tennessee Press, 1976.

Hulbert, Archer Butler, ed. *The Crown Collection of Photographs of American Maps, Series III.* Cleveland: Arthur H. Clark, 1915.

Hunt, Freeman. "Cotton Warehouses, Steam Presses, Etc. at Mobile." *Hunt's Merchants' Magazine* 24, (1851): 266.

Hunter, Louis C. *Steamboats on the Western Rivers: An Economic and Technological History.* Cambridge: Harvard University Press, 1949.

Ingraham, J. H., ed. *The Sunny South; or The Southerner at Home.* Philadelphia: G. G. Evans, 1860.

"Interesting Transcriptions from the Mayor's Court, " 1820–1825. Prepared from original data by the Municipal and Court Records Project of the Works Progress Administration, 1939. Mass.

Irion, Jack B. *Archaeological Testing of the Confederate Obstructions, 1Mb28, Mobile Harbor, Alabama.* Austin, Tex.: Espey, Hutson & Associates, 1985.

Jackson, Harvey H. *Rivers of History: Life on the Coosa, Tallapoosa, Cahaba, and Alabama.* Tuscaloosa: University of Alabama Press, 1995.

Jefferson, Thomas. *Writings*. New York: Literary Classics of the United States, 1984.

Johnson, Cecil. *British West Florida, 1763–1783*. New Haven: Yale University Press, 1943.

Jones, Thomas G. *Reports of Cases Argued and Determined in the Supreme Court of Alabama during December Term 1876*. Montgomery: Joel White, 1878.

Joint Rivers and Harbor Committee. *Report of Sub-Committee on Harbor Improvement to Joint Rivers and Harbor Committee of Mobile*. Mobile: Privately printed, 1910.

Key, Watt. "A Camp Man and His Tools." *Mobile Bay* 28 (October 2012): 76–77.

Knight, Vernon James, Jr. *The Search for Mabila: The Decisive Battle Between Hernando de Soto and Chief Tascalusa*. Tuscaloosa: University of Alabama Press, 2009.

Knight, Vernon J., Jr., and Sherée Adams. "A Voyage to the Mobile and Tomeh in 1700, with Notes on the Interior of Alabama." *Journal of Alabama Archaeology* 27, no. 1 (1981): 32–56.

Koch, Albert C. *Journey through a Part of North America in the Years 1844 to 1846*. 1846. Reprint, Carbondale: Southern Illinois University Press, 1972.

Kremer, Gary R. *George Washington Carver*. Santa Barbara, Calif.: Greenwood. 2011.

Krivor, Michael. "Remote Sensing Investigations for the Slave Ship Clotilda." Mobile: Museum of Mobile: 1998.

Land, John E. *Mobile: Her Trade, Commerce and Industries, 1883–4*. Mobile: Mobile Printing, 1884.

Laws of the United States Relating to the Improvement of Rivers and Harbours from August 11, 1790, to March 4, 1907. 2 vols. Washington, D.C.: Government Printing Office, 1907.

Lloyd, James T. *Lloyd's Steamboat Directory and Disasters on the Western Waters*. Cincinnati: James T. Lloyd, 1856.

Lumber Trade Journal 68 (July 1, 1913): 12.

Lyell, Sir Charles. *A Second Visit to the United States*. Vol. 2. New York: Harper, 1849.

Maffitt, Emma Martin. *The Life and Services of John Newland Maffitt*. New York: Neale, 1906.

Mansfield, Mike. "An Onerous and Unnecessary Burden: Mobile and the Negro Seaman Acts." *Gulf South Historical Review* 21 (Fall 2005): 6–28.

Marley, David. *Wars of the Americas: A Chronology of Armed Conflict in the Western Hemisphere from 1492 to the Present*. 2 vols. Santa Barbara: ABC-CLIO, 2008.

Matte, Jacqueline Anderson. "Extinction by Reclassification: The MOWA Choctaws of South Alabama and Their Struggle for Federal Recognition." *Alabama Review* 59 (July 2006): 163–204.

Matthews, Catherine Van Cortlandt. *Andrew Ellicott: His Life and Letters*. New York: Grafton Press, 1908.

Mayo, Anthony J., and Nitin Nohria. *In Their Time: The Greatest Business Leaders of the Twentieth Century*. Harvard: Harvard Business School Publishing, 2005.

McCann, Thomas P. *An American Company: The Tragedy of United Fruit*. New York: Crown, 1977.

McDonald, Alfred Hudson. *One Man's Message: An Autobiography*. Mobile: Alfred Hudson McDonald, 2010.

McGehee, Tom. "Ask McGehee: A 'Warehouse District' in Mobile?" *Mobile Bay* 28 (April 2012): 92–93.

McKenna, Joseph. *British Ships in the Confederate Navy*. Jefferson, N.C.: McFarland, 2010.

McKinstry, Alexander. *Code of Ordinances of the City of Mobile*. Mobile: Goetzel, 1859.

McLaurin, Melton, and Michael Thomason. *Mobile: The Life and Times of a Great Southern City. An Illustrated History*. Woodland Hills, Calif.: Windsor Publications, 1981.

McMillan, Malcom C., ed. *The Alabama Confederate Reader*. Tuscaloosa: University of Alabama Press, 1963.

McSwain, James B. "Fire Hazards and Protection of Property: Municipal Regulation of the Storage and Supply of Fuel Oil in Mobile, Alabama, 1894–1910." *Journal of Urban History* 28 (July 2002): 599–628.

McWilliams, Richebourg Gaillard. *Fleur de Lys and Calumet: Being the Pénicaut Narrative of French Adventure in Louisiana*. Baton Rouge: Louisiana State University Press, 1953.

———. *Iberville's Gulf Journals*. Tuscaloosa: University of Alabama Press, 1981.

"M.E.B.A. No. 14." *American Marine Engineer* 8 (October 1913): 34.

Mellown, Robert O. "Steamboat Travel in Early Alabama." *Alabama Heritage* (Fall 1986): 2–11.

"Memorandum of Research Regarding CSX Main Line Track Rights," n.d. MHDC.

Memorial of the Mayor and Aldermen of the City of Mobile, December 29, 1820. Washington, D. C.: Gales & Seaton, 1820.

Meriwether, Colyer, ed. "'A Southern Traveler's Diary in 1840' by William Wills." *Publications of the Southern History Association* 8 (1904): 129–38.

Merrill, William E. "Report on the Present Condition of the Harbor of Mobile, Ala., February 6, 1866." Executive Documents Printed by Order of the House of Representatives, during the First Session of the Thirty-ninth Congress, 1865–66. Washington, D.C.: Government Printing Office, 1866.

"Mobile's Piers in the Bridge to France." *Electric Railway Journal* 51 (June 22, 1918): 1185–86.

"Mobile's Rich Tradition of (War) Shipbuilding," *Alabama Seaport* (Summer 2013): 28–31.

Morris, John, ed. *Wanderings of a Vagabond: An Autobiography.* New York: Privately printed, 1873.

Morrison, Andrew, ed. *Mobile: The New South.* Mobile: Metropolitan and Star Publishing, 1887–1888.

Morse, Jedidiah. *The American Gazetteer.* Boston: S. Hall, Thomas & Andrews, 1797.

Nelson, Bruce. "Organized Labor and the Struggle for Black Equality." *Journal of American Historians* 80 (December 1993): 952–88.

Neville, Bert, ed. *Ante-Bellum Floating Palaces of the Alabama River and the "Good Old Times in Dixie."* 1904. Reprint, Selma: Bert Neville, 1960.

———. *Directory of Steam—Some Motor-Towboats & U.S. Engineer Department Vessels on the Mobile-Alabama-Tombigbee-Warrior Rivers, 1881–1947.* Selma: Coffee Printing, 1964.

"New Floating Dry Dock Built at Mobile," *International Marine Engineering* 25 (March 1920): 215–18.

Newman, Johnny. "A Brief History of Choctaw Point Lighthouse." *Alabama Lightkeepers Newsletter* (Fall 2009).

New South Associates. *From Alluvium to Commerce: Waterfront Architecture, Land Reclamation, and Commercial Development in Mobile, Alabama.* Stone Mountain, Ga.: New South Associates, 1995.

Nolan, Charles E. *A History of the Archdiocese of Mobile.* Mobile: Archdiocese of Mobile, 2012.

Nordmann, Christopher Andrew. "Free Negroes of Mobile County, Alabama." Ph.D. dissertation, University of Alabama, 1990.

O'Brien, Jack, Jr. "Where Was the *Hunley* Built?" *Gulf Coast Historical Review* 21 (Fall 2005): 29–48.

O'Brien, Sean Michael. *Mobile, 1865: Last Stand of the Confederacy.* Westport, Conn.: Praeger, 2001.

Oldmixon, John W. *Transatlantic Wanderings.* London: Routledge, 1855.

O'Meagher, Casimir Joseph. *Some Historical Notes of the O'Meaghers of Ikerrin.* New York: Joseph Casimir O'Meagher, 1890.

Otto, William T. *Cases Argued and Adjudged in the Supreme Court of the United States. October term, 1880.* Vol. 12. New York: Banks Law Publishing, 1910.

Owen, Thomas McAdory, ed. "Burr's Conspiracy." In *Transactions of the Alabama Historical Society, 1898–99.* Vol. 3. Tuscaloosa: Alabama Historical Society, 1899: 167–77.

———. *History of Alabama and Dictionary of Alabama Biography.* 4 vols. Chicago: S. J. Clarke Publishing, 1921.

Parton, J. *The Life and Times of Aaron Burr.* New York: Mason Bros., 1858.

Patterson, Benton Rain. *The Great American Steamboat Race: The Natchez, The Robert E. Lee & and the Climax of an Era.* Jefferson, N.C.: McFarland, 2009.

Perry, Milton F. *Infernal Machines: The Story of Confederate Submarine and Mine Warfare.* Baton Rouge: Louisiana State University Press, 1965.

Phares, Earle. "Huxtry! All Aboard the U-Boat Scoop," *Pep* 2 (September 1917): 11.

Phillips, Ulrich B. *Plantation and Frontier Documents: 1649–1863, Illustrative of Industrial History in the Colonial & Ante-Bellum South.* Cleveland: Arthur H. Clark, 1909.

Pickens, Israel. *Acts Passed at the Fourth Annual Session of the General Assembly of the State of Alabama, November 3, 1822.* Cahawba: Wm. B. Allen, 1823.

Pickett, Albert James. *History of Alabama.* Charleston: Walker and James, 1851.

Pitts, Dr. J. R. S. *The Life and Confessions of James Copeland.* 1909. Reprint, Jackson: University Press of Mississippi, 2008.

Porter, David D. *The Naval History of the Civil War.* New York: Sherman Publishing, 1886.

Powell, Gerald R., Matthew C. Cordon, and J. Barto Arnold III. *Civil War Blockade Runners: Prize Claims and the Historical Record, Including the* Denbigh*'s Court Documents.* College Station, Tex.: Institute of Nautical Archaeology, 2012.

Power, Tyrone. *Impressions of America, During the Years 1833, 1834, and 1835.* Vol. 2. London: Richard Bentley, 1836.

Prelini, Charles. *Dredges and Dredging.* New York: D. Van Nostrand, 1912.

Priestly, Herbert Ingram, ed. *The Luna Papers, 1559–1561.* 2 vols. 1928. Reprint, Tuscaloosa: University of Alabama Press, 2010.

Professional Memoirs, Engineer Bureau, United States Army. Vol. 5. Washington, D. C.: Engineering School, 1913.

Public Health Reports Issued by the Surgeon-General Public Health Marine Hospital Service. Washington, D.C.: Government Printing Office, 1906.

Rayford, Julian Lee. *Cottonmouth: A Novel.* New York: Charles Scribner's Sons, 1941.

Rea, Robert Right. "Madogwys Forever!: The Present State of the Madoc Controversy." *Alabama Historical Quarterly* 30 (Spring 1968): 6–17.

———, and Milo B. Howard Jr. *The Minutes, Journals and Acts of the General Assembly of British West Florida.* Tuscaloosa: University of Alabama Press, 1976.

Reed, Walter. "Geronimo and His Warriors in Captivity." *Illustrated American* 3 (August 16, 1890): 231–35.

Register, Robert. "Andrew Ellicott's Observations While Serving on the Southern Boundary Commission: 1796–1800." *Gulf Coast Historical Review* 12 (Spring 1997): 6–43.

Reid, Whitelaw. *After the War: A Southern Tour.* New York: Moore, Wilstach & Baldwin, 1866.

"Removal of the Apaches from Alabama to Indian Territory, The." *Southern Workman and Hampton School Record* 23 (November 1894): 198.

Report. In *Message from the President of the United States to the Two Houses of Congress* [*Senate*], *at the Commencement of the First Session of the Thirty-third Congress.* Part 2, 521–26. Washington, D.C.: Robert Armstrong, 1853.

Reynolds, Bernard A. *Sketches of Mobile, from 1814 to the Present.* Mobile: B. H. Richardson, 1868.

Reynolds, Sarah. "Safeguarding a Perilous Harbor: The First Line of Defense." *Sense Magazine* 3 (May 2013): 19–20.

Riccio, Joseph F., and Conrad A. Gazzier. *History of Water Supply of the Mobile Area, Alabama.* University, Ala.: Geological Survey of Alabama, 1973.

Rix, William. *Incidents of Life in a Southern City during the War: A Series of Sketches Written for the* Rutland Herald *by a Vermont Gentleman, who was for Many Years a Prominent Merchant in Mobile.* Mobile: Iberville Historical Society Papers, 1865.

Robertson, Natalie S. *The Slave Ship* Clotilda *and the Making of AfricaTown, USA: Spirit of Our Ancestors.* Westport, Conn.: Praeger, 2008.

Roche, Emma Langdon. *Historic Sketches of the South.* New York: Knickerbocker Press, 1914.

Romans, Bernard. A *Concise Natural History of East and West Florida.* New York: For the author, 1775.

Rowland, Dunbar, ed. *Letters and Enclosures to the Secretary of State from Major Robert Farmar and Governor George Johnstone.* Vol. 1. Nashville: Brandon Printing, 1911.

———. *Encyclopedia of Mississippi History.* 2 Vols. Madison, Wis.: Selwyn A. Brant, 1907.

Russell, William Howard. *My Diary North and South.* Vol. 1. London: Bradbury and Evans, 1863.

Saltus, Allen R., and Sidney H. Schell. *The* CSS Huntsville *and* CSS Tuscaloosa *Project Mobile River, Alabama: Report of 1985 Activities.* Museum of Mobile, 1985.

Saxe-Wiemar Eisenach, Duke of (Bernard). *Travels through North America During the Years 1825 and 1826.* Vol. 2. Philadelphia: Carey, Lea, and Carey, 1826.

Scharf, J. Thomas. *History of the Confederate States Navy from Its Organization to the Surrender of Its Last Vessel.* Albany, N.Y.: Joseph McDonough, 1894.

Schell, Sidney H. "Submarine Weapons Tested at Mobile during the Civil War." *Alabama Review* 45 (July 1992): 163–83.

Schwartz, Rick. *Hurricanes and the Middle Atlantic States.* Alexandria, Va.: Blue Diamond Books, 2007.

Scroggs, William O. *Filibusters and Financiers: The Story of William Walker and His Associates.* New York: Macmillan, 1916.

Sexton, Rebecca Grant, ed. *A Southern Woman of Letters: The Correspondence of Augusta Jane Evans Wilson.* Columbia: University of South Carolina Press, 2002.

Shepherd, J. W. *Cases Argued and Determined in the Supreme Court of Alabama, during January Term, 1855*. Vol. 26. Montgomery: Cowan and Martin, 1859.

Shingleton, Royce. *High Seas Confederate: The Life and Times of John Newland Maffitt.* Columbia: University of South Carolina Press, 1994.

Shippee, Lester B., ed. *Bishop Whipple's Southern Diary, 1843–1844.* New York: Da Capo Press, 1968.

Silverstone, Paul H. *Civil War Navies, 1855–1883.* New York: Taylor and Francis, 2006.

Simpson, J. H. "Annual Report of Colonel J. H. Simpson, Corps of Engineers for the Fiscal Year Ended June 30, 1872." In *Annual Report of the Chief of Engineers to the Secretary of War for the Year 1872,* 589–612. Washington, D.C.: Government Printing Office, 1872.

Skinner, Woodward B. *The Apache Rock Crumbles: The Captivity of Geronimo's People.* Pensacola: Woodward B. Skinner, 1987.

Sledge, John. *Cities of Silence: A Guide to Mobile's Historic Cemeteries.* Tuscaloosa: University of Alabama Press, 2002.

———. *The Pillared City: Greek Revival Mobile.* Athens: University of Georgia Press, 2009.

Smith, David Barton. *Health Care Divided: Race and Healing a Nation.* Ann Arbor: University of Michigan Press, 1999.

Smith, James Morton. *The Republic of Letters: The Correspondence Between Thomas Jefferson and James Madison, 1776–1826.* New York: Norton, 1995.

Smith, Robert Leslie. *Gone to the Swamp: Raw Materials for the Good Life in the Mobile-Tensaw Delta.* Tuscaloosa: University of Alabama Press, 2008.

Smith, W. Evertt. *A Field Guide to Mobile Delta Geomorphology.* Tuscaloosa: Geological Survey of Alabama, Information Series 80, 1997.

Smith, Winston. *The People's City: The Glory and Grief of an Alabama Town, 1850–1874.* Demopolis: Marengo County Historical Society, 2003.

South Carolina Geographic Alliance. "The *Hunley:* Interactive Geography." Educational CD-ROM. University of South Carolina, 2010. Online at http://artsandsciences.sc.edu/cege/resources/cdroms/THIG__Lesson__Book.pdf.

Spies, Gregory. "A Line of Demarcation and Ellicott's Survey of the 31st Parallel." *Backsights* 15 (January 1996): 4–10.

———. "Major Ellicott's Triangulation." *Professional Surveyor's Magazine* (September 2004): 1–3.

"Steamboat Bill of Facts." *Journal of the Steamboat Historical Society of America* 14 (1955): 2.

Stein, Albert. *Brief Notes on the Report of the Board of U.S. Engineers upon the Improvement of the Harbor of Mobile.* Mobile: Privately printed, 1873.

———. *Report on the Improvement of the Mobile River and Bay.* Mobile: Middleton, Harris, 1855.

Still, William N., Jr. "The Confederate States Navy at Mobile, 1861 to August, 1864." *Alabama Historical Quarterly* 30 (Fall and Winter 1968): 127–44.

———. *Iron Afloat: The Story of the Confederate Armorclads.* Nashville: Vanderbilt University Press, 1971.

Stumpf, Stuart O., ed. "The Arrest of Aaron Burr: A Documentary Record." *Alabama Historical Quarterly* 42 (Fall and Winter 1980):113–23.

Surrey, N. M. Miller. *The Commerce of Louisiana during the French Regime, 1699–1763.* 1916. Reprint, Tuscaloosa: University of Alabama Press, 2006.

Swanton, John R. *Early History of the Creek Indians and Their Neighbors.* Washington, D.C.: Government Printing Office, 1922.

Symonds, Craig L. *Confederate Admiral: The Life and Wars of Franklin Buchanan.* Annapolis: Naval Institute Press, 1999.

Tenney, W. J. *The Military and Naval History of the Rebellion in the United States.* New York: D. Appleton, 1867.

"Tenn-Tom Waterway," *Mobile* (October 1981): 14.

Terkel, Studs. *And They All Sang: Adventures of an Electric Disc Jockey.* New York: New Press, 2005.

Thomas, Mary Martha. "The Mobile Homefront during the Second World War." *Gulf Coast Historical Review* 1 (Spring 1986): 55–75.

Thomason, Michael V. R., ed. *Mobile: The New History of Alabama's First City.* Tuscaloosa: University of Alabama Press, 2001.

Toulmin, Harry. *A Digest of the Laws of the State of Alabama Containing the Statues and Resolutions in Force at the end of the General Assembly in January, 1823.* New York: Ginn & Curtis, 1828.

Trickey, E. Bruce, Nicholas H. Holmes, Jr., and Janet R. Clute. "Archaeological and Historical Investigations at Pinto Battery or Battery

Gladden, Site 1Mb17, Mobile Bay, Alabama." *Journal of Alabama Archaeology* 32 (June 1986): 40–62.

Turner, Erin, ed. *Wise Women: From Pocahontas to Sarah Winnemucca, Remarkable Stories of Native American Trailblazers.* Kearny, Nebr.: Morris Publishing, 2009.

Turner, Wesley B. *The War of 1812: The War that Both Sides Won.* Toronto: Dundurn Press, 2010.

United States Commission of Fish and Fisheries. *Report of the Commissioner for 1885.* Washington, D.C.: Government Printing Office, 1887.

Usner, Daniel H. *Indians, Settlers and Slaves in a Frontier Exchange Economy: The Lower Mississippi Valley before 1783.* Chapel Hill: University of North Carolina Press, 1992.

U.S. War Department. *War of the Rebellion: Official Records of Union and Confederate Armies.* 128 parts in 70 vols. Washington, D.C.: U.S. Government Printing Office, 1880–1901.

———. *War of the Rebellion: Official Records of Union and Confederate Navies.* 30 vols. Washington, D.C.: U.S. Government Printing Office, 1894–1922.

Utley, Robert M. *Geronimo.* New Haven: Yale University Press, 2012.

Van Doren, Mark, ed. *The Travels of William Bartram.* New York: Dover Press, 1955.

Vestal, Stanley. *The Missouri.* New York: Farrar & Rhinehart, 1945.

Von Scheliha, Viktor Ernst Karl Rudolf. *A Treatise on Coast Defense: Based on Experience Gained by Officers of the Corps of Engineers of the Army of the Confederate States, and Compiled from Official Reports of Officers of the Navy of the United States, Made During the Late South American War From 1861 to 1865.* London: E. & F. N. Spon, 1868.

Voogd, Jan. *Race Riots and Resistance: The Red Summer of 1919.* New York: Peter Lang, 2008.

Wade, William W., Jason R. Plater, and Jacqueline Q. Kelley. *History of Coastal Alabama Natural Gas Exploration and Development: Final Report.* New Orleans: U. S. Department of the Interior, 1999.

Wallace, John William. *Cases Argued and Adjudged in the Supreme Court of the United States, December Term, 1866.* Vol. 5. Washington, D. C.: W. H. & O. H. Morrison, 1870.

Walter, Eugene. *Milking the Moon: A Southerner's Story of Life on This Planet.* New York: Three Rivers Press, 2001.

———. *The Untidy Pilgrim.* New York: Lippincott, 1953.

Walthall, John A. *Prehistoric Indians of the Southeast: Archaeology of Alabama and the Middle South.* Tuscaloosa: University of Alabama Press, 1980.

Walton, Ivan W. and Joe Grimm. *Windjammers: Songs of the Great Lakes Sailors.* Detroit: Great Lakes Books, 2002.

Ward, Geoffry. *The War: An Intimate History 1941–1945.* New York: Knopf, 2007.

Ward, Rufus. *The Tombigbee Steamboats: Rollodores, Deadheads and Side-Wheelers.* Charleston, S.C.: The History Press, 2010.

Waselkov, Gregory. *A Conquering Spirit: Fort Mims and the Redstick War of 1813–1814.* Tuscaloosa: University of Alabama Press, 2006.

———. *Old Mobile Archaeology.* Mobile: University of South Alabama Center for Archaeological Studies, 1999.

——— and Bonnie Gums. *Plantation Archaeology at Rivière aux Chiens, ca. 1725–1848.* Mobile: University of South Alabama Center for Archaeological Studies, 2000.

Waterman, George S. "Afloat, Afield, Afloat." *Confederate Veteran* 9 (January 1901): 24–29.

"Watershed Assessment, Tracking and Environmental Results." http://iaspub.epa.gov/tmdl__waters10/attains__watershed.control#assessment__data. Accessed November 17, 2013.

Weber, Alma B. "Mobile Harbor: Problems of Internal Improvement 1865–1900." *Journal of the Alabama Academy of Science* 39 (January 1968): 13–20.

Weddle, Robert S. *Spanish Sea: The Gulf of Mexico in North American Discovery, 1500–1685.* College Station: Texas A & M University Press, 1985.

Welborn, Aaron. "A Traitor in the Wilderness: The Arrest of Aaron Burr." *Alabama Heritage* (Winter 2007): 10–19.

"West Florida, Its Attempt on Mobile, 1810–1811." *American Historical Review* 2 (July 1897): 699–705.

Wilkinson, General James. *Memoirs of My Own Times.* Philadelphia: Abraham Small, 1816.

Williams, Kimberlyn, et al., "Sea-level Rise and Coastal Forests on the Gulf of Mexico." Washington, D. C.: U. S. Geological Survey, Vol. 99, Issue 441, 1999.

Windham, Kathryn Tucker. *13 Alabama Ghosts and Jeffrey.* Tuscaloosa: Strode Publishers, 1969.

Wise, Stephen R. *Lifeline of the Confederacy: Blockade Running during the Civil War.* Columbia: University of South Carolina Press, 1991.

Woodrum, Robert H. "'The Past Has Taught Us a Lesson': The International Longshoremen's Association and Black Workers in Mobile, 1903–1913." *Alabama Review* 65 (April 2012): 100–136.

Ziebach, Elmo B. *The Second Head of Chocalata: Short Stories.* Victoria, B.C.: Trafford, 2003.

Internet Sources

"About General W. K. Wilson Bridge," https://www.facebook.com/pages/General-WK-Wilson-Jr-Bridge/112866822060298. Accessed July 13, 2013.

"Africatown Listed," http://www.nuzzapp.com/2012/12/18/africatown-listed-on-historic-place-registry/. Accessed October 12, 2013.

"Caesar Pipelay Vessel Joins Helix ESG Fleet," http://gcaptain.com/caesar-pipelay-vessel-joins-helix?11496. Accessed July 21, 2012.

"Coalition against a Raised Expressway," http://law.justia.com/cases/federal/appellate-courts/F2/835/803/296813/. Accessed July 13, 2013.

"Concatenated Order of Hoo-Hoo." *Encyclopedia of Arkansas History & Culture,* http://www.encyclopediaofarkansas.net/encyclopedia/entry-detail.aspx?entryID=1199&type=Category&item=Organizations+and+Civic+Leaders. Accessed July 4, 2013.

"Dishonorable Discharge: The Fifty Most Polluted Rivers in the Country," http://www.ewg.org/node/20399. Accessed July 21, 2012 and July 14, 2013.

Drago, Chip. "Bridging the Divide or the Snarl Ahead?" *Mobile Bay Times* blog, http://www.mobilebaytimes.com/bridge.html. Accessed July 13, 2013.

Encyclopedia of Alabama, http://encyclopediaofalabama.org/. Various access dates.

"E. R. Boston," http://www.marinetraffic.com/ais/shipdetails.aspx?MMSI=636091947. Accessed July 21, 2012.

Hogue, Sean. "Caesar Pipelay Vessel Joins Helix ESG Fleet," http://gcaptain.com/caesar-pipelay-vessel-joins-helix?11496. Accessed July 21, 2012.

Kammerer, J. C. "Largest Rivers in the United States," http://pubs.usgs.gov/of/1987/ofr87-242/. Accessed October 7, 2012.

"MAWSS Facilities," http://www.mawss.com/facilities2.html. Accessed July 14, 2013.

Mobile Baykeeper website, http://www.mobilebaykeeper.org/. Accessed July 14, 2013.

"Mobile Gets First Post Panamax Ship Call," http://article.wn.com/view/2012/06/04/Mobile__Gets__First__PostPanamax__Ship__Call/#/related__news. Accessed July 13, 2013.

National Archives at Atlanta. "The *Clotilda:* A Finding Aid," http://www.archives.gov/atlanta/finding-aids/clotilda.pdf. Accessed October 9, 2013.

"National Water-Quality Assessment Program: Mobile River Basin," http://tn.water.usgs.gov/MOBL/mobl-fact.pdf. Accessed September 9, 2012.

"Navy Names Combat Ship USS *Coronado,*" http:/www.navy.mil/search/display.asp?story__id=43396. Accessed July 21, 2012.

South, Gareth Platt. "January 4, 1861—Two Federal Forts Seized!," http://www.7score10years.com/index.php/south/81-south/143-january-4-1861-two-federal-forts-seized. Accessed March 2, 2013.

"Southeast Shipyards Mobile," http://www.thisismyshipyard.com/your-locations/southeast-shipyards-mobile/. Accessed July 13, 2013.

"State Pilotage Commission Functional Analysis Records Disposition Authority," http://www.archives.state.al.us/officials/rdas/pilotage.html#__1__12. Accessed August 3, 2013.

"Stauffer Chemical Co. (Cold Creek Plant)," http://www.epa.gov/region4/superfund/sites/npl/alabama/stacocreal.html. Accessed July 14, 2013.

"*Tai Honesty,*" http://www.marinetraffic.com/ais/shipdetails.aspx?mmsi=372506000. Accessed July 21, 2012.

Thomas, Susan. "Climbing the Branches of My Family Tree," http://climbingthebranches.blogspot.com/2011/10/saturdays-structures-frascati-park.html. Accessed July 4, 2013.

"*Torm Camilla,*" http://www.marinetraffic.com/ais/ru/shipdetails.aspx?MMSI=22040200. Accessed July 21, 2012.

"Watershed Quality Assessment Report," http://iaspub.epa.gov/tmdl__waters10/attains__watershed.control#assessment__data. Accessed November 17, 2013.

U. S. National Transportation Safety Board. "Railroad Marine Accident Report," http://www.ntsb.gov/investigations/summary/rar9401.htm. Accessed September 2, 2013.

"Welcome to the World of ThyssenKrupp Steel," http://www.thyssenkruppsteelusa.com/. Accessed July 13, 2013.

"Wetland and Habitat," http://www.alabamawildlife.org/stecoship/?pageID=54. Accessed September 11, 2012.

Wills, Rich. "The *H. L. Hunley* in Historical Context," http://www.history.navy.mil/branches/org12–7b.htm. Accessed April 1, 2013.

Wilson, Bill. "Bridge Stands Up to Katrina," http://www.roadsbridges.com/bridge-stands-katrina. Accessed September 8, 2013.

INDEX

ABOUT THE AUTHOR

John S. Sledge is senior architectural historian for the Mobile Historic Development Commission and a member of the National Book Critics Circle. He holds a bachelor's in history and Spanish from Auburn University and a master's in historic preservation from Middle Tennessee State University. Sledge is the author of three books on Mobile's historic architecture, as well as a collection of literary criticism, *Southern Bound: A Gulf Coast Journalist on Books, Writers, and Literary Pilgrimages of the Heart,* published by the University of South Carolina Press. He and his wife, Lynn, live in Fairhope, Alabama, half a mile from Mobile Bay.